THE CHOCOLATE SOLDIERS

THE STORY OF THE YOUNG CITIZEN VOLUNTEERS AND
14TH ROYAL IRISH RIFLES DURING THE GREAT WAR

STEVEN MOORE

COLOURPOINT

Published 2016 by Colourpoint Books
an imprint of Colourpoint Creative Ltd
Colourpoint House, Jubilee Business Park
21 Jubilee Road, Newtownards, BT23 4YH
Tel: 028 9182 6339
Fax: 028 9182 1900
E-mail: sales@colourpoint.co.uk
Web: www.colourpoint.co.uk

First Edition
First Impression

Text © Steven Moore, 2016
Illustrations © Various, as acknowledged in captions

Designed by April Sky Design, Newtownards
Tel: 028 9182 7195
Web: www.aprilsky.co.uk

Printed by W&G Baird Ltd, Antrim

ISBN 978-1-78073-059-2

Front cover: A photograph of his comrades by George Hackney, semi-official photographer of 14th (YCV) Royal Irish Rifles.
The Germans had ensured that they held the high ground on the Western Front, with the result that the British trenches
were generally further down the slope and inclined to flood, making life difficult and unpleasant for the men. (*George Hackney*)

About the author: Steven Moore, formerly News Editor with the *News Letter*, the oldest English language daily newspaper
in the world, and currently Deputy Editor of *FarmWeek*, the leading agriculture newspaper in Northern Ireland,
was born and educated in north Belfast, but has lived in Bangor, County Down, since 1982.
He is also the author of *The Irish On The Somme: A battlefield guide to the Irish regiments in the Great War and the monuments to their
memory* and *Hanged at Crumlin Road Gaol: The Story of Capital Punishment in Belfast.*

CONTENTS

Acknowledgements 5

Maps. 7

Chapter 1   An Oddity of History. 9

Chapter 2   The Swirl of the Pipes 15

Chapter 3   Discipline of the Highest Order. 24

Chapter 4   Drill, Brothers, Drill. 31

Chapter 5   A Lorry Loomed Out of the Darkness 40

Chapter 6   Soldiers of the King 46

Chapter 7   Bun Fights and Card Schools 58

Chapter 8   Arrival of the Wild Irish 72

Chapter 9   Standing in the Shelter of the Dugout. 83

Chapter 10   Sweeping their Way Across France 101

Chapter 11   Waiting like Cattle in a Slaughter House 117

Chapter 12   The Supreme Test. 128

Chapter 13   Picking up the Pieces 146

Chapter 14   We are Merry and Bright. 160

Chapter 15   The Hell that was Passchendaele 173

Chapter 16   Cursed in the Worst Cockney Irish Ever 184

Chapter 17   There Wasn't a Shot to be Heard 191

Chapter 18   The Last Post. 199

Appendices   1: The YCV Constitution and Bye-Laws 206

               2: An Irish Corps d'Elite 208

               3: Units of the 36th (Ulster) Division 211

               4: Armchair Generals and Afternoon Frocks. 212

               5: The Soldier Boy of the McFadzeans. 216

               6: Late Lieutenant Victor H Robb 220

               7: 14th (YCV) RIR Dead of July 1916 221

               8: 14th (YCV) RIR Dead of Early June 1917 225

               9: 14th (YCV) RIR Dead from 16–31 Aug 1917 . . . 226

               10: 14th (YCV) RIR Dead from 6–18 Dec 1917 . . . 230

               11: 14th (YCV) RIR/23rd Entrenching Battalion Dead from 21 Mar–27 Apr 1918. . 231

               12: Young Citizen Volunteers Revisit Mesnil 233

               End Notes 236

               Notes on Sources 249

               Index 251

For my grandchildren Ria, Jacob, Isla and Sophia,
for whom the future promises so much

ACKNOWLEDGEMENTS

THIS IS A BOOK that arguably has been in the making for close on 40 years. It was as a teenager, interested in collecting military cap badges, that I first came across the Young Citizen Volunteers and the 14th Royal Irish Rifles. Two of my grandfather's brothers had served in both organisatons and I was fortunate back then to be given some of the papers, postcards, letters and, the most important to me at the time, badges that the family still possessed. Over the years, however, it was the 'paperwork' that came to mean more to me and that sparked a passion and a thirst for knowledge about the Great War, the role of the Irish regiments and particularly that of the 36th (Ulster) Division.

In the intervening years I have been to the Western Front many times, including helping, in a particularly modest way, with the excavations of the front line trenches in Thiepval Wood and writing extensively on the period. Always in the background, however, I felt the need to further explore the war from as close a perspective as I could get to that of my great uncles, William Moore and John Reid Moore. It took the encouragement of Craig McGuicken, then Curator of the Somme Heritage Centre at Newtownards, to provide the necessary push. He was at that time compiling an exhibition on the YCVs and 14th Rifles and his enthusiasm for the subject convinced me that I needed to look beyond self-indulgent research and instead to create a work that would give readers a glimpse – for that is all that words can do – of what it was like to be a soldier during the First World War. Craig introduced me to Andrew Totten and Bobby Storey, both of whom were incredibly generous in providing me with a huge volume of information and photographs on the YCVs and 14th Rifles that they had gathered up over the years. What developed from there has been, for me, a labour of love and I can only hope it comes close to doing justice to the men of the Young Citizen Volunteers and 14th Royal Irish Rifles. I have been greatly assisted, as always, by Carol Walker, director of the Somme Museum, and the late Noel Kane, archivist and tour guide, who despite being in poor health spared no effort to turn up many of the images that grace the pages that follow. Alastair Harrison, a true gentleman whose father Samuel not only came through the war with the YCVs but left behind a journal of his experiences, postcards of where he had served, and a variety of documents and letters, allowed me to borrow these items and to quote freely from them.

David Truesdale and Sylvia McRoberts kindly gave me permission to quote from *Young Citizen Old Soldier*, the journal of Rifleman James McRoberts, and to use some of the photographs; Lester Morrow provided some rare images; Dr Sarah Ferris gave me permission to quote from the papers of *Young Citizen* and poet Thomas Carnduff; Robert Orr provided photographs and aided in the return of YCV mementoes to the family; Joanne Lowry and Dianne Leeman at Belfast City Hall showed great patience and much assistance in facilitating the taking of photographs within the building; Catherine Mulvenna and Mary Coffey at Belfast Met made me aware of, and aided in the copying of photographs held of staff members who served in the 14th Rifles during the war; Paul Callaghan helped with research and photographs; and Amanda Moreno and her colleagues at the Royal Ulster Rifles Museum were exceedingly helpful and generous with their archives and guidance on the use of the George Hackney images.

The staff at the Belfast Central Library, and particularly the Newspaper Library, were unfailingly helpful and polite, as were those of the Public Record Office of Northern Ireland. Indeed, I am indebted to so many people for their assistance, guidance, advice and practical help throughout the preparation of this book that it would be impossible and impractical to name them all but, to each and every one, goes my sincere thanks. For any errors in this book – and with the conflicting and often confusing array of information available, mistakes, or at least differences of interpretation, may be inevitable – I alone accept responsibility.

Steven Moore
January 2016

MAPS: Locations referred to in the book

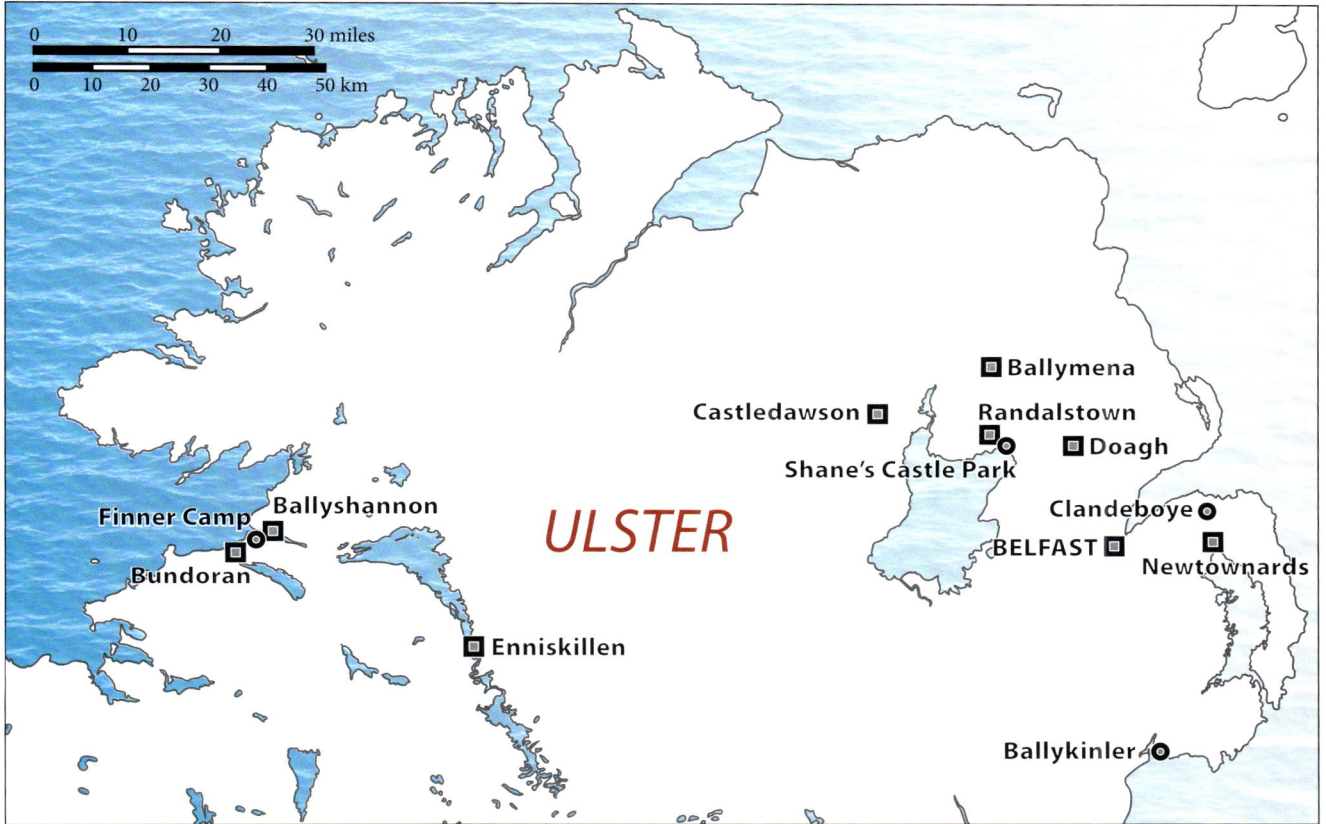

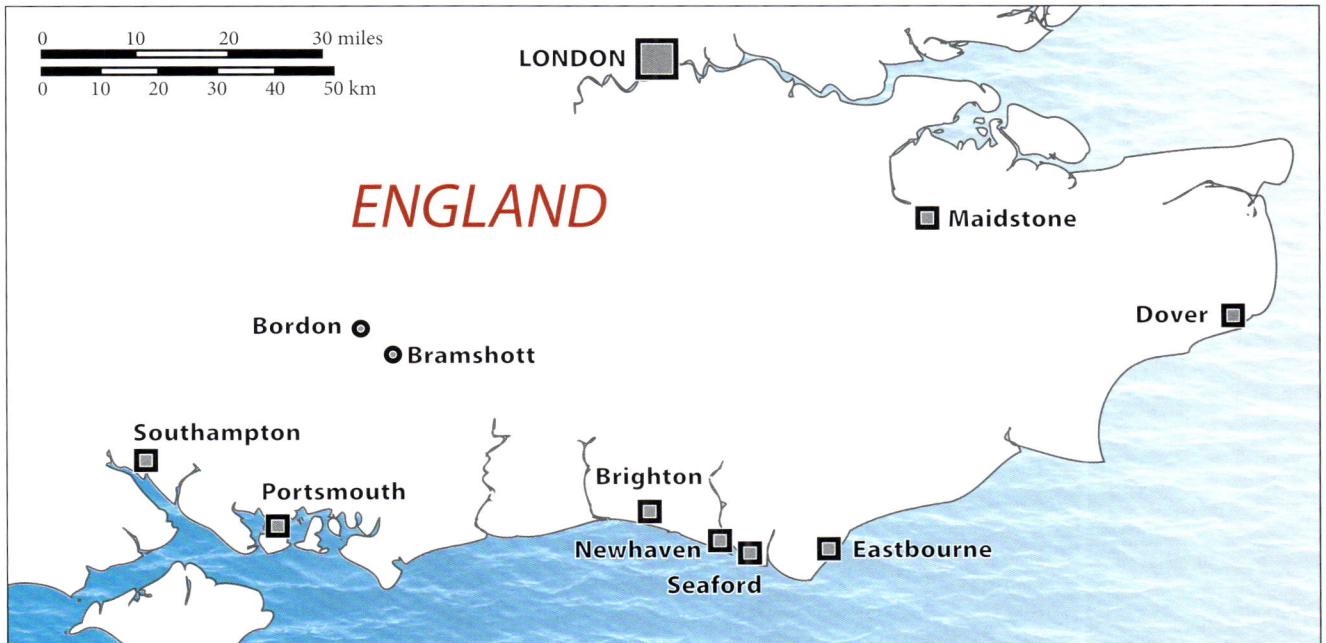

0   10   20   30 miles
0   10   20   30   40   50 km

Ballymena

Castledawson

Randalstown

Doagh

Shane's Castle Park

Clandeboye

Finner Camp   Ballyshannon

BELFAST

Newtownards

Bundoran

ULSTER

Enniskillen

Ballykinler

0   10   20   30 miles
0   10   20   30   40   50 km

LONDON

Maidstone

ENGLAND

Dover

Bordon

Bramshott

Southampton

Portsmouth

Brighton

Newhaven

Seaford

Eastbourne

BELGIUM

FRANCE

0   10   20   30 miles

0   10   20   30   40   50 km

Dunkirk

Calais

Passchendaele

Vlamertinge

Winnezeele   Watou   Ypres

Kortrijk

Serques   Berthen   Westoutre   Locre

Caestre   Kemmel   Messines

Nortbecourt   Hondeghem   Dranoutre

Boisdinghem   Saint   Arques   Bailleul   Ploegsteert

Omer   Neuve Eglise   Romarin

Boulogne

Berguette   Western Front   Lille   Tournai

1 Jan 1915

Bethune

Etaples   Lens

Vimy   Douai   Valenciennes

Arras

Conteville   Fonquevillers   Auchonvillers   Moeuvres   Cambrai

Doullens   Forceville   Bapaume

Berneuil   Beauval   Couin   Auchonvillers   Hermies

Abbeville   Ergnies   Acheux   Hamel   Mesnil   Barastre

Pernois   Varennes   Thiepval

Pont-Remy   Martinsart

Herrissart   Albert

River Somme   Maricourt

Poulainville

Amiens

Villers-Bretonneux   Saint-Quentin

Moreuil   Canizy   Grand Seraucourt

Rethonvillers

Chapter 1

AN ODDITY OF HISTORY

It is undoubtedly good for young men to band themselves in this way for mutual improvement, and with the worthy ambition of doing the city if not the State some service. Man in his highest development is essentially a gregarious animal. His solitary virtues are not those which make much for civilisation and progress.

An 'Old Fogey', *Northern Whig*

THE YOUNG CITIZEN VOLUNTEERS is an oddity of history. Its name, or at least the initials YCV, adorn many a gable wall today but it is likely that few have more than a fleeting understanding of its history as folklore and perception have overtaken the facts. To a modern generation, the YCV, if known at all, will be as the youth wing of the present-day Ulster Volunteer Force, an organisation which lays claim to the heritage of 'Carson's UVF' though it was not formed until more than 40 years after the latter had ceased to exist. The original YCV, however, was as far removed in concept, nature and purpose as it was possible to get from its later incarnation.

References to the Young Citizen Volunteers, usually in the form of the shamrock badge and initials, can be found on many gable walls in Belfast. This example, from the east of the city, is clearly referring to the original YCVs and 14th Royal Irish Rifles. *(Author)*

The Young Citizen Volunteers of Ireland was, by stages, a youth movement conceived as an emergency peace-keeping force; a paramilitary body prepared to take up arms to prove its loyalty; and the core of a military unit of the British Army that fought in virtually all the major battles on the Western Front during 1916 and 1917, with its remnants involved in halting the final German offensive of 1918.

The threat of war was as much a major driver in the establishing of the YCV as the declared desire to promote the physical and moral well-being of its members. Discipline and military-style training were already incorporated in the activities of youth groups such as the Boys' Brigade and Boy Scouts. The YCV, it was proposed, would take this to a higher level by including arms training for a membership that was of military age combined with drill, huge doses of patriotism and an injection of social responsibility – exactly the sort of training, as secretary Frank Workman pointed out at the inaugural meeting of the organisation in September 1912, already then being given to young men in Germany. There was a need, he argued, to be similarly prepared in the United Kingdom, adding that the YCV could also assist the Lord Mayor at home in the event of civil disturbance.

The political scene in the Ireland of 1911–14 was dramatic and tense. The Third Home Rule Bill was working its way through parliament and with each stage completed it became clear that the final act was likely to be played out on the streets of Belfast and beyond rather than at Westminster. The road to what was to become known as the Ulster Crisis had arguably began with the Reform Act of 1885, which had effectively tripled the number of eligible voters in Ireland. The result was a huge surge in the number of Irish Parliamentary Party MPs elected in the general election of that year, its 86 representatives (including one who took a seat in Liverpool) effectively holding the balance of power, allowing them to decide whether the Conservatives or Liberals, evenly matched, should form the government. With the Tories unwilling to grant Home Rule, they offered their support to William Ewart Gladstone, making him Prime Minister and securing his support for a limited form of self-government from Dublin. The First Home Rule Bill was introduced on 8 April 1886 and, though ultimately defeated by parliamentary means, it stirred up opposition on both sides of the Irish Sea. Conservative leader Lord Randolph Churchill famously declared he was willing to play the "Orange card" and proclaiming "Ulster will fight, and Ulster will be right". Gladstone made another attempt following the general election of 1892 and though the Commons passed his Second Home Rule Bill, the House of Lords rejected it. As before, the feeling in Ulster had been adamant, with 100,000 loyalists parading past the White Linen Hall, site of today's Belfast City Hall, on 4 April 1893 to register their opposition. The Conservatives returned to power in 1895 and the prospect of Home Rule for Ireland disappeared from the political agenda. It returned in 1910, however, when, despite winning two elections that year, the Liberals still required the support of Irish MPs to form a credible government.

Lord Randolph Churchill, photographed here in 1883, was Conservative leader at the time of the First Home Rule Bill, and proclaimed: "Ulster will fight, and Ulster will be right".

Even before the introduction of the Third Home Rule Bill in 1912, unionists were preparing plans to resist its implementation by force of arms if necessary. One of the first signs of the growing resistance was the reforming of Unionist Clubs to provide a focus for opposition. First created in 1893, they were revived in April 1911. By the end of that year some 164 clubs were in existence, which more than doubled to 316 clubs by August 1918. The vast majority were in the nine counties of Ulster, though a few were formed elsewhere in Ireland. A number of the Ulster Clubs formed rifle clubs, a clear sign of their intent to prepare for conflict outside the political arena. The opposition took a step forward, quite literally, when in January 1912 the Orange Order's County Grand Master Colonel Robert Hugh Wallace obtained leave from magistrates in Belfast to drill and practise "military exercises, movements and evolutions". Born in Downpatrick, County Down, the Colonel had been commissioned into the Royal South Down Militia as a 19-year-old and saw action in the Boer War. He headed up the family firm of solicitors and so was able to combine his legal and military experiences to challenge the law. He commanded the North Belfast Regiment of the Ulster Volunteer Force and was later to raise the 17th Royal Irish Rifles and to command the 19th Rifles at Newcastle from 1915–18.

The law permitted such activity provided its aim was the maintenance of the Constitution

– a sweet irony for the loyalists who were determined that the Union of Great Britain and Ireland would remain unchanged. By the end of the year, thousands of men were receiving rudimentary training, with drilling often taking place in public places as a show of strength. Behind closed doors, usually inside Orange halls, the small number of weapons that had been smuggled into the country were also getting an airing, as much as a morale booster for the volunteers as for the purposes of training in small arms.

It is perhaps remarkable that from amidst such a politically charged atmosphere emerged the Young Citizen Volunteers (YCV), an organisation that claimed no such allegiances or sectarian baggage. Nor was its arrival unheralded or lacking confidence. Belfast at the turn of the century did not consider itself to be in anyway a backwater of the United Kingdom or indeed the British Empire, and likewise the founding fathers of the YCV did not lack ambition. They intended to grow the Young Citizen Volunteers of Ireland movement into a national, conceivably even an international, organisation. Taking over from where youth organisations such as the Boys' Brigade, Boy Scouts and Church Lads ended, this was to be a body on which King and country could depend. Starting in Belfast, the YCV movement was expected to sweep Ireland, then Britain and the Empire, and possibly beyond. In the event, only one battalion was formed and that was based in the city of the YCV's birth, Belfast, though there was interest shown in surrounding towns. A contributing factor for its stunted growth was unquestionably the attitude of the authorities in Great Britain. The government, rather than being grateful for this display of patriotism, exhibited its usual, and perhaps not unnatural, suspicion of any organised grouping in Ireland and withheld its blessing, refusing it permission to carry or train with arms. The organisers pressed ahead with their educational talks, route marches, military drills and strict discipline nonetheless but while the membership remained strong on paper, it began to dwindle in reality.

John and James Fitzsimons signed up together in the YCV with a third brother, Ernest. John was later killed on the first day of the Battle of the Somme, 1 July 1916. *(Courtesy of the Somme Museum)*

And, of course, by this time it had a serious rival in the form of the Ulster Volunteer Force. The UVF was politically driven, considerably more exciting and, from the outset, carried the promise of armed conflict. It was inevitable, it might seem with hindsight, that, given the tensions of the day, the YCV would ultimately be swept up into the ranks of the UVF, which it pre-dated. Even before the merger took place there was a degree of crossover in membership. Poet Thomas Carnduff, who joined the YCV prior to the war, was convinced that the men of Ulster were up for the fight:

> "They were ready and willing to shed blood for the cause, their own or that of anyone else, so long as Ulster remained in the United Kingdom. There was nothing comic regarding their determination to resist. They would have martyred themselves wilfully and recklessly. One shot fired would certainly have set Ulster ablaze. They allowed Carson to lead them, but he could not have held them back."

The political landscape of Ulster, however, was changed overnight by what Carnduff termed a 'coincidence' – the outbreak of the Great War. Many of YCV's active members, like their Ulster Volunteer comrades, enlisted in the Army, with the Young Citizens becoming the core of the 14th (YCV) Battalion of the Royal Irish Rifles, part of the 36th (Ulster) Division. The remainder of the YCV, now part of the UVF, continued as a civilian organisation but in 1916 it was put into suspended animation from which it was never revived. In the 90-plus years since its disbandment, the battalion has taken on a virtually iconic status yet, as this history will show, it had to defend its reputation during the war years. A tension existed between it and the other Belfast battalions of the Rifles, largely composed of the pre-war UVF regiments from the North, East, South and West of the city. This was in part due to the belief that the YCVs were given an easier time and probably exacerbated by the generally higher social standing of its members. The tension appears to have continued to an extent post-war, with the 14th holding its own functions and generally only sending representatives to the larger divisional old comrade gatherings.

Photographer George Hackney evidently had the blessing of his commanding officer to create a photographic record of the 14th (YCV) Royal Irish Rifles. Many of his photographs appear elsewhere in this book. *(George Hackney)*

In the pages that follow you will get to walk in the footsteps of the men of the YCV and 14th Royal Irish Rifles as they were transformed from the naïve young men who trudged around the roads of Donegal in their Sunday best suits to the battle-hardened troops of the Western Front. Many are named in the text or appendices, including all those who could be verified, through the Commonwealth War Graves Commission and Soldiers Died databases, as having died with the 14th Rifles. Experience suggests that there may be others omitted from these lists, and certainly a few names have emerged through the surviving dairies and journals whose reported deaths could not be confirmed. The story of the YCVs and 14th Royal Irish Rifles is told largely through the words of the soldiers themselves, such as Jim Fitzsimons, who lost a brother serving with the battalion; the concise Charles Sheridan; one time bomber and later signaller H Berry; Downpatrick-born Samuel Harrison, who served from September 1914 until wounded in November 1917; Jim Maultsaid, who joined the YCV as a means of getting into the army after initially being rejected as a recruit; George Mullin, who clearly enjoyed his soldiering days; and many more. The battalion's newspaper, edited by Stanley Monard, provided a window into the thinking and sense of humour of the men, while the *War Diary*, much of it written by long-time adjutant Alan Mulholland, not only provided a timeline but contained much detail, comment and even speculation at times. Many amateur photographers existed within the ranks of the Young Citizens but it is the pictures of George Hackney, who clearly had his commanding officer's permission to record day-to-day life in the battalion, that stand out as capturing their daily life.

The men (the military in the First World War was almost exclusively a male preserve) came from a wide range of social and economic backgrounds. Virtually all were young and most were from Belfast, though only a minority who served had been members of the Young Citizen Volunteers prior to the outbreak of war. Two of these young men in particular inspired this book. John Reid Moore and William Moore, the author's great uncles, exchanged the grey of their YCV uniforms for khaki in 1914. John was made a sergeant and later transferred to the 109th Trench Mortar Battery. He was killed, aged 22, on 1 July 1916, the first day of the Battle of the Somme, and is buried in Connaught Cemetery, his headstone looking out from the front row towards the 'Bloody Road' and with Thiepval Wood to the rear. His brother, William, was company quartermaster and

John and William Moore, great uncles of the author, served in A Company of the 14th Royal Irish Rifles. In this photograph of company sergeants, John is standing to the extreme right and William is sitting, second from the left. *(Author)*

was later commissioned into the 12th Royal Irish Rifles. He was wounded at least twice and won the Military Cross in 1917. After the war he moved to England, working as a district manager for a Manchester roofing company. He was a founding member of the Leicester Ulster Society, holding the posts of treasurer, chairman and president at different times. He died in 1969 at the age of 79. Their father was leading Orangeman Thomas Gourlie Moore, of Baltic Avenue in Belfast. At the time of his death in 1936 he was Deputy Grand Master of the Grand Lodge of Ireland.

By coincidence, another young man to join the 14th Rifles was Edwin Sterritt, great grandfather of the author's wife. He had been posted to the YCVs from the 19th Royal Irish Rifles, based at Newtownards, on 7 October 1916. He was allocated to A Company, in which both William and John Moore had served at one time. Already a married man with a wife and young family living at Vistula Street in Belfast, he was severely wounded in August 1917 resulting in the loss of a lung.

The perception, which persists to this day, that the YCVs were from privileged backgrounds would have irked them. Battalion member John

Already a married man when he enlisted in 1915, and despite losing a lung at Third Ypres in 1917, Edwin Sterritt lived long enough to celebrate his Golden Wedding anniversary with wife Isabella. *(Author)*

Kennedy Hope, a reluctant lance corporal with strong socialist beliefs, radiated bitterness in his account of his service, written in the winter of 1928, as indicated by the opening passage:

"I tell very little of the nights when the sentry stood shivering on the steps for hours watching the sandbags grow a beard of frost or 'watching the barbed wire moving about'. I tell not my thoughts as I stand on sentry and know that our fearful gas is creeping over a quick German line and carrying death to hundreds of terror stricken Huns. I tell not what I thought when ordered to present arms to a DMS as he passed my post in the front line, an unheard of thing but nevertheless truth. I tell not what I thought when pulled out of a cavity in the trench, where I was sleeping, by our officious Colonel and ordered to take a piece of 4×2 flannel out of the muzzle of my rifle as it might ruin the barrel. Ex-Service is one thing. Ex the trenches is the man who counts. The man who holds the front line. The man in constant danger of being blown out of the trenches or pinched by the scruff of the neck in a raid or unceremoniously shot dead."

The YCV battalion in which he served was unique not only within the 36th (Ulster) Division but in the army as a whole. The Young Citizens were members of a non-sectarian, non-political group who opted to become members of an armed paramilitary force; they took oaths to be good citizens but were prepared to face down the forces of law and order; most came from Belfast yet were shunned by their comrades in the other city battalions; they did their duty on the field of battle yet the 'Chocolate Soldiers', as they were unkindly dubbed, were continuously accused of getting it easy and became the first northern Irish recruited battalion that needed to employ English conscripts as replacements after volunteers from home dried up. They were, in short, the odd men out.

Ria Moore at the grave of her great great great uncle John Reid Moore, buried in Connaught Cemetery on the Somme. *(Author)*

Chapter 2

THE SWIRL OF THE PIPES

We feel that the young men of our country have been seriously handicapped in the past in not having any general organisation capable of continuing the good work done by the Boys' Brigade, Church Lads' Brigade, and Boy Scouts' Movements, and of affording opportunity for like training to the larger number of young men who have not had the advantages conferred by membership of those organisations. The Young Citizen Volunteer Corps has been originated to supply this want.

**Letter seeking guarantors for £1,500 bank loan
to finance the setting up of YCV**

TO THE SWIRL OF a lone piper in traditional highland dress, the first company of the Young Citizen Volunteers of Ireland swung into the large banqueting room of Belfast's City Hall. In its wake followed several hundred more would-be recruits, who quickly merged with other young men waiting inside. Their purpose was to officially bring into being an organisation that had already captured the imaginations of many and which, it was hoped, would ultimately spread throughout Ireland, Great Britain and possibly beyond. Advertisements trailing the meeting had been running in the local press for days beforehand and word of what was proposed, discussed in private for months, had spread far and wide.

On this late summer evening of 10 September 1912, however, the focus was on Belfast, with many of the most influential men of this blossoming city, including a number of military figures, making up the platform party. Opening proceedings, the soon-to-be honorary secretary HG Stevenson[1] read out messages of support from as far away as London.

These, tellingly, included a telegram from Major R McCalmont, of the Irish Guards, suggesting that Army officers might have a role to play in the new body. Lord Mayor Robert James McMordie then rose to his feet. A man of immense stature in the city he had led for more than three years, he outlined the ambitions for the organisation

The Banqueting Room at the City Hall in Belfast was packed to overflowing on the evening of 10 September 1912, at the inaugural meeting of the Young Citizen Volunteers of Ireland. *(Author)*

The Platform Party at the first YCV meeting included some of the most influential men in Belfast. Lord Mayor Robert McMordie is the central figure sitting behind the table. (*Belfast Telegraph*)

that would begin where the existing youth groups left off. The *Belfast News Letter* reported of his speech:

> "They knew the excellent physical and moral training received by the Boy Scouts, and if they reflected at all they would recognise that physical training and moral training must of necessity produce a good mental training. So it was thought that drill might be continued with great advantages after the age of eighteen, when youths passed out of such organisations as the Boy Scouts, the Boys' Brigade, and the Church Lads' Brigade (Applause).
>
> That was the period when young men were open to the greatest risks. It was, therefore, a time when they should get together and have a continuous training up till they entered on their own accounts upon the practical affairs of life. (Applause).
>
> They also recognised that there were many other lads who had not had the benefit of being associated with the Boy Scouts, the Boys' Brigade, and the Church Lads' Brigade, and the idea was to gather them into the ranks of the Young Citizen Volunteers, and put them on a level with their fellows in the matter of training. In that way there could be brought into one organisation a very large proportion, if not all, of the young men of their city, and of other cities too, to undergo moral training and physical training until they became mature men. (Applause)."

Moral obligations would be insisted upon from members who would be an asset to their community and state. The young men accepted into the ranks of the YCV, in addition to improving their own physical and mental well-being, would be prepared in an emergency not only to defend his own home but ultimately come to the nation's aid.

RH Kinahan, of the Boys' Brigade in Belfast, in seconding the motion put forward by Alexander Cooke, president of the Belfast Citizens' Association,[2] to form the new body, emphasised the military nature of his own and other such groups.

He expressed the hope that the YCV[3] would be supplied with rifles and equipment, though pointed out that his own organisation had declined an approach to become army cadets.

After the formal acceptance of resolutions, including the adoption of the previously prepared constitution (see Appendix 1), officials were elected with the Lord Mayor becoming president and shipbuilder and city councillor Frank Workman treasurer, with a headquarters address of 7 Chichester Street in Belfast.

It was Fred T Geddes, also confirmed that night as an honorary secretary, who was the man behind the concept of the Young Citizen Volunteers. He had found a ready accomplice in Lord Mayor McMordie, who he had approached with his idea. On 6 June 1912, the First Citizen hosted a meeting of prominent men in his parlour at the City Hall to consider the proposal to form a "young citizens' volunteer corps". Expressing his "anxiety to associate himself with any movement calculated to assist in the intellectual and physical development of the young men of Belfast," he called on Geddes to address the gathering, which he did with such affect that a proposal to form the body was put forward by Mr GW Ferguson, JP, and seconded by Mr EM Reid, with those present agreeing to make up a committee to prepare the way. The committee met again the following week, again in the Lord Mayor's Parlour but with Councillor Gilliland presiding this time. It was reported that Geddes submitted a "very comprehensive set of rules, which, with a few slight alterations, were unanimously approved of, and which will be placed before a public meeting which the Lord Mayor has arranged to call later, and of which due notice will be given," reported the *Northern Whig* on 13 June 1912.

Now, at the first public meeting some three months later, Geddes outlined his concept. Members of the YCV would be physically, intellectually and morally fit and well-balanced citizens, he told his audience. The activities planned would appeal to "the average, full-blooded, young fellow" with energy to expend. The Young Citizen Volunteers would be unique as nowhere else in the world, to his knowledge, did such a similar organisation exist and so they would not interfere with any existing body of young men. Members would be free to form companies of their own that would be strictly non-political and non-sectarian. The well-being of any community depended upon the patriotism of its citizens, with messages of approval having already been received from representatives of every religious creed in the city. "The object of the organisation was twofold," he told the hall. "First, there was the development of a spirit of responsible citizenship and municipal patriotism by means of lectures and discussions on civic matters and, in the second place, there was the development of manly physique and all that meant in the way of self-respect, self-control and chivalry by means of modified military and police drill." The YCV would bring together young men who had previously served in the youth organisations and their halls would become "splendid training grounds" for aspiring athletes of all kinds. He ended his speech by calling for support across the community "so that their rising manhood might be trained and prepared to play a worthy part in their affairs of their large and growing city".

Former Lord Mayor and MP for East Belfast, Robert McMordie's statue looks out over the city centre from the City Hall grounds. *(Author)*

The premise of the new body had clearly struck a chord with young and old alike. The *Northern Whig* newspaper's popular columnist 'An Old Fogey' saw huge possibilities for the new organisation. In an article published on the morning of that first meeting, he sang the praises of the YCV or, as he termed it, the YCC (Young Citizen Corps):

> "Boys' organisations for the inculcation of discipline and duty, for the cultivation of moral and religious sentiment, for the improvement of physique are legion. Boys' Brigade, Church Lads' Brigade, Boy Scouts, Boy Bluejackets – all these are admirable in their character and their work. But the day comes when the trousered youth quits the knickerbockered battalion. Boys leave the Brigade at sixteen, the Scouts are super-annuated at seventeen, the Church Lads at nineteen. Youths who have belonged to either of these organisations and have come to regard as essentials the comradeship, the exercise, the emulation, and the spirit de corps which all of them supply feel the pinch sorely when they are unceremoniously thrust outside by that bald sexton Time ... Here proposes to come in the Young Citizens' Corps. It will take hold of ex-brigadier, ex-scout, and ex-bluejacket, and put them in the position of again enjoying the warm comradeship of the ranks, the healthful discipline of the company. It will take, too, the raw youth who has never known these influences and assist in shaping him into a well set-up, self-respecting, moral citizen, able to assist intelligently when called upon in the government of his city, to assist patriotically should the need arise in the defence of his country." (See Appendix 2)

The City Hall played a major part in the formation of the Young Citizen Volunteers, including hosting committee meetings in the Lord Mayor's Parlour and as a venue for the first YCV gathering at which the organisation was officially brought into being. *(Author)*

The Council of the YCV held its first meeting in the Lord Mayor's Parlour on Monday 16 September 1912, with Mr McMordie in the chair and set about forming a range of committees to take the organisation forward. Just over a fortnight after the initial City Hall meeting, a second was held, this time at the Ulster Hall, at which a Belfast battalion of the YCV was officially formed. Such was the level of interest the hall was full long before the members of the platform party took their seats. Mr McMordie again occupied the chair while Sergeant Bentley[4] spoke about the training that was to be undertaken. The *Belfast News Letter* reported:

> "Dr A Trimble, JP, expressed the belief that a city passed through phases of growth and development similar to the individual. Judging by the splendid and enthusiastic audience of young men which he saw before him, he thought he might say that Belfast has passed through its phases of childhood and youth, and had entered on the glorious period of virile manhood. Such an organisation as the Young Citizen Volunteers seemed to him worthy of the heartiest support of every citizen, since it would seek to develop and foster a sense of brotherhood and love of public duty, and, above all, love of country and city. Already,

THE SWIRL OF THE PIPES

wherever Belfast men were found, their thoughts and affections turned to home, and every effort should be made to encourage and strengthen a tie which would make life's hardships less harsh and willingness for public service a natural result of citizenship."

The motion proposing the formation of a Belfast battalion was put forward by Martin H Turnbull, seconded by WJ Gilliland, and unanimously passed. To applause from the floor, secretary HG Stevenson announced that eight companies had already been formed with another 13 in the process of being created, bringing the initial membership up to 1,000.

Following a public meeting held at the Good Templar Hall on the Hamilton Road, Bangor, in November 1912, a YCV company was formed in the seaside town with hopes expressed that it might grow into a battalion in due course. *(Author)*

Among them was a company formed by the Central Presbyterian Association, which held its inaugural meeting in Assembly Buildings in early October. After tea was served at 7.30 pm, Mr TH McCleery, convener of the CPA's Recreation Committee, addressed the gathering. Sergeant Bentley, a member of the YCV's Executive Committee, explained the objectives of the organisation, and HG Stevenson answered questions from the floor. The meeting concluded with the election of office-bearers, with John Sinclair as President; Mr McCleery, KM Alexander and JH Ireland vice-presidents; secretary was Thomas Rainey; and JH Martin was made honorary treasurer. SJ McIlrath, TI Cole and R Alexander made up the company committee. The CPA company would later provide a number of volunteers to the 14th Royal Irish Rifles, including its only Victoria Cross winner, Billy McFadzean.[5] Most companies were, naturally, formed in Belfast though there was interest expressed elsewhere, including Londonderry, Ballymena, and even as far away as England.

A public meeting in the Good Templar Hall in Bangor, County Down, in early November, resulted in a company being formed in the seaside town. A "fairly large number of young men" filed into the hall where John McMeekan, chairman of Bangor Urban Council, presided. He told the "men in the making" present that the future lay in their hands and the YCV, which he hoped would grow into a battalion in the town, would equip and discipline them for the responsibilities they would face as they grew older. Fred Geddes was able to tell the new recruits that membership had grown to more than 1,000 in Belfast alone since inception. The *County Down Spectator* reported:

"As this was (the) inaugural meeting of the movement in Bangor, he earnestly trusted that it would receive the hearty support of the best elements of the community, and that the young men in Bangor would, in the future, take an important part in the life of that important town. (Applause.) Mr E May explained the workings of the organisation, and on the motion of Mr Bertie Little, seconded by Mr John Cleland, it was unanimously decided to form a company of the Young Citizen Volunteer Corps in Bangor."

Mr McMeekan was elected president, with Thomas Wilson vice-president, A Breeze became secretary, Mr Irvine the treasurer and Samuel T Coulter was given the role of instructor. On the first Friday evening in December a further meeting was held, this time at the Central Auction Mart on Main Street, at which some 35 young men enrolled in the Bangor company with the local newspaper speculating that it would be "one of the finest in Ireland and it is anticipated that when the company is in full working order the number of applications for enrolment will be greater". The YCV constitution allowed for the establishment of a reserve corps of members aged over 35, with a meeting held on 22 November 1912 at Brice's auction mart to form a Bangor 'Veteran's Corps' under the leadership of Thomas Wilson.

In Belfast, meanwhile, training of volunteers was already underway. The city council's Market Committee had sanctioned the use of St George's covered market in May Street as a drill hall, with the first meetings taking place from 8.00 pm–10.00 pm on Mondays, Tuesdays and Wednesdays from 14 October. The decision to allow municipal property to be used in such a way wasn't universally popular, however, and at the November meeting of the council an objection was aired – though, as the *Northern Whig* reported, it only provoked laughter:

> "Councillor McEntee called attention to the proposal to allow the use of St George's Market for the Young Citizen Volunteers for the purpose of drilling. He thought unsectarian and unpolitical drilling at the present time was an impossibility – (laughter) – and he disapproved of the proposal. He moved as an amendment that the paragraph be omitted.
>
> Alderman Tyrrell said it was very strange that the last speaker should object on political grounds to this proposal, considering that his own son was a member of the Young Citizen Volunteers. (Laughter and 'Hear, hear.')
>
> Councillor Workman tendered the thanks of the association, of which he was treasurer, to Councillor McEntee for the advertisement which he had given to the organisation."

Belfast council granted the YCV the use of St George's covered market to train in, with meetings held there on Monday, Tuesday and Wednesday evenings initially. *(Author)*

On 10 December 1912, the first general meeting of the YCV's Belfast corps was held in the Central Hall of the Municipal Technical Institute with Mr McMordie in the chair. Members formed up in companies at St George's Market and marched to the venue "attracting a good deal of public attention" according to press reports. The Lord Mayor, introducing what was the first in a series of lectures to increase the young men's knowledge of municipal matters, said they were engaged in a great "educational movement". The institute's principal, Francis Charles Forth[6] delivering the address, told them it was impossible to conceive any citizen who could place before himself higher or worthier aims and ambitions than those to which they had pledged themselves.

"Your constitution also includes as a cardinal rule, that the organisation shall be strictly non-sectarian and non-political, and you have thus rendered it possible for every citizen to take part in this splendid movement for securing and maintaining a high standard both of civic efficiency and of individual development," he told them. Noting that many of the first recruits had come from the ranks of the Boys' Brigade, and so were already well-trained and of the right spirit, he also acknowledged that the organisation would be viewed with suspicion by some because of its emphasis on the sort of discipline associated with soldiering, warfare and bloodshed. Their task, however, was to train themselves up to be ready to serve and – citing the example of the Birkenhead disaster of 1852, during which some 500 men gave up their lives in order to save women and children – be prepared to sacrifice themselves for the greater good. Referring to the loss of the *Titanic* eight months earlier, a "disaster which we cannot even think of without heartache, and which for the same reason we would hesitate to speak of, were it not that our grief is softened by the knowledge that those heroes – our kinsmen – established, for all time, yet another inspiring example of magnificent discipline in time of deadly peril", he said it was in the nature of the male to join disciplined organisations, the importance of which had been argued by eminent opinion formers such as Lord Roberts, General Sir Robert Baden-Powell and Lord Rosebery:[7]

Francis Charles Forth, the first principal of Belfast Technical College, was a keen supporter of the Young Citizen Volunteer movement and personally delivered the first of a series of lectures on municipal responsibility. He later became a captain in the Royal Irish Rifles. *(Courtesy of Belfast Met)*

"As a proof of that I would point to the numbers who join such movements as the Boys' Brigade, the Boy Scouts, the Legion of the Frontiersmen, the Officers' Training Corps, the British Boys' Training Corps, the various Territorial Corps, the Navy and the Army. Some people will tell you that there are too many volunteer organisations. I have heard it said that there was no opening in Belfast for an association such as the Young Citizen Volunteers. But if you take the total numbers enrolled in those various local organisations which are included amongst the list just enumerated, and if you note the limitations as to length of service imposed in some of the organisations by the maximum age regulations, and then compare the numbers with the total population, you will find that the field of work open to you is very

extensive and that you have come in to occupy a gap which badly needed filling with such an association as yours."

The creation of the Young Citizen Volunteers could be viewed as a natural progression of what had become known as the 'Brigade Movement'. It had evolved from around the middle of the 19th century when social reformers and religious groups concerned about the moral, spiritual and physical development of young people had set up the first groups. Based on the religious teaching and military-type training available to public school boys, a number of these organisations spread across the nation, offering those in their teens, who then often started work at the age of 13, an interest and social life that contrasted with the boredom of their jobs.

The first of these to catch the national imagination was the non-denominational Boys' Brigade, established by William Smith in Glasgow in 1883. An officer in the reserve forces and a Sunday School teacher, he combined his knowledge of military drill with religious fervour to create a body that is still a leading youth organisation today not just in Britain but across the world. It was William McVicker, secretary of the Mission Sunday School connected with St Mary's Magdalene Parish Church in Donegall Pass, Belfast, who founded the first BB company in Ireland after initially reading about Smith's work in Scotland then travelling to Glasgow to meet him in person in 1888. The authorities – despite seeing such organisations as potential army cadets in Great Britain – were suspicious of anything remotely military coming to Ireland, with Dublin Castle lodging an objection to the application to begin enrolment. It was finally granted, however, on 31 December 1888, with the company's home being Charlotte Street Hall. Other churches followed suit, with a dozen companies in and around Belfast in existence by 1890, allowing a brigade to be formed.

A youth group with a strictly Anglican background was next to be established in the north of Ireland with the arrival of the Church Lads' Brigade, the first company formed by St Luke's in Belfast in 1895. A company had been formed at Christchurch, Leeson Park, Dublin, two years earlier. The organisation's roots went back a further decade when, in 1885, a Mr Goldstraw started The Gordon Boys' Brigade in Liverpool. Although taking its name from General Gordon, the hero of Khartoum, it was closely modelled on the BB. In 1891, the Gordon Boys merged with St Andrew's Lads' Brigade, established by Walter Mallock Gee, another officer with the voluntary reserve and secretary of the Junior Branch of the Church of England Temperance Society, at Fulham, London, and the London Diocesan Council for the Welfare of Lads to form the Church Lads' Brigade. In 1911, the Church Lads' Brigade became part of the government's Territorial Cadet Force. On the outbreak of the First World War current and former members formed the nucleus of both the 16th and 19th Battalions of the King's Royal Rifle Corps, with many dying at the Battle of the Somme and subsequent engagements.

The last of the major youth organisations to arrive on the scene was the Boy Scouts. Its inspiration was the Boer War hero Major General Robert Baden-Powell. He held an experimental Scout Camp at Poole in the summer of 1907. Scouting groups began to spring up across the country and, in 1910, Parliament granted a charter to officially bring into being The Boy Scout Association. Part of the training received by the boys was marksmanship though, as one scoutmaster, Robert Patterson of 1st Holywood Troop, pointed out, there

Julia McMordie, wife of the Lord Mayor, was also active in encouraging youth movements and was particularly involved with the 10th Belfast Scout Troop. *(Courtesy of Andrew Totten)*

was no support for this coming from the government. Writing on 31 August 1912, to correct an error in a newspaper article, he said:

> "The Holywood Boy Scouts Miniature Rifle Club was formed in December, 1911, by my predecessor, Scoutmaster Downing, and was affiliated with the NRA[8] in January of this year. As the Boy Scout movement is not recognised in any way by the government, the statement that a dozen rifles were supplied to the troop is far from being correct. We have four .22 rifles in the troop, supplied by the Boy Scouts Headquarters, London, out of a gift of 1,000 pounds made to them some eighteen months ago. Rifle shooting forms a very small part of the boy scout's training, and is only indulged in when the scout wishes to obtain his marksman's badge."

Nationalists, unhappy that Boy Scouts took their allegiance to the King, set up their own youth organisation, Na Fianna Eireann. Established by Countess Constance Markievicz[9] in 1909, it was overtly political, requiring its members to promise not to join the British Army and to strive for Irish independence.

Boys received military training and were given lessons in Irish history and Gaelic. Like the YCV, its name was still being used decades after its founding for the youth wing of a republican paramilitary organisation.

Chapter 3

DISCIPLINE OF THE HIGHEST ORDER

In times of difficulty men had to carry their guns while they followed the plough.

Belfast Lord Mayor
Robert James McMordie

Former Irish Guards officer Lieutenant Colonel Robert Chichester, who was to be the Young Citizen Volunteers' only commanding officer, demanded a free hand on the 'military side' of the organisation. *(Belfast Telegraph)*

THE MAN WHO WAS to shape the Young Citizen Volunteers was Robert Peel Dawson Spencer Chichester, the son of a lord and grandfather, though he was never to know it, of a future Prime Minister of Northern Ireland. In 1912, he was a retired lieutenant colonel of just 39 years of age with service in both the Irish Guards and Royal Irish Rifles.[1]

Born on 13 August 1873, to Lord Adolphus John Spencer Churchill Chichester and Mary (nee Dawson) of Castledawson, he entered the army as a teenager. He saw action in central Africa from 1897–99 on attachment to the Central African Rifles then proceeded to South Africa to take part in the Boer War, for which he was awarded the Queen's Medal with clasp for his service. From 1904–13 he commanded the 6th Battalion of the Middlesex Regiment, though clearly this didn't fully occupy his time. In addition to acting as Assistant Commissioner and commanding the combined escorts to the Anglo-German Boundary Commission for Nyasa and Tanganyika in 1908, he was also a Deputy Lieutenant of County Londonderry; a magistrate for Antrim, Donegal and his home county; High Sheriff for County Londonderry from 1907–8 and for County Antrim 1911–12. Lieutenant Colonel Chichester, who set up home at Ormiston[2] in Belfast on his retirement from the army, listed among his other interests being a member of several sporting clubs, including Killultagh Old Rock and Chichester Harriers and the National Coursing Club, as well as an interest in outdoor pursuits such as fishing, shooting and playing cricket.

Naturally, for a man of his standing, he enjoyed the comforts of two private clubs, the Junior United Service Union in Brighton and the Ulster Club in Belfast. A member of the Ulster Unionist Council with a genuine interest in politics, he was an ardent loyalist who would soon become heavily involved in raising and training the East Belfast Regiment of the Ulster Volunteer Force. Before that, however, he had accepted the responsibility of leading the Young Citizen Volunteers, a task he undertook with considerable enthusiasm, passion and obvious pride.

Colonel Chichester had not been the first choice, however. At a meeting of the Uniform Committee, held at 7 Chichester Street, Belfast, on 7 October 1912, Fred T Geddes proposed, with Mr GJ Elliott seconding, to "ask Major Ferrar to take the position. Councillor Workman and the mover and seconder of the resolution to wait upon him with this purpose in view." He presumably declined, for at a meeting on 22 October it was suggested that Colonel Chichester be approached. A month later, on 28 November, Chichester was introduced to the Volunteer Committee at a meeting held in the Lord Mayor's Parlour. The YCV minute book records:

"The Colonel expressed his willingness to take up the duties on the understanding that he would have a free hand with regard to the military side of the organisation. He mentioned that several of the rules would probably require to be revised, but that this could be gone into at a later date. He also stated that it would be necessary to engage additional instructors, as it would be impossible for one man to deal with such a large body of men in such a way as to get the best results."

It adds: "Colonel Chichester expressed the hope that at an early date it would be possible to secure rifles for the men." It was later confirmed that General Sir William Adair had consented to be Honorary Colonel of the Belfast battalion.

The organisation headed by Colonel Chichester was to be based on military lines. Membership was confined to men between the ages of 18 and 35, though there was no upper age limit for officers or officials. Each had to be at least five foot in height and able to present credentials of good character. They were formed into companies which were to have at least 30 and no more than 50 members and be commanded by a captain, with one or two lieutenants according to size, and several staff sergeants. The YCV regulations, written in anticipation of continued expansion, stipulated that six companies were enough to form a battalion, which in turn was to create a Battalion Council whose duties included the appointment of a president, surgeons, treasurer and secretary, the admission of new companies, the selection of officers and organisation of a training schedule. Where isolated companies were formed, a Volunteer Executive would manage their day-to-day running, issuing of uniforms and the raising and collection of subscriptions and donations.

The Young Citizen Volunteers was to be "strictly non-sectarian and non-political" according to its constitution, though that aspect of the organisation is unlikely to have caused anyone any difficulty for the bye-laws on political activities were, at best, ambivalent. Rule 6, for example, stated: "Members shall not, as such, take part in any political meeting or demonstration; nor shall they wear the uniform of the Corps if attending any political meeting". As early as 19 September 1912 – just days after the official launch of the organisation – the honorary secretaries were softening the line on the non-religious, non-political element of the constitution. On that date a letter, published in the *Belfast News Letter*, and nominally aimed at clarifying the situation regarding the formation of a senior corps, stated:

"Some people are under the impression that they must sacrifice their religious and political activities by joining the volunteers. This is altogether wrong, for members can hold whatever religious and political views they please and engage in any religious and political work they please so long as they do not do so as volunteers. Being a civil force, it is open to all, and is strictly non-political and non-sectarian."

Some of the most influential men in Belfast wanted to be publicly identified with the Young Citizen Volunteers. *(Courtesy of Andrew Totten)*

A steering committee, or 'Volunteer Council', set up at the inaugural City Hall meeting to oversee the establishment of the organisation, was far from a-political. Growing to almost 70 members, it included many of Belfast's well-to-do and better-known citizens, many of who were prominent unionists. Members included the Rt Hon Thomas Sinclair, a staunch opponent of home rule; Sir W Crawford, a Belfast magistrate and soon to be Chairman of the York Street Flax Spinning Company; linen manufacturing brothers John Milne Barbour and Harold Barbour; Workman's shipbuilding partner George Smith Clark; Robert Henry Reade, serving Chairman of York Street Flax Spinning Company; Lt Col Walter Edwin Carson McCammond,[3] commanding 4th Royal Irish Rifles; businessman and loyalist gunrunner Major Fred Crawford; tea importer Samuel David Bell; industrialist James Mackie; flour merchant ST Mercier; Belfast Town Clerk Robert Meyer; city councillor Henry Joy McCracken, a descendant of the 1798 rebel leader of the same name; engineer and councillor Henry Riddell; and Kirker Robb, whose son was to die as an officer with the 14th (YCV) Royal Irish Rifles.

Indeed, the only notable non-unionist appeared to be solicitor Francis Joseph Bigger, a prominent nationalist and exponent of a Gaelic revival. Born at Mallusk, he was a respected historian and antiquarian with a particular interest in the 1798 rebellion. The committee members were to remain in office until 15 December 1913, when a further meeting was to be held to look at progress. In the event, their term of office was never officially terminated.

By the middle of January 1913, Fred Geddes was able to claim that applications were coming in from a wide area, including Holywood, Bangor, Newtownards, Lisburn, Ballymena and Londonderry. Speaking at a Central Presbyterian Association discussion on the role of the YCV, held on the 16th of the month, he said Lord Raglan, governor of the Isle of Man, had shown interest in setting up a similar organisation on the island.[4]

Throughout that first winter drills were held every week, reducing to once a month from May 1913. While there was the teaching of first-aid techniques and occasional route marches, the bulk of the training given consisted of "modified military and police drill, single-stick, rifle, and baton exercises, signalling, knot-tying, and such other exercises as the Company's Executive may select, or as may be directed by the Volunteer Executive".

Those missing two drill nights in succession without leave faced a fine of sixpence for each absence, while those arriving late could also find themselves out of pocket. Serious or regular breaches of the rules could result in a member being expelled.

Organised lectures were held regularly as a means of promoting responsibility and loyalty. The Municipal Technical College was again the venue in March 1913 when EJ Elliott gave an address on 'Citizenship'. On 1 May it was the turn of the Town Clerk, Robert Meyer, to deliver a lecture on the 'The History of Belfast'. Some 500 members attended the address, which was accompanied by lantern slides provided by the celebrated Belfast photographer Robert Hogg.

Belfast's Municipal Technical Institute hosted many of the Young Citizen Volunteers' lectures, including one illustrated by the celebrated photographer Robert Hogg. *(Courtesy of Belfast Met)*

It would be wrong, however, to suggest that life as a member of the Young Citizens was all work and no play. The social element of the corps not only took many forms but was also clearly very important both in bonding the young men together and in relieving the more militaristic aspects. In April 1913, for instance, the men attended a concert held in the Ulster Hall, at which the YCV band made its first official public appearance. That such an addition to the organisation was required was first mooted in the letter columns of the morning newspapers in January 1913, when someone signing themselves "Imperialist" wrote:

> "Sir – In order to give a completeness to above organisation a thoroughly efficient military band (brass and reed) is essential, and I would suggest that those in authority should take immediate steps to have this accomplished. There should be no restrictions in regard to age-limit, so that qualified players would be eligible."

Town Clerk Robert Meyer, in addition to being a member of the YCV's steering committee, delivered a lecture on the History of Belfast. *(Belfast Telegraph)*

Within days the idea had been officially taken up and in March the embryo band took to the streets to lead members from St George's Market to the Municipal Technical College for that month's lecture. By the time of the Ulster Hall concert, however, it had been much more refined and, under the direction of former Royal Irish Fusiliers Drum Major May, its playing earned the accolade from the *Belfast News Letter* of being "distinguished by a delicacy of tone and a decision of style which promise well for the future". Lord Mayor McMordie, in his opening remarks before the programme of entertainment began, praised the work of the drill instructors, joking that he would not allow any man to vote, or even marry, unless he had undergone such training.

That same month the No 2 (Cliftonville) Company, the largest in the organisation, was treated to tea in Ye Olde Castle Restaurant by company president John Tyrrell. More than

Right: Football was always popular within the Young Citizen Volunteers, with this side evidently proud of collecting a piece of silverware. *(Courtesy of the Somme Museum)*

Below: The YCV band was a popular addition to the organisation and always drew a crowd when it made public appearances. *(Courtesy of Andrew Totten)*

Under I.A.A. and B.L. (Boy Scout) Associations.

ULSTER BOY SCOUT SPORTS and RALLY.

Organisers:
OFFICERS OF THE 10th BELFAST TROOP.
Patrons:
VISCOUNT MASSEREENE AND FERRARD.
SIR R. KENNEDY, K.C.M.G., D.L.
THE LORD AND LADY MAYORESS.
SIR OTTO AND LADY JAFFE.
and others.

at The Oval, Belfast,

:: ON ::

Saturday 28th June, 1913,

Flag Signalling commences at 2 o'clock.   Sports at 3 o'clock.

Band of the 1st. Batt. Y.C.V.I.

Ulster Flag Signalling Championship.

=== Great Ulster Rally. ===

The Finest Sports of the Year.

OVER 250 ENTRANTS.

NUMEROUS COMIC EVENTS.

Admission   -   Sixpence.
Grand Stand inclusive,   -   One Shilling.
Official Programme and Tickets on Sale everywhere.

R. Nicholl & Co., Printers, High Street, Belfast.

100 guests attended, including Colonel Chichester, Adjutant Captain HO Davis, Dr A Trimble, Captains FWL May and FT Geddes, Lieutenants WB Bulloch, W Shaw, J McMinn and H Tyrrell. The men, who wore their distinctive uniforms, were entertained by a variety of artists, most of whom came from within their own ranks, including W Tyrrell, J Moore, J Laird, J Williamson, F Doherty, WJ Hopper, W Uprichard, S Johnston, R Graham, with Messrs Hanna and Crone providing the accompaniment. A motion of thanks forwarded by Nelson Leech[5] and seconded by WW Buloch was passed, thanking the sub-committee that had arranged the programme, consisting of H Tyrrell, W Crone, WH Calvert and RW Flack.[5]

At the invitation of its commanding officer, Lieutenant Colonel Chichester, some 335 men and 19 officers attended the second performance at the Royal Hippodrome in Belfast city centre on 22 January 1914. Forming up at St George's market at 7.45 pm in dress uniform, and led by the band, they marched along May Street and Howard Street to the theatre, where a large crowd had gathered to watch their arrival. Filing into the stalls and circle, they cheered a message of welcome flashed on the screen by 'hipposcope' and at the conclusion of the evening "joined in singing the National Anthem, and in giving cheers for the King and for their officers". All was not rosy, however, as a number of factors had contributed to falling numbers attending drill nights. The *Belfast News Letter* took the opportunity to review the organisation's progress to date in its report of the theatre outing:

"Since the cordial send-off given to the organisation in October last the Young Citizen Volunteers have made steady progress in every direction save that of actual numbers. At the time of the inception of the corps a wave of enthusiasm swept many young men into the ranks who failed to settle down to the military routine and discipline, and now the genuinely earnest members who remain undoubtedly form one of the finest bodies of drilled citizens to be found in the kingdom – men of whom any officers might well be proud. And though the Government and the military authorities have thus far given the movement the cold shoulder, and have refused to allow the corps to be equipped with rifles, the organisation has achieved a very creditable measure of success, thanks largely to the substantial support given by many of the leading citizens of Belfast, and to the keen interest shown by the President, the Lord Mayor, Mr RJ McMordie, MP; the honorary treasurer, Mr Frank Workman; the assistant honorary treasurer, Mr GD Coates; and the representative council which has been formed; together with the work of the secretary, Mr HG Stevenson. The battalion has been exceedingly fortunate in its officers. Colonel Chichester has not only taken a lively interest in the work of the corps, but has generously placed the grounds of his residence, Ormiston, at its disposal for drill purposes, and has also given facilities for the sports and pastimes of the men. The other officers of the corps include – Major JE Gunning, second-in-command; Captain and Adjutant HO Davis, Captain FWL May, Captain J Harper, Captain W Glass,[6] Captain JW Coulter (acting quartermaster), Captain E May, Captain WH Whann, Lieutenant E Workman, Lieutenant W Bullock, Lieutenant J Shaw; and Second-Lieutenants C Hirst, J McKee, A McKee,[7] V Robb, V Hindman, J McMinn, and TH Mayes. The Markets Committee having permitted the use of the spacious covered markets for the work of the battalion, drills are held on three evenings each week, and there is also a special class for officers and non-commissioned officers with a view to giving special training to company and section commanders. Up to the present, the drill has been almost wholly without the use of rifles, but, this fact notwithstanding, the facilities afforded have been such that the men have had a very thorough training in field work of every description, while the discipline which obtains is of the very highest order."

William Glass, a pre-war captain in the Young Citizen Volunteers, was to be killed with the 11th Royal Irish Rifles in June 1917. *(Central Presbyterian Association Magazine, June 1917)*

It was a fair and accurate summary of what had been a difficult 16 months for the fledging organisation. From more than 1,000 young men who had flooded into its ranks in the first few weeks of its creation, perhaps a third remained as active members. Those who had failed to stay the distance would, no doubt, have had many reasons to leave but clearly the most common would have been the level of discipline they had been expected to maintain. Colonel Chichester along with Major Gunning, his second-in-command and formerly of the Irish Guards, had brought to the YCV a standard of compliance that would have wearied many an army recruit, let alone the former BB boys or Boy Scouts who had sought to continue their innocent youthful pleasures within the ranks of this new organisation.

Expense was another aspect of being a YCV member. Two shillings and sixpence was demanded from each recruit on enrolment and a further sixpence at the beginning of each month in subscriptions. In addition, members had to buy their own uniforms at a cost of approximately 30 shillings, though that could be paid by monthly instalments after "giving such security for the cost of the same as the Volunteer Executive may require". Many young men would have struggled to find such sums that, though pitiful by today's standards, represented sizeable expenditure in 1912–14. Such charges, no doubt, contributed to the perception that the YCV was an elitist organisation that only the sons of clergy, shopkeepers and managers could enjoy. For some, remaining a Young Citizen was simply a luxury they couldn't afford.

The distinctive YCV uniform consisted of a grey tunic with Prussian blue facings, piping, slashes and a crow's foot at the cuffs set off with white metal buttons bearing a crown, red hand of Ulster and YCV lettering. The collar and cap badges featured the red hand of Ulster and crown on a shamrock. While officers wore shirt and tie with a Sam Brown belt, the rank and file had to make do with an uncomfortable stand-up collar and striped belt at the waist. The organisation decided "not to adopt recognised military badges for distinguishing officers as this system was open to abuse and lead to misunderstanding and unpleasantries". The shamrock cap badge could be adopted by allowing the envisaged "battalions of the various provinces to introduce their own coat of arms in the centre". Concerns were raised as to whether or not the Young Citizens were allowed to use the crown, but, as the YCV minute book notes, "after discussion it was decided that while the Volunteers were not really legally established to use it that it be adhered to".

Thomas Carnduff, who was to go on to make a name for himself as a working class poet and author, joined the Cliftonville company of the YCV aged 26. It was one of 18 companies listed in the Young Citizens minute book as existing in Belfast as at 22 October 1912, the others being City Hall, Ormeau, Central, Balmoral and Malone, Cliftonville No 2, Knock, GPO, 9th Old Boys, Fortwilliam, 37th Old Boys, Ormeau Swimmers, Duncairn, Shankill, Donegall, Connswater, Strandtown, and CIYMS. Carnduff was impressed with its goals and content that politics was banned within its ranks. He promptly paid up for his uniform and silver regimental badges "displaying a three-leafed shamrock with the Hand of Ulster embossed on the centre". Most of the drill instructors were former soldiers who soon had the raw recruits "licked into shape, similar to a British territorial infantry battalion of today," he recorded. Organisers persisted in the hope that the government would make an exception and recognise the YCV as qualifying for support under the Territorial Act of 1907, which did not apply to Ireland. That would have resulted in financial support and a supply of rifles. A number of applications were submitted but the authorities were having none of it, with the rejections generating resentment and disappointment in the ranks and beyond.[8]

Carnduff noted: "Lieut-Colonel Chichester, an Irish Guards reserve officer, took over command, with Major Kerr-Smiley[9] and Captain Harry Mulholland as second and third officers. We made a brave show on our first route march through the city streets but we carried no firearms, which caused much comment."

Chapter 4

DRILL, BROTHERS, DRILL

When traitors, drunk with party zeal,
   Made known their secret plan
To place beneath the rebel heel
   The loyal Ulsterman,
With steadfast courage undismayed
   By angry threats or jeers,
Our leader spoke, and called to aid
   The Ulster Volunteers.

   Drill, brothers, drill
For the danger's drawing near;
   March, brothers, march,
For the hour may soon be here;
   When together we shall stand,
Ranked and ready at command,
   For home and faith and freedom
And the land we love so dear.

by HCW, 1914

ON SATURDAY 5 JULY 1913, men began gathering along roads in north Belfast. Many wore their working clothes; others were dressed in the same garb they would be sporting the following day at church. Members from the Ligoniel area met at the corner of Cliftonpark Avenue and the Crumlin Road; further along the avenue the men of the Cliftonville and Duncairn branches formed up and moved off. They would be joined later by contingents from Fortwilliam and Greencastle where Royal Avenue meets Donegall Street. At their head were bands from Ligoniel and Whitehouse, and the pipers of Castleton. After a circuit of the City Hall, the parade made its way through the Shankill, Cliftonville and Antrim Road districts, with crowds of people lining the route to applaud. Amongst those striding out in front were shipyard owner George Clark and leading linen yarn and flex merchant Boughey WD Montgomery,[1] both founding members of the YCV committee.

On this occasion, however, all those taking part in this show of strength wore armbands bearing three different initials: UVF.

Without a uniform as such, the Ulster Volunteer Force relied on their armbands to distinguish them from other civilians. *(Author)*

The *Belfast News Letter* reported the following Monday:

"A spectacle full of interest was provided the citizens of Belfast on Saturday, when the first parade in connection with the recently organised Ulster Volunteer Force took place. The units that joined in the display belonged to the Northern district, and their bearing and appearance created an excellent impression. All marched with the dash and swing of regular troops, results of the strict course of training to which they had been submitted from the very commencement of the movement. Unfortunately owing to other demands upon the attention of the members, many of them were unable to participate in the turnout, but the numbers on parade were sufficient to give critics some idea of the strength, solidarity, and efficiency of the force. As the men marched in fours through the leading thoroughfares they were viewed with admiration by thousands of spectators."

Above: Lieutenant Colonel WEC McCammond would ultimately be associated with the Royal Irish Rifles, the Young Citizen Volunteers and the Ulster Volunteer Force. *(Belfast Telegraph)*

Below: The grounds of Craigavon House on 23 September 1911, as Orangemen and members of the Unionist Clubs arrive. *(PRONI D961/3/001)*

By an odd coincidence, elements of the 3rd, 4th and 5th Battalions of the Royal Irish Rifles arrived in Belfast on the same day as they returned home, led by a military band, from a four-week training camp at Ballykinlar to Victoria Barracks. They were under the command of Lieutenant Colonel WEC McCammond, also associated with the YCV and soon to become a UVF leader.

The YCV and UVF had evolved in tandem, with more in common than divided them. The latter, however, was overtly a product of the political turmoil that was now threatening to engulf the north of Ireland. The man at its helm, at least politically, was Sir Edward Carson. A Dublin-born barrister, he had been elected leader of the Unionist Party in 1910, just a year before the Liberal Party returned to power and the unfinished business of granting Home Rule to Ireland. Carson loved a good fight and, despite his legal background, was not overly concerned that it should only be fought within the law. He was passionate about the cause and was prepared to put his career and even his freedom on the line.

It was at a demonstration at Craigavon House, the Belfast home of Carson's right-hand man James Craig, that the unionist leader spelled out his commitment and what he would need of his supporters. Standing on the platform overlooking Belfast Lough on the eastern fringes of the city, he told the estimated 50,000-strong crowd that they would have to be prepared to take control of the province the day that Home Rule became law. Physical resistance would require an army, of course, and the seeds of the UVF were reportedly planted that day, 23 September 1911. Among the groups at the mass demonstration was a contingent of Orangemen from County Tyrone under the leadership of

Captain Ambrose Ricardo – a future Brigadier in the 36th (Ulster) Division – whose drill and appearance impressed those waiting in the field. Other Lodges and the Unionist Clubs began to follow their example by engaging in paramilitary-type training.

Over the following year the unionist leadership stepped up the political pressure both at Westminster and in Ulster, where Carson undertook a series of political rallies that accumulated on 28 September 1912 – just 18 days after the meeting that had created the Young Citizens – with the most impressive display of domestic political resistance of the 20th century: the signing of the Ulster Covenant.[2]

After attending a religious ceremony at the Ulster Hall, during which the three main Protestant churches gave their blessing to the great show of strength which was to follow, Carson led the unionist leadership to the City Hall where they were greeted by robed city councillors, Harbour Board members, Water Commissioners and representatives of the Board of Guardians. With Lord Mayor Robert McMordie at their head, they then made their way inside to where a Union Flag draped table had been placed under the impressive City Hall dome so Carson could be the first to sign the Covenant. They were followed throughout the day by thousands of men who signed forms set out on the rows of specially constructed tables lining the City Hall corridors. In total, some 218,000 men and 234,000 women were to sign the declaration at centres throughout Ulster, including many YCV members.

Thomas Carnduff and another Young Citizen, Willie Baxter (who was later to be killed in France with the 14th Royal Irish Rifles), were among the thousands who queued at the City Hall to sign the solemn league and covenant. "Baxter was, like myself, a shipyardman, and I am afraid neither of the two of us were keen politicians at the time, but we didn't want to miss any of the fun," recalled Carnduff.

> "Carson arrived with his staff at the City Hall early in the day and was the first to sign. A flag was borne into the chamber supposed to have been carried by the Inniskilling regiment at the Battle of the Boyne. The flag was woven of silk with a crimson five-pointed star in the centre of its orange folds and the cross of St George of England in the top left hand corner. No one had ever heard of the existence of this standard previous to the demonstration. It was handed back to its owners and has never been heard of since."

For a year since the planting of the seeds at Craigavon, the belief that a military organisation would be required to resist Home Rule had steadily been growing. The Ulster Unionist Council, formed in 1905 as a broad church unionist body, gave its blessing to the formation of such a body and in January 1913, the Ulster Volunteer Force officially came into being. Its membership was to be confined to men who had signed the solemn league and covenant and, though it got off to a sluggish start, its numbers were ultimately to reach close to 100,000 men of all ages and backgrounds. A headquarters was established at the Old Town Hall and with the help of the elderly Lord Roberts, the most distinguished and highly decorated soldier of his generation, an old Indian Army officer, General Sir George Richardson, was found to command it. Although not an Irishman, Richardson had taken up residence in the north of Ireland after retiring from the army in 1907.

William Baxter joined the Young Citizen Volunteers with his friend Thomas Carnduff. He served throughout the war until he was killed on 21 March 1918, the first day of the major German offensive on the Somme. *(Courtesy of Belfast Met)*

General Sir George Richardson, a former Indian Army officer, was selected to command the UVF on the recommendation of Lord Roberts. *(Library of Congress, Prints & Photographs Division, Washington DC, USA. Reproduction Number LC-DIG-GGBAIN-15693)*

Structured on the lines of the British Army, the UVF had regiments, battalions and companies based on geographical divisions, with the Orange Order and the Unionist Clubs proving fruitful recruiting grounds. The size of regiments varied greatly according to the size of the Protestant community they were drawn from. Consequently in Belfast, where there was a regiment for North, South, East and West of the city, each could claim several battalions while in the west of the province an entire regiment might be less in number than a city battalion. In addition to 'infantry' the UVF boasted a Motor Car Corps – an innovation that was ahead of the professional army – Signalling and Dispatch Rider Corps, cavalry units in Enniskillen and Ballymena, and a Medical and Nursing Corps that included many women volunteers. Indeed, the role of women generally in the UVF made it ahead of its time. When possible, retired army officers were recruited to provide professional training and leadership. The majority of units, however, were led and drilled by men of limited or no military experience. The growing strength of this civilian army alarmed the authorities in Dublin and London though there was little that they could do but sabre rattle. By July 1913 the Commissioner of the Royal Irish Constabulary was reporting that 20,000 men were drilling in Belfast with growing evidence of "religious and political feeling". He added:

"To sum up the situation you have in Belfast some 300,000 Protestants and 100,000 Catholics – the latter mainly dependent on the former for a livelihood – the Protestant population also are bitterly opposed to Home Rule . . . I am convinced that there will be serious loss of life and wholesale destruction of property in Belfast on the passing of the Home Rule Bill."

The further through the parliamentary process that the Third Home Rule Bill progressed, the greater the tension and the more the UVF stepped up its public displays. Battalions and regiments were regularly paraded for ceremonies, such as the presentation of Standards or Colours by prominent citizens. Church parades were regular occurrences, as were training marches and musters, all aimed at attracting the attention of the Government.

As 1913 gave way to 1914, there were few who didn't believe that it would all end in bloodshed on the streets of Ulster, not least as there was now a new player in the game. At the end of November 1913, a public meeting held at the Rotunda Rink in Dublin had seen the creation of the Irish Volunteers. The hall, capable of holding 4,000 people, was packed to overflowing. Nationalist MP Thomas Kettle, who was to die at the Somme in September 1916 among some of the same men he was that night appealing to for support, could barely be heard by the reporters at the front. "To drill, to learn the use of arms, to acquire the habit of concerted and disciplined action, to form a citizen army from a population now at the mercy of almost any organised aggression – this beyond all doubt is a programme that appeals to all Ireland, but especially to young Ireland," he told those pressing forward at the front.

"We begin at once in Dublin, and we are confident that the movement will be taken up without delay all over the country. Public opinion has already, and quite spontaneously, formed itself into an eager desire for the establishment of the Irish Volunteers. The object proposed for the Irish Volunteers is to secure and maintain the rights and liberties common to all the people of Ireland. Their duties will be defensive and protective, and they will not contemplate either aggression or domination."

The political debate over the Third Home Rule Bill also became increasingly more savage, with little goodwill apparent and, despite the constant talking behind closed doors, no sign of compromise. Indeed, there emerged within the Cabinet a group of individuals who seemed more inclined to call the Ulstermen's bluff rather than find a peaceful way forward. This special committee, which included Winston Churchill – who three years earlier had effectively been run out of town by unionist protestors when he attempted to address nationalists on the merits of Home Rule – War Minister Colonel John Seely, Lord Lieutenant of Ireland Augustine Birrell and Attorney General Sir John Simon, was chaired by Lord Crewe, another long time advocate of Irish self-rule and himself a former Lord Lieutenant of Ireland, though illness made him unavailable at a critical moment.

Battalions and regiments of the Ulster Volunteer Force throughout the province were engaged in shows of strength aimed at discouraging the Government from attempting to force the issue. *(Author's collection)*

Orders had been issued on 12 March requiring the Army commanders in Ireland to step up security, particularly at arms dumps, amid intelligence reports of planned raids. However, following meetings in London on 18 and 19 March involving at various times the members of the Cabinet sub-committee, Prime Minister Asquith, Army Council representatives and senior military figures including Lieutenant General Sir Arthur Paget, commander-in-chief of military forces in Ireland, fresh instructions were sent out that went much further than merely doubling guards at key installations. Troops were to be dispatched to both Newry and Dundalk; Victoria Barracks, considered vulnerable to civilian protest, was to be evacuated and the men sent to Holywood barracks, just a short distance away from Craigavon, home to James Craig; the Carrickfergus garrison was increased while detachments of men were sent to Omagh, Armagh and Enniskillen. Battalions of soldiers based in England were to be made available to cross the Irish Sea at short notice. Two light cruisers, HMS *Attentive* and HMS *Pathfinder*, were ordered to sail from Bantry Bay for Kingstown, where they were to pick up companies of soldiers and transport them to Carrickfergus by daybreak on 21 March before seeking orders on what further assistance they might be to the army. Other ships were ordered to be ready to carry troops from Portsmouth to Kingstown and Dundalk, while elements of the Royal Navy's Third Battle Squadron, then off the coast of Spain, was ordered to gather in the Firth of Clyde and to be prepared to sail for Ireland if required; another eight war ships received similar orders for possible deployment. In addition, Major General Sir Nevil Macready, an officer with a well-earned reputation for the skilful use of soldiers in support of the civil powers and Director of Personal Services at the War Office, was secretly appointed General Officer commanding Belfast.

The Ulster Volunteer Force engaged in military style exercises to show the Government the seriousness of its intent.

While all this was contemplated in secrecy, rumours abounded that some sort of action to rein in the loyalists was afoot. The newspapers predicted that mass arrests, including those of Carson and Craig, were only days away. The UVF, which had sources both within military and political circles, prepared as best it could for all eventualities. Its leaders were warned to stay away from their homes for fear of being caught up in the expected military sweeps and the Old Town Hall was evacuated, with headquarters staff moved to a heavily guarded Craigavon.

In the event, however, the Government had its own bluff called. The army, while traditionally politically neutral, could not avoid but be influenced by events that were threatening to engulf not just Ireland but Great Britain in an increasing spiral of uncertainty verging on crisis. Many officers, some through birth or family connections and others with straight-forward Tory leanings, sympathised with the unionist population. Dozens at the Curragh camp, led by Brigadier General Hubert Gough, were prepared to resign or accept dismissal rather than move against the north. Faced with what was at best an embarrassment and at worst the forerunner of similar mass resignations across the armed forces, the Government took cold feet.

In public, the YCV had carried on as normal throughout the emerging crisis. On the evening of 5 March 1914, more than 300 men and officers, including Colonel R Spencer Chichester, found the time to pack into the Exhibition Hall in Belfast for a smoking concert, a common means of both bonding and fundraising. The *Belfast News Letter* noted that "since its formation some eighteen months ago the organisation has received a gratifying measure of support, and is now established on a firm basis, the strong spirit of comradeship obtaining in all ranks being one of the most satisfactory features, while the discipline and enthusiasm are splendidly maintained." The volunteers, who wore full-dress uniform, presented a "very smart appearance", and "thoroughly enjoyed themselves". It was, however, to prove to be the final night's entertainment for the YCV as an independent organisation, as the growing disquiet within its ranks and leadership came to a head.

The one voice that was to be absent from any debate, however, was that of the man who had been most influential in bringing about the creation of the Young Citizens, Belfast Lord Mayor Robert McMordie. Away on holiday at Hyeres in the south of France from the start of March, he had returned to his east Belfast residence, Cabin Hill, on 24 March as the situation at home worsened. Suffering from influenza, he consulted his doctor who advised rest. The following day, however, his condition had deteriorated and Professor Sir William Whitla was sent for. He diagnosed acute bronchitis and pneumonia but was hopeful a full recovery could be affected. That afternoon, however, the Lord Mayor suffered a fatal heart attack. A strong supporter of both the UVF and

The death of Belfast Lord Mayor Robert McMordie came at a crucial point in the YCV's history. The Young Citizens and the Ulster Volunteers paraded together for the first time at his funeral. This photograph of Mr McMordie was taken just months earlier at the opening of a Belfast abattoir. *(Courtesy of Belfast City Council)*

YCV, his views on the future path to be followed would have carried considerable weight. As it was, his funeral on Saturday 28 March, provided the first occasion when the two organisations paraded together. The *Belfast Telegraph* reported:

"Each of the city battalions sent fifty men, who marched behind the Young Citizen Volunteers. The YCVs were in uniform, and the UVF in civilian attire. As the cortege passed out of the gates of Cabin Hill bearing its manly owner through familiar scenes for the last time, the Volunteers lined on either side of the Newtownards Road stood to attention."

The Ulster Volunteers again lined both sides of the Falls Road as the cortege reached the City Cemetery, joining the crowds of on-lookers in bearing their heads as the hearse passed through the gates. The newspaper continued:

"There was a brief halt at the portals of the cemetery while the casket was being placed on the shoulders of a party of Young Citizen Volunteer sergeants. Then, with slow and measured tread the short remaining stage of the journey was traversed till there came the final halt opposite the McMordie vault, which is almost under the shadow of the mortuary chapel, but on the other side of the avenue. A deep and impressive solemnity rested o'er the scene as the casket was reverently committed to the keeping of the tomb…"

Eight YCV sergeants, under Sergeant Bowman, had carried the casket. In total, some 223 YCV men and officers attended the funeral under Colonel Chichester, who later placed a wreath of clove carnations and red roses by the tomb on behalf of his Young Citizens.

The drive for the organisation to join the Ulster Volunteers came from within the membership, and particularly from the commanding officer, with the YCV committee only realising it no longer had a body to govern when reports of the merger appeared in the newspapers. Carnduff recorded:

"Some eight hundred volunteers paraded in St George's Market where Colonel Chichester proposed we join forces with the UVF, threatening to resign on the spot if the majority refused. The vote was practically unanimous and the Young Citizens ceased to be an independent force. A Special Service brigade had been organised from amongst the rank and file of the UVF members and the Young Citizens were attached to this body because of their standard of training. The Special Service brigade were to be ready for hazardous work if the occasion should arise."

It was the Young Citizens themselves, with the encouragement of their commanding officer, who took the decision to combine with the Ulster Volunteers. *(Courtesy of the Somme Museum)*

The Special Service Section of the UVF had only been formed in recent months as a direct result of the increasing threat of military action being taken against Carson and his volunteers. Each regiment had its own unit, its members being made up of former professional soldiers, reservists or militia. The idea was to have this unit ready for active service at a moment's notice, buying time for the rest of the UVF to be mobilised. In addition, efforts had been made to recruit professional soldiers to command the UVF regiments, resulting in the introduction of Colonel GHH Couchman as head of the Belfast division and Colonel

JH Patterson, Major Tempest Stone and Captain Malone as commanders respectively of the West, South and North Belfast regiments. Only Colonel Chichester, the YCV commanding officer, had remained at the head of the East Belfast regiment of the UVF.

An emergency meeting of the YCV's Volunteer Committee was called for Thursday 2 April 1914, at the Lord Mayor's Parlour. Colonel Chichester failed to attend, sending along his second in command, Major Gunning, to represent him. The minute book records:

> "Mr Workman stated that the Council had been summoned to consider recent developments in connection with the military side of the organisation as reported in the daily papers, and stated that if there was any truth in the rumours, that Colonel Chichester and those responsible, had no authority for identifying the organisation with political affairs. Mr May explained that it became necessary to take the action referred to as no support was being given to the civic side of the organisation. After some discussion Mr Geddes proposed, and Capt Mitchell seconded the following resolution: 'That the Office Bearers and Council of the Young Citizen Volunteers of Ireland deeply regret that they were not consulted prior to the recent amalgamation of the 1st Battalion Young Citizen Volunteers, with the Ulster Volunteer Force, and take this opportunity of informing the public that it was done without their authority or consent.'"

Mr May, however, pointed out that the council was technically no longer in office as it had failed to hold a general meeting in December 1913, as demanded by the YCV's constitution. The committee then passed a second motion, opposed only by Mr Geddes, watering down the first by simply expressing "surprise" at the merger with the UVF and forming a sub-committee to look at what to do next. It also urged Colonel Chichester to attend a meeting within the next week to explain his actions. Leon McVicker, of Cantrell and Cochrane Ltd, a member of the YCV committee, was unable to attend the 2 April meeting. In his letter of apology he wrote: "I fancy our minds are in unison on the subject and although I am a member of the UVF, I am not in favour of the YCV being 'turned over,' especially so, remembering the object – 'Non-Pol' and 'Non-Sec'. My idea was to grant men leave of absence during the present crisis. By being taken over it completely destroys forever the YCV and leaves the organisation open to criticism." The commanding officer again failed to appear, though Frank Workman[3] was able to report to a committee meeting on 20 April that "he had a conversation with Colonel Chichester without any satisfactory results".

Mr Geddes, who obviously felt betrayed by the organisation he had created, demanded that the council either approve or repudiate the Colonel's actions and look at the steps necessary to take the organisation back within its control or disband it. His fellow committee members decided instead to write to the Colonel demanding an explanation. The last entry in the minute book is for a meeting held at 7 Chichester Street on Tuesday 19 May at noon, with Councillor Workman presiding. It was reported that a letter had been received from commanding officer suggesting a meeting be held on finances "but nothing on the UVF move". Workman had already replied, telling him "this was a matter in which he was not specially interested". The committee discussed taking legal action against the Colonel, and adjourned for a fortnight for legal advice. It appears to have never met again.

Chapter 5

A LORRY LOOMED OUT OF THE DARKNESS

All differences of rank and social status were forgotten in face of a common danger, all were animated by the one desire to maintain their priceless heritage of civil and religious freedom, and all were determined to put everything to the hazard in defence of their liberties.

The *Belfast News Letter* on the YCV being inspected
by Sir Edward Carson, June 1914

O N THE EVENING OF 24 April 1914, messengers were sent out across Belfast armed with the addresses of members of the Young Citizen Volunteers. That Friday night, as they pedalled down side streets or steered their motorcycles up the driveways of the well-to-do, one of the largest mobilisations of a civilian army was underway in support of an act of rebellion that was to rock the British establishment to its core. It had been four months since Fred Crawford, a member of the YCV steering committee and prominent UVF figure, had suggested to the unionist leadership the purchase and landing of thousands of weapons and millions of rounds of ammunition. For years he and others had been attempting, with some success, to slip arms into the country under the noses of the authorities. The scale of such activities, however, was always going to be too small to arm the Ulster Volunteers who were, in any event, becoming impatient with parading the streets with wooden dummy weapons. Now, after an adventure worthy of a fiction novel, he had arrived off the coast of Ireland with a shipload of rifles and barrels of bullets.

Thomas Carnduff[1] was playing with his young son when the knock came to the door. Opening it he found one of his sergeants in uniform, still astride his bicycle propping himself up against the house wall with an outstretched arm. "Get into your uniform and

A niche industry grew up in Belfast in 1913–14 making wooden guns so that members of the Ulster Clubs, Orange Order and Ulster Volunteer Force could practice arms drill and still be within the law. *(Belfast Telegraph)*

report at Ormiston House. Make it fast," he snapped before disappearing again into the darkness. Making his excuses to a wife who was less than impressed that he was heading off in uniform with no idea what he was going to do or when he was likely to return, he made his way to Colonel Chichester's home. There he was given a rifle with a full magazine and paraded with the rest of the battalion in the darkness.

> "We were all keyed up with excitement. It was a beautiful spring night and the slight wisp rustling the overhead branches intensified expectation of mystery and adventure. There was no shouting, usual with military parades. The NCOs collected their sections swiftly, but quietly and without fuss. A cordon of volunteers was placed round the grounds and patrols sent out along the roads to intercept any inquisitive policemen and see what could be done regarding the telephone wires in the neighbourhood. Shortly afterwards, all telephones, in our district, at any rate, were rendered harmless."

All across Ulster men were on the move, many to Larne where the port was sealed off in preparation of the arrival of the *Clyde Valley* and its shipment of arms from Germany. In Belfast, all the UVF battalions were fully mobilised by early evening. While most were sent out to patrol their respective areas, a contingent from East Belfast was despatched to Musgrave Channel, by the docks, where it was to spend the evening apparently waiting for rifles to be unloaded from a ship. For company they had Customs officials and police officers who were equally interested in the contents of the SS *Balmerino*. At the same time, volunteers from North Belfast had marched to the Midland Railway Station, which they cordoned off outside while taking over the platforms inside. The real action, however, was taking place elsewhere.

Fred Crawford, who had received the last minute order as he was passing the Copeland Islands, off the coast of County Down, to land at Larne rather than Belfast, finally tied up about 11.00 pm, some two hours later than expected. Men swarmed aboard the *Clyde Valley*, renamed the *Mountjoy II* by Crawford, determined to make up the lost time. As one group loaded rifles into the succession of cars that nosed their way up the quayside before, fully laden, disappearing again into the night, others loaded waiting ships that were to sail for Belfast and Donaghadee. The *Clyde Valley* had one last call to make, sailing across Belfast Lough to take the remaining rifles and ammunition on board

The gunrunners aboard the *Fanny* in the Kiel Canal, Germany. The *Fanny* transported the weapons to the Irish Sea, where they were transferred to a second ship, the *Clyde Valley* to avoid detection.

Back row: Fred Crawford (the UVF's Director of Ordnance), Captain Andrew Agnew (captain of the *Fanny*) and Bruno Spiro (the Berlin gunsmith from whom the guns were purchased).

Front Row: Captain Marthin Falck (former owner of the *Fanny*) and Helen Crawford (Fred Crawford's wife). *(PRONI D961/3/002)*

to Bangor where the North Down Regiment of the UVF rapidly unloaded it, the last of the weapons only leaving town around 7.00 am, well after the cover of darkness had given way to the glare of daylight.

At Ormiston, the YCV waited patiently for something to happen. All were expected to remain silent, with Carnduff roasted by a sergeant after he let out an oath when struck on the shin by a rifle butt. By midnight the roads, normally still at that time of night, were becoming noticeably busier with lorries and private cars rumbling by. A couple more hours passed then word was passed round to be ready for action. "A motor cyclist swung past

Today Ormiston House lies empty and decaying, as evidenced by the state of the Gate House and stables, the only buildings now visible from the roadway. (*Author*)

Thomas Carnduff was a member of the Cliftonville company of the YCV. During the war he served with the Royal Engineers and later found employment as a Belfast gas inspector. (*Courtesy of Dr Sarah Ferris*)

us through the gates of Ormiston," remembered Carnduff. "A lorry loomed out of the darkness and the driver sang out a greeting as he turned the vehicle into the carriage way. The tarpaulin was stripped from the lorry in a few seconds and rifles and ammunition were soon being transferred to the cellars." YCV patrols were mounted in the surrounding streets and anyone who could not identify themselves as a Volunteer was turned back but there were no unsavoury incidents. Had police or soldiers arrived on the scene, Carnduff had little doubt that lives would have been lost but, like all the other lads who had been training for months past with the hope of seeing action, it was not fear but exhilaration that was the over-riding emotion. Weary but happy, the men made their way home again in the full knowledge that they were in the thick of things at last.

The temporary arms dumps set up by the UVF on the night of 24 April were cleared over the following days, with the weapons distributed across the province. Belfast was allocated bales of German rifles, each containing five weapons accompanied by bayonets and 500 rounds of ammunition, though for the most part they remained locked away. The army, which at one time seemed on the verge of declaring martial law, kept a low profile, leaving the enforcement of order to the police. There was little to concern the Royal Irish Constabulary, however, for though the Volunteers were making themselves visible, their instructions were to avoid confrontation and maintain the peace. With all sides endeavouring to keep order, the Third Home Rule Bill had its final reading in the Commons on 25 May without provoking incident in Belfast. The UVF kept its members busy by mounting training days and ceremonial parades, while church services and the presentations of colours were regular occurrences.

The YCV, headed by Major JE Gunning, was back at Ormiston a month after the gunrunning, together with the six battalion strong East Belfast UVF Regiment – No 1 Ballynafeigh and Newtownbreda, No 2 Willowfield, No 3 Mountpottinger, No 4 Victoria, No 5 Avoniel and No 6 Strandtown and Knock – to take part in a Drumhead Service on Sunday 24 May, the eve of the Commons debate. An estimated 3,500 men, having paraded from various parts of the city headed by three bands, including the Willowfield Temperance Flute Band and the Duke of York Pipe Band, formed three sides of a square in a field off the Wandsworth Road, close to Colonel Chichester's house. A large crowd had gathered to watch the service, with a detachment of 'Volunteer Police' keeping them off the parade ground. Among the guests were Belfast Lord Mayor Crawford McCullagh and his private secretary FW Moneypenny. The men were drawn up to form three sides of a square, with the drums of the Young Citizen Volunteers piled in the centre of the open side. The service opened with the singing of that old loyalist battle hymn, 'O God, our help in ages past,' with the YCV brass band, led by Fred May, conducting.

The Young Citizens, in their distinctive grey uniforms, also put on more warlike performances for the benefit of both the Government and public. Carnduff remembered the men being ordered to march through the streets of Belfast city centre armed with rifles and bayonets: "The city was full of rumours on the morning of the route march. There were whispers that operations on a warlike scale would commence that day. But the authorities merely stood by." Headed by Colonel Chichester and Major Kerr-Smiley, both on horseback, and encouraged by lively tunes from the regimental band, the men enjoyed the cheers, applause and hat waving from the crowds that had rapidly gathered along the roadside.

"Bringing up the rear, guarded by a strong escort, was a brace of machine guns mounted on tripods and bogies," he recorded, adding an interesting insight into how the Volunteers saw themselves: "… one was apt to remember such another demonstration in the same thoroughfare, one hundred and twenty years earlier, when the old Irish Volunteers demonstrated their defiance of the English government of the day and their sympathy with the French people in the taking of the Bastille."

On 7 June 1914, the Young Citizen Volunteers paraded alongside the UVF's Special Service Force at the Royal Ulster Agricultural Society show grounds at Balmoral to be reviewed by Sir Edward Carson. Colonel Chichester, riding at their head, led the battalion

The YCVs took on a much more warlike pose when they paraded through the streets of Belfast with a pair of machine guns being pulled on bogies. *(Courtesy of the Somme Museum)*

through the gates at Balmoral Avenue at 4.45 pm sharp. Second-in-command Kerr-Smiley accompanied him with Adjutant Gunning bringing up the rear, also on horseback. The *Belfast News Letter* reported:

> "Their arrival evoked a loud roar of satisfaction from the spectators, and the display of enthusiasm was renewed with vigour as the five companies composing the battalion were drawn up in quarter-column facing the grand stand. To the inspiring strains of a military tune played by their own band, under the conductorship of Mr Fred May, the corps marched like a crack battalion of infantry of the line, their smart appearance being enhanced by their attractive uniforms, which looked at their best in the glorious sunlight. This was the first occasion upon which the Young Citizen Volunteers had paraded before Sir Edward Carson since they became attached to the East Belfast Regiment of the Ulster Volunteer Force, and their conduct on parade bore striking testimony to the efficient training they have received under the experienced direction of their commanding officer, who devotes a good deal of time and energy to the improvement of the corps, with a view to making them one of the most effective units of Ulster's army. The step taken by the men some time ago in linking themselves with the Volunteer Force has earned for them the highest appreciation not only of the citizens of Belfast, but of the loyalists throughout the Imperial province, the significance of the movement being all the more striking by reason of the fact that the initiative was taken voluntarily by the rank and file, and the Unionist leader carried the vast audience with him on Saturday when he gave the corps a hearty welcome."

With the Young Citizens formed up on the right of the line, with the Special units of East, South and North Belfast lined up next to them in that order, Sir Edward – who had arrived

The Young Citizen Volunteers always drew a crowd when they paraded through the streets of Belfast, particularly after merging with the Ulster Volunteer Force. *(Courtesy of the Somme Museum)*

at Balmoral after presenting drums and bugles to the West Belfast Regiment of the UVF at Glencairn in front of 25,000 spectators – addressed them. The crisis facing them was coming to a head, he stressed: "We will go on to the end, not in any spirit of aggression; nay, even if necessary in a spirit of humility, but with a grim determination that come what will we cannot, and we will not, be conquered," he warned. Sir Edward also had specific praise for the YCV:

> "And now I want to take this opportunity of saying how pleased I am that the Young Citizens' Army – such a splendid body of men and so well equipped – have resolved to join their forces with ours. We give them a most hearty welcome. They will find in your ranks men with the same ideals, men with the same loyalty towards their King, and the same determination to uphold the rights of their country. I hope, men, it may not be very long till I see every one of you with his rifle on his shoulder."

The men, raising their caps in the air, gave three cheers for the King followed by three more for Sir Edward. The 3,000 men on parade, formed up in companies and marching four abreast, were then led from the field by Colonel Couchman and Captain Scriven to the strains of El Abanico and Imperial Echoes. The *Belfast News Letter* reported: "The great gathering of spectators cheered themselves hoarse as the Volunteers came on, the Young Citizens being accorded a particularly warm reception, and Sir Edward Carson was deeply touched by the appearance of the men and the conduct of the spectators who surrounded the enclosure."

The Third Home Rule Bill was now only days from completing its legislative passage through the Lords, and even though there had been further attempts in the wake of the gunrunning to find an accord, with even the King hosting talks, all had foundered. On 10 July Sir Edward Carson attended a specially-convened meeting of the Ulster Unionist Council in Belfast at which the wheels were set in motion to create a Provisional Government in Ulster which would, according to its constitution, protect the province "for the constitution of the United Kingdom" until proper government was restored. The Twelfth parades, held on Monday 13 July as was traditional when the 12th fell on a Sunday, passed without incident, and the following day the Lords, again with amendments that they knew would be ignored, completed their deliberations on the Bill. King George V called a conference of his own for 21–24 July, held at Buckingham Palace, in a bid to break the deadlock but to no avail. There were, however, much more serious events taking place elsewhere in Europe, though most people in Britain and Ireland were blissfully unaware of their significance until just days before the declaration of war with Germany on 4 August 1914. Now with a common enemy, everything changed overnight. Although the Government of Ireland Act received its Royal Assent, it was to be suspended until the end of hostilities with the promise of further discussions on an amending Bill. Instead of Ulster Volunteers peering down the sights of their German rifles at British soldiers, they prepared to don the khaki to defend the United Kingdom against a different foe.

GG Paton and JW Paton, who were both on the teaching staff at Belfast Technical College in Belfast, joined the YCVs together and later both served as sergeants in the 14th Royal Irish Rifles. *(Courtesy of Belfast Met)*

Chapter 6

SOLDIERS OF THE KING

Wherever you go you will hear them shout,
We really won't be knocked about,
And we won't drink chloride-of-lime,
We won't drink chloride-of-lime.

YCV marching song

THE YCV HAD ITS own command structure and formation, and it was this which came into play as the new recruits to what was to be known as the 14th (YCV) Battalion Royal Irish Rifles met at Davidson's Yard in east Belfast for their first experience of soldiering. The Young Citizen NCOs, supplemented by UVF comrades and old sweats called out of retirement, gave the orders. Friends stuck together, choosing one of the eight companies formed. While the small builders' yard might have lacked the 'glamour' of the military barracks, for George H Mullin it was still a grand occasion. "No member of the battalion present will ever forget that memorable assembly of the Young Citizen Volunteers of Belfast as 'Soldiers of the King'." Each company paraded separately under its own sergeant, who issued the commands and called the roll. The eight companies then assembled in columns, 18 ranks across, with A to the front through in alphabetical order to H in the rear, forming the battalion for the first time. The adjutant, Captain Bentley, ran his eye across the assembled ranks. "Grave doubts must have crossed his mind about the possibility of these fellows ever being licked into shape, and welded into an efficient unit of Kitchener's Army," recorded the newly anointed Rifleman Mullin.

"One may well ask what did the Adjutant see as he looked around that sunny morning in Davidson's Yard. He saw a crowd of happy, eager, carefree young men, with smiling faces, not in army uniform, but all dressed in their ordinary every-day civilian clothes. Many were wearing straw hats, which were popular, and some were carrying walking sticks. The Adjutant disapproved of the walking sticks on parade, and gave orders for them to be left against the boundary wall. All were anxious in case the war would be over before they reached the firing line."

Recruitment to the YCV battalion had officially opened at the Old Town Hall in Victoria Street in central Belfast on 14 September 1914. However, some of those who had passed through it in the days previous had already opted to join the then unnamed 14th Rifles. The building, which had served as the headquarters of the UVF throughout the crisis of the previous two years, had been rapidly adapted for its new purpose. Hundreds were passing through its heavy wooden doors every morning flushed with patriotic ardour, eventually re-emerging a shilling richer as soldiers of the King. The fact that almost six weeks had passed before the first official YCV recruits had been able to volunteer was down to the fragile political situation in Ireland. It had taken time for a compromise to be reached between the government and unionist leadership, with the latter agreeing to allow the Home Rule Bill, which had brought Ulster to the brink of civil war, to become law unopposed but with its operation suspended until the end of the war. Sir Edward Carson, meanwhile, had won approval for the creation of an Ulster Division despite the initial reluctance of Minister for War Lord Kitchener. On 3 September the unionist leader addressed a parade of the North Belfast Ulster Volunteers at Dunmore House on the Antrim Road, telling them:

> "You may have many difficulties – you will have many difficulties – you will have plenty of suffering and sacrifice before you, but from what I know of you I am confident that you will acquit yourselves as Irishmen in the field, and above all, as Ulstermen, proud of your British connection."

The men then marched to the Old Town Hall to enlist, with the first man to emerge being 44-year-old Boer War veteran William Hanna, of Brussels Street, who, the *Belfast News Letter* reported, "smiled cheerfully as his papers were completed, securing for him the distinction of being the first member of the Ulster Volunteer Force to be accepted as such by the military authorities".

Each of the UVF battalions took their turn to sign up en masse, with the newspapers reporting the intense rivalry, particularly between north and east Belfast, as to which could get up to strength quickest. There was also confusion as to the names of the new battalions, with the newspapers assuming that the North Belfast UVF would become the 7th Royal Irish Rifles, the other three Volunteers regiments in Belfast forming respectively the 8th, 9th and 10th, and the YCVs becoming the 11th Rifles. In the event, however, the North Belfast Regiment became the 15th Rifles (the title of 7th Rifles belonged to a battalion serving with the 16th (Irish) Division) while the Antrim and Down UVF regiments were allocated the 11th, 12th and 13th Rifles titles, with the YCV granted the title of the 14th Rifles. The pioneer battalion, the last fighting unit formed, was recruited as the 16th Rifles. The name change, which only came to light in early October, caused some of the newspapers to accuse the War Office of treating Ulster "very shabbily". The *Belfast News Letter,* pointing out that many English and Scottish units had been named after cities and the South had regiments with Leinster, Munster and Connaught in the title, complained: "Why not call the Young Citizens the 1st Battalion City of Belfast Regiment and add some of the other battalions of the Rifles to it as 2nd, 3rd, and 4th Battalions?" It added:

Fred Barker, an original member of the YCVs and the South Belfast Regiment of the UVF, joined the Black Watch in 1914, later being commissioned into the 14th Royal Irish Rifles. He was to see action in Dublin during the Easter Rising, and was wounded at the Somme in July 1916, again in October that year, and at the Battle of Messines in June 1917. *(Royal Ulster Rifles Museum)*

"Ulster and Belfast have been studiously ignored. Proud as we are of the Royal 'Irish' Rifles and the Royal 'Irish' Fusiliers, there is nothing territorial about the title 'Irish'. It applies to every part of Ireland. Why not the Royal Ulster Rifles? It is to be hoped that this matter will be brought under the notice of the powers that be."

On 9 September 1914 "all NCOs and men who have volunteered for foreign service" paraded before Colonel Chichester at St George's Market at 8.00 pm "for inspection and final approval". It was to be the last occasion on which the Young Citizens would muster as a purely citizen army. Days later the men gathered again at the Town Hall, queuing with friends and no doubt joking and jostling with each other as they waited their turn to enlist. Among the first through the doors was Mullin, accompanied by "my two staunch friends" Joseph Hawthorne and James Russell. "All the prospective recruits were impatient, and in a hurry to get through the necessary procedure of enlistment," he recalled. "The work of completing the attestation forms proceeded at top speed all morning. Doctors were working at high pressure making the medical examinations. There was a good deal of banter. In the evening after tea, magistrates were in attendance for the swearing in process. This was not done individually, but in large groups. This was the final act." The men signed on for three years "or the duration of war". Samuel Harrison, who signed up with the Townsley brothers, Billy and Wilson, thought the medical arrangements particularly efficient:

The Townsley brothers Billy and Wilson signed up to join the 14th Royal Irish Rifles with their mate Samuel Harrison. *(Courtesy of Alastair Harrison)*

"In batches we were marched into a ground floor room where our UVF cards were examined. We then stripped to the waist and removed our shoes and stockings. Then in turn we passed through a series of rooms where various physical tests were carried out. In one room the height and weight of each man was registered, and a sight test applied. In another the examination covered heart, lungs, legs, feet, hernia, and varicose veins. In yet another room sat numbers of clerks who recorded the colour of the eyes, hair, the complexion, any body marks, etc. Finally, we entered a room where more clerks recorded our personal details such as name, place of birth, age, trade or calling, address, former service (if any), religious denomination, etc, and then we took the Oath".

For Jim Maultsaid it was his second time inside a recruiting office. He had attempted to sign up on 5 August but had been rejected. Realising that Carson's Volunteers would eventually be incorporated in the new armies to be formed, he joined the YCVs as a means of outflanking the system.

The battalion, which was shortly to be reduced to four companies by amalgamation, continued to muster at Davidson's yard while alternative arrangements were being made.

The men were put through their paces for approximately two hours a day before being sent home again. There were no uniforms or rifles and the drill was restricted to the most basic kind. Companies fell-in in two ranks and numbered from the right. They then received the command to "right dress" to straighten the lines. The sergeants and NCOs, some of whom were veterans of the Boer War, attempted to demonstrate the correct way to salute or execute simple manoeuvres. After a few days Second Lieutenant Hanna[1] joined the battalion from the Officers' Training Corps.

Deftly turned out in his straw hat, he gave commands in a loud and clear voice that carried across the yard. The ranks were also swelling as the week went on, as noted by John Kennedy Hope: "The crowd is getting bigger every day. Most of them have belonged to the 'gun runners' and know the game." A pay parade was held at the yard on the first Saturday morning after recruitment began, with each man given a 10 shilling allowance to cover the wear and tear on their civilian clothes, then sent home to bid family and friends farewell as the battalion received its first orders to move. The Saturday was spent by many collecting together pieces of kit, with hurried purchases of canvas bags, enamel mugs and plates, and gathering together personal items such a knife, fork and spoon, razor and shaving brush, and comb. Sunday, the traditional day of rest, meant attending church for some, perhaps a lie in for others. Many of the lads made final arrangements for the storage of possessions, squared up accounts and took the opportunity to visit friends and family.

On Thursday of the following week an advance party consisting of two officers and 42 men left from the Great Northern railway station on Great Victoria Street in Belfast, their destination being Finner Camp, on the Donegal coast. It was convenient for the boys of the three Inniskilling battalions that made up the 109th Brigade of the Ulster Division (see Appendix 3) but a long way from home for the Belfast lads. On Friday 25 September, the men of A, B, C and D Companies began gathering at the City Hall shortly before 6.00 am, where their commanding officer and the YCV band awaited them. The *Belfast News Letter* reported:

> "The men fell in at the quadrangle in the City Hall, Colonel Chichester being early on the scene, and headed by the battalion band, they marched via Donegall Square South and Howard Street to the Great Victoria Street terminus. Notwithstanding the early hour of the parade there was a very large gathering of spectators, including many relatives of the Volunteers, and the route to the station was lined by a large crowd which cheered with enthusiasm as the men swung past to the strains of 'It's a long way to Tipperary'. Amongst yesterday's departures were a divinity student, a Pressman, two photographers, a commercial traveller, insurance agents, clerks, members of the Fire Brigade, and many skilled tradesmen."

YCV members who had not enlisted lined the approaches to the station, dressed in their grey uniforms, forming a guard of honour under the command of Captain HM Moore and Lieutenant JW Storey, and acting as crowd control. Rifleman Mullin, forever cheery, tells of a crowded platform punctuated with spontaneous laughter and fun.

> "When roll-call was completed, company commanders gave the command to board the train. Very soon the kitbags were stowed on the luggage racks, and all ranks

were safely in the carriages, with only a few officers left on the platform. After some delay, all formalities having been completed, the officers entered their first-class compartment and signalled the guard for the train to depart. Obediently the guard blew his whistle, waved the green flag to the engine driver, when the engine's shrill whistle gave the alarm that our 114 miles journey to Ballyshannon had now started. All the carriage windows were crowded with smiling faces and waving hands as the train pulled out of the station."

It was approximately 7.00 am and the band struck up 'Auld Lang Syne' "amidst a hurricane of cheering". The process was repeated as the remaining companies, under the command of Major JE Gunning, caught a second special train at 9.00 am. All told, 15 officers and 956 men were despatched. For many this was their first substantial train journey and they moved from one side of the carriage to the other and back again to catch the sights. Mullin again: "The journey could not have been undertaken with greater zest, it could not have been more enjoyable if it had been a Church or Sunday-school excursion to any seaside rendezvous. During the whole journey there was a continuous babble of talk and laughter."

In the late afternoon the trains finally pulled into the station at Ballyshannon. The men were herded out into the street outside. Some were issued with stores to carry, including Hope who was "presented with two old South African rifles which we have to carry into camp – one over each shoulder". The battalion's arrival at Finner was a "thrilling moment" for some like Mullin: "The fresh air blowing from the Atlantic Ocean was most invigorating, and the scenery along the road was delightful. Very soon the YCVs were marching through their camp entrance, to halt at their own lines." Rifleman Berry thought it "an ideal place for a military camp, situated on the main road between Ballyshannon and Bundoran. Ground is sandy and dry" but Hope had a different take on it: "It's a God forsaken place – as bare as a golf ball," he recorded. Another, unnamed, recruit declared: "Things are comfortable, generally speaking, and if they weren't we wouldn't say a word. There are so many chums of us together it is like a bit of Belfast transplanted to the shores of the Atlantic."

This view of Finner Camp, taken from a postcard, shows Colonel Chichester's hut at top left, while the officers' cookhouse, complete with chimney, is on the right close to the wall. The officers' tents are in the foreground with the 96 tents for other ranks beyond. *(Courtesy of Andrew Totten)*

The YCVs now met up for the first time with the other battalions in the 109th Brigade – the 9th, 10th and 11th Royal Inniskilling Fusiliers, which had been raised largely from the UVF units in Tyrone, Londonderry, Donegal and Fermanagh. The Young Citizens' former comrades, the Belfast battalions of the UVF – now the 8th (East Belfast Volunteers), 9th (West Belfast Volunteers), 10th (South Belfast Volunteers) and 15th (North Belfast Volunteers) Royal Irish Rifles – were at Ballykinlar in south Down as the 107th Brigade. The remaining brigade, the 108th, consisting of the 11th, 12th and 13th Royal Irish Rifles, and 9th Royal Irish Fusiliers, was sent to Clandeboye and Newtownards for training.

There is no question that Finner was basic. It had no cookhouses, washing facilities or permanent buildings. All accommodation was in standard army bell tents, arranged in rows of 10, with larger marquees serving as the likes of the Quartermaster's Stores, Sergeants' Mess and canteen, where stout and beer could be purchased. The officers' tents were separate, and to the Bundoran side of the camp. While the men slept at least 10 to a tent, only the lieutenants were expected to bunk up, with all other officers having a tent of their own. Colonel Chichester, as battalion commanding officer, had the luxury of a wooden hut.

Two large water tanks on a rise supplied the camp with water, while a low stone wall was all that separated it from the road. In time proper latrines were added, running water provided and washhouses built as the numbers arriving in camp grew. The cooks, who increased in number as the battalion came up to strength, worked in the open for the most part. Most were new to the profession and the men did not always appreciate their efforts. Hope, applying his usual sarcasm, noted:

George Mullin proudly poses for the camera outside his 'living quarters' at Finner camp. The standard issue military bell tents generally slept at least 10 men. *(Courtesy of Andrew Totten)*

> "The grub is good, it is always stew, sometimes it is curry stew. Somebody says the curry is added when the meat is rotten to disguise the damned thing. There is no hot water so the dixie is wiped out with sods and sand; the grease is always thick in the inside when it is filled with water for tea. The tea is a beautiful blend of soup."

The conditions and lack of experience of the cooks were mitigating factors according to the more understanding Jim Fitzsimons: "Feeding a problem – amateur cooks, strong winds blowing sand all over the place, including the food, causing a lot of overtime at the latrines (trenches)." Indeed, there was a standing, or should that read 'sitting', joke:

> "Sentry – 'Halt, who goes there?'
> Phantom – Diarrhoea.
> Sentry – Pass diarrhoea, all's well."

Men from each tent would come and collect the food for their comrades, which would be ladled into large dixies from which 20 men would be served. A commercial canteen supplied basic necessities and a few luxuries such as cakes and ginger beer. A Belfast businessman and member of Belfast Corporation, Alderman Tyrrell, operated it as a sideline to his main business, a grocery store on the Crumlin Road.

Plates and mugs were at the ready as the dixie arrived, though there was still time to pose for James Fitzsimon's camera. Note the variations in dress as uniforms were still scarce at this stage of the war. *(Courtesy of the Somme Museum)*

Reveille was at 6.30 am, the camp alarm clock being the bugler attached to the guardroom. Mullin recalled: "Believe it or not, the camp was instantly astir. Early morning tasks had to be performed with speed. The mess orderly doubled to the cooks and fetched a dixie full of hot cocoa. This was left between the two tents, the boys helping themselves by dipping their enamel mugs into the dixie. There was always enough cocoa to satisfy everyone. It took only a few minutes to fold the blankets in the prescribed manner. A quick wash and shave in cold water were undertaken with zest."

At 7.00 am the "fall in" was sounded, the battalion parading by companies under Adjutant Captain Bentley. A pattern quickly emerged designed to improve the men's fitness. Initially the captain, "a sparse wiry figure in running shorts" according to Harrison, would march them towards Bundoran, returning after a mile. This then became a double march and the distance increased at regular intervals, or a run across the sand dunes at a sprightly pace was substituted. "God help the man who fell out – falling out on this run meant extra fatigues or extra guard duty," recalled Rifleman Berry. Most, though, seemed to have enjoyed their 'constitutional'. Longer route marches were carried out at least once a week, growing in frequency to virtually every day, and not simply to improve fitness or discipline. One particularly cold day the alarm was sounded at the camp and the battalion rapidly formed up with the four companies in line as for a Commanding Officer's parade. The order was then given to march off with Captain Bentley at the head setting a brisk pace.

> "The Adjutant's secret was soon to be revealed. He did not head for the road; instead he led the battalion to the sand hills, between the camp and the sea. And then came the command 'Double March'. Captain Bentley kept a steady double for a few miles. Up hill and down hill, the pace was maintained. After some time he reverted to the quick march, returning to camp by a circuitous route. It can safely be assumed that there were no cold feet when the boys arrived back, with a healthy appetite, to wait for tea."

The YCVs were shocked by the backwardness and poverty of the west of Ireland as their forced marches took them throughout Donegal, Fermanagh and even into Leitrim. "We halt one day beside a house well off the beaten track and go to explore the place," recalled Hope. "The primitive state of the dwelling amazes us. A woman appears, apparently in a state of terror and we ask for a drink. She has no bread but proceeds to make scones, not a word does she say. Has she heard of a war, probably not. Maybe she thinks the country is invaded. She's still silent. We pay her handsomely for her hospitality and depart while she gazes at the money."

The conclusion of one particular route march provided the boys with something to laugh about and brought about one former Boer War veteran's time with the battalion to a crashing end. Captain Charles St Aubyn Wake,[2] described by Hope as having a "face like King William and a cork leg" which left him with a pronounced limp, endeavoured to carry out as many of his duties as possible on a "white horse which has to be kept perfectly steady while he gets the game leg over its back". Following a 10-mile route march he had the men "mark time" before giving the order to "Halt". Mullin takes up the story:

> "Captain Wake's next command was 'Fall Out the Gentlemen'. For some unknown reason he then fell off his horse. He lay where he fell, apparently unhurt. He made no attempt to rise. He then gave the final command 'Battalion Dis-miss', whereupon the parade did a right turn, saluted and then dispersed. Only then did Captain Wake get up, and hand his mount over to the groom, who was waiting. Captain Wake remained only a short time with the 14th Battalion."

A favourite choice for the men as they marched through the County Donegal countryside was the little ditty, quoted at the start of this chapter, composed following an incident that, quite literally, left a bad taste in their mouths. Two large water tanks were situated on a rise, next to the Inniskillings' lines. They were treated regularly with chloride-of-lime to ensure the water remained safe to drink but the man in charge was somewhat over zealous with its application, giving the water a bitter taste which was to taint everything from the tea to the evening stew for weeks to come. The officers refused to drink it and had fresh well water brought in every day by fatigue parties, but everyone else had to lump it.

The golden sands and lapping Atlantic waves were a huge attraction to men brought up in the back streets of Belfast and some, including Berry, bathed every day until the weather grew too cold. Indeed, within the military regime bathing parades were a regular feature of camp life at Finner. Each man stripped on the sand in his place in the ranks and then, when everyone was ready, they splashed into the sea together. But, as Mullin almost found to his cost, it had inherent dangers with only the intervention of the YCV's champion swimmer, Sergeant Ralph Cole,[3] coming between him and death:

> "One morning I had a most unpleasant experience. Swimming out too far, I was unable to get in again, as it was difficult to swim through the surf. Each time I swam in, the backwash carried me out again. Fortunately for me, Ralph Cole noticed that I was in difficulties, and he immediately swam over to me with powerful strokes. Sergeant Cole's presence gave me confidence, and I had just sufficient strength left to reach the beach. I was a very sick man due to the large quantity of sea water that I had swallowed. It was well that most of the boys were out of the water when this incident happened. I was able to hide my sickness and march back with 12 Platoon. After a short rest in my tent I fully recovered, and was none the worse for my experience of being nearly drowned. None of my platoon knew what had occurred. It was a secret between Sergeant Cole and me."

Meal times at Finner Camp, due to the absence of proper facilities, were very casual affairs. (Belfast Telegraph)

Mullin's experience must not have been that unusual as Harrison mentions how precautions were taken to ensure everyone made it back to shore on each occasion: "As the surf can be very heavy there those of us who were expert swimmers stayed further out to sea than the others, to see that nobody got into trouble by going out of their depth. This was because on our very first outing someone did get into trouble and had to be rescued by one of his pals."

Mornings were largely given over to platoon training, with the junior officers putting the men through basic parade drills such as numbering, dressing, forming fours, marching in step, saluting and signalling, and later, when weapons were available, rifle drill was introduced. Occasionally the battalion would parade together for drill, usually under the adjutant. Captain Bentley, who took advantage of a slight rise on the parade ground to get a clearer view, evidently enjoyed this opportunity to test the officers as much as the men and would issue his orders in quick succession. Captain Charles Owen Slacke, commanding A Company, was one of those who came under his notice. Mullin recalls such a parade when the order for the battalion to advance in column with A Company leading failed to elicit the correct response from Slacke: "He, however, instead of advancing, proceeded to retire. Thereupon the adjutant's wrath descended on his head. 'Captain Slacke' roared the adjutant, 'Do you not know your front from your rear?' This remark caused many subdued smiles. There were many other similar incidents." Hope also holds Slacke up for ridicule, recording: "Our soldier Company Commander is replaced by one Captain Slacke. He is a round-faced, fat bellied gentleman with a cynical smile. We have at last got something to amuse us. Slacke is a genius at drill. We like to get on a parade of this sort to see how he will unravel the company when he gets it into a mess. We snigger when he says Carry on Sergeant Major."

The dress code at Finner was almost exclusively civilian initially, though there were exceptions. Some of the original YCV members wore their distinctive grey uniforms while others who had been associated with Cliftonville Football Club wore red jerseys that had been presented to them by the club. The Quartermaster issued uniforms as soon as they arrived at Finner though, as they were from a variety of manufacturers, they differed slightly in shade, material and detail. "The YCV battalion was issued with an additional suit, the tunic of which had blue edging, with breeches in place of trousers," recalled Mullin. "The breeches had a blue stripe, and were fastened below the knees. The boys were proud of their distinctive cap badge, which consisted of a shamrock in the centre of which was the Red Hand of Ulster, the whole surmounted with the Crown. The letters YCV were worn on the shoulders instead of RIR which was worn by other units."

With the issuing of uniforms and other bits of equipment came regular kit inspections and Sergeant Major Herron was always on the prowl through the tents to make sure everything was as it should be. The camp guards, posted at the Orderly Room and the Quartermaster's Stores, were rigorously put through their paces so they were ready to respond at a moment's notice to the arrival of the brigadier or divisional commander. The bugle was the main means of communication, dictating the men's day from Reveille to Last Post, as Samuel Harrison discovered. "We speedily became familiar with the different calls, the most popular being 'Cookhouse' and the 'Post Call'. When the weather was inclement we welcomed the 'No Parade Today' call."

As with the khaki, it had taken several months to supply sufficient new rifles for the battalion, though the men had received drill in their use and gotten to fire them at Finner on the ranges constructed on the beach below the camp, resulting in "gun-shock shoulder".

Harrison recalled the good-humoured lessons delivered by Sergeant 'Charlie' Chaplin during which "we were often treated to an imitation of the well-known radio comic, much to our unfailing delight". He added: "One day we found ourselves under fire from a nearby rifle range, and had to beat a hasty retreat, fortunately without any casualties."

Sundays meant compulsory church parades and in the evenings some of the men would walk into Bundoran to attend services. Mullin had been a member of the choir at his home church and had the blessing of the Rev Elias Francis Naylor, Rural Dean, to sit with the choir in Christ's Church in the town for the hymns and Psalms.

Despite all the effort being put in to turn soft civilians into hardened soldiers, good manners remained at all times. Mullin recalled: "It can be said with truth that training was always given in a leisurely manner. There was no sarcasm, the NCOs being always polite and cheerful." In time, however, the acting NCOs were replaced. Company commanders, often only newly commissioned themselves, were ordered to submit for the Colonel's approval a list of names to be awarded stripes. These were subsequently published in 'Battalion Orders'. Hope, as usual, had a take on it: "Old soldiers and young ones too get their ranks. Officers are commissioned. McKee says 'he's Kimmy no longer by King's this, that and the other thing'. Their necks all get bigger. The rubbing in has commenced." For Samuel Harrison, the imposition of a stricter regime meant he, as a private, and good friend Sergeant Billy Stephenson were forbidden to "pal about" together.

The battalion was rapidly coming up to full strength, helped by an influx of 'Glasgow Ulstermen' who arrived at Finner in October 1914. It was reported around this time that the battalion had 22 officers and 1,120 other ranks with vacancies still for "carpenters, smiths, butchers, shoemakers, cooks and grooms" as well as "musicians, buglers, drummers, pipers and flute players". The officers included captains Harper and Slacke, lieutenants McMinn, TH Mayes, McMaster,[4] Hyndman, Clokey, Robb and Dobson, Adjutant Bentley and Quartermaster Sergeant Elphick, all of whom had been with the battalion when it travelled to Donegal from Belfast. More than 100 of the recruits were from the Belfast Technical College according to one of the YCV's benefactors, FC Forth, who reported to his governors in November that more than 520 students and lecturers had joined up to that point with the biggest contingent going to the 14th Rifles.

An effort was made to get the men home on a reasonably regular basis, with huge scale weekend leave arranged. Special trains were laid on to and from the Great Northern Railway terminus, with the men arriving home on Friday evening and returning to Finner on Monday morning. One half of the battalion would leave usually around 9.00 am and the remainder half-an-hour later, not arriving back at Ballyshannon until lunchtime. Family and friends inevitably ensured they got a hearty send-off on each occasion. Off-duty hours in the evenings and non-leave weekends tended to be spent in Bundoran. The town boasted all the delights of a seaside resort in winter with a few additional amenities provided for the soldiers' comforts. Two recreation huts served snacks at a reasonable cost, supplementing

Basic training was undertaken at Finner, including teaching the raw recruits how to sight a gun. A makeshift firing range was constructed on the beach below the camp. (Belfast Telegraph)

Most Fridays those with passes would be paraded then marched to the halt to catch the train for Belfast, returning the following Monday morning. *(Belfast Telegraph)*

the rather questionable Army food dished out at the camp, and did a roaring trade. The Great Northern Railway tearooms in the town were exclusively for the use of the troops as reading rooms on Sundays, while Bundoran's skating rink was given over by its directors as a recreation room. Harrison had a particular favourite:

"None of us ever got used to the food generally provided for the British Tommy in those days, and precious parcels from home were a Godsend. The local 'ham and egg' teas were very popular on pay days, and these we would purchase at the Manchester House Café in Bundoran, at the modest cost of one shilling. I fear the rest of our pay, such as it amounted to, was spent on 'Liffey water', but we never got enough of this to want to go treading on the tails of anyone's coat."

At the end of the evening the boys gathered together before 'marching' to camp as they sang the popular songs of the day, arriving back in time for the sounding of the "Last Post" followed by "Lights Out". The authorities frowned on drunkenness, with the Colonel parading the whole battalion, including the sick, to warn the men that they were now under military law and could face imprisonment or other punishments for stepping out of line. The occasion coincided with a fresh outbreak of illness in the camp, with three men and an officer fainting, as the letter from the War Office was read out.

During the milder autumn evenings camp-fire concerts would be held, the men sitting on the grass around the fire to be entertained by the likes of Lieutenant Johnny Long,[5] the Quartermaster, who sang a "silly comic song about Andy, Bandy and Biddy, on their way to the fair".

In October preparation work began for the erection of huts in which the men could winter, though the weather that month was mild and dry. November, however, brought heavy rain, sleet and snow, and with it the threat of a severe winter. That same month Major General Hickman Powell, commanding the Ulster Division, risked the rains to inspect the battalion and declared himself pleased with its appearance and progress. The 11th Inniskillings was moved from Finner to new accommodation in Enniskillen and other troops took up residence in the first completed wooden huts that now stood in a camp that was rapidly becoming a sea of mud. The canvas tents offered little protection from the elements at the best of times, and some were blown down in the storms that rolled in from the Atlantic. According to Harrison, conditions were becoming so bad that there was virtual rebellion in the ranks. Some of the boys "packed their kits and paraded in spite of anything their officers could say to them. They got their own way and billets were found for them in Bundoran and in Ballyshannon". The Great Northern Railway Hotel on the cliffs at Bundoran was requisitioned and, with its furniture and affects removed, was turned over to the 14th Rifles who took up residence on 3 December 1914. There was sufficient space to accommodate B, C and D companies, with A Company's platoons distributed around the town and beyond. The change from tents to hotel rooms was like "ship-wrecked seamen rescued from a small, lonely island," thought Mullin:

> "The spaciousness of the rooms increased the buoyancy of everyone immensely. The exhilaration for the first few days was intense. The boys kept rushing round the corridors like dogs just released from the leash. Sociability was more marked. Friends could visit each other without trouble. Many new friends were made."

Relationships were also improved at Ballyshannon, where some of the A Company men were billeted. According to Harrison "the 'khaki' was not particularly popular there and it was eventually put out of bounds. Only the flooding of our camp at Finner had brought about the relaxation of that order, but the boys who were billeted there managed to win a few friends . . ." A Company's accommodation was centred around O'Gorman's Hotel in Bundoran and it was there that it held a smoking concert a week after taking up residence. Captain C St Aubyn Wake presided with Captain Slacke and Lieutenants A Mulholland, RV Gracey and GC Wedgwood all present. Lance Corporal TA Burrows, said to be "well-known in musical circles in the north of Ireland", drew up the programme with Lieutenants Mulholland, Mayes and Holmes along with Sergeant Uprichard, Sergeant Gray, Corporal Stewart, Lance-Corporal Burrows, Corporal Yates, Privates Martin, Downes, McCausland, Armstrong, Cass, Gifford, Harper, Frazer, Baird, and Pierpoint all on the bill.

The improved accommodation and deteriorating weather did not halt what Harrison claimed was "becoming known as the smartest battalion in the Ulster Division" from continuing its military exercises. "I went in over the knees in a quagmire during a sham attack on a railway today," he confided to his diary. "We are getting this sort of thing daily now, one platoon being sent out to hold a position, the others forming the attack."

Christmas was fast approaching, with its promise of home leave. The battalion was divided in two by means of drawing numbers out of a post bag. Those with a "1" were able to head off on 19 December to enjoy Christmas Day and Boxing Day with family. Mullin, who had fancied himself "swanking around Belfast, proudly displaying our YCV uniform with our own special cap badge," pulled out a "2" and had to wait until the first group's return before he got away with the remainder of the battalion on 28 December. That meant celebrating Christmas Day in Bundoran, with the hotel's large dining room decorated and a special menu laid on, followed by the "usual Christmas festivities". Rifleman Berry was similarly unlucky with the draw but appeared content with the new arrangements: "The quarters in the hotel are quite comfortable and a change from living under canvas," he recorded. "This is where I spent my first Xmas in the army. Had a most enjoyable day and a splendid dinner under the circumstances. Xmas afternoon was devoted to sports, etc." Samuel Harrison and his mate Billy Townsley bathed off the rocks below the hotel on Christmas Day, an act of bravado that drew caustic comments from their comrades.

Chapter 7

BUN FIGHTS AND CARD SCHOOLS

A profound and curious sense of unreality haunts the most vivid and intimate impressions of a present which is to be followed by such a momentous future... The 14th Battalion, at any rate, will go far, and it will have the hearty good wishes of hosts of friends in Ulster, who will watch its record with keen interest in the days to come.

The Weekly Telegraph, April 1915

IN EARLY DECEMBER 1914, the justices of the peace at the monthly petty sessions ordered all pubs in the Randalstown district to close early. They were to shut their doors at 8.00 pm during the week and 7.00 pm on a Saturday. The order was proof positive that the long awaited move of the 109th Brigade from Finner to the newly constructed camp in County Antrim was imminent.[1]

Work on laying out the grounds and constructing the wooden huts in Shane's Castle Park was already well advanced by October 1914. A local man, Robert Smith, formerly of the Ballymena firm of Gault Brothers, was acting as foreman carpenter under the direction of two officials from the War Office. The camp, the fifth to be established since the outbreak of war, was described as being on a "suitable and picturesque site" with its own water supply. The *Ballymena Weekly Telegraph* was already predicting, two months before the move, that the new tenants would include the YCVs.

> "The constitution of the camp has not yet been finally decided upon, but it is probable that the Young Citizen Volunteers, now the 14th Battalion Royal Irish Rifles, will form one unit, being transferred from their present quarters at Finner camp. If carried out this change will be greatly appreciated by the YCVs, as Randalstown will be more accessible to their homes in and about Belfast."

On 12 December the Press ran a six-day timetable of the troops' expected movements across Ireland, beginning the following day and ending with their arrival at Randalstown on 18 December. The troops back in Donegal, however, snug in their newly-acquisitioned hotel, were largely oblivious of such loose, and generally inaccurate, talk.

When the move did eventually come, it caught them on the hop. The orders arrived after the second group had left for home on 28 December for their week of festive leave. While

Kit inspections, such as this one taking place at Randalstown, were never among soldiers' favourite occasions. *(George Hackney)*

the newly-returned lads packed up their kit in preparation to relocate, letters went out to the remainder to report to Randalstown, a special train being laid on from Belfast's York Road station. A railway siding had been built for the use of the new camp, and the special train pulled into it a little before dusk on 8 January 1915. The boys piled out onto the newly built platform, formed up and marched off to their new home to discover a familiar enemy from Finner waiting for them. "Mud, such mud. You never saw anything like it in your life," complained Mullin. The building work combined with the wet weather had turned the ground between the huts into a quagmire that could only be transcended by using the duckboards that ran between them. "Randalstown may be all right in the summer but at present round about the huts it is over the boot-mouth in mud," recorded Harrison. "Of course it is carried inside on our boots, consequently the floors, which were originally white, are getting badly soiled. There are huts being built here to accommodate the whole brigade. I can't say how many men are here at present, but if it weren't for its proximity to Belfast we would sooner have remained in Bundoran." Berry was a little less severe, though conceded the camp was "very muddy and damp but eventually we got it clean and shipshape, but what a job." Even the normally upbeat Mullin, who was allocated to hut No 14, was disappointed at first: "The outlook was bleak and desolate. Each hut was provided with a round Army-type stove placed in the centre close to one side. For some days no fuel was supplied and, as it was bitterly cold, the camp had to be searched for scrap wood to burn in the stove."[2]

Facilities were basic, with the brigade chaplains making a public appeal in mid-January for help equipping and maintaining the four planned recreation rooms. Subscriptions were sought for a cinematograph, books, games and periodicals, with donations to be sent for the attention of the Earl of Leitrim. Gifts of books, magazines, illustrated weeklies and newspapers not more than a day old, as well as games such as draughts, chess and bagatelle, could be left at the Shane's Castle estate offices care of Lady O'Neill. On the first Sunday after their arrival, the men played host to invited guests from Belfast, including members of the Press. One recorded:

"Owing to the bad weather, the camp did not look its best, the ground being mud cut by the transport and passage of fatigue parties. The huts are comfortable, roomy and will be heated by stoves. About 25 men occupy each hut. Low wooden bedsteads are provided, racks for clothing and accoutrements are on the walls, and the approaches are being made in wood or road metal. In the course of a week or two electric lighting will be installed and other improvements added."

The minute book of the YMCA noted on 15 January that its buildings at Randalstown were not yet ready and even as late as 23 April it was saying that the new building at the camp was "just on the eve of completion and we are now arranging the staff of workers and the equipment for all-round social Christian work . . ." The following month the minute book noted: "The hut at Randalstown has proved too small . . . we have the loan of three smaller huts in different parts of the camp."

Likewise, it was some time before the large dining-hall was completed and ready for its proper purpose, though it did serve as a convenient venue for a memorable evening on 26 January 1915, as reported by Rifleman James McRoberts:

"In the evening a concert was held in the new dining-hall to which everyone was admitted free. The chief artist of the night was Percy French, author of the song: 'Mountains of Mourne'. . . He sang and played on the mandolin, but his most amusing contribution was his series of drawings. French would portray the picture of a baby crying, turn the paper upside down, and the face was distorted with laughter. He made a fine sketch of clumps of pines, growing on a landscape of snow, turned the picture upside down and we looked at a number of ships on a beautiful sea. He had quite a number of such entertaining freaks of the pencil."

The 'wee Jew' Cecil Marcus, as Hope described him, was a member of the card school at Randalstown. *(Courtesy of Belfast Met)*

Normally the dining hall was equipped with tables with the men sitting on forms and eating off proper dishes, though they still needed to bring their own knives, forks and spoons. With so many young men gathered together in one place there were the inevitable bun fights: "One day I was unlucky enough to be the victim," recorded Mullin. "I well remember that I was sitting at the table, my basin of tea in front of me, enjoying the evening meal. Private Robinson, the Colonel's chauffeur, was sitting directly in front of me, at the next table. He threw a bun, which landed in my basin of tea, the contents splashing over my face. I was annoyed, but what action could I take, by way of retaliation?"

The fooling around, of course, could continue in the huts in the evening. Hope found his room-mates divided into two rival groups, with one crowd listening to an old gramophone while at the other end of the hut was a card school "run by 'Scotty' Wilson from Kilmarnock, Wooter Cross from Lytham in Lancashire, and the 'wee Jew' Marcus. At night there is pandemonium. Sleep is impossible till the rowdies settle. The tricksters are always on the prowl. A rope is tied to the foot of somebody's bed. Everything is perfectly quiet. The rope is pulled and the victim is pitched out. There is a curse, a plate or a bowl flies through the air, and sometimes passes through a window." It wasn't the only thing going bump in the night: "We hear all kinds of noises. The farmers are removing the contents of the swill barrels and other receptacles. The carts rattle past and some wit says in half sleep 'Ships that pass in the night." Not even the presence of senior NCOs could guarantee respect of the rules. Company Sergeant Major Griffiths,[3] known as 'Porky' for obvious reasons, slept behind a wooden partition close to the door of the hut occupied by Harrison, who remembered him fondly:

> "He was a tubby little Newtownards man, an old soldier who had served his time in the Boer War. His accent was real 'County Down' but he knew what he was talking about and was very articulate when lecturing us about the rifle. The boys used to 'pull his leg' as we sprawled round him on the grass while he told us about the trajectory of a bullet, and what happened to it when it left the barrel."

Each morning, as he made his way to the ablutions with soap and towel in hand, he delivered his own brand of greeting, though it usually had the opposite to the desired effect: "They were usually anything but complimentary to us as we watched him go, and we determined to stay between the blankets just as long as Sergeant 'Stevie' would let us."

Discipline generally seems to have been of a high order within the 14th Rifles, though there were always those prepared to try it on. One such incident came in the wake of the funeral of the Young Citizens' first casualty in February 1915. Rifleman James Cobain, a 26-year-old from Evelyn Gardens in Belfast, had been home on weekend leave and was, according to his father, apparently in the best of health. However, on his return from a route march on Tuesday 16 February he complained of having a headache and feeling unwell. He went to bed rather than going for dinner but at 3.45 am the following morning his moaning woke Corporal Potter, who went to seek help. Dr MacKenzie,[4] examining Cobain, found him virtually paralysed and ordered his immediate removal to the Ulster Divisional Hospital on the Donegall Road in Belfast.

But, as the ambulance passed through Templepatrick, Sergeant Kerr, of the Royal Army Medical Corp, realised he was turning black. He stopped the vehicle and examined Cobain but could find no pulse or other evidence of life. A post-mortem, carried out by Professor W St Clair Symmers, found he had died of cerebrospinal meningitis, of which, he told the inquest held the following day in Belfast Union Workhouse, there had been an epidemic in Belfast within the past five years.[5]

James Cobain was buried in the Church of the Holy Evangelists' churchyard extension at Carnmoney, on the outskirts of Belfast. *(Author)*

Rifleman James Cobain was the 14th Royal Irish Rifles' first casualty. His funeral to Carnmoney was attended by many officers and was accompanied by a guard of honour made up of YCVs. *(Belfast Telegraph)*

Lieutenant McMinn offered regrets to the family on behalf of the officers and men of the battalion. Rifleman Cobain, he said, was of an exemplary character and had the makings of a good soldier. A joiner in civilian life, he was buried with full military honours on 19 February. His remains were removed from the Ulster Divisional Hospital on the Donegall Road at 1.00 pm and, led by the battalion's band and flanked by a firing party, were carried on a gun carriage to his parents' home at Evelyn Gardens. Then, covered in the Union Flag, the coffin was borne to Carnmoney for burial in the Church of Ireland graveyard. Among the wreaths was one in the form of a YCV crest from Colonel Chichester and the officers of the 14th; a shamrock and crown from his messmates in hut 20 at Randalstown; a harp and crown from the men of his own C Company; and floral tributes from each of the other companies.

A dozen men and a bugler, under Sergeant Powell, had received training in ceremonial drill before being sent by train on the Saturday morning to Belfast to take part in the funeral. Their instructions were to return afterwards, via York Street station, to hand in their rifles before going on leave for the weekend. In their absence, however, a brigade order cancelled all leave, much to the annoyance of the men. Mullin records how one, Private Hawthorne, surrendered an expired pass before returning home on that weekend's cancelled chit. His cheek paid off, as his stunt escaped detection. Another member of the party, however, Rifleman McIlroy, was not so clever. "McIlroy also returned home, without a pass," records Mullin, who had a theory as to why so few comrades fell foul of the full rigours of military law at this time.

> "At roll call on Saturday night, Corporal Woodside[6] reported Private McIlroy absent without leave. When McIlroy returned to camp on Sunday night, he was placed under arrest for disobeying Brigader-General Hickman's order stopping further leave. This was considered a serious breach of discipline. It was thought at the time that Private McIlroy would be tried by Court-Martial. He was kept under arrest for a long period, but was subsequently released without any trial by Court-Martial, or otherwise. The only explanation is that Colonel Chichester had sufficient influence with Hickman to get the charge withdrawn. It seemed the incident was hushed up and forgotten. One day Captain Bentley addressed the assembled battalion, and told them that he was tired of saving this battalion from courts-martial, and that he was not going to do it any longer. Nevertheless, there were no courts-martial in the 14th Battalion during the period of the Adjutancy."

Generally, however, leave was not only plentiful for the YCVs at Randalstown, but it was even possible to get a last minute extension. Mullin discovered the post office, operating from a cottage on the edge of the estate, was particularly useful. He volunteered on his weekends in camp as a telegraph boy, learning that a telegram to the commanding officer asking for longer at home usually received a positive response. Even on the odd occasion when all leave was cancelled it was possible to get a ticket home. Mullin recalls an occasion when Sergeant Major Herron, with whom he had become friends, not only secured a weekend pass for him but give him five shillings to spend in Belfast. On another occasion the men who had reported sick on a Saturday morning were granted weekend leave by medical officer Captain WR MacKenzie while everyone else was confined to camp. "The incident was the

subject of idle talk and such banter by the wags of the battalion. After all, it was a thoughtful action by Dr MacKenzie, for the benefit of the sick men under his charge," thought Mullin.

The regular battalion route marches had continued unabated but now a weekly brigade route march of 20–25 miles was added, usually combined with a field exercise or mock battle. While the manoeuvres were designed to have the brigade gel as a unit, one particularly strenuous exercise ended up with a falling out. Based round the hills to the east of Randalstown, the battalions "fought" up and down the slopes, some acting as defenders and the others in attack. It was not until late in the afternoon that the "ceasefire" rang out from the bugles. The YCVs were at this stage dug in on the lower slopes of Drumadarragh Hill, some 12 miles away from the camp. The prospect of the three-hour march back to Shane's Castle Park appealed not at all to tired and hungry men. Grumbling began among some, with the perception growing that the men would refuse to make the journey by foot. In the event, a more acceptable form of transport was provided, though Mullin suggests this was more through thoughtfulness, rather than pressure: "No one guessed the pleasant surprise that Colonel Chichester had arranged for his battalion. Instead of having to march back to camp, the boys had only to march to the nearest point on the railway, and entrain on the special train, which the Colonel had ordered. The 14th Battalion arrived in camp a long time before the other three Inniskilling battalions marched in." The Skins were raging that the "soft" Belfast lads had received special treatment, with relations between them and the Young Citizens strained for some time. Mullin, in a letter to Major WR Charley written in September 1961 as thanks for the hospitality shown on Old Soldiers Day, recalled:

"In the early spring of 1915, the 109th Infantry Brigade (Brigadier General Hickman) were engaged in a training skirmish embracing the hills ENE of Randalstown. The mock battle lasted all day, and ended in the late afternoon, when Colonel Chichester's 14th Battalion RIR were on the slopes of Drumadarragh Hill (929 ft).

Now, not withstanding the Adjutant's dismay, our Colonel ordered a special train, which soon had us back in Camp. The poor Inniskillings had to walk. We were long living that down."[7]

Such exercises were not only good training for what lay ahead but were appreciated by troops who, in the words of Harrison, now "swung along like veterans". Berry enjoyed the war games involving the entire brigade. "We dug trenches on top of the hill, heavy work, chalky soil, slept in our great coats until dawn and then marched home to camp where a glorious breakfast was awaiting up. This is a great life," he enthused. The route marches often doubled up as recruitment drives. In a series of events on Wednesdays in April, for example, the YCVs joined the 9th and 11th Battalions of the Royal Inniskilling Fusiliers and, accompanied by up to five bands, paraded to surrounding towns. At Ballymena the divisional

The bivouac at Drumadarragh where the YCVs slept under their great coats.
(George Hackney)

commander, Major General C Herbert Powell, addressed the crowd at Fair Hill. A week later it was the turn of Brigadier General TE Hickman to speak at Castledawson. He told the young men in his audience that they would regret not enlisting "when those men whom they saw in uniform came back with glory and honour" and urged the women to "influence the young men. You can tell them to go and do their duty. And, what is more, you can refuse to walk out with them if they will not do their duty".

When not on duty the men had limited options to enjoy themselves. Nights out to Ballymena or Antrim, often in a taxi "which the driver drove at a breakneck speed along the deserted road, the loose floorboards lifting our feet as we hit the bumps in the road," according to Harrison, were possible though it was necessary, unless they had a late pass, to return to camp by 9.30 pm when the Orderly Sergeant called the roll. Men were then detailed to their various tasks the following day, such as guards, cookhouse assistants or duty in the orderly room. Sometimes the pleasures came to Randalstown. The 10th Boy Scouts, for example, when they had cakes left over after a fundraising competition in aid of Belgian relief, sent them to the YCVs in which a number of their old boys were serving. Innocent amusement was also to be had from the battalion's pets, a drake by the name of Sammy, who was in the charge of cook H Bingham, and which had a tendency to follow the men onto the parade ground, and a fox terrier, dubbed Mick, which is said to have taken "an intelligent interest in military affairs". Towards the end of April the battalion officers organised a smoking concert featuring more than a dozen performers who had travelled up from Belfast in a fleet of cars provided by well wishers, including Richard Dawson Bates, a future Minister in the first Northern Ireland parliament. Most of the acts were singers, with recitations, a conjuring routine, mandolin player, paper tearing, sketches and a female impersonator appearing. The evening concluded with a singing competition among the men, with privates Smith and McCormick being selected by a panel of the artists as having given the best renditions of Tipperary. Other prize-winners were Privates McCausland, Daly, Gafficken, Hindman and Irwin. A report in the *Weekly Telegraph* noted the good relations that existed between officers and men. It went on:

"Perhaps the most thrilling experience to the layman and music-lover was the immense verve of the chorus when the men joined in the refrain of a song. This was fairly rousing; the tone was rich and strong… with an energy that only the vocal power of four or five hundred lusty throats could compass. They took up Mr Gemmell's song 'Cheery-O' at once, and this looks like a promising regimental ditty."

Major Bruce,[8] in a speech thanking the artists for their contributions, said he had only one message for them to take back to Belfast. Turning to his audience, he asked "Are we down-hearted," and received a roar of "No" in response.

The commanding officer had been unable to make the concert but Harrison and his mate Billy Townsley were to meet the Colonel unexpectedly one Saturday afternoon as they indulged in another favourite past time. "The River Bann flowed past our camp, which was surrounded by magnificent trees, and we knew trout could be caught in it, though we had heard that one required a permit," he records.

"But the lure was too strong for us, so being 'off duty' we got our tackle out, slipped over the fence, through the trees, and had a fair-sized fish out on the grass beside us in no time at all. Suddenly a voice behind us spoke, 'Any luck, boys?' and we wheeled round. It was the Colonel himself, and he had caught us red-handed! To our relief he seemed to look on us as a pair of fellow sportsmen and promised to get us permission himself to fish the river. We had fully expected to be 'crimed' for our adventure. But that one fish was our sole catch that evening, and we cooked it on the stove in our hut under the envious eyes, and noses, of some of our non-fishing pals."

This group of characters posing with the battalion's mascots, Sammy the drake and Mick the fox terrier, includes, standing, CQMS White, Rifleman Joe Wright, Rifleman William McBurney, Sergeant Patton, CSM White; sitting, Sergeant Smyth, Sergeant Cole, Cook H Bingham, CSM Griffith, Sergeant R J Elliott and Sergeant Diamond. *(Belfast Telegraph)*

Among the old soldiers who had returned to the Colours to help train the YCVs was Sergeant Kinnaird, a veteran of the South African War. Always immaculately turned out, he didn't simply walk about the camp but marched everywhere, perfectly erect, with shoulders square and head back, swinging his arms from the shoulder, the elbows slightly bent. To the young men of the YCVs he cut a humorous figure and they dared mock him one morning at Randalstown. Mullin takes up the story: "As the boys watched the sergeant's mechanical movements, a few were unable to resist the temptation to whistle loudly the 'Signallers Call'. One wag sang 'Oul Kinnaird' to the three notes of the 'Signallers Call'. The sergeant looked back for an instant, and then proceeded on his way, seemingly unconcerned." However, he reported the incident and all the men of one tent, members of No 16 section, were brought up on a charge, found guilty, and sentenced to complete a route march the following evening. The lasting legacy, however, was that from then on the 'Signallers Call' was always referred to in the battalion as 'Oul Kinnaird'. Sergeant Kinnaird earned a lengthy, if not totally complimentary, tribute in the May 1916 edition of the battalion magazine, *The Incinerator*:

> "No one who ever saw him could forget his curious parade manner – walking up and down with hands behind his back like a street preacher. It is reported that at one period he was chief of a little Bethel until such time as a rival from the fold caused him to break with the brethren and abandon preaching for the more lucrative calling of a bookmaker. But this is mere gossip. He had a genius for mispronouncing names and manufacturing words, a reel he called 'a creel,' and an earthpin was an 'earthenspike.' 'Ignorantist' was one of his pet vituperatives, and his pronunciation of the word 'deafening' in a stirring recitation entitled 'Asleep at his Post' was a constant joy to his auditors. As a tactician in the art of 'swinging the hammer' he was without a rival. Orderly Room held no terrors for him and he faced any CO with a great deal more assurance than the officer who brought the charge against him. Nothing was more amusing than to watch him hurrying onto the parade ground ten minutes late, as if he held the cares of a State on his shoulders. His excuse never varied. 'I've just been to the Quartermaster's Store to see about them stores of ours.' On my asking the Quartermaster about this one day I was treated to a generous display of artistic profanity. The Quartermaster also added a rider to the effect that if JK came within a mile of his Store he would shoot him. But the next morning it was the same. 'I've just been to the Quartermaster's Store, etc, etc.' As a disciplinarian he laboured under the disadvantage of being a character, although he was really too soft-hearted to crime any man. It was on one occasion, however, that he broke all records by criming a hut and waking his Company Officer at some unearthly hour to tell him about it. Some irreverent youths made up a new version of the signaller's call, introducing his name in a frivolous manner, and as he was unable to identify the offenders he wrote on the crime sheet 'Hut 13' under the heading 'Name of offender.' He was quite chagrined when he was told one could not charge a building. Amongst the men he was a never-failing source of humour and surprise."[9]

Everyone knew that the Ulster Division's days on home soil were numbered and that the parade planned through the streets of Belfast for Saturday 8 May 1915, while dressed up as a recruiting initiative, was in essence its final farewell. The 9th and 11th Royal Inniskilling Fusiliers travelled up in a series of trains to the Midland terminus at York Road on the morning of the parade. Forming up in Duncrue Street, they marched through the city to Deramore Park South. The YCVs had marched up from Randalstown on the Wednesday before, leaving camp at 7.00 am and, according to Charles Sheridan, "arrived in the city at 6.00 pm almost on our hands and knees but greatly excited and in good spirits". They returned to their original parade ground of Davidson's Yard, from which they set out to join the brigade. The 10th Skins remained at Finner though a battalion recruiting party made the journey from Tyrone.

The Belfast battalions of the Rifles that made up the 107th Brigade had arrived in the city the day before from their base at Ballykinlar, and started off for Balmoral from their respective ends of Belfast. The 108th Brigade travelled from Newtownards and Bangor by special train that morning, marching from the County Down terminus to their muster point in Ormeau Park. Some 400 men of the 17th Rifles and Divisional Signal Company arrived up from Newcastle; the 121st, 122nd and 150th Field Companies of the Royal Engineers from Antrim; the 16th Rifles, the divisional pioneers, travelled from Lurgan; the 12th Inniskillings, another reserve battalion, from Enniskillen; and so on.

By mid-morning on the day of the parade all the men were in place at Malone, where they stacked arms and had tea and sandwiches. For the YCVs it had been a long morning. They had left Davidson's Yard early, marching along the Mountpottinger Road, Ravenhill Road, Ormeau Park, across King's Bridge, to the Stranmillis Road, Malone Road and Deramore Park South, arriving shortly before 9.00 am. The *Belfast Telegraph* reported:

> "The fall-in sounded at noon, the troops instantly springing to the ranks. Sir Edward Carson and party returned to the enclosure, where the spectators were on the *qui-vive* for the arrival of Major General Sir H McCalmont, the inspecting officer. There was something very business-like in the sight of the Division standing silently on parade. There was none of the glitter and pomp associated with spectacular events of this kind in times of peace. Scarlet uniforms and nodding plumes of general officers had given way to the familiar khaki, the blare of the brass band was replaced by the fife and drum and the skirl of the pipes. Over all brooded a sense of solemnity. The spectators realised that these brave men were shortly going forth – many of them to find graves in a foreign land, and others to endure wounds and suffering, but all to serve the Empire loyally, which is the keynote of the Ulster Volunteer Force."

For almost 45 minutes the general, on horseback and dressed in full ceremonial dress with cocked hat and plume, trotted back and forth through the lines carrying out his inspection. He then took up his position among the other dignitaries on the saluting base as the division marched past, led by a squadron of the Inniskilling Dragoons, followed by the Cyclist Company, dismounted of course, and the Royal Engineer companies led by their band. The *Belfast Telegraph* again:

> "The 107th Brigade headed the infantry, and as battalion after battalion of sturdy Ulstermen in column of platoon marched past with bands playing, the scene was truly impressive. The weather was ideal, a gentle breeze tempering the rays of the sun, which gleamed out at intervals. The General took his salute from the leading battalions and then rode off to take his place at the City Hall, where the march past in column was to be seen at its best. The troops all marched to the Malone Road, and the march through the city then began, the route being via Malone Road and Lisburn Road. The head of the parade arrived eventually at the city centre, wheeling round the end of Wellington Place heading up past the City Hall, the regulation pace of three miles per hour maintained like the rhythm beat of a clock. On, like a restless flood, four deep, tramp, tramp, tramp, past the saluting base, where every

head turns like well-oiled machinery. On down Chichester Street the long line goes, clean-limbed, muscular fellows, brown-faced, clear-eyed, pulsing with health and vigour – what a splendid sight! The three miles from the parade ground has meant nothing to these trained and athletic lads. They tread lightly, their equipment and accoutrements, say some sixty pounds or so in weight, borne without the slightest apparent effort. One does not need to be a trained military expert to see that they are men who would hold their own with any trained forces in the world."[10]

Second Lieutenant Reginald Lambert Lack, as scout officer, led the 14th Battalion with him and his men wearing their summer shorts. It was, as Mullin pointed out, "only on rare occasions, such as this, that the public have an opportunity to see an infantry battalion on the march, complete with field kitchens, transport and other details" and the crowds gave them a rapturous reception, applauding and cheering throughout the route. Others threw treats to the men, which was a mixed blessing for some, according to Charles Sheridan: "The most 'interesting' event in my own case was when someone threw an orange and I caught it 'in the neck'." As the 14th Rifles neared the City Hall there was a noticeable rise in the cheering from the crowds, according to the *Belfast News Letter*:

The Young Citizens, according to newspaper reports, received a warm reception as they paraded through their home city for the last time. *(Courtesy of the Somme Museum)*

"There was, however, no more popular battalion than that recruited from the Young Citizen Volunteers. The Young Citizens, as they are usually styled, had a place towards the rear of the extended column, and their progress was made one of unbroken triumph by the cheers of the spectators."

At the junction of Royal Avenue and North Street the parade effectively finished with units either dispersing to their temporary bases within Belfast or marching to the railway stations for the return trip to camp. The YCVs wheeled right down Donegall Street and along Waring Street on their way back to Davidson's Yard and dispersal.

The following evening the men gathered again at Davidson's Yard around 7.30 pm and, headed by pipes, bugles and fifes, and drums bands under the command of Sergeant Major Elphick,[11] they marched to the Royal Hippodrome where a large crowd had gathered to applaud them on arrival.

The men filled the stalls and circle, with a number of the 'old YCV' invited to join their former comrades. The officers, who were paying for the evening, were the last to enter the theatre and were greeted with cheering. That evening the star performer, Miss Dorothy Ward, who was presented with a bouquet of flowers by D Company, wished the battalion good luck at the Front and a victorious and safe return.

The men again paraded on the Sunday afternoon at St George's Market before marching to the Ulster Hall to attend a military service. They filed into their seats in the main body of the hall, with family and friends among those occupying the gallery and orchestra seats. The Rev George Wedgwood[12] led the service, taking as his theme "Watch ye, stand fast in the faith, quit you like men, be strong." The service concluded with the singing of the National Anthem, after which the men filed out, forming up in the roadway before being dismissed and sent home for a final night.

The journey back to camp, predictably, involved a brigade field exercise with a company of the Royal Engineers and the Antrim squadron of the North Irish Horse taking part along with the 9th and 11th Inniskillings. They detrained at Dunadry in the early afternoon, where they had a meal and awaited the arrival of the sappers. Harrison recalled:

> "The Engineers had their pontoons with them to build a bridge across the river that lay between Dunadry and Randalstown. Two of our companies, C and D, some of the Skins and the North Irish Horse, provided the opposition. We, that is A and B Companies, had the Dragoons, the rest of the Skins, and the Royal Engineers on our side. My platoon was told off to guard the transport, so we lay down in our greatcoats to get some sleep after arranging guard duties. Firing commenced about 11 o'clock and a rocket or two shot up into the darkness on our right front. These were used in an effort to disclose the 'enemy's' whereabouts. Then a heavy burst of firing from each side broke out. About 3.30 am we were sent along at the double but it was all over before we got into action. The march back to camp was pure hell for me as I had developed a large blister on my heel, but I felt better after a cold shower, followed by breakfast."

Mullin saw even less action, though the night was memorable to him because of the kindness of a stranger:

> "My officer placed me on sentry duty, high up on the railway bridge at Muckamore. The bridge was on our lines of communication, and had to be defended. If it had been daylight, the bridge would have been an excellent observation post. About 11.00 pm a kind lady living close by brought me tea and tasty sandwiches, which were much enjoyed."

The spring brought an improvement in the weather and a return to the fold of the 10th Inniskillings, who had remained behind in Donegal when the other three battalions had relocated to Randalstown. It meant for the first time that full brigade training could be undertaken. By now there was an 'end of term' feeling in the camp as everyone knew that they were soon to move on. Speculation was rife about the ultimate destination with the smart money on the Dardanelles. Hope, for one, was satisfied with his time spent here, which he summed up in characteristically few words: "We are shown the way of a rifle and bayonet, we dig trenches, and sleep in the open at night. Manoeuvres and night marches take us as far afield as Ballymena, Castledawson and into Doagh."

The battalion band, which had provided so much entertainment and accompanied the men on some of those marches, was effectively disbanded (though didn't disappear entirely), the musicians being sent back to their normal duties and leaving

Route marches were virtually an everyday occurrence for the lads of the 14th Royal Irish Rifles, while the halts for rest were golden opportunities for George Hackney to set up his camera. *(George Hackney)*

regimental Sergeant Major Elphick, who was in charge of the baton, to rue the end of his evening tattoos. Towards the end of May, under glorious sunshine, the YCVs paraded in the Deer Park of Shane's Castle Demesne to be inspected by the Lord Lieutenant and Lady Wimborne, on their first visit to Ulster. Accompanied by their daughter, Miss Grosvenor, they had motored from Belfast Castle, arriving at the camp at 11.30 am. The battalion, along with the rest of the 109th Brigade, was drawn up in columns of double companies with the massed bands in the centre. After the playing of the National Anthem, the Lord Lieutenant, accompanied by the divisional commanding officer General CH Powell and Brigadier General TE Hickman, inspected the ranks. The brigade then marched past the party before returning to its original position from where it advanced in review order and gave the Royal salute with fixed bayonets.

Around this time the battalion notched up a notable scalp at its favourite past time – football. In a hastily arranged match, played at Cliftonville's Solitude ground in Belfast, the YCVs ran out four-nil winners over the Fermoy-based Irish Brigade. The scorers in the game, which was a fundraiser for the Wounded Soldiers Fund, were Walker (two), Pierpoint and Captain McKee. On Friday 18 June, the 109th Brigade held its sports day in the Deer Park, with invited guests and family travelling from Belfast on the Midland excursion train. All four battalions took part, with the 14th Rifles doing particularly well by winning the 100 yards, sack, quarter-mile, and mile races, the sack fight, and tilting the bucket. It would be the last major battalion event for 200 of the men who, the following week, were transferred to the 16th Rifles to bring it up to strength, an indication that recruiting was still going well. Indeed, an advert run previously in the local newspapers proclaimed: "14th (Service) Battalion Royal Irish Rifles (YCV): the above battalion has permission to recruit beyond its established strength. Recruits desirous of joining this crack corps should apply at

No 68 Scottish Provident Buildings between 9.00 am and 6.00 pm. Only those recruits who are willing to join for General Service and are of good character need apply."[13]

The Randalstown camp[14] had overcome many of its failings by the early summer. One observer on a visit noted: "The 'hutments' covered with corrugated iron, were neat and tidy, sometimes they were guarded by men with rifle and bayonet; they were slightly raised from the ground – possibly a reminder of the wet days of the late winter and early spring." Each hut had a name, with titles such as 'Shankill Road' and 'Liverpool', and were clean and tidy throughout. He went on:

> "This Randalstown camp perfected under the necessities of training for the terrible world war is a triumph of organisation. Whatever may have been its defects heretofore, it is now a revelation of what can be affected by skill, experience and preparation. Well made paths as hard as Macadam 'meander' – the word is chosen deliberately – through the wilderness of huts and latterly there are under footways leading to the several quarters."

There was even a dash of colour as some of the men had taken the trouble of creating flowerbeds outside their huts or on spare bits of ground. Men took to sleeping outside as the huts were becoming stuffy of an evening. With the sunshine came a further relaxation as families and friends were allowed to visit the YCVs at weekends. "The 'boys in khaki' welcome their friends with hearty good wishes; they take and shake their hands with cordial and warm grips; they laugh whole-heartedly like up-grown schoolboys long imprisoned but now free," it was reported.

The lads of 12 Platoon, C Company, 14th Royal Irish Rifles, pose for the camera at Randalstown camp. The huts, despite their shortfalls, were an improvement on the tents at Finner. (Courtesy of Andrew Totten)

Chapter 8

ARRIVAL OF THE WILD IRISH

Any man worthy of mention by us, will come under the eye of that future Macaulay who writes: 'The History of the Great European War, 1914–' What solace for that man in his maturer years. When his children, gathering round his knee, in the cool of a summer evening, lisp the glorious question: 'And what did you do in the Great War, Daddy?' what a tale will he tell! Concluding his narrative, he will place his hand on his eldest son and heir's head and say, triumphantly: '– and for those achievements, Thomas Henry, my name was mentioned in The Incinerator. That's why you read your Daddy's name in your history books today."

**From *The Incinerator*, battalion magazine of the
14th (YCV) Royal Irish Rifles**

A BRASS BAND PLAYED as the men of the 14th Royal Irish Rifles made their way up the gangplanks to board the *Connaught*, a G&J Burns ship, at Kingstown, on the outskirts of Dublin. It was early evening on 6 July 1915, and the lads were finally leaving Ireland to begin their great adventure. From early morning special trains had been bringing them south, with the first companies of the YCV leaving Randalstown at 10.30 am. Each man had been given a bag of food to sustain them on the journey, with chocolates, biscuits, an orange, two bananas and cigarettes included. And, of course, they had the standard tin of bully beef and packet of tea and sugar in their packs. "The train ran into Lisburn station about one o'clock that afternoon," remembered Harrison. "I opened the compartment window and stood at it as we passed through, in the hope that I might catch a glimpse of someone I knew, and to whom I might be able to shout a message for my family, but saw nobody I recognised." Tea with bread and butter was served on arrival at the quayside. The 9th Inniskillings had remained behind, however, having been afflicted by an outbreak of German Measles, much to their embarrassment. While they settled into partial quarantine at Ballycastle, the remainder of the division began its journey. Around 9.00 pm, the boat, with its portholes covered by blackout curtains and no visible lights above decks, pulled away from its berth for the night crossing to Holyhead at Anglesey in north Wales. "The crossing was smooth and uneventful," recalled Harrison. "I stopped below for most of the journey, as it was really quite cold and I didn't want to have to unroll my greatcoat." At Holyhead they boarded trains again around 1.00 am for the trip to Seaford, on the Sussex coast, stopping at Rugby for half-an-hour during which tea with bread and butter was served by children on the platform. After brief stops at Willesden and Lewes, where the YCVs were able to stretch their legs, they finally pulled in at Seaford.[1]

"We detrained and loaded our gear into the transports, which were waiting for us, formed up and marched off towards the camp," noted Harrison. "This proved to be only 10 minutes or so from the railway station, and, to our joy, we found it was about the same from the sea."

The accommodation was again in huts, though as the weather was warm and dry and the construction complete, a lot more pleasant than their earlier experience. To Hope "Seaford is a delightful watering place midway between Eastbourne and Brighton" with his only concern being "ants which move about in millions around the foundations of the huts." Rifleman Berry saw it as a "fine camp, on top of a hill overlooking the town." He added: "We bathed daily and trained for war. It doesn't seem very far away, as we can hear the guns firing

J Ewing does a bit of letter writing during his spare time at Seaford while Austin McCleery prefers to catch up on his sleep. *(George Hackney)*

in France whenever the wind is in the proper direction." Mullin, who had turned down the chance of corporal's stripes and the temporary safety of a place in a reserve battalion alongside the over-age Company Sergeant Major Herron, was equally delighted with his new surroundings. "The hutted camp at Seaford was conveniently situated near the town; a well-known residential coastal resort with a steep shingle beach and excellent promenade." The locals, on the other hand, were more than a little anxious to have thousands of young Irishmen arrive on their doorsteps. Indeed, according to Charles Sheridan, the arrival of the Ulster Division was "much to the alarm of the inhabitants of that place who on hearing the 'Wild Irish' were coming promptly hide themselves indoors for a few days until they realised we were not nearly as 'wild' as we were supposed to be and they ended by liking us very much or so they said for I must admit we were very quiet during our stay there."[2]

The timing of the Ulster Division's move to England had been influenced in part by the authorities' desire to avoid having them still at home for the Twelfth demonstrations that year. As a result, many experienced a far from traditional day of celebration. The Rev WJ Robinson, Methodist chaplain with the division, described the day in a letter home. He wrote:

"We were curious to see how the 12th would be passed. The morning was spent in bathing parades, whole battalions in the sea at a time. In the afternoon the men were free, and crowded the various homes and halls. Seaford streets in the evening were packed with khaki-clad men – clear, smart, steady men. A few drums and fifes were procured, and an impromptu procession formed up and marched through the streets singing 'Rule Britannia,' and other patriotic songs. Perfect good humour prevailed, and though I was in the town from 7 to 9.30, I never saw, nor heard of any untoward incident."

A local newspaper reported how many soldiers were "gaily bedecked with the sashes and regalia of the Loyal Orange Institution, while it would have been an impossibility to discover a man in uniform without an orange-coloured decoration in hat or buttonhole." A number of English Orangemen visited the town during the day to take part in a service that began with the traditional unionist hymn, 'O God, our Help in Ages Past' and closed with 'Fight The Good Fight' and a collection for the Lord Enniskillen Memorial Orphan Fund.

For many of the Belfast lads this was as far away from home as they had ever been and, as Berry indicated, their thoughts were on what lay ahead. The town had long been viewed as a location vulnerable to attack, with a barracks established there in the 18th century. In 1810 a Martello tower was built, using half-a-million bricks, to oppose any attempt by Napoleon to invade. The YCVs found the people of Seaford and the surrounding coastal towns and villages were again on a war footing. Because of its closeness to the French coast, trenches had been dug and barbed wire defences erected along part of the shoreline to thwart invaders, while those living along the coast itself were not allowed to show lights after dark. At Seaford's military camps, of which there were several, the windows were covered with blankets and outside lights shaded for fear of attracting enemy attention. The men mounted sentry duties at important installations, such as the Blatchington Reservoir, and watched bemused as airships and aeroplanes regularly passed overhead. When one came down in a field close to the camp with engine troubles, the embarrassed pilot found himself the centre of the attention of several hundred excited Ulstermen.

Men prepare dinner on the Sussex Downs, which provided plenty of space for large-scale war gaming and training. *(George Hackney)*

The extensive South Downs, running from Winchester to Eastbourne with Seaford sitting on the valley floor, provided the necessary space for divisional training, with huge exercises being staged both day and night involving infantry, cavalry, cyclists and ancillary services such as the Royal Engineers, Royal Army Service Corps and Royal Army Medical Corps. Only the divisional artillery, raised in London and still undergoing intensive training, was not able to take part.

An article written by the Rev John Pollock, minister of St Enoch's Church, Carlisle Circus, Belfast, who holidayed in Seaford in the summer of 1915, is worth quoting at length.[3] He described a pleasant town, its architecture largely from the 19th century, which depended on those seeking convalescence and education to survive "having three large sanatoria of different kinds to its thirty high-class boarding schools". "Under normal conditions summer visitors are not encouraged for Seaford desires to remain 'select'," he added. Sussex, and especially the South Downs, resembled County Down, he thought, with low billowy hills that rolled from Beachy Head to the Hampshire border.

"Seaford is less than sixty miles from London and rather more than a hundred miles from the nearest point of the Flanders firing line. Standing in a field last evening away from the lights and noises of camp and town I could see the glow of London like a faint aurora on the northern horizon and hear the soft 'puh' of the heavy artillery at the front… think of it. A man can actually look at the lights of London and listen to the death dealing explosion of German shells."

Nearby Newhaven, with its harbour full of Royal Navy ships, was out of bounds to all, while the surrounding country was extremely beautiful, with "quaint old villages" dotting the landscape.

Mr Pollock had a keen eye and a wicked sense of humour, noting: "Shops that were threatened with extinction are doing a roaring trade, one modest little stationery emporium selling, I am told, something like a thousand picture postcards a day. If ever a Seaford shopkeeper says to you as he hands you your parcel, 'Isn't this a dreadful war?' he says it with a smile." Soldiers were everywhere, with the cleric finding himself "in the heart of a very realistic battlefield, with infantry advancing in open order, a bayonet attack, and clattering cavalry rushing forward to their support, while snipers crept stealthily from cover to cover. It was an oppressive day, and every man carried his kit; but no field of footballers ever threw themselves into their sport more heartily than those boys of the Ulster Division played their exciting war game." Morale was sky high, with no grumbling about the long hours and hard work or food, and general contentment with the living accommodation, claimed the clergyman. "Our boys at Seaford are the healthiest crowd you will see anywhere. When they swing down the street whistling, with their bathing-towels over their shoulders, caps thrown back, shirt sleeves rolled up, sunburnt breasts bare to the breeze, you pity the sickly civilians in the side walk. How glorious it must be to be young these days, and a British Tommy." Mr Pollock concluded his article in similarly romantic fashion:

The string of clergymen who visited the YCVs at Seaford might have been of the opinion that drink wasn't a problem but this photo, entitled 'The Morning After the Night Before', suggests otherwise. *(George Hackney)*

"As I sit here at my door in the cool of the evening, the sound of the 'last post' comes up from the North Camp, stretching like a strangely symmetrical city along the valley. Every window is alight, but all is perfectly still. Behind the opposite high ground you can see where London lies. It is a scene suggestive of anything rather than conflict, and the red riot of war. 'Lights out!' The last note of the bugle has barely died away when a section of the camp, the YCV, is instantaneously switched into darkness. Then another section, and another, and others in quick succession, till only the officers' huts in the distance remain visible. No need to wish the boys a good night's sleep! Already some of them are dreaming of Royal Avenue, 'good old Shankill,' and the old folks at home – to say nothing of that 'sweetest girl I know,' who is also busy dreaming, further off than Tipperary."

Being a man of the cloth, he was obviously concerned about the moral well-being of the soldiers, and suggested "no Belfast mother need tremble for her boy in such a clean and wholesome environment" at Seaford. Claiming that he had not seen any soldier the worse for drink, he added: "No body of soldiers ever had more done for their moral and spiritual welfare. The military chaplains of all denominations ire with each other in self-sacrificing thoroughness with which they do their work, though grievously short-handed. The Salvation Army, the Church Army, and especially the YMCA are doing priceless service, for which it is hoped the historian of the Great War will give them full credit." However, in a sermon on his visit to Seaford, delivered at St Enoch's on 5 September 1915, he was more realistic about the religious aspect of the men: "I cannot say that all our men are 'good soldiers of Jesus Christ' – would to God that they were! But there are many praying lads among them, and the spirit that dominated the whole is the spirit of serious optimism that is not easily distinguished from Christian faith." Religion was clearly important to many of the men and even those less church minded are likely to have sought comfort in it as the prospect of going to war drew closer. A gospel temperance campaign that rolled into Seaford at the end of July 1915 found the men of the Ulster Division were quite literally willing to queue up to sign the non-drinking pledge and join the Pocket Testament League. Mr Tennyson Smith and his wife, who had been touring army camps for the previous eight months under the auspices of the National Council of the YMCA, could not keep up with demand with reportedly more than 200 men stepping forward to sign on the first evening and well over 100 on each of the following three nights. Some 502 Belfast men alone are said to have taken the pledge while close to 300 applied for testaments on one particular evening, with more having to be ordered in.

To the YCVs the real importance of Seaford's location was that free time, of which there was plenty at weekends, could be spent at the popular seaside towns of Eastbourne or Brighton, while London was comfortably within reach. Restrictions were relaxed, with the men allowed to return to camp at whatever hour suited them provided they kept the noise and disturbance down. Invitations to social events, such as dances and whist drives, were sent to the camp from the various organisations in the area, with nearby Haslemere being particularly open to entertain the troops. Mullin and Bob Douglas were among those who liked to spend weekends in the capital, staying in the Union Jack Club that catered specifically for services' personnel. There they met fellow volunteers who were intrigued by their battalion insignia. "In the club we were often asked what regiment? And what did the letters YCV stand for? In answer to the latter question, Douglas usually replied "Young Chocolate Volunteers" or some other witty remark." The nickname 'Chocolate Soldiers', which came with a number of variations, was used both as a form of endearment and of scorn, depending on who was delivering it. The Inniskillings liked to tease 'their' Rifles battalion with it but would come to the defence of their comrades if others did the same. The other Belfast battalions of the Royal Irish Rifles were the most likely to use it as a taunt as tensions grew between the YCVs and units in the 107th Brigade, with the latter – which had spent months in the front line at the end of 1915 while the rest of the 36th Division continued its training – of the view that the Young Citizens got it easy.[4]

Hope, whose circle of friends appeared to contain more 'characters' than most, has a less happy tale to tell from a visit to the capital:

> "We get leave to London. On the way back to Lewes, Paddy Wallace in a daft fit, pulls the communication cord and stops the train. Paddy's name is taken, the train proceeds and is half-an-hour late, so late that the connection at Lewes is missed and we have to walk some miles to camp. Hundreds have to do this owing to Paddy's madness. The railway company writes to Paddy pointing out the seriousness of the offence and the penalty if no explanation is offered. Paddy and I make up some awful lie about the 'accident' and nothing more is heard."

The food now being served up in the mess hall was regulation Army issue for the first time, though no more inviting for that. There were, however, plenty of places within easy reach where spare cash would buy more readily digestible fare. Harrison was not a man to complain, even recording that "altogether we are having a great time here, not being overworked as we had been at home," but he too had a gripe about the food, both in quality and quantity, though as always saw the silver lining in terms of how it improved his social life. "The bread! Well, seven small loaves between 14 men doesn't go very far. That means 1 lb per man daily. Some of the boys here could eat two men's share. I manage to do on it, but if I am not satisfied I just go over to the YMCA or the Salvation Army hut, and have a cup of tea or coffee, with cake and buns. One can get a decent book out of the Lending Library in the YMCA and there is a fine platform and piano for impromptu concerts. Concert parties come down from London on Saturday evenings, and these are very popular."

Despite the water being colder than off the Donegal coast, the bathing parades remained popular though, as at Finner, the dangers were ever present. Harrison recalled:

"Two of the ASC were drowned while bathing. Some of the Citizens who were there saved two or three others. I had quite an experience in this line myself on the very first bathing parade we had after we arrived in Seaford. The water deepens very suddenly here and a chap called W----- was swept off his feet by a receding wave. He shouted at me and I went to his assistance, telling him to place his hands on my shoulders. Instead of doing this he gripped me by the neck and both of us went under. I eventually got him ashore, and it was only then that I realised my danger. That taught me a lesson and in future I shall be more careful. W----- has since given up bathing altogether."[5]

A number of men lost their lives at Seaford, including some through drowning in the cold and sometimes choppy sea. Here the chaplains walk behind the Union Flag draped coffin of an Inniskilling on its way to the cemetery in the seaside town. (George Hackney)

A series of high-profile visitors made their way to Seaford to see the men. Lieutenant General Sir AJ Murray, Chief of the Imperial General Staff and a former commander of the 2nd Skins and honorary colonel of the regiment, spent two days at Seaford inspecting the Ulster Division in mid-July. Secretary of War Lord Kitchener followed him. The Field Marshal, who was nearly unseated from his horse after it was spooked by the cheering of schoolchildren who had come out to greet him, expressed the view that the Ulster Division was "too good to be left behind". He instructed that, once it had completed its musketry course, it should be sent to France – but not before some 200 men who were "too fine" for the RAMC were sent to the artillery. In the event, only 150 men switched to the Royal Artillery. A divisional order issued later recorded:

> "Field-Marshal Earl Kitchener expressed to the General Officer Commanding his great pleasure with the appearance of the Ulster Division, and congratulated him on the appearances of the men and their steadiness on parade and on their drill. He further said he was glad to find a division so well advanced. Lord Kitchener greatly regretted that time did not permit him to inspect the Divisional Train and Reserve Park."

On 18 July, the Sunday between the top brass visits, the Church of Ireland Primate the Most Rev Dr Crozier came to see the division at Seaford, staying as the guest of Lieutenant Colonel Chichester. He celebrated Holy Communion in a church hut in the North Camp assisted by the 14th Rifles' padre Canon King and later preached to some 8,000 soldiers in the grounds of Seaford golf club. At noon he held a confirmation service in the South Camp church with one officer and 18 men receiving the blessing.[6]

The following month Presbyterian Moderator the Right Rev Dr Hamill conducted services at Seaford for the Ulster Division troops. Perhaps the most popular of the VIPs, however, was unionist leader Sir Edward Carson, though the report of his visit in the *Belfast News Letter* ruffled a few feathers. It read:

> "Sir Edward Carson recently paid a visit to the Ulster Division at Seaford, Sussex, and made a tour of many of the huts occupied by the volunteers from the North of Ireland. The right honourable gentleman saw the 14th Battalion, Royal Irish Rifles (Young Citizens), Lieutenant Colonel RPD Chichester commanding on parade on Thursday, and was accorded a most enthusiastic reception by the rank and file as well as by the officers. He expressed great pleasure at the discipline and splendid bearing of the men – it is understood that Sir Edward Carson will visit other units of the Ulster Division at an early date."

A letter to the paper, published on Saturday 14 August and signed by an "Ulster Volunteer, South Camp, Seaford," pointed out: "Sir – In your issue of 9th August I see an announcement to the effect that Sir Edward Carson recently paid a visit of inspection to the 14th Royal Irish Rifles (Young Citizens). The visit referred to extended to the entire Ulster Division, very few if any, of the various units of which were not inspected by the right honourable gentleman."

The first anniversary of the declaration of war was commemorated at Seaford on 4 August with a series of church services. In the Garrison Church, in South Camp, a voluntary service attended by more than 1,000 soldiers was held at noon. That evening Lieutenant Colonel Chichester and his senior officers down to battalion commanders attended a service in the Parish Church in Seaford town, which was immediately followed by an open air service in a field adjacent to the church from which clergy addressed the congregation from a platform specially built for the purpose.

This, presumably, is a self-portrait as the man in the picture putting pen to paper is George Hackney, the battalion's semi-official photographer. *(George Hackney)*

Sporting events were organised on a regular basis at Seaford, sometimes taking up most of a week. The 14th Rifles enjoyed mixed fortunes during the five-day boxing tournament – interrupted with a route march between bouts – held in August. On the middle Saturday the boxing took a back seat to allow 21 teams to take part in a divisional cross-country championship that took the form of a time trial over a 4.5-mile circuit of the camp. D Company of the YCVs won by less than a minute – only for the second-placed team, from the 8th Royal Irish Rifles, to lodge an objection that not all the men in the team were from the one company. Rifleman James McRoberts, who only discovered an ability and love for long-distance running after joining the Army, noted: "At first there was an understanding that this battalion had beaten us, and the virulent ridicule the 'Young Citizens' had to listen to for a time was amusing rather than otherwise. When we reached our camp we were loudly cheered and all had our tea in the Sergeants' Mess."[7]

Outside of sport, concert parties, a favourite entertainment of the YCVs, continued at Seaford, normally at Steyne Hall, the Wesleyan Soldiers' Home, with Captain Harper presiding.[8]

Towards the end of August the division received orders to move from Seaford to use the ranges at Bordon and Bramshott in Hampshire. The 14th was assembled in its new camp by early September in preparation to take the musketry courses using a very unsatisfactory supply of American ammunition. Sheridan thought Bramshott camp a "rather isolated place but we had a good time while there as we constantly paid visits to the villages or towns which were nearest to us…" Berry recorded "weather is warm and dry, we bivouacked here for a week and enjoyed ourselves." The bivouac was made of two ground sheets linked together and shared by two men. In Berry's case his sleeping companion was a mate, Herby Bowden. As at Seaford, the men made a good impression on the local community. A Bramshott resident, writing to a friend in Belfast, told her:

"It was a joyous day to me when I heard that the Ulster Division was coming to these camps. They have made a good impression, and everywhere it has been the same thing. It is a pleasure to see them riding and marching through the place.

One notices their fine physique and good features. Last Sunday there were route marches. We are a bit off the village, which is large one, and the people told me it was beautiful to hear the hymns and the harmonies of the voices as the men went past in companies to camp. Our Soldiers' Club here is called 'Home'. In it lies the reward for all effort and fatigue, and our work does not stop there, as we correspond with many of the men who go to France. We have already the names and numbers of many brave Ulster boys. We had numbers of your Young Citizens yesterday. It is pleasant and interesting to all to record that our English friends have been so kind."

There was also an additional course on the ranges at Bisley for the machine-gun sections, of which Mullin was nominally a part. He recalled how he and four companions, out for a stroll, became lost and disorientated there when fog came down on the open plains. "It was near midnight before we found our camp. Fortunately for us, the bugler kept sounding the YCV regimental call every ten minutes. That saved us." It would have been obvious

The Longmoor rifle ranges at Bordon were not just used for musketry courses. This photograph appears to show the men being taught battlefield tactics with the use of a blackboard. *(George Hackney)*

to all, even those who didn't pay heed to camp gossip, that training was all but over. The message wasn't lost on Kennedy: "The end of the picnic is in sight," he concluded, adding: "We are getting a final rub up. It would take an acrobat to do the handling here in the course of intensive training."

With the courses completed, final preparations were undertaken for the move to France. The men were granted a last home leave – though not before an ugly scene was acted out. James McRoberts recalled:

"One evening a rumour reached us from the huts that no leave was going to be granted before going to the Front, and that several of the battalions had – to use the only possible word – mutinied. That night we were paraded and addressed by Major B--, at that moment in a lamentable, intoxicated state. Was it so bad at the Front? If we did not get leave he said, we were not to mutiny, no matter what other battalions might do and what they might say about us. We had joined the Army for King and Country and had undertaken to obey its rules and commands. This was the first war most of us had been in and probably it would be the last, thus it behoved us to abide by the rules like men. So let us play the game and to hell with the Pope! The proceedings were a scandal and a shame to the British Army, but the reckless, dare-all manner of the Major had a great influence with the troops."

It was difficult for the men to say farewell to family and friends with the knowledge they were finally heading off to face the enemy and there were those who abused the privilege. "I was very glad to get home again," remembered Sheridan, adding: "It was rather rotten having to leave after four days… I did not take any extra days like some of the boys and I have been sorry ever since that I didn't." New equipment "as hard as the gates of perdition" according to Kennedy, was issued, including boots that not only had to be broken in but also were a size too big to allow for extra socks to be worn in winter. Harrison was impressed with his new webbing, though puzzled by the number of straps.

> "No doubt it will all become clear when we actually get our hands on it. Respirators are also to be handed out and a special pocket is conveniently placed in our new tunics in which to carry this. There are actually 13 items of woven webbing straps, bags, and cases that have to be assembled. We then realised that these bits and pieces had to carry everything that a soldier possessed except his rifle and the clothing he stood up in."

The men were also required to fill-in a will, indicating where they wanted their few bits and pieces of personal items to be sent in the event of their deaths. Surely a sobering thought on the eve of going overseas.

There was one final change, which was to leave a bad taste in the mouths of many. Major General Powell, who had overseen the Ulster Division's training from the beginning, was sent off to France for instruction only to discover on his return that Major General Oliver Nugent, who had battle experience on the Western Front, had replaced him as commanding officer. One of the new CO's first tasks was to parade the division on 30 September 1915, to be inspected by King George V and Kitchener. Kennedy was far from impressed: "We are going to see the King. Over the country for miles we march till we arrive at a big open space. George

Another photograph at the Longmoor ranges. Here the men are given a demonstration on how to don one of the earliest gas protection masks. *(George Hackney)*

with Kitchener and all the 'knobs' take the grand salute as the division marches past." The "knobs" included UVF commander Sir George Richardson who was told by the King "what a fine Division had been given by his Ulster Volunteers". Cyril Falls, in the divisional history, adds: "As the King's motorcar overtook some of the troops marching back to camp the men burst out into cheering, so that the car swept along a loud roaring line – an unrehearsed spontaneous exhibition of loyalty."

Not everyone was going to war, of course, as many of the NCOs who had supplied the bulk of the training along with some of the volunteers were too old for overseas service. This provided a further opportunity, not to be missed by the battalion wags, of stirring it up. Kennedy records: "The battalion is over war strength. Old soldiers are keeping quiet. We are ragging them about going overseas. We hear they are going home and tell them they are for France. One fellow, a cook of our company, has been told to appear that he thinks he is going. He is ragged till he's nearly out of his mind."

There was also a question mark over the YCV's commanding officer, Lieutenant Colonel

Chichester who, at the beginning of October, had to step down as he required surgery in a London nursing home. Major HR Bliss, of the 3rd Battalion Royal Irish Regiment, temporarily took his place. Bliss had served in West Africa in 1900, saw action at Ashanti, been present at the relief of Kumassi and was mentioned in despatches during active service in Nigeria in 1901–2.

The final few days on British soil were spent in clearing up the camp in preparation for its handover to the next unit. Even in this task Hope managed to find controversy and difficulties. After cleaning out his own sleeping accommodation he was ordered by a corporal to help out at an adjoining tent but refused – not realising the regimental sergeant major was standing behind him. "He hears the cross talk and orders the corporal to put me in 'clink'. I am up on a 'crime' for the first time. The corporal doesn't 'put me in' and the RSM fetches up the corporal for disobeying his orders, and brings me up also. I am marched in before the CO and get three days pack drill. The corporal is hasty tempered and throws in his stripes." Hope, however, escaped entirely as the punishment was forgotten about amid the imminent move.

In a final message, the King promised he would be watching the division's progress on the Western Front:

> "You are about to join your comrades at the Front in bringing to a successful end to this relentless war of over twelve months' duration. Your prompt patriotic answer to the nation's call to arms will never be forgotten. The keen exertions of all ranks during the period of training have brought out to a state of efficiency not unworthy of my Regular Army. I am confident that in the field you will nobly uphold the traditions of the fine regiments whose names you bear. Ever since your enrolment I have closely watched the growth and steady progress of all units. I shall continue to follow with interest the fortunes of your Division. In bidding you farewell, I pray that God may bless you in all your undertakings."

Chapter 9

STANDING IN THE SHELTER OF THE DUGOUT

You are ordered abroad as a soldier of the King to help our French comrades against the invasion of a common enemy. You have to perform a task which will need your courage, your energy, your patience. Remember that the honour of the British Army depends on your individual conduct. It will be your duty not only to set an example of discipline and perfect steadiness under fire but also to maintain the most friendly relations with those whom you are helping in this struggle. The operations in which you are engaged will, for the most part, take place in a friendly country, and you can do your own country no better service than in showing yourself in France and Belgium in the true character of a British soldier.

**Part of a confidential note, from Lord Kitchener, placed inside
the Active Service Pay Books of soldiers leaving for France**

A SILENCE FELL OVER those on deck as the paddle steamer *Empress Queen*, carrying the men of the 14th Royal Irish Rifles, gently eased past "a large hospital ship with thousands of lights".[1]

The sight, remembered Hope, gave the boys 'food for thought' as they prepared to disembark at La Havre. The shivers of fear which passed up some spines were matched by the buzz of excitement felt by others as they watched in wonder the French troops on the quayside, still wearing the red trousers which had cost them dear in the early fighting by making them standout as targets. This was the great adventure, the chance of a lifetime to test a man's mettle, to serve one's country and earn the respect and gratitude of a nation – provided you returned alive, and preferably not in a hospital ship like the one they had just passed. Senior officers of the 36th Division, led by the now displaced General Powell, had travelled to France at the end of the summer of 1915 to gain some first-hand experience of trench war and even as the King was completing his inspection at the end of the previous month, the advance parties were already making arrangements for the battalion's arrival. Much of the division had sailed into Boulogne, with General Nugent and his staff arriving there around midnight on 3 October, with the horses and transport travelling the same route as the YCVs. They had left Bramshott camp on 4 October, their special trains having the blinds drawn for fear that German 'spies' (a national pre-occupation at the time) might realise they were on the move. At Southampton they piled up their equipment in the huge quayside sheds and attempted to find a place to get their heads down for a few hours sleep.

A number of men, including Mullin, were posted about the deck of the former Isle of Man Steam Packet Company ship to keep an eye out for submarines as it set off on 5 October 1915. "Dawn was breaking as our boat steamed into harbour," recorded Rifleman Berry. McRoberts noted: "Signs of the war met the eye on every hand. Trainloads of English

Passing a hospital ship as they arrived in France was a sobering moment for many of the 14th Rifles on board the troop transporter. *(George Hackney)*

wounded were continually arriving. Some bore injured men who were quite helpless and these were carried on the platform on stretchers, others had only minor wounds and travelled like ordinary passengers." The men were formed up on the quayside and marched through Le Havre and up a hill to the camp, struggling to keep their grip on the square-set pavers. McRoberts, who had stayed behind to help with the unloading, goes on:

"In the evening we followed the battalion, and after a weary march reached the so-called rest camp, a canvas abode situated in a veritable quagmire. We had seen no French soldiers except sentries in an assortment of uniforms and all along the route there were notices written in English posted up: 'Keep to the Right'. We were packed, about a dozen in each bell-tent where we had a meal of tea and iron rations."

Mullin was likewise far from impressed with what he found there: "The accommodation in Cinder City turned out to be much worse than we expected. Our sleeping quarters were bell tents, pitched in a sea of ankle deep mud. It was necessary to remove boots on entering the tent". Berry found himself one of 16 men squeezed into a tent: "What a hell of a crush! Jammed together with equipment, etc."

The following day proved to be an anti-climax, with the men virtually confined to their tents as the thick mud made it all but impossible to move around. The canteen, when it eventually opened, was the only distraction. Some were lucky in having a wise-cracker in the company: "In my tent Private Billy Oliver has many useful humorous philosophical sayings, which relieve the monotony," remembered Mullin. He was also quick to attempt putting his lessons learnt at French classes at Randalstown into practice, accosting the first native speaker he could find: "Accordingly I seized the first opportunity to ask a garcon "Quel est votre nom?" I was surprised how quickly the boy responded, telling me his name. Evidently he understood my pronunciation without difficulty. This raised hopes for the future. Very soon I was to find plenty of time for practicing French speaking, with varying degrees of success."

After just the one night at Le Havre the men marched off around 3.00 am to the railway station and were disappointed to discover waiting for them a long line of cattle-trucks. Painfully slowly – men were able to alight and run alongside to exercise their stiff legs and still not fall behind or, as Mullin put it, "you could have got out to pick flowers along the line" – the train carried them eastwards. The wagons, considered fit enough for just eight horses, were packed with dozens of men. Berry felt he "could scarcely breathe," adding:

> "Rifles that had been slung up where continually falling on top of us when asleep and occasionally some chap would kick in his sleep. Usually the boot met some other poor devil's face. What a journey! It seemed endless… We sat with our legs swinging out; we played cards; we smoked; we sang the hours away – and ever crawled nearer the Front."

There were many unofficial halts along the way until, mid-afternoon, a scheduled stop was made during which strong black coffee without sugar or milk was served, much to the disgust of Mullin who craved a decent cup of Belfast tea.

Eventually the train pulled into a siding at Amiens, the only city in the Somme region, and the men were formed up on the side of the track to march off to their billets. An unusually deflated Mullin recorded:

> "We don't know where we are and we care less. We are glad to get on the move, and sincerely hope our guides know the way . . . in silence and perhaps a little depressed we march through the night, each wrapped up in his own thoughts. At length weary and tired out we arrive at our billeting village, where we wait on the roadside for a long time. The darkness of the night increases the difficulty of placing platoons in their allotted billets."

Mullin's platoon finally got to lay down their weary heads in a dilapidated barn in what the men were to discover was Poulainville. It had taken them all day and half the night to travel barely 100 miles.

The village school at Poulainville was turned into the Orderly Room and a makeshift firing range constructed on the edge of the village. The working routine remained much the same as in England, with parades, inspections, route marches and a series of exercises, two at brigade level and one a divisional field day as General Nugent had his first look at what he had inherited. As with many new commanding officers, he gave his officers a dressing down for the perceived shortfalls in training. For the men, however, country life was not entirely disagreeable. The village, which transpired to be their home for the next two weeks, was much in need of attention, so they set about cleaning up their billets, introducing as many comforts as possible, and searching the locality for cheap eggs and milk. Harrison, whose main complaint was the lack of sufficient water to wash in, was accommodated in a loft above a stable. He recalled:

> "Opposite our billet is the chapel, a building of considerable size and beauty. To get to our 'bedroom' we enter a stable door, risk a backward lunge from the iron-shod hoof of its equine occupant, mount a staircase, and find ourselves under the roof, knee-deep in straw. The yard down below is inhabited by rooting pigs, clucking hens and their broods, ducks, stray dogs, cats and pigeons, all these wallowing about in the mire common to the stable and pigsty. The stench is awful!"

The lads soon ran out of the cigarettes they had brought from home and tried the French tobacco "with lamentable results," according to Harrison, while the regular trips to the village's cafes soon meant the likes of "vin rouge, vin blanc, du pange, de buerre" came into daily use. Rifleman Charles Connolly kept his mother, who lived in Drogheda, and a brother who had a home at Templemore Avenue, Belfast, well abreast of everything he was involved in, including giving them a taste of his daily routine: "Since arriving in France we get up at 5.30 am, and are in bed at 8.00 pm, when in billets," he wrote. "Very often we are in bed earlier, as there is absolutely nothing else to do. You can't even go for a walk as all the roads from the village are out of bounds. The two cafes the town boasted of were not desirable as rendezvous." Although Amiens, just a short distance away, was off-limits to the rank and file, a trip was arranged to see the city's beautiful cathedral. The men, caps in hand, were in awe of their surroundings. "We had a route march, in full marching order, to Amiens where we piled rifles in the square, in front of the Cathedral and entered the building in single file," recorded McRoberts. "It had a noble, magnificent and rich appearance which made everyone talk of it with wonder and delight. On the outside the doors and several of the windows were protected by sandbag structures which were piled up to an amazing height." Always with an eye for the ladies, he added: "We expected to see some fine specimens of French maidenhood in Amiens but had to return much disappointed. We found many fellows who readily gave us full instruction as to the location of and rates charged by 'their sisters' for sexual entertainment. 'She is tres bonne ici et ici,' (very good here and here) said one, pointing to his breasts and crotch." In fact, according to Connolly, when they emerged from the cathedral they found many French people had gathered to see the 'Tommies'. "We were speedily on terms of intimacy, and though Amiens was 'out-of-bounds' to individual soldiers, there were, to my personal knowledge, many clandestine visits afterwards," he wrote home.

On 21 October, they quit Poulainville for Beauval in preparation for training in the trenches and completed a field exercise along the way. Moving out shortly after 8.00 am, with the 107th and 109th brigades forming up initially in 'artillery formation' then into extended line, the men 'battled on' until around 5.30 pm when the exercise was called off. The *War Diary* noted "men billeted down after much confusion, owing to proper arrangements not having been made for billeting". The following day the confusion was put right with companies reunited in the same locations and a huge clean up of the town and billets undertaken to improve sanitation. For Sheridan, sent out to buy some fresh supplies, his arrival at Beauval was to be the start of a friendship with a French family that ensured he, at least, was better fed than his comrades:

"On our arrival I went to a house to buy milk and bread and although I did not know it the people were very well to do and were just having dinner. One of the daughters of the house was very much amused at my efforts to speak French but managed to understand and after heating the milk for me she – backed by the rest of the family – asked me to sit down to dinner with them and as I had marched and skirmished across ploughed fields for a distance of 18 kms I was only too delighted and accepted after feebly trying to express my thanks. We stayed there two weeks during which time I became very friendly with the French family I have mentioned. I had a free run of the house at all hours and I had only to express a wish for anything (in the food line) and it was granted at once."[2]

Beauval, just a few miles south of Doullens, was closer to the front line and caused some to ponder what lay ahead. Mullin again: "When a little strafe starts I listen to the thunder of the guns and wonder how anyone or anything could possibly live up there. At night I can trace the line by the position of the gun flashes."

Harrison was happier in the bigger town: "There is plenty of room in this billet, the streets are wider, and after the little village with its many odours, it was a relief to stroll around and gaze into the windows of several pretentious shops, without holding one's nose in places." Some of the cafés served chips, much to the delight of the men, while many took the opportunity of visiting a barber shop where the proprietor was a woman so, according to Harrison, as to "enjoy a new sensation – that of being shaved by one of the fair sex".

All officers were provided with horses, though horsemanship had to be learned. Here Captains Harper, Hyndman and McKee appear to be being pulled in different directions by their mounts. *(George Hackney)*

The King, on a tour of the front, was in the vicinity of where the Ulstermen were now based and the battalion was ordered to line the roadway south of Beauval as a guard of honour. It was a bitterly cold day and the men, in position hours before the scheduled arrival of the entourage, which included the Prince of Wales, the French president, Field Marshal Sir John French and his French counterpart Marshal Joffre, had to endure freezing temperatures as they waited on the briefest of Royal visits. "The 'circus' is very much overdue and we are nearly frozen to death waiting on the roadside," noted a less than enthusiastic Hope. Mullin, on the other hand, recalled:

"We march to the position, and then in single file line both sides of the road. The lines are made longer by the ranks opening out to one yard apart. We are nearly frozen stiff owing to the long wait. We are warned the procession of cars is approaching.

The battalion present arms as the first car containing the King and Marshal Joffre is about to pass. I have a clear view of His Majesty, as his car slows down to five or six mph. Statesmen and some Allied generals complete the entourage."

On the same day the King swept past, the battalion had been preparing to move to the trenches for instruction from the 143rd Brigade, and the following day, as the men moved up to the tented camp at Couin, in the grounds of a chateau, they passed the 13th Rifles and 9th Royal Irish Fusiliers returning from their spells in the line. Connelly recalled:

"We halted for the night at one of the so-called 'rest camps,' some miles in rear of the firing line. We had a jolly time of it that night in the tent. We had been down to the village, and purchased some eatables from the Bucks canteen, and brought them up for our supper... After getting in a supply of apples we set out for the much talked of trenches. Naturally all were babbling over with curiosity to see what they were like."

The YCVs were met by guides of the 5th and 7th Battalions of the Royal Warwickshire Regiment at Souastre on 27 October. They led them into the trenches at Fonquevillers, which were "French in style – wickerwork sides," according to Hope. "The dugouts are big and have wire beds. Seems as if it is an exhibition line to show to greenhorns." On the way blankets were passed out to the men as they made their way up by platoons at 100-yard intervals with the officers' horses, baggage and kitchens sent back to Bayencourt. This was one of the quietest sectors at this time but it was still a shock to the system to men experiencing trench conditions for the first time. "We almost crawled there in the darkness, and on the way reached a deserted village in ruins, not a house having escaped untouched," Connolly reported home. "Our platoon was brought through endless communication trenches, the passage being very tiring owing to our slipping about in the mud and falling into holes. At length we reached a regular maze of trenches following our guide like sheep. We were pushed into a dugout, and being worn out just fell down and slept as we were." Mullin recalled:

"The entrance to our communication trench passes through a farmhouse which has not been completely wrecked. We follow our guide up the trench, my section is led into a shelter, a so-called dugout. It is a trench with a roof, at right angles to the communication trench. Along one side there are wire-netting beds. I am lucky as I am the last man in. First in claims the first bed. My place is at the extreme end furthest from the door. A candle is lit. The walls are revetted with branches of trees. I am not in long, until I hear rats squealing and scampering about. There is nothing else for it but to lie on the bed and try to sleep. I protect myself with my rubber ground sheet. While I remain awake I keep knocking the rats off, as best I can. A candle is kept lit, but it makes no difference. Pte S Dunlop hangs (by a cord from the roof) his Mother's food parcel, thinking it would be safe. It was for a short time. It was not long until the rats were in the cardboard box. We all had to learn by experience. The bread ration was kept in my mess-tin. It was a relief to get out into the trenches on duty at dawn."

Life in the reserve lines could be tedious during the day. Here a couple of Young Citizens appear very relaxed as they read the papers sent from home. *(George Hackney)*

Hope had a similar experience, but was quicker to source an answer: "We examine the wire beds. They are very comfortable, but there is too much water dripping from the roof. We cover ourselves with the rubber sheet which we should lie on. There is an uncanny feeling, something is jumping over the wet sheet – rats, and they are as big as cats. They are after our haversack where we have our rations. This is something we have discovered and we keep our bread in our mess tins so that these boys won't eat the heart out of the quarter loaf."

The village the trenches ran through was badly beaten about, according to Berry, as it was continually under observation and artillery fire. "Strange sounds emanated from some of the tumbledown buildings on either side of us as we proceeded down the street," recalled Harrison of his journey to the front. "These issued from the throats of British Tommies who were doing a spell 'in reserve'. Barriers were erected at intervals along the village street. Proceeding in silence we marched through, and, passing through the last barrier, found ourselves almost in the 'support trench'. A sentry was posted there, who challenged us as we approached, coming to the 'ready' in a business-like manner." By 10.30 pm everyone was at his post in the trenches for the first time. After a sleepless night in a dugout, Harrison was relieved to turnout at "stand to". "It was an eerie sensation we experienced for the first time, standing in the shelter of the dugout, listening to the angry crackle of machine guns and the 'snap' of the bullets through the frosty air overhead." Connolly had his slumber similarly rudely interrupted just before daybreak, and was taken aback to find himself closer to the enemy than he had realised:

"I was rather surprised to find that we were in the first line fire trench. We looked over the parapet one at a time, and in the dull light could dimly discern the German lines at a short distance. As the light increased so did the firing. It is startling at first, especially the artillery fire, but before long we become so used to it that you don't even notice it."

The CO and adjutant passed along the line, speaking to the men as they went. There must have been an air of the surreal for many, for this was neither the normal training nor could it have felt entirely like the real thing. Instead they were visitors and not unduly welcome ones at that. Fitzsimons recalled: "Wiring parties were conducted by an Irish major who walked about with a blackthorn stick whacking everyone and telling them to 'keep your heads down'. A demonstration by a sergeant on how to fire a rifle grenade (10 inch rod) – stuck it in a rifle without removing the black enamelled tin case in which they were packed or inserting a detonator. We waited expectantly but no bang." The Germans had a few words of "welcome" as well, according to a "young Belfast businessman" who had enlisted in the YCVs. He wrote home at the end of October to report: "One of our officers told us today that the minute the first batch arrived in the trenches the Bosches started to yell – "Get up and show yourselves, you ------- Ulstermen". The boys were determined not to be overawed and, according to an account carried in a newspaper published on 12 July 1919, the YCV's baptism of fire signally failed to impress:

This section of trench system, almost certainly part of a communication line well back from the front, illustrates how difficult it was for stretcher bearers to negotiate with a wounded man. *(Courtesy of the Somme Museum)*

"A sergeant of the Warwicks, our trench instructor, told us that there was going to be a 'big do' at 3.00 am, consequently everyone was on the tip-toe of expectation, and eagerly awaited the coming bombardment. Suddenly, at three, a few 18-pounders opened up somewhere in our rear, a dozen or so shells howled overhead, a red flickering across the sky followed by several dull explosions as the shells burst in Gommecourt Wood. Instantly a German whiz-bang battery retaliated, spitting a few shrieking missiles into our village; then – silence. For a moment we stood waiting. 'When's this strafe coming off?' asked an impatient Ulsterman. 'Strafe, mate,' ejaculated a Warwick, 'didn't you 'ear it? Blimey! It's just finished.'"

On the second night in the trenches the word was passed down the line of the possibility of a gas attack, which soon became distorted into one word: "Gas". Hope recalls the fear that went with the threat of such an attack:

"We pull on the early pattern cloth bag mask and begin to fire. After what seems an age of suffocation we are relieved when someone appears and tells us there is no gas. Only those in such a predicament can realise what a gas attack means. Two kinds of gas are used, Chlorine and Phorfene which turns the lungs into water in a few seconds. The gas is really a liquid which, when it comes into contact with the air, goes off in the form of a vapour. It can't be seen – only detected by smell."

Connolly had spent the day digging trenches, having to duck down on a regular basis as they weren't deep enough yet to offer the men cover and, just to add insult to injury, were filled to a depth of nearly two feet with water. "We were separated some distance from one another, and after toiling for some time an officer came splashing along and asked me if I were enjoying myself, to which I replied, 'I don't think'," he moaned. That evening, however, he thought was "very exciting and well worth experiencing". "We got orders to open fire, and for the first time got our chance of pouring lead at the Huns. However, the Germans were not asleep, and soon the bullets cracked round us in all directions, and we were obliged to keep down. Then our artillery sent over some shells. I looked over to see what was happening and it was a glorious sight to see the blue effect of the star lights which illuminated the whole scene and to witness the shells burst, with deafening reports. So night and day we 'strafed' the Huns." Harrison's platoon was in support and was engaged moving bricks from the ruined village into the lines to floor the communication trench when they came under direct attack for the first time. The men had been watching a couple of British planes flying back and forth across the lines for about 20 minutes, defying German attempts to bring them down, when the shelling began. "Our boys, watching this new sensation, got quite excited, and some of them recklessly sat up on the edge of the trench, cheering our brave airmen. The first intimation that we had been observed came in the shape of a shell that burst in close proximity to our trench. Another and another followed. The boys were undismayed and laughed and joked as they stumbled along the muddy trench."

Connolly's inexperience almost got him killed when out in No-Man's-Land, though his elementary trench training came to his aid. Ordered to provide cover for a wiring party, he told the family in a letter home:

> "We climbed over the parapet about 2 o'clock in the morning, and advanced clear of our wire, where we lay flat on the ground, and then went forward very cautiously. After lying some time in the wet slush I began to get cramped with the cold, and stood up to get relief, when to my horror a star shell from the enemy lit up the country, exposing me in full relief against the skyline. Remembering instructions I stood motionless, praying that the Germans would have sufficient intelligence to take me for a post, which I think they did. We still kept on the look out with eyes and ears, while the party behind seemed to kick up a most horrible row hammering in posts. More than once I imagined someone was coming towards us. On one occasion I felt sure I saw something move, and nudged the fellow next me. We both watched, and surely something was creeping towards us. It hardly seemed large enough for a man, and not till it was quite close on us when we had our rifles levelled, did we recognise that it was only a cat. It was the most horrible cat I have ever seen, and apparently quite wild."

On 29 October the battalion suffered its first casualty in the trenches when splinters from a rifle grenade wounded a sergeant. It was also reported that Private Robert Robertson had suffered a bullet wound to the arm. From a well-to-do family that ran a plumbing business, Robertson & Company in Mill Street, he was well-known back in Belfast as he had played for Cliftonville Football Club while one brother, Jordan, was an Irish international player and two others, John and George, accomplished cyclists. The relief felt as the men came to the end of their first spell in the trenches, however, was not so much at having escaped injury but at having faced the unknown and found it less disagreeable than most had thought. "This was a novelty and we had been looking forward to it with mixed feelings but were glad to find it so much better than we had expected and much more interesting," noted Sheridan. Another unnamed YCV, whose letter home was published in the *Belfast News Letter,* told the family: "We have had our first experience of the trenches. It was safe enough if you kept your head down, except when they took it into their heads to shell us. We have only had one casualty so far. I was out the other night 100 yards in front of the trenches repairing wire entanglement, but the beggars did not annoy us, and we got through ok." At 4.00 am on 2 November, a "wet miserable morning", the first platoon began pulling out of the front line, the battalion not forming up again until well clear of Fonquevillers. Hope was downbeat:

> "We move along the road mechanically, every man is silent. We have had our first shock of trench warfare – shock not of warfare I should say but the shock of having existed for four days and nights without sleep in a filthy, rotten, slimy atmosphere. We go on and on knowing that we are going to our billet. There is not a word. We are probably thinking – thinking that that terrible experience is just the forerunner of what will happen again and that in the end we shall die, die – not from a shell or bullet – but from exposure."

Everyone was covered from head to foot in mud and tired for want of sleep as they stopped at the Couin rest camp for the night. Hot baths awaited them that the *War Diary* notes "were very acceptable, the men not having had their clothes off for eight days". It was badly needed, thought Connolly, "for one would not have recognised the smart men of the crack corps who used to parade Royal Avenue".

Officers were charged with censoring their men's letters home, and probably should have stopped some of the information that made it into the Belfast newspapers from ever leaving France. Certainly, as the war went on, there was a clampdown on the leaking of such material with the papers themselves undertaking not to carry stories that might be of use to the enemy. One officer – who actually complained about the trouble his men gave him when censoring their letters because of the detail contained – was fortunately guilty of the same himself, giving us a very detailed account of the YCV's first stint at the Front. Even though his letter, published in the *Belfast News Letter* on 12 November 1915, revisits much of the above, it is still worth quoting at length:

> "The labyrinth of trenches and dugout is amazing. A prosperous village used to be here, but is mainly a mass of ruins now. We are here for instructional purposes, and are learning trench warfare by easy stages. We had to march in by night in small parties, with considerable intervals, as the road is commanded by German machine-gun fire, but the journey was made without mishap. They say this is a quiet part of the front, but one wouldn't think so at times, with the big guns from both sides playing over and into the trenches. Our artillery preponderates easily. An English territorial regiment occupies this part, and we are provisionally attached to them; very nice chaps they are. The trenches are named after the streets, &c, of a big English town I was once in. The Terriers come from there, but I daresay they notice a difference

This group of YCV officers, evidently enjoying the weather on a fine day, was taken by Captain Val Hyndman. *(Courtesy of the Somme Museum)*

between this place and their own 'leafy' country. The first part of my stay here was in a 'dugout' – the name is very apt. We are reverting to the prehistoric age, and I'm sure the boys are beginning to grow hair on their legs. The 'residents' don't trouble themselves about shell-fire, &c. At first you are inclined to duck, but when you see them going on with their work without lifting their heads you feel it would be intra dig, so you refrain. When one does bust close at hand it only draws forth facetious comments. I have not yet reached the 'facetious' stage! This morning shrapnel burst in my vicinity, and up till now I haven't seen the humorous side. However, I may. The boys are getting on well, and are enjoying themselves. They are getting quite expert at knowing the different guns and what they are doing. In the morning the troops 'stand to' (5.30 am–6.15 am), all under arms. If the Germans are up first they sound 'reveille' with machine guns and rifle-fire, and if the British happen to waken first – they return the compliment. No harm is done by these exchanges of courtesies. We have had one casualty – a sergeant got pelted with bits from a rifle-grenade. One or two minor injuries have also occurred, but nothing serious."

He described how his platoon was working at deepening and draining a trench when the aeroplane mentioned previously appeared over the German lines. He continued:

"It was bombarded by anti-aircraft guns, and I'm sure not less than one hundred shots were fired at it, but without effect. It was a fine night. I counted thirty shrapnel bursts in the air at one time. (The smoke, like a white ball of cotton, lingers a good while before dissipating.) The Germans seemed annoyed at their failure, and when the aeroplane was out of range they treated us to a few rounds. One burst close to us – we came away from there. It has been very wet since we came here, and the back trenches are very muddy and wet – ankle deep in some places. It is very sticky and clayey. The 'dugouts' are comfortable if not roomy, and have stoves in them. Rats abound, and a good revolver shot can have some sport. As I have to buy my own ammunition, I didn't try to bag any. The Germans occupy a wood with a village behind it. The trenches are about 400 yards apart here, but much closer on either side of the wood. Our front is concave, and in front of both sets of trenches are barbed wire entanglements. Every night we go out erecting new wire and repairing old, but haven't been molested so far. A sort of unwritten law prevails; the Germans send out their working parties and so do we, with a tacit understanding to let each other alone – at least that is what it looks like. At present I'm 'billeted' in the village – it isn't a billet, for there are no civilians here at all – but we are in the kitchen of a farmhouse – we three YCVs sleep in the kitchen on the floor, and three Terriers officers occupy the cellar below. One window is boarded up, and the other can boast of, I think, the only whole pane of glass in the village. The Germans have been in the habit of sending over, about once a week, an aerial torpedo. It is a Minenwerfer, which is about 3 ft 6 in long and 9 in in diameter, filled with 280 lbs of high explosive. When 'Minnie' falls she makes quite a depression in the ground – and shakes up everything for about half a mile radius. She should be due one of these evenings – I don't want to meet her. We expect to return to our former billets on Tuesday for a rest – which, I suppose, will mean drill and route marches and attacking imaginary enemies, &c."

The unnamed officer, who clearly finished his letter after returning to billets, said the weather had been "wretched" with heavy and continuous rain that left the men covered head to foot in mud. He concluded:

"We had to leave in half platoons, with 300 yards interval, and find our way in the dark back from the trenches. The move was made without mishap, and we reached the place at which we halted on our way out. We were under canvas amongst the trees near a chateau. The men were paraded in fifties and sent down to baths which had been erected for troops leaving the firing line. The apparatus is crude, but effective. The water is heated, and the men get it in shower baths. They enjoyed it, and it was needed. Officers get plunge baths, and I got my clothes off for the first time in a week. When in the trenches you daren't take off anything, boots or equipment included. Revolvers and pouches are uncomfortable bedfellows. It poured with rain incessantly all day, and the place, which was soaking when we arrived, soon became a swamp. I procured a brazier, and after a good deal of trouble got it going, so we were comfy enough in the tent. We sat round and coughed and shed tears for quite a while, and then when it burned up we burst into song, mainly items from the 'Students' Song Book', with improvisations suitable to the circumstances. We were very happy under what would ordinarily be considered very miserable and adverse conditions. Fortunately, next day was fine, and we arrived here in the afternoon and reoccupied our old billets. Today the men are washing clothes, &c., as we leave again tomorrow for some other village. The men enjoyed their visit to the trenches, and are rapidly becoming old soldiers, not to say veterans. I have since heard that 'Minnie' arrived in the section of trenches which we occupied on Monday night. She landed about 9.00 am, and now the 'dugout' which I had been in is non est. I am glad I was not 'at home' when she called."

It had been shortly after lunch when the men arrived back at their old billets at Beauval, though their stay was to be very brief. The decision had been taken to exchange the 107th Brigade with the 12th Brigade of the 4th Division, allowing the Belfast battalions to experience prolonged spells in the trenches in the company of seasoned troops. Likewise, battalions of the English brigade were now to be temporarily placed within the Ulster Division. As a consequence, the 14th Rifles was ordered to move to Pernois on 5 November along with the 11th Rifles on attachment to the 12th Brigade in which the 1st King's Own Royal Lancashire Regiment and 1/5th South Lancashire Regiment both remained. The 2nd Essex and 2nd Lancashire Fusiliers took their places in the 109th and 108th Brigades respectively. Brigadier General TE Hickman addressed the YCVs before they left, expressing the hope that they would soon be back within the ranks of his 109th Brigade.

The 14th Rifles' new brigadier was a veteran of Mons and the subsequent retreat, and had been on active service ever since. He now "rubbed it into us Ulstermen with a vengeance," according to Harrison, instilling the need for fitness and discipline, and a new regime of long route marches and field exercises were introduced. "Much attention was given to proper alignment and keeping in step," recalled Mullin. "It seems the most comfortable pace is 112 paces to the minute, set from the rear of the column." Rifleman McRoberts didn't mind the field days or company and platoon drill, but was scathing of his officers:

> "Once again we were under the control of our officers who were nearly all ignorant, conservative and bullying, to an intolerable degree. In the trenches we rarely saw even one of them. Not one was ever seen in our dugout, not one was ever observed giving a direction of any kind, their voices were never heard. Captain S- was intoxicated for most of the time we were in the trenches. I believe he once visited our guard at night. He asked the sentry his name and then what were his duties. The sentry replied. 'Is that right?' asked S. of the Sergeant of the guard, who was a Warwick. 'Yes Sir,' replied the Sergeant. 'And what would you do in the case of an alarm?' was the next question of the reeking Captain. The sentry gave an answer. 'Is that correct?' queried the Captain a second time. 'Not exactly Sir' was the answer. 'You are absolutely wrong,' said the Captain turning upon the unfortunate Sergeant, 'you are a sentry and you do not know your duty, you should be court-martialled'. Such arrogance from an ignorant, drunken officer was unbearable to flesh blood. Our Lieutenant was scarcely more visible during our stay in the trenches. He never came round to see how we fared for food, he never visited our dugouts and our rifles weren't even inspected once."

In between the bouts of training the battalion was heavily engaged as working parties, felling trees and preparing billets for the new divisions yet to arrive. There were lighter moments as well, such as when a rumour circulated that a German spy was in the area and, according to Sheridan, "half the battalion" went in search of him. A staff officer was detained for questioning in error, sparking the wrath of Lieutenant TH Mayes but providing the boys with something to joke about for months to come. There was also tragedy, with the battalion suffering its first fatality in France on 13 November when Private William Lorimer, a member of the original YCV, died of pneumonia at No 4 Casualty Clearing Station. A member of C Company, he had lived with his wife Mary in Mountcollyer Avenue, Belfast, before the war and had worked as a motor trimmer for W Denby and Sons on the Antrim Road.[3]

It turned very wintry as November moved on, with John Reid Moore, writing home on the 22nd of the month that they were "having very cold weather just now with any amount of snow and it looks as if we are in for a serious winter". He added: "It's very hard and cold getting up at 6 o'clock these mornings and I often think of the old song I used to sing 'It's nice to get up in the morning but it's nicer to lie in bed'. However, I suppose I will just have to put up with it." The village of Pernois, he complained, had little to offer the boys in terms of shops with even acquiring a couple of eggs a major coup. He evidently had not enjoyed his spell at the front line as he went on: "There is no word of us going back to the trenches again and as far as I can hear we won't be back again until after Christmas and I don't care as it's not much of a picnic."

On 27 November, the battalion moved from Pernois to Franqueville, where the men spent the night before travelling on to Ailly-le-Haut-Clocher the next day. The division was now concentrated in the Abbeville area, with its headquarters at Pont-Remy on the banks of the Somme, well away from the front. The YCVs found the billets were filthy and much time was spent cleaning them up and building incinerators to burn the rubbish. Despite the weather having turned cold and wet, Mullin was happy in his new surroundings: "We are now as far back as we can go, and are engaged on the same type of work. When we are free, some of the boys explore and have the personality to persuade Madame to frire pommes de terre for three paying guests. When the good lady had the chips ready, we sat round the table and had an enjoyable supper."

Late November and early December were largely spent on fatigues and training – two companies at a time involved in digging trenches near Bussus while the machine-gun

Digging trenches during the winter months, even for training purposes, was extremely hard work on frozen ground. *(George Hackney)*

teams constructed new emplacements in the support line, and wood cutting parties were sent to Pont-Remy. Mullin found such activities congenial: "Another big job is repairing holes in the lath and mud walls of barns, which will be fitted up with bunks, to provide billets for the fresh divisions arriving to help us to win the war. Just now we have some RE to take charge of our party. They supervise and show the amateur infantry the proper way to do the job. I like working with the RE, because any job is easy when you know how to do it." The signallers, meanwhile, managed to annoy the local priest by running a telephone line through the village cemetery, wrapping the wire round some of the headstones and memorials to keep it taut. "When the priest saw this I am afraid the words he used are not often heard from the pulpit," remembered Sheridan.

A few familiar faces disappeared at around this time while others arrived: Major Gunning[4] had to be carted off to hospital after he broke an ankle falling from his horse on 1 December, while a few days later Lieutenant Colonel Bliss[5] relinquished command of the battalion to return to the 2nd RIR; the following day, 7 December, his replacement, Lieutenant Colonel CCG Ashton took over command. Among the new officers to arrive were Lieutenant VH Robb from the reserve battalion, and Second Lieutenant H Cansdale from the 4th Rifles.

A 14th Rifles Lewis gun section in the trenches. Machine guns and artillery were responsible for most deaths on the Western Front. (George Hackney)

After a month with the 12th Brigade, the order returning them to the 109th came through on 9 December, with the men moving off the next day. A Company were put up at Gorenflos and the remainder of the battalion took over the billets at Ergnies – where they were to remain for the next three weeks – vacated by the 2nd Essex Regiment who were heading the opposite way. Harrison's platoon was delighted to find its billets were practically new and well finished – until the following day when it was discovered the straw on the floor was alive with vermin. "Many a warm comfortable shirt had to be consigned to the incinerator, with many regrets," he notes. "It was no uncommon sight there to see the boys, stripped to the waist, busy 'chat' hunting. All hands had to 'stand to', everyone doing their bit to get the place thoroughly cleaned out and disinfected. The straw was carted away, and after a couple of braziers had burned for an hour or two on the earthen floor, it was really a pleasant place to spend the night." He goes on to paint a picture of young men who, as yet, still had not truly faced the horrors of war:

"Many a singsong we had, sitting with our backs to the walls as willing hands piled on the fuel. I can see the ruddy faces of our Irish boys yet, beaming with health and good nature, as the firelight danced, the sparks flew, and eddies of smoke rose to the rafters. 'Part singing' was popular, and songs lending themselves to the blending of three or four voices were never tired of through repetition."

The manual work continued and though there was more hard labour, including trench digging north-west of Ergnies, there was more variety in the tasks undertaken. Lieutenant Renwick,[6] for instance, supervised the erection of a building to accommodate 500 men and later cleared out a barn and converted it for use as a temporary cinema.

An old barn accommodated 10 wooden tubs, each capable of allowing half-a-dozen men to bath at a time. The warm water was "turned white by cresol, a strong disinfectant," remembered Mullin.

Back in Belfast, efforts were being made to provide a few home comforts for the YCVs as temperatures plunged. Dehra Chichester, wife of the battalion colonel, along with the partners and relatives of other officers, formed a committee headed by the Lady Mayoress to arrange to have woollen items knitted and sent to the men. Working under the auspices of the Ulsterwomen's Gift Fund, they appealed to the public to send in such comforts, along with cigarettes and cash donations, specifically marked for the benefit of the 14th Rifles. Writing to the newspapers in December 1915, she felt the need to point out that the YCVs were not privileged but needed support as much as any other unit:

"An entirely mistaken idea has gained ground in Belfast – vis, that all the men of this battalion are so well-to-do that they require no help. This impression is certainly incorrect. Many of the men, certainly, do not require any assistance in the way of comforts, and are amply supplied from their own homes, but this by no means applied to the whole battalion. I am kept regularly informed as to the requirements of the battalion by the adjutant (in the temporary absence of Colonel Chichester on sick leave). My committee and I, with the help of the Ulsterwomen's Gift Fund, endeavour to send out all that is asked for. Some time ago the adjutant wrote that many of the men had no mufflers and no covering on their hands. This want has, at any rate for the present, been remedied. I hope that the citizens of Belfast, in their desire to keep their four divisional battalions (North, South, East and West) well supplied, will not forget the battalion which is recruited from all four divisions."

The origins of *The Incinerator*'s title lay in the constant need to build furnaces to dispose of the waste an army on the move naturally created, hence the 'siting' of the Editor's chair. *(Courtesy of the Somme Museum)*

THE EDITOR'S CHAIR.

Around the same time the men started an Orange Lodge within the battalion – one of six established within the Ulster Division and the first since 1815 when warrants had been granted to the 6th Inniskilling Dragoons and 7th Inniskilling Fusiliers after Waterloo. The first meeting of YCV LOL 871 was held in a barn. The majority of its members were Orangemen belonging to lodges back home but others joined out in France for the first time. Private William A Greer, a member of Donegall Road Total Abstinence LOL 883 in Belfast, was present and recalled: "We carry out everything as far as we can in orthodox fashion. The meeting was quite enjoyable and the circumstances under which it was held reminded one of the old style meetings at home…" Even Harrison, who normally took no interest in such matters, allowed friends to "persuade" him to become an Orangeman.

As Christmas approached the work schedule was pegged back, with the afternoon parades cancelled entirely on 20 December and the men encouraged to take part in a range of sporting activities. The Christmas dinner included turkey, goose and chicken followed with plum puddings. Judges were appointed to select the best-decorated billets, with A Company walking away with the £2 prize. There is no record of how they divided it among the men! Reports of B and C companies' Christmas festivities later appeared in the battalion magazine, *The Incinerator*. The former set up a committee to oversee the preparations and ensure that all the necessary ingredients were provided. Their methods, it was suggested, might have been less than totally ethical as "so busy were they that, even yet, when one of them passes a farmyard the ducks, instead of quacking, fall to quaking, and as for geese and hens, well any intelligent person can easily read signs of alarm in their eyes". The day began with carol singing which, apparently, sparked much mickey-taking and banter. Number six platoon excelled itself with a Christmas tree on which empty bully-beef tins, lumps of cheese and Army biscuits served as decorations. The long-anticipated dinner did not disappoint and was accompanied by a visit from the officers to the platoon billets:

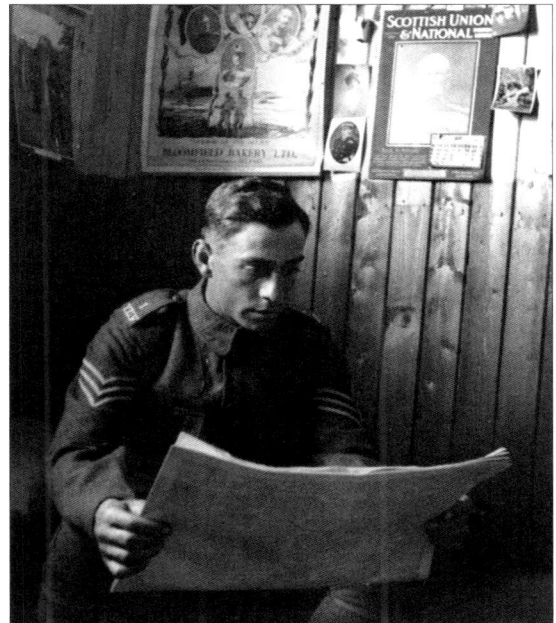

Company Sergeant Major R Mortimer, seen here relaxing at Seaford camp, proved himself an able soldier in France. *(George Hackney)*

"After dinners had been drawn for the various sections, came a pilgrimage round the billets to receive comments and see how the men were enjoying the geese, ducks, fowl, and last, but not least, the Christmas plum pudding. The Pilgrims consisted of Captain Harper and Captain McKee, Lieutenants Hooton, Lack and O'Neill, who need not fear to receive 'characters' at the hands of their respective platoons, Company Sergt Major Mortimer, a first-rate successor to the 'crown' of that fine soldier whom everyone misses, Sergeant Major Griffiths; and Sergeant Kenning, Acting Quartermaster-Sergt., whose capacious smile and jovial jests were worth at least a couple of extra courses to each billet."

The C Company festive report was written even more tongue-in-cheek by "A. D." with so many digs at the officers and senior NCOs who served up the meal and delivered speeches to a less than receptive audience that Lieutenant Stanley Hopkirk Monard, as *The Incinerator* editor, felt the need to add a disclaimer. It describes how a series of ad hoc tables were constructed from doors balanced across tree branches and stepladders. These were then draped with Army blankets and lighted candles in empty jam tins were placed at intervals, despite the meal being served at 2.00 pm. "Perspiring sergeants came trotting in with huge steaming turkeys, corporals followed with geese, and the lance-corporals made up the rear with the less conspicuous, but nevertheless necessary, cabbage and potatoes. Due order of seniority was strictly observed!" Roast beef and plum pudding was also on the menu, washed down with two barrels of "commandeered" Bass thanks to the company scavenger Private H Moore. The mood was obviously boisterous, as it took two attempts to have "three cheers" for the Commanding Officer and, once the officers had retired, "everybody now proposes three cheers for everybody else, and the proposals are duly carried out". The NCOs had their dinner at a second sitting at the same tables, in what is described as a "very formal affair" during which the officers again visit and deliver speeches, the captain staying for a "Black and White" whiskey, and the quartermaster-sergeant and sergeant major both speaking, at which point a ladder "which has been serving as a temporary form, collapses, depositing a number of sergeants on the floor". Hope and his companions, true to character, managed to find trouble even at Christmas. Feeling the cold, and with no fuel of their own to burn, they sent out scouts with one discovering that a barn just across the road held "black peat". He goes on:

> "A raiding party goes out at night and knocks a hole in the wall and the peat begins to trickle into our billet. We have a great fire in a brazier which threatens to reach the roof. Madame of the house is in a state of nerves and is giving off at a great rate. Her head, arms and stomach are all keeping time. We must shut her mouth some way. McKeown gathers all the surplus tins of jam and tobacco lying round the billet and pushes the whole lot into her lap. She is quite subdued and apparently doesn't now care whether the barn goes on fire or not."

The Young Citizen Volunteers spent what, for most, was their first Christmas away from home in France 1915. This postcard greeting was sent by Company Sergeant Major William Moore to his family back in Belfast. *(Author)*

Boxing Day, apart from the church parade, was a holiday, while the highlight of 27 December was two football games. In the first, played in the morning, the sergeants took on the officers, the latter emerging 1-0 victors after what the *War Diary* described as a "close and strenuous game". Lieutenant Monard sent off a report of the games to the *Ireland's Saturday Night* newspaper in Belfast and included it in the battalion magazine. Previous clashes between the rugby-loving officers and 'footballing' sergeants had been a walkover for the NCOs but, much to the disdain of the men standing on the touchlines, there was now a reversal of fortunes: "Nobody can explain it. The officers (at one part of the game three of them were off the field quarrelling with intractable stomachs – Christmas feeding!) were complacent, chiefly, but much amused. The sergeants were dumb-founded, and have issued another challenge. The men are uncommunicative on the subject, but dark hints seem to suggest that they resent being deprived of what was to have been their best alternative to a visit to the Belfast pantomime." During the afternoon the battalion team was 'away' to the 11th Royal Inniskilling Fusiliers, the match ending in a 1-1 draw before a crowd of 1,500 men. Both goals were scored from penalties with only the "tenacity of the Rifles" thwarting the Skins, who had an Irish League player, Bingham, playing at centre forward.

The last day of the year marked a return to the business in hand, with companies sent to the trenches for training and instruction on how to mount an attack. On their return they found that Colonel Chichester had resumed command of the battalion, receiving, according to the *War Diary*, "a very warm welcome from both officers and men".

Chapter 10

SWEEPING THEIR WAY ACROSS FRANCE

We've got a sergeant-major,
Who's never seen a gun;
He's mentioned in despatches
For drinking privates' rum,
And when he sees old Jerry
You should see the bugger run
Miles and miles and miles behind the lines!

From the First World War song 'Behind The Lines'

THE STANDING JOKE AMONG the Young Citizens was that they were "sweeping their way across France" – with the brush that is, not the bayonet. In their first few months of overseas service they were more likely to have a trowel, hammer or saw in their hands than a rifle. As they were out of the line much of this time, a seemingly endless list of manual tasks was found to keep the men busy and improve the infrastructure of the rear area. In fairness, the 14th Rifles' obsession with cleanliness and tidiness didn't help dispel the impression that soldiering was secondary, with the battalion priding itself on leaving every billet in better condition than it was found. The *War Diary* is full of comments about the poor state of the accommodation the YCVs inherited, with the men sent out to repair and clean up, often with the task barely completed when orders came through to move again.

The battalion was again under the guiding hand of Colonel Chichester, who had returned from his spell of illness. "YCVs delighted to see Colonel Spencer Chichester on parade this morning for the first time in France," noted Mullin on 1 January 1916. "He brought a message from Sir Crawford McCullagh, the Lord Mayor, Aldermen and citizens of Belfast, wishing the battalion a Happy New Year." The Colonel went on an inspection of the billets to see how the men were living and to renew acquaintances.

On 3 January the 14th Rifles, minus A Company, practiced trench attacks as part of a brigade exercise, earning the praise of the brigadier general for the "satisfactory way in which the attack on the trenches was carried out by all ranks yesterday. He considers that this performance reflects great credit on the way in which company and platoon commanders have instructed their NCOs and men, and on the way in which the NCOs and men have paid attention to and benefited by such instructions". A Company, meanwhile, was at Beauval working under the direction of the 122nd Field Company of the Royal Engineers and a similar task now awaited the remainder of the battalion. It moved from Ergnies to Berneuil – "the muddiest village we had struck so far" according to Harrison – on 6 January, spending the first few days improving and cleaning the billets and village beyond while a rear party under Second Lieutenant H Cansdale did the same at the vacated barracks. "Repairs of all sorts were undertaken, and we became jacks-of-all-trades, carpentry, bricklaying, plastering, etc, being the order of the day until the village became really habitable," recalled Harrison. On 10 January, Captains James McKee and Val Hyndman were detailed as works officers on the hutment scheme at Berneuil, Berteaucourt and St Leger, with all available men formed into working parties shortly afterwards to make and fit bunks in the new billets, work that was to continue throughout the remainder of the month. Colonel Chichester made his presence felt on 16 January when, shortly before 6.00 pm on that Sunday evening, he had all officers summoned to him, who in turn called out the orderly sergeants at the double and told them to turn out the battalion. The CO delivered a "stinging lecture reprimanding certain members of the battalion for misconduct," according to Mullin, though he leaves us in the dark as to the cause of the rumpus by simply adding "as the charge did not apply to me, I was ignorant about the matter". He gives the colonel the credit for burying charges laid against 40 members

With the knowledge of the looming 'Big Push' that everyone knew was coming that summer, *The Incinerator* decided that 1916 was the year of reckoning for the Kaiser and Germany. *(Courtesy of the Somme Museum)*

of C Company who around the same time were accused, following a kit inspection, of losing their emergency rations which, along with other items of equipment, had been swallowed up in the mud of the trenches at Fonquevillers. Shortly afterwards the same company was marched to nearby Berteaucourt, where it was to stay for the next few days while repairing billets. It was not all labouring, of course, and on Monday 24 January a divisional exercise was held in which Mullin, to his delight, found himself acting as battalion scout. "I have an exciting day. My job is to find out where the enemy are. I am alone and I run into enemy's concealed car patrol," he noted.

January was also a month of visits and reorganisation, with more than the usual to-ing and fro-ing. The Archbishop of Armagh, the Most Rev Dr John Baptist Crozier, paid the 36th (Ulster) Division a visit, conducting a battalion church parade on 23 January, and later addressing the men. Lieutenant Colonel CCG Ashton, relieved of his command by the returning Colonel Chichester, left for Vaux-en-Amienois to take over at the helm of 1/7th Gordon Highlanders. Second Lieutenant Gilbert Colclough Wedgwood joined the battalion briefly before his transfer, along with Lieutenant Clokey, two sergeants – one John Reid Moore – a corporal, two lance corporals and 26 men to the 109th Brigade Machine Gun Company. The four Vickers guns they took with them were replaced with Lewis guns. Lieutenant Hanna was sent to Le Meillard as an assistant at the School of Instruction. Second Lieutenant WAP Willson[1] reported for duty on 10 January, being sent back to base for three weeks to help in the training of reinforcements.

Sergeant William Henry Calvert[2] accompanied him but was to meet an unfortunate end a week later. The 24-year-old from Knuteford Drive in north Belfast, an original member of the pre-war YCVs, was instructing a group of soldiers on how not to throw a 'bomb' when he apparently lifted a live grenade in error. He was killed in the subsequent explosion, with a number of the training group injured.

The soldiers of the 14th Rifles had spent the winter by no means disagreeably, and the break had allowed them to continue to have a social life alongside the demands of training and working. Harrison recorded in January 1916:

> "We have held two or three concerts here lately, the programme being strengthened by a gramophone. This made things quite home-like. There is plenty of talent in the battalion, singers both grave and gay, a mandolin player, reciters, both comic and otherwise, and, of course, the band. Last night there wasn't standing room even. We have football matches every Saturday, and there is keen competition between the companies as to which have the best team. A concert party, known as 'The Follies' has been formed in our Division, and three of the 'Citizens' have gone to make up the number. These chaps have a jolly fine time of it I hear, having practically nothing to do but practice pieces. They haven't toured the Division yet, being still in the chrysalis stage, but we hope to hear them when they emerge from their retirement. They have no military duties of any kind to perform."

The first men to be granted leave left for home on 28 January. Only eight places were available, though this was to be increased to 12 in April, with married men given priority. A different destination was planned for the rest of the battalion with orders to move to the trenches arriving at battalion headquarters on 1 February. The working parties were recalled and the next day was spent getting men and their equipment clean and ready. "Rifle inspection by Armourer Sergeant RAOC," recorded Mullin in his diary. "We took the bolts out of the rifles and the AS looked down each barrel as he moved along." The 3 and 4 February were devoted to range training, with the officers given a special course in the use of grenades, while all ranks took part in a route march, taking in Bernaville and Fienvillers before returning to Berneuil. Final preparations for the move were undertaken the next day, a Sunday, after the church parade.

Monday morning, at 7.00 am, the battalion moved off, halting for the evening at Puchevillers. Rain had fallen overnight and it had snowed in the afternoon, leaving the roads in a poor state: "Bitterly cold, snow falling and no blankets," griped Berry. "However, being dog tired, I got to sleep and was pretty well frozen when I awoke the following morning." The troops in Bernuil left on the Tuesday to make the journey to Puchevillers, struggling to cover three miles an hour according to Mullin and taking seven hours in total to cover the 13 miles because of the need for regular stops. On 9 February the battalion moved on to Varennes along a "very muddy road all the way". They were observed, at one point, by a German plane, possibly the one referred to by Harrison: "A German aircraft passed overhead, being identified by one of our fellows as a Taube, and our anti-aircraft guns opened a furious bombardment. This was the first enemy aircraft we had seen, and naturally created a good deal of excitement, the boys crowding into the village street to watch the shells bursting all around the machine, but without the satisfaction of seeing it brought down." Berry was billeted with a French woman: "She wouldn't give us water, so we took it ourselves and were blessed with her curses. I'm sure she was pleased to see us leaving, as we were."

The next day some 600 men were paraded at 8.00 am and marched to Acheux to help the Royal Engineers construct a railway line between Candas and Acheux. The divisional pioneers, the 16th Royal Irish Rifles, had already been engaged on the project for weeks past. "Thank goodness there is an Expeditionary Force canteen within easy reach," confessed Mullin. "I repair here as often as I dare. The ground has to be levelled, the sleepers laid and the rails fastened to the chairs. I become an expert navvy." Each day for the next week they returned to the task, often in very poor weather that on occasion caused the working days to be cut short.

Around the same time the 10th Rifles and Young Citizens exchanged two platoons for four days to allow the 14th detachment, under Captain Samuel Willis, instruction in the front line. Although the remainder of the battalion was left in reserve, it did not mean the men were excused from going up to the front. On 20 February, a Sunday, Samuel Harrison was among those selected to visit the front lines. They entered the communication trench via a ruined house on the edge of Auchonvillers where each man was handed a pair of 'gumboots': "They proved to be very awkward for walking the greasy roads and trenches, and the journey up the 'communications trench' was attended by many falls. The mud was knee-deep in places, but this did not dampen our spirits by any means. The darkness, added to the rifle, equipment, boots, shrapnel helmet, and the new footwear, impeded our progress, but we eventually struck the first line." Harrison was given sentry duty, the man he was relieving warning him to "keep a sharp lookout, as a German patrol is reported out" but he could see nothing in front of him but the mass of wire and iron stanchions. He was later sent out to a sap in the company of two "seasoned campaigners" who did their best to make him feel at ease. The following night he was again posted to a sap head with a number of others, spending 12 hours – he later realised that two hours was the normal – gazing into the darkness:

> "Several times a flare went up from the German trenches and I fancied I saw a skulking figure or two beyond our wire. It was hard to concentrate one's gaze on a certain point, as the strained eyesight seemed to see an enemy, or anything that could be construed into the bulk of a man's body, where the wire supports were thickest. Then again they seemed to dance about, and do all sorts of contortions, until one has to pass a hand across one's eyes, or fix them on a certain nearby object, to make sure one saw alright."

Mullin was also in and out of the trenches and gives a matter-of-fact account of his time leading up to the YCVs entering the front line in their own right. After having lunch at Varennes, he set out for the trenches, arriving at Mailly-Mailet around 6.00 pm where he had tea, then on to Auchonvillers where he was billeted. His task was to supply the lines with rations and that evening at around 11.00 pm he set out with tea for the front line, returning at 2.00 am. "Owing to a stupid guide going up the wrong avenue, the wrong platoon got the tea," he moaned. At 7.00 am he was back on the road, carrying bacon dip to the lines for breakfast, returning at 9.30 am. From 1.00–5.00 pm he was on a working party attached to the 10th Rifles, attempting to improve a trench in which lay mud "like thick glue" that rose to the knees. On the Tuesday he was part of a working party in the front line from 1.00–5.00 am:

> "This trench was dug by the 8th Rifles (East Belfast Volunteers) but was never revetted. A hard frost was followed by a thaw, the parapet and parados both gave

way and fell into the trench. Progress along the trench was exceedingly slow. Had to clean rifle, etc. After breakfast we received order to pack up ready to leave. Fell in at 6.30 pm. We were kept waiting on B Company and we did not march away until 8.10 pm. We arrived back at Varennes at midnight. We had tea before going to bed to enjoy a much needed sleep."

The following morning he was back working on the railway at Acheux, finishing at noon, then in the afternoon marched from Varennes to Beaussart, passing through Forceville on the way, in thick snow. After spending the night in a "rotten billet," new accommodation was found for his section, which had been granted the day off. "We are as free as the birds all day. I spent a good part of the day in a cafe close to the stove, drinking citron and grenadine," he recorded with obvious glee. The next day he was back in the trenches at Auchonvillers working in the front line under the supervision of the Royal Engineers making a fire step, returning to Beaussart by 4.30 pm.

On the Monday morning there was an hour-long route march, followed by a pay parade, after which blankets and kit had to be left in the store as A, C and D companies prepared to enter the front line for their own stints, with B Company in reserve. The 14th was in the centre of the divisional line, at Auchonvillers, and was to enjoy a fairly quiet spell of duty. A

The Germans had ensured that they held the high ground on the Western Front, with the result that the British trenches were generally further down the slope and inclined to flood, making life difficult and unpleasant for the men. *(George Hackney)*

German counter-mine exploded close to the Redan but caused little damage, though some of the sappers had to be rescued. The British artillery, alerted by battalion observers, shelled an enemy wagon train, with frightened horses heard galloping away from the scene. YCV patrols were sent out into No-Man's-Land but did not encounter any Germans. The Young Citizens, however, had another enemy to deal with and were coming off second best.

The *War Diary* records: "Found trenches in exceedingly muddy and wet condition due to thaw after severe frost and snow. Owing to bad arrangements for changing gum-boots most of the men in front line trenches had to stay in with their feet and legs wet." The diaries of the rank-and-file are more scathing. "I am placed on sentry, No 3 Post. Mud everywhere," complained Mullin, who wasn't relieved of this duty until 10.30 am the next day.

> "Trenches in shocking condition. One hole called a dugout for all 12 platoon. Mud everywhere, and everything covered with it. It is really a feat of strength and courage progressing along the new trench. It takes hours. The trench has not been revetted, consequently the mud is three feet deep."

The following evening he did sentry duty at No 9 post, closer to his dugout, from stand to: "It is better than where I was last night. Only once per night I see an officer or sergeant. The mud is responsible for no visitors."

A German shell found the store where the gumboots had been kept, destroying the majority of them. Although more were later brought up from another depot, it came too late for the likes of Berry who, despite being issued with a pair of boots, still ended up in a casualty clearing station for a week with trench foot. "We have been issued out with trench waders, but the mud and water seems to get in somehow," he said, adding: "We have to do duty in awful discomfort, wet through and through – no chance of drying anything. However we got a few pumps going which dried up the trenches a bit." Harrison, who had to carry up rations with comrades from B Company, found the communication trench "thigh deep in icy-cold water, chunks of ice floating on top, and a miniature landslide had taken place here and there." He added:

> "…the boys in the front line were in a bad light during our spell, they having to stick it without any means of getting their socks, puttees and wet trousers dried. One company was in an exceptionally bad place, our progress carrying hot tea in large flasks, and 'dixies' containing soup, etc, to them, having to be made through a mill-stream of swirling water, this finding its way into their dugouts and down the communication trenches."

The men in this part of the front line, he discovered, had no gumboots and were standing waist deep in mud and water in places. Mullin was feeling the strain: "I am sleepy but I have nowhere to sleep. I cannot find any place to sit. Nothing but mud." The food, when it arrived, was cold though that was the least of his problems as breakfast the next morning "had been dropped in the mud and picked up again. That accident made no difference, we ate it just the same and were glad to get it. Hunger is a good sauce." Hope was similarly disgruntled by the state of the front line as he attempted to settle down to trench routine. "The duty is two hours on the step, two hours beside the step and two hours in a dugout for sleep. The dugout is twenty or thirty yards away from the post and is approached through a trench full of slush and slime over the knees. It is a case of find this hole in the dark – throw oneself into it wet, cold and slimy, and try to rest. It's the fourth day in and we are more dead than alive."

The fellow Belfast men of the 10th Rifles relieved the YCVs after nightfall, though there appeared little kinship with relations as frosty as the weather. "They are old soldiers now, having been in the trenches for months with the regular army brigade," conceded Mullin, adding: "It is very dark wet miserable night. We were leaving the trenches after only four nights. I was pleased and happy with thoughts of sleep and dry billets. As the boys of the 10th Battalion passed me in the trench they made it clear they were very much annoyed at having to return to the line so soon. We had no sympathy for the 107th Brigade. We did not understand."[3]

Another member of the YCV, in a letter published in the local press in February 1916, hints at similar rumours doing the rounds at home:

The 14th Rifles, by virtue of the fact its origins lay with the YCV rather than the UVF, was often singled out for both praise and criticism in equal measure. The latter was not kindly received and particularly so when it was perceived to come from the comfort of the gentlemen's clubs. "Such delusions are easy for some people, especially when they happen to be a few hundred miles from the firing line," concluded the June 1916 edition of *The Incinerator. (Courtesy of the Somme Museum)*

"I wish through your columns to relieve the minds of the friends and relatives of the men of the 14th Battalion Royal Irish Rifles (Young Citizens) of the unfair and unsporting rumours that have been circulated by certain people in Belfast. Where these rumours have arisen from, and by whom circulated, we know very well, and can only emphasise the well-known fact that where the green-eyed monster creeps in, a certain class of people are not responsible for their actions. This battalion, in company with the other battalions in their brigade, have won nothing but praise from the Army Corps to which they have been attached since coming to France. The good reputation they have in every village speaks for the general conduct of the regiment. The many friends of the regiment may rest assured there is no disgrace attached to our name, which is the oldest in the Ulster Division, and only a few days ago the corps commander paid us one of the greatest compliments a regiment could wish for, and coming from such a soldier, and an Irishman, meant a great deal. One thing I am assured of is they have proved themselves men under many trying circumstances, and have taken their baptism of fire as a matter of course, and now their turn has come again, I, for one, do not wish to fight beside better men. The men of the battalion know what consideration to give these rumours and where they arise from, but, as they have done in the past, they will continue to play the game."

Hope, who considered the Belfast brigade to be the 'arch-enemy', was, like the rest of the YCVs, just glad to be relieved. He wearily moved out, the few 'whizzbangs' that fell nearby helping him quicken his pace and adding to his downbeat mood. Back in Forceville the next day, the men began cleaning up themselves and their equipment. "Rifle, uniform, in particular my overcoat, and equipment, all covered with mud. I keep at it, until the job is done," records Mullin, who had the good sense to pin up his great coat to save it trailing in the mud. Others cut their overcoats off just below the waist, infuriating Major Bowen,[4] a Royal Artillery officer and the newly-arrived second-in-command.

He was also annoyed that some 30 men had to be taken to hospital for treatment for trench foot after coming out of the lines. "I would have had 'trench feet' too, only I took the precaution of moving my toes and feet during my spell of sentry duty," mused Mullin. "My own gumption told me to do this. The trouble was worthwhile."

During the first week in March, the 36th Division extended its front, with the 109th Brigade taking over a sector south of the Ancre and moving into Thiepval Wood for the first time. By the end of the month, however, they were reduced to effectively their positions on 1 July, with the 31st Division coming in on their left, and the 36th straddling the River Ancre, the two sub-sectors being known as Thiepval Wood and Hamel. The 14th Rifles spent four days at Forceville during which B and D companies rejoined from Varennes and an enemy Taube aeroplane dropped three small bombs close to the Headquarters Mess without doing any damage, though did spark a scramble for souvenirs. Marching to Mesnil via Englebelmer and Martinsart on 7 March, it took over billets vacated by the 11th Royal Inniskilling Fusiliers. Hope felt comparatively safe, as they were "not troubled much by the Hun" in the village: "In fact we sleep in comparative safety in the kitchens of the houses in the main street." Harrison, whose platoon was billeted in a cellar beside the church, didn't share his view: "It is positively heart breaking to see the way it has been smashed by the German artillery. Stained-glass windows have been stove in, the walls and roof are gaping in places, and the interior is a perfect wreck. There must surely come a day of reckoning for all

Left: A note sent to the brigade headquarters on 4 March 1916, and signed by the commanding officer, seeking an assortment of materials for trench life. Judging by the ticks and crosses, not everything was forthcoming. (Courtesy of the Somme Museum)

Right: A further request, on 25 March 1916, lists a number of the same Items previously asked for by the CO. Signed by Adjutant Alan Mulholland, it includes 18 latrine buckets! (Courtesy of the Somme Museum)

this!" A series of wire netting and cloth camouflage was placed about the village to obscure it from German view, with the road leading out of the village towards the line closed to traffic during daylight, obviously with good reason. Berry, who was on a working party repairing the nearby Jacob's Ladder communication trenches, recalled seeing an artillery transport wagon that tried to pass along the road during the day shelled. Another of their duties was to guard the dump at Mount Keep, within a wooded area, and to man the reserve trenches if it was thought necessary, such as on 10 March when the enemy heavily bombarded the front line trenches held by the 10th Inniskillings. A private, whose account of military life in a letter home was reproduced in the newspapers, wrote:

"About 10.30, when all had retired to bed except the sentries, and were enjoying that rarest and most precious of army privileges, a good night's sleep, the sound of whistles was heard. Immediately the troops were aroused, and those who did not sleep in cellars had to quickly don a few clothes and seek their respective holes. I was awakened by the sergeant, and in a couple of minutes found myself in a fairly large cellar occupied by some signallers. The sky all round was lighted up with vivid flashes, and the air was rent with the deep booming of the guns, the loud crashes of the shells, and the sharp rattle of the machine guns. At frequent intervals one could hear a boom, followed by a whirring through the air, followed by a loud crash, betokening that a shell had landed quite close. Down in our cellar, with this storm of death raging over head, we listened to the various messages received from all quarters by the signallers operating at the telephone. It was a wonderful illustration of the power and ingenuity of modern invention, as we heard how troops in the firing line were faring though hundreds of yards away. Excitement reached its height when a message from Brigade Headquarters was received and interpreted. 'Hun prepare.' There were several minutes of breathless silence while this message was despatched to the headquarters of the companies and to the commanding officer, who immediately gave orders for a general stand to arms. By this time the firing had decreased considerably, and at about 12.30 am a message from headquarters informed us that the bombardment was over, and that we could return to our slumbers, from which we had been so rudely awakened. It was our first experience of this kind, and the excitement and the novelty of the thing completely did away with any thoughts of the danger."

The following day, the 14th relieved the 11th Skins in the trenches at Hamel, the march, according to the same accidental newspaper columnist above, only taking half-an-hour to reach "a village which showed considerable signs of wear and tear":

"Indeed, not a single house was standing intact, and in the gloom the ruins had quite an awesome effect. Here we proceeded to a communication trench, which we followed for several hundred yards, till we arrived at the front line trench. We remained in the trench till the platoon we were relieving had gone, and then sought the 'dugout'. And it was 'some' dugout. We had to adopt the 'every picture tells a story' position, and then gradually descended about ten feet into the earth. It was pitch dark, and our progress was rather slow owing to the frequent collisions between our heads and the roof. When we succeeded in reaching the bottom we found ourselves in the dugout. Picture to yourself a passage about 80 ft long by 8 ft broad, and you have the refuge of forty-four men for some days. Here we had to sleep, eat, drink, and be merry; and how it was possible to do it was an army secret. Our attitudes in sleeping would have been the delight of a teetotal crank, who would have labelled the dugout 'A Drink Den at Night.' Stretching oneself was, of course, absolutely out of the question, but really the flexibility of the human body is wonderful. I will never again see anything extraordinary in the antics of a contortionist or of a boneless wonder."

The weather had picked up considerably and working parties toiled long hours repairing the trench system. When darkness fell it become more exciting, as our correspondent found out on sentry duty:

"One night I was standing looking out into the darkness when suddenly I saw a great flash. Something whizzed over my head, and then bang, and the ground shook with the shock. About four more followed in quick succession, and I flattened myself against the parapet and watched them burst some yards in the rear. Then silence again till my time was up. Another night I heard distinctly the German transports as they drove along the road to the rear of the German line, and even the shouts of the drivers urging on the horses could be distinguished."

Both Allied and enemy aircraft regularly flew over this sector, often duelling for dominance. For Jim Maultsaid this passed as entertainment on a fine day: "In the blue sky thousands of feet above a battle is in progress. We gaze up and take a deep interest in the war of the clouds. Friend and foe are all one to us but the antics of these small dots give us something to look at!"

On the afternoon of 15 March, a trench mortar shell fired from a German forward sap killed Lance Sergeant Charles Penman, in some accounts referred to as Carl, who had the dubious distinction of becoming the battalion's first trench war casualty. The 19-year-old, a former member of 36th Company of the BB, was from Lyle Street in Belfast and had been a popular figure, with his death felt across the YCVs. "I feel sorry for his mother, as she is a widow," wrote Mullin. The news of his death was broken to her by the family clergyman, the Rev Dr Henry Montgomery, of the Shankill Road Mission, who organised a memorial service at the Albert Hall for Sunday 26 March.[5]

An attempt had been made to remove Sergeant Penman's body immediately after his death but the carrying party had been forced to drop him and dive for cover after just 15 yards as another shell dropped from the skies. A graphic description comes from Harrison:

"One of the German weapons was their deadly 'minewerfer,' a sort of aerial torpedo. They are very costly, I believe, and they can be seen as they travel through the air if a sharp lookout is kept. Unfortunately the first one wasn't seen, and this dropped beside a young sergeant of ours, in a reserve trench, killing him instantly and wounding two

Left: The death of Charles Penman came as a shock to the men of the 14th Royal Irish Rifles. A popular figure among his comrades, he holds the distinction of being the first trench casualty of the battalion. YCV officer Val Hyndman took this photograph of his grave. *(Courtesy of the Somme Museum)*

Right: Today Charles Penman's grave in Hamel Military Cemetery, Beaumont-Hamel, is marked by a standard Commonwealth War Grave Commission headstone. *(Author)*

or three others. A fearful explosion, followed by a cloud of salmon-coloured smoke, with bricks, sticks and everything in the vicinity going up in the air, convinced us that some new atrocity was being perpetrated upon us. However, the next one was spotted in its flight, and then we knew. About twelve in all came over."

Around this time some of the men of the 14th Rifles decided the German bombardments were too accurate and that a 'spy' must be tipping them off as to when troop movements were taking place. Suspicion fell on the church tower at Mesnil, with the belief growing that the clock on the tower, which was clearly visible from the German lines, was being used to rely messages. In frustration, the Young Citizens removed the clock hands, bringing them back with them to Belfast (see Appendix 12). Hope provides another illustration of the strange juxtaposition that continually existed between normality and the surreal: "We are in the Dollys Brae sector for a spell and it is anything but pleasant. The Hun is now employing minewerfer against the village of Hamel and has already reduced some of the houses to powder. Although almost in the front line, one of the outhouses contains a cow which supplies the milk for the officers. Each battalion when it 'takes over' the trenches also 'takes over' the cow and attends to it when in the line."

A few other basic necessities were being addressed on 15 March, with the list of items requisitioned by Adjutant Captain Mulholland from 109th Brigade trench stores that day including trench signs marking Joffre Avenue and shelters, along with "eight buckets or biscuit tins for urinating at night in firing trench". Another 18 "Latrine buckets" were requested on 25 March.

After being relieved by the 11th Inniskillings, the YCVs returned to Mesnil, from which they supplied working parties to construct new dugouts. The Young Citizens replaced the Inniskillings again on 20 March, with the following day providing Berry with his first view of the enemy. "Remember seeing my first German at dawn today," he noted. "We were on a height overlooking part of their trenches; had a shot at him but don't know whether I hit him. Anyway he disappeared into his trench." After holding the line for six days, during which time Lieutenants R Walker and Matt Wright took out a bombing patrol to an old mill in No-Man's-Land, they were again relieved by the 11th Battalion on the evening of the 26th. The battalion suffered two more fatalities, with 20-year-old Private W Leitch, from the Donegall Road in Belfast, killed on 21 March and Private Lawrence John Lewis, who had previously been wounded by shrapnel, dying the following day.

The battalion returned to Hamel, falling back into the routine of providing working parties. Working under the direction of the Royal Engineers, teams of men dug narrow trenches in which cables were to be buried. The battalion's return to the front line, again near Mesnil, was to mark another milestone in its blooding. The length of trench to be covered had been extended so the relief, completed shortly after 9.30 pm on 2 April, saw three companies in the front line – B to the right, A in the centre and D on the left – with each having to do their own carrying of supplies. The following afternoon the Germans shelled the trenches, and sent over several 'oil cans'. There were no casualties but the line was damaged badly enough to have all other working parties suspended in order to carry out repairs. Mullin, who was in the reserve line but on a working party, recorded: "We had to stop work and take cover for a short time owing to shells falling rather close." It was the same story the next day, with more 'oil cans' launched from the enemy's forward saps. The battalion responded by having a howitzer battery shell the position known as the Railway Sap as a deterrent. A patrol under the command of Second Lieutenant Robert Gracey went out in search of Germans but none were seen.

The 5 April was much quieter, though the enemy was reported to be registering its guns in the late afternoon. A dud shell landed beside the dugout where Mullin was working. "If it had gone off, I am afraid for us the war would be over," he concluded. Further 'Minnies' fell in and around the front line positions held by D Company that evening. At 9.00 pm the next night, 6 April, the German guns opened up in earnest and for two-and-a-half hours blasted the left of the YCV lines, killing six men and wounding at least that number again. "The bombardment was increasing in intensity and everybody was ordered by Sergeant Major JJ Mackay to stand-to," remembered McRoberts.

"Coming out of the dugout into the open, the sight was terrible and the din astounding. We took up our places in the front line, fixed bayonets and loaded up ten rounds. I was a little frightened at first for the high explosive was tearing up our trenches. As I glanced along the line, great clouds of smoke could be seen rolling up to the sky where the explosions had lighted. Whiz-bangs came bursting over our heads, spreading their deadly shrapnel and trench mortars were crossing over thick, their course traced through the air by a trail of sparks. Machine guns were pumping and pumping. At last, Mr R Renwick came round, and we received the joyful instruction to blaze away. We got up on the fire step and starting off, each and all of us obtained his nerve. Our artillery had got going and the shells were roaring overhead like so many rushing, express trains. Our rifle fire was sweeping the ground and glancing off our wire."

The men sent round after round into the darkness for fear of a large scale raid, earning them praise in Divisional orders for their courage and coolness under fire. Hope had been making his way back to the line when the firing started:

"I am one of the ration party passing through Hamel with rations for the following day. Each man carried two sandbags tied together and filled with loaves over one shoulder and rifles over the other. A Hun bombardment opens right in the communication trench up which we are passing. All the shells in Europe seem to be falling round us. Hell is let loose somewhere. We are in the middle of our baptism of fire. We hurry into the line with the grub and throw it into a dugout. Every man, and we are at full strength, is on the fire step with barely elbow room waiting for the first sight of the fellow from over the way – we haven't seen one yet. Thousands of rounds of ammunition are fired into the dead of night but the Hun doesn't venture into our line. We have had a terrible hour and lose seven (sic) killed and 30 wounded."

Men were ordered out of the trenches to lie among the wire in No-Man's-Land, such was the intensity of fire on the front line. "During the strafe we had to do our 15 rounds rapid fire," noted Berry. "I could hardly hold my rifle. It was damned hot. I think this was what kept Jerry in his trenches – rapid fire augmented by our guns."

A direct hit on a Lewis gun killed both gunners and destroyed the weapon. Harrison, whose "old and good friend" Sergeant Billy Stephenson[6] was among the dead, was proud of the battalion's actions: "Our boys stuck to their guns as only Ulstermen can do, and our artillery gradually wore theirs down. Our trenches were in a bad state however, after two hours of it." Captain Willis, writing to Stephenson's minister, the Rev TA Smyth, said: "He was a fine lad and showed, in common with the men under him, the coolest courage during a heavy bombardment of our trenches by artillery, machine gun and rifle fire, and all the devilish ingenuity that the Germans could bring to bear on our trenches." A letter from a member of the battalion, sent to the family in Belfast, gives a bit more detail on the circumstances of his death, though obviously the writer was not speaking from first-hand experience:

Attempts to remove the body of Sergeant William ('Billy') Stephenson had to be abandoned temporarily so severe was the enemy shelling. *(Central Presbyterian Association Magazine)*

"On our way up we got the first news of the casualties inevitable in such a bombardment, and the first one was our sergeant, W Stephenson. He was shot doing his utmost to cheer up the men, and regardless of personal risk, making sure the other fellows were all right. He was one of the most popular sergeants in the battalion, and was absolutely fearless. Under his leadership we had the utmost confidence and the assurance that if it were humanly possible we would be safe. On the night of the shelling he went up and down the trenches visiting all the sentries. One of them, a very small chap, was quite terrorised at the whizzing shells, but in five minutes Billy S had him firing away like the others. He was killed visiting the loneliest and most dangerous sap for the fifth time to make sure that the sentries were all right. Whether he gets any award for his self-sacrificing conduct or not, his platoon will long remember him as a good sergeant and a brave soldier."

Those killed with Sergeant Stephenson in the bombardment were: Private Randolph Churchill Bestall Campbell, 21, from Cyprus Park in Belfast though born at Ballynahinch, County Down. A member of A Company, he had worked for Richardsons, Sons and Owden

A cluster of Young Citizens' graves, the result of the German bombardment of 6 April 1916. This photograph is part of the Hyndman collection. *(Courtesy of the Somme Museum)*

Limited prior to the war and a wreath on behalf of the firm was laid in remembrance of him at the City Hall in July 1916. George Dorrity, 21, of Elaine Street, Belfast, who had worked at the Bank Buildings. George Foster, also 21, a former boilermaker with shipbuilders Harland and Wolff from Beechfield Street, Belfast. He was a past member of 20th Company of the BB and had attended Willowfield Parish Church. His family appears to have been well-connected, with his father, Alexander Foster, associated with the Sirocco Works, his uncle George Stewart with the Royal Bakery, and a grandfather, James Foster, having run a coaching business between Downpatrick and Belfast. William Henry Reid, 24, had lived with an uncle at Glenbrook Avenue from boyhood. He had been a member of both the YCV and UVF, played cricket and football for the 5th BB Old Boys, trained at the McQuiston Gymnasium, attended St Donard's Parish Church and, as an Orangeman, went to meetings of the Royal Schomberg LOL 1690 and Union Temperance LOL 691. Maultsaid recorded in his diary: "He died firing his machine gun. All that was found of him was his right hand clasping the trigger of his gun. That old red head would dodge my punches no more (we often had a few rounds with the gloves), no more would I share my little parcels from home with him. This was my greatest blow so far". Alec Campbell, 19, of Nore Street, Belfast, a former apprentice plumber with John Reilly, Brunswick Street, Belfast, and an original member of the YCVs, was injured in the bombardment and died of his wounds the following day, 7 April 1916. The first named five lie side-by-side in Hamel Military Cemetery, Beaumont-Hamel, while Alec Campbell was buried at Forceville Communal Cemetery.

A large body of men, under Sergeant J Makesom, had been out in No-Man's-Land to repair the barbed wire and found itself pinned to the ground by the shelling. Jim Fitzsimons was one of those who found himself in a very exposed position: "I had a front seat view of it all as I was near the sunken road halfway between the lines at the time with my nose stuck in the ground being shot at by both sides." The most dangerous part, he concluded, was getting back to his own lines when things quieted down as everyone was "trigger happy". Dr Gavin arrived in the trenches and McRoberts was sent to fetch the stretcher-bearers.

"In the firing line once more, I found we had a lot of casualties; the firing had ceased now, the bombardment having lasted two hours. Until almost daybreak, I helped to remove the wounded, first Alec Campbell, then S McAdam and then H Coates. Alec Campbell was usually known as 'Fatty' to distinguish him from Ronnie Campbell as they both belonged to the same Section. It was strange that they both should be our only fatal casualties in that section that night, for 'Fatty' died in the ambulance before reaching hospital. This was severe work; the patients had received bad wounds which had been dressed in the nearest shelters. The stretcher-bearers stripped to the shirt, smeared up to the elbows in hot blood, were pulling off tunics and trousers, cutting away shirts and applying first-aid dressings. When ready to be shifted, the patients had to be hauled along the narrow fire trenches to the communication trench, where they were put on stretchers. At every sharp turn they had to be hauled off the stretcher, pulled round the corner and placed on the stretcher again. All this had to be done in a narrow passage where there was no room to stand sideways and support the body of the poor, wounded fellow. Simpler turns could be mastered by raising up the stretcher, outside the trench. Down in the Medical Officer's place the wounded had accumulated and a dead Sergeant, W Stephenson from 'D' Company, was laying there, his face covered with a ground sheet."

According to Fitzsimons, there were "terrific complaints from the higher up about the amount of .303 ammo we used up and we had nothing left when it was all over." In fact, Second Lieutenant Jim Walker, as acting adjutant, had to send in a requisition request to the Quartermaster Stores on 7 April for 35,000 rounds of ammunition. Despite the huge expenditure of small arms and artillery fire, and, indeed, claims to the contrary, the Germans had not been persuaded to remain in their trenches but had launched a raid in force against the neighbouring 29th Division, snatching more than 30 men. The division had not long arrived in France after earning for itself a formidable reputation at Gallipoli.

Working parties were sent out to repair the barbed wire as soon as the shelling died down, while others began restoring the communication and front line trenches. Another group, under Sergeant Murphy, was given the sad task of making "six graves to be ready early tomorrow after stand to". Relieved by the 11th Inniskillings, the 14th returned to Mesnil tired and weary. Over the next few days the men were allowed baths and time to clean equipment, though the rest was brief with working parties and company training undertaken. In an entry on 12 April the *War Diary* blandly notes another casualty: "Pte J Stewart wounded himself with revolver while on working party". It may have been an accident or it could have been a desperate action by a desperate man, though there were others whose efforts to escape the terrors of the front were more cunning. Jim Maultsaid recorded some of the tricks used by men to "work their ticket" back home, such as eating noxious substances like soap or, in one case, working fragments of a copper coin into the blisters caused by route marches so they became infected: "What a leg! It went up like a balloon! Did he lose the leg! I cannot say…"

The day after the shooting incident, 13 April, all leave was cancelled and officers and men already away recalled as the battalion was ordered back to the trenches, moving out at 7.45 pm the next evening to relieve the 11th Royal Inniskilling Fusiliers. This spell at the front was relatively quiet with only the German machine gunners causing concern until four carefully aimed howitzer rounds silenced them. The heavy rain made it necessary to have working parties continuously manning the pumps. There were worse jobs, of course. On 19 April a party consisting of two officers, four sergeants, three corporals and 60 men was tasked with "clearing ground of killed". They left the trenches at 2.00 am to spend three hours in their gruesome task, being sent back to 'Gordon Castle' at 5.00 am. That same evening Mullin was out in No-Man's-Land as cover for a wiring party: "Nice job. Nothing to do but lie there waiting and ready for Jerry coming over," he decided. Relieved by the 9th Royal Irish Fusiliers the following evening, the battalion marched to a hutted camp outside Martinsart, where a rum ration was issued. The men again enjoyed the baths at Mesnil, which was just a couple of kilometres away, and were excused some of the working parties organised by the Royal Engineers due to the severe weather. There was little chance of catching up on missed sleep, however. Berry recalled "there is a big gun just a few yards from our hut and every time she fires, our equipment, rifles, etc, come down in a shower about us. Water is scarce. I have to shave in cold tea." He added a couple of days later: "Got very little sleep tonight. Our friend, the big gun, is firing every half-minute or so – crash is deafening. The hut was in a state of tremor all night." Despite this reminder that the enemy were just a short distance away, it was necessary for an order to be issued to all company sergeant majors on the 21st regarding the wearing of protective equipment: "All NCOs and men are again cautioned about going without steel helmets when out of the trenches, the CO states that he will deal severely with any NCO or man walking out of their billets without them."

The YCVs marked Easter in the huts, with men not on working parties given time off. Mullin and his mate Bob Douglas headed into the town of Albert on the Monday to see for themselves what was becoming the most famous landmark of the war.

> "We saw the great ruined cathedral of Notre Dame de Brebieres with the leaning figure of the Virgin holding the infant Christ above her head. For over a year she had hung at an angle of 15 degrees below horizontal face downwards to the street below. It is said that the French people believe that the day the holy figures would fall, would see the end of the war, and that the German shell that would bring down the blessed Virgin of Brebieres would shatter the throne of the Hohenzollerns."[7]

Harrison ventured a look inside the church itself, "now a mass of ruins, most pitiful to behold," adding: "A few families still carried on business in its ruined street, but thousands had left their homes at the approach of the Hun, many of these being utilised as billets for our soldiers."

The weather was growing warmer by the day, and with it the mood among the men brightened according to Mullin: "Summer must have arrived as we have to hand in one blanket," he mused on the 26th, while two days later he was able to report how some of the lads had stopped for a swim in the River Ancre on their way back to the camp.

A view of the church in Albert during the fighting. The town was a 'must see' for the troops in the Somme sector because of the 'leaning Madonna' with a myth developing that the war would end when the statue eventually fell. *(Author's collection)*

Chapter 11

WAITING LIKE CATTLE IN A SLAUGHTER HOUSE

Censoring letters is my chief trouble here. This lot is a set of war correspondents in disguise. I hear the YCV mail is as large as the rest of the division put together. Our company gave in 400 letters in one night – I had the curiosity to count them – and that is the usual rate.

Officer of the 14th Royal Irish Rifles

JEROME LENNIE WALKER, or Jim to his friends, was an exceptional man. Despite having such poor eyesight that he was virtually blind without his glasses, none were keener than he for a fight. He had been the first to get involved in the war after finding himself in Courtrai, Belgium, as the Germans invaded. The then 25-year-old had opted to stand his ground while the remainder of his family fled and worked alongside the Red Cross, using his car to ferry about aid and people. He then travelled to Ypres, remaining there throughout the early bombardments when he was forced to shelter in a cellar for weeks at a time. During the breaks in the fighting Walker helped in the removal of 3,000 inmates from the lunatic asylum to Paris. Returning to Belfast, he sought a commission and, as a gifted linguist, served on the divisional staff for a period before being sent to the 14th Rifles. Lieutenant Walker also had the misfortune of being the first officer of the battalion to be killed and to be among the first Ulster casualties in Thiepval Wood during a period that brought home to many just what lay ahead of them.

On Easter Monday, 1916, B Company moved up to the wood for the first time, becoming the first Young Citizens to occupy the trench line from which the Ulster Division was to attack on 1 July, the opening day of the Battle of the Somme. It was two days later that officers from each company were taken on a conducted tour of the wood's defence systems as the 14th Rifles was to take over a section of the line from the 11th Inniskillings. On 1 May, as the men began their first full day in their new surroundings, the battalion *War Diary* reported: "Thiepval Wood looking at its best". However, by the following morning rain accompanied by thunder and lightning had brought flooding to the trenches. Even Berry seemed taken by his new surroundings: "This has been a fine wood at one time but now most of the trees are blasted and splintered by enemy guns," he noted. "The River Ancre runs close by which affords ample supplies. Occasionally we bathed, but had to beware of enemy snipers who were good shots." He added: "It is fine to listen to the birds

Despite the relaxed appearance of these two 14th Rifles men, they were obviously within striking range of the enemy. Note the Keep Down sign to their right, warning those passing along the trench that there were German snipers at work. *(George Hackney)*

singing just after 'stand to' – cuckoos and larks – and one could believe there wasn't a war on, listening to these birds except for an occasional explosion. When off duty I spent most of my time lying in the sunshine or either reading or writing." Harrison was equally impressed, recording: "The trenches are splendid, clean and dry, and the dugouts are good."

There was little enemy activity initially, apart from the usual trench mortars coming from Thiepval village and a few shrapnel bursts, though there were casualties. Lance Corporal William McLaughlin, a 19-year-old from Milford, County Armagh, was killed on 2 May; Private William Grainger, of Elm Street, Belfast, the following day; and Private Arnold Hayden, from Ashley Avenue, Belfast, died on 5 May from wounds sustained in an earlier bombardment. The 23-year-old, described by Berry as being "a decent chap," had a brother, Second Lieutenant WA Hayden, who had been commissioned a short time before into a reserve battalion at home. The response of the British artillery, or rather its lack of effectiveness, was clearly a frustration to the troops. On 4 May the *War Diary* noted how retaliatory strikes by the heavy guns and 18-pounders had a lamentable success rate:

> "A record was kept of both heavy and light with the following result:- Heavies, out of 24 shells 15 failed to explode; 18-pounders, out of 12 fired 8 were duds. It is most discouraging to men in the front line who have to put up with this sort of thing. Shrapnel and trench mortars at intervals fired into Thiepval Wood and front line about 11 o'clock closing up trench – George X Street which connects us with battalion on our right. This could not be cleared till next night as it was in full view of the enemy."

The following day the YCVs were told to be on the alert as the division to their right was planning a raid that evening. In the afternoon, emphasising the importance placed on the attack, Brigadier General TE Hickman and some of his staff officers toured the 14th Rifles' front accompanied by the commanding officer and adjutant. The enemy, aware something was in the offing, got the night's activities started by sending over a number of 'Minnies' followed by what was termed a "slow bombardment". At the stroke of midnight, however, the British heavy guns opened up on the German front line and the enemy, deceived into thinking the raid was coming from the Ulster trenches – an impression reinforced by the fact the battalion steadfastly held its fire – retaliated in kind. Within hours the Young Citizens had suffered its greatest loss to date, with 10 men killed and close to two dozen wounded. At one point a "devil of a mortar" exploded close to headquarters.

D Company took the greatest pounding, with men buried alive in blown-in trenches. According to Hope, they were doubly unfortunate as they should have been on the left of the section rather than the right but had been wrongly directed. "A lucky error we think but not so lucky for our D Company. They get an awful strafing of minewerfer and some of them are blown to bits including an officer. A sandbag full is all that is found of some of the boys." McRoberts is even more graphic in his description:

> "When matters cooled down, the work of digging out the bodies began, but some had to remain buried up to the neck for several hours before they could be extricated. One poor fellow, if he had been uncovered sooner, would have been saved, but he had to remain buried and bled to death from a wound in the leg. Lieutenant JL Walker[1] and many others were fatally injured and a still greater number were severely wounded. It was a bad night. With the breaking day the work continued and eight sandbags of flesh remains were gathered up and sent down to the burying ground."

The adjutant wrote:

> "I made my way to the front line at stand to and an awful sight it was to see the procession of dead and wounded being carried down. The pioneer squad were digging hard saving all they could possibly get out alive. Many of them died at their post although they could possibly have saved themselves by retiring, but their orders were to hold the front line at all costs. Second Lieutenant Walker, the officer in charge of this sector, was unfortunately killed and had given them orders not to give way and like true soldiers they stuck till they fell."

The German trenches had taken a similar pounding and when the firing died down both sides counted the cost. Berry, who had been on sentry duty when the bombardment kicked off, recorded: "Our trenches were knocked about very badly but of course Jerry's line must have been as bad or worse. Dawn came at last. Jerry was quiet but was busy repairing his trenches and getting in his killed and wounded same as ourselves."

Lieutenant Walker, whose family owned a flax business with a home at Wynard, Helen's Bay, County Down, as well as in Courtrai, had always shown fighting spirit. A month after his death, Lieutenant Stanley Monard, editor of the YCV magazine, *The Incinerator*, recalled in the June edition his last meeting with the commander of 13th platoon:

"Well, cheerio, laddie. We're all prepared, and one thing you can bet your life on, 13 will never retire" were his last words. The pair of them had returned to the front line shortly after 10.30 pm after a couple of 'Minnies' had shook the mess dugout and heralding the start of the German bombardment. Lieutenant Walker, who had spent nights in the trenches sleeping on the firestep amidst his men rather than in the officers' dugout, relished the prospect of action: "During the whole of the bombardment, this brave chap wandered up and down his men, cheerfully, and in the highest spirits. It was the nearest approach – was that shell storm – to his greatest ambition. That ambition was well-known to all his comrades. 'You wait, laddie,' he would say, with an enthusiastic glint in his eyes, 'you wait until I lead old '13' against the Blankey Boche. You'll see some pretty work.' Without a doubt there would have been. Jim Walker possessed that rare combination, clear thinking and tremendous – almost abnormal – enthusiasm, and certainly he would have been incomparable in a hand-to-hand tussle with the enemy. Such pluck as he possessed is very seldom met with. He should never have been in the Army at all, from one serious defect. Without his spectacles he could not see more than a few inches from his face. How many men would have seized upon his disqualification to spend a safe and comfortable time far from the sound of guns. The efforts Walker made to overcome his serious impediment to his candidature were prodigious, and – need it be said – entirely successful. It was his one fear in the trenches. 'Without the jolly old "specs",' he would humorously remark, 'I should be absolutely blind. So if I start sticking the bayonet into you – mistaking you for a Boche – just try and tell me who you are. But you'll have to be damnably quick, laddie, to save that precious life of yours.'"

Monard lamented the loss of a fellow officer who was the "life and soul" of the mess and hinted that Lieutenant Walker may have had a premonition of his death:

"During the tour in the trenches he had been wearing a private's tunic. An hour or so before the 'strafe' commenced, however, he went to his dugout. 'Hanley,'[2] he said to his orderly, 'Give me my proper tunic. If I'm killed to-night I have a fancy to die as an officer.' Prophetic words, truly. But then he was always one to make provision for possible contingencies. Before going out on a patrol, he always left a letter, to be posted in the event of… On the evening preceding his death he actually sent a letter to his brother-in-law, asking him to post an enclosed communication in case of the great eventuality."

Colonel Chichester[3] had previously returned home again through ill-health leading to a succession of commanding officers. Major FO Bowen – who had only taken over on 3 May after his immediate predecessor, Major Llewellyn,[4] was transferred to the King's African Rifles, East African Forces – issued a battalion order expressing his "high appreciation of their great gallantry and devotion to duty under trying circumstances".

The men killed were: Private Edward Adams, from Cullingtree Street, Belfast, who had formerly worked for Harland and Wolff and had been a member of the JH Stirling Masonic Lodge 345 and King William Temperance LOL 369. Private Albert Beattie, a

20-year-old from Belfast, a former member of the Balmoral Industrial School Band and the Rescue Tent Brass Band. Lance Corporal John Lowe, who was 19 and originally from Kidderminster, England. Private Tom Martin, 22, from the Springfield Road in Belfast, an accomplished gymnast and member of St Mathew's Temperance Lodge and Donegall Square Methodist Church. Private TH McBratney, 24, from Killyleagh, County Down, and a member of Second Comber Presbyterian Church. Private David McKeown, 24, from Dromore, County Down, who in civilian life had been a bus conductor with Belfast City Tramways and a member of

A row of 14th Rifles' graves in Authuile Military Cemetery tell their own story of 6 May 1916. Many of the bodies had to be dug out of the collapsed trenches. *(Author)*

Waringsford Rising Star LOL 545. Private Thomas Sloane,[5] 26, from Elswick Street, Belfast. Private George Tollerton,[6] a married man who had been working and living in Portadown prior to the war. Private 'Jimmie' Walker, 24, from Clady, Dunadry, County Antrim, who had formerly played football for Belfast club Linfield and was one of the battalion's 'greatest players'. Private George Kirkwood, from Alexander Park Avenue, Belfast, who was so badly wounded that he died at Forceville three days later on 9 May.

In each case, as was customary, officers wrote letters of comfort to the dead soldiers' families. Lieutenant SH Monard wrote of Private Walker:

> "It is with great regret but extreme pride, that I write to give you details of the death of your gallant son on the morning of the 6th May. Private Walker was, with a comrade, responsible for holding a most important forward trench in our line, the insertion of which would to a certainty have meant the loss of a portion of our sector. During two hours' bombardment your son struck to his post under a storm of high explosive shells, until finally a flying fragment struck him. He remained conscious and cool, and his wound was hurriedly dressed. The loss of blood, however, was tremendous, and he died on his way to hospital. Private J Walker was a most popular man in our company. He was a sportsman, and particularly a good footballer. His brilliant play was the delight and pride of all ranks. Frequently he saved his company from defeat at football, and undoubtedly on the morning of the 6th May he assisted materially in keeping the flag flying. Your sorrow will be intense; but I want to ask you to take comfort in the fact that he died a glorious and heroic death. We have the greatest pride in his achievement and in D Company, his own company, his name will never be forgotten."

Private Martin's father was told:

> "The shells were so thick that the place was a perfect inferno, and I shall never be able to understand how your son and his comrades stuck to their posts. Their

steadiness and bravery prevented the enemy from entering our lines, and while your bereavement is tremendous, I want to ask you to try to be comforted in the fact that your son died a glorious death while doing his duty to his King and country. During two hours' bombardment your son was absolutely cool and steady, and his good spirits were of the greatest encouragement to the men on his right and left. Your son's comrades speak in the highest terms of his gallant conduct."

Lieutenant Renwick, officer in charge of the machine-gun section, was a little more personal when he wrote to the parents of Private Martin:

"During a very heavy bombardment of our trenches on 5th May,[7] while on duty with his machine gun, a trench mortar shell exploded in the trench, killing him instantaneously. He was buried at 3.00 pm the following afternoon in a little graveyard beside the village where we are located, our chaplain conducting the service. The graveyard is one set apart for British soldiers, and a cross has been erected on his grave. Although only in my section a short time, I had always found him to be a capable, willing soldier and a good comrade. During the action he stood by his gun with great courage, and his name has since appeared in battalion orders for gallantry. To my assurance of deep sympathy is added the sincere regret of his comrades in the section."

The Incinerator, published little more than a month after, carried a much more hard-edged comment on the bombardment. It reported:

"Poor Kirkwood of 'B' Company, who died from his wounds, spoke some memorable last words: 'And to think,' he moaned, while being taken down Elgin Avenue on the stretcher, 'And to think I shan't be able to avenge Leitch and Dorrity.' That's the spirit we like. Our pals have been killed by a nation of murderers and by all that's true we are not going to be satisfied until we have had the lives of a dozen Huns for every comrade of ours who is lying in a lonely church yard in Flanders. Revenge! Revenge! Let us once get through the hideousness of waiting like cattle in a slaughter house – which is what trench life means – and then go mad until we have had an eye for an eye and a tooth for a tooth. Once near enough to the Boche to be free from his Trench Mortars and other horrors, we will show him a few conjuring tricks with rifle and bayonet. And each time the steel finds a temporary home we will snarl: 'That's for Martin, and that for Sloane. Take that for Walker, McLaughlin, McKeown, Campbell,' and so on."[8]

The battalion was relieved on the evening of 6 May, arriving at Martinsart Wood at 1.00 am, where the men collapsed into their beds for their first sleep in 48 hours. At 9.00 am on 8 May they were again on the march, taking over billets from the 8th Rifles at Lealvillers near Acheux. As usual, they were in a poor state with no incinerators, latrines or other basic necessities considered essential by the YCVs. "Why," the *War Diary* wondered, "we do not work on a proper system for this billeting". It went on:

"Many months of weary toil we spent behind the line building and patching half of France and now when we come out of months fighting we have to start this navvies' work again. If the soldiers and officers, especially of the new armies, would only bear in mind what they will find in every book of instruction 'remember other troops may occupy the billets after you,' or words to that effect. It is the system that is all wrong, and one is afraid of offending the other."

As it turned out, however, they had plenty of time to make themselves comfortable as the battalion was to remain at Lealvillers for a month preparing for the long talked about 'Big Push'. The training schedule was to be intense and varied, though entertainments, including visits by the Divisional Follies of The Merry Mauve Melody Makers, and football challenge matches were interspersed as a means of easing the tension. Most importantly, they were assured of an extended spell out of the line. Brigadier General TE Hickman, in a Special Order of the Day, urged the men to make best use of their rest time:

A group of Young Citizens, some armed with spades and others apparently happy to watch the work, are captured on Val Hyndman's camera. *(Courtesy of the Somme Museum)*

"Officers and men of the 109th Infantry Brigade, I desire to express my best thanks for the splendid behaviour of officers and men during their three months in the trenches. The work was hard, and the casualties numerous, but both were borne cheerfully, which shows their gallant spirit, determination and above all good discipline of all ranks concerned. I hope that you will enjoy the short period of rest allowed you, so that when the time comes for going back to the firing line, that you will do more good and valuable work for your country."

Physical fitness sessions were organised; military drill practiced; and courses held in bayonet fighting, gas precautions and procedures and wiring. And, of course, the working parties continued as always. The most important task awaiting the men, however, was to become familiar with the enemy trench system by practising over a mock-up laid out in the pattern of the German lines in front of Thiepval Wood. "It all seems so simple and above ground. I don't think we quite realise what is before us," commented the *War Diary*. Berry described how most days were spent "practising an advance over dummy trenches – these were shallow trenches and were exact in every detail as Jerry's trenches which we were to capture later on at Thiepval". Part of the training involved working in conjunction with the artillery, trench mortar batteries, Royal Flying Corps and machine-gun teams. Mullin, as a runner, realised how important it was that he learned how to recognise the layout of the German trenches so he could find his way round them delivering messages. His task was made a little easier as many of the key points had been given the names of towns and villages back home in Ireland. "I am runner from Cavan to battalion HQ. Let me say

Cavan is a strong point (on the 140 contour) between Lisburn and Moy," he notes in a diary entry about a brigade attack across the dummy trench system on 26 May. Both men were impressed with a demonstration set up for the whole 109th Brigade of the effectiveness of trench mortars on the trenches and barbed wire. "The damage done by these handy little guns is terrific. The noise drew the people from their houses – perhaps they thought Jerry was coming again," wrote Berry, while Mullin said: "It certainly was devastating."

During this period they had a number of important visitors, including Sir Douglas Haig, who expressed himself highly pleased with the clean and smart turnout of the men. Mullin had been taking part in a company drill shortly after breakfast when "I was delighted to see Sir Douglas Haig, the C in C, with an escort of 17th Lancers approaching slowly at a trot and halt a short distance from where C Company were drilling. A sergeant on his lance carried a small Union Jack, the flag denoting the C-I-C. Sir Douglas watched our drill for a short time and then moved off. It was a treat to see Sir Douglas and his escort as beautifully turned out as in peace time. The cavalry horses were much admired." Sergeant Maultsaid, a bomber, put on a demonstration for the general, tossing a grenade into a target area 40 yards away with deadly accuracy. Haig, a veteran of set-up exhibitions, wanted more proof and told him: "Very good, sergeant. Now let me see your men throw". Maultsaid recorded in his diary: "I picked my crack throwers. Bang, bang, bang! All bulls-eyes. I was delighted." Haig was clearly pleased: "Are your boys all Irishmen, sergeant?" he asked, then in response to being told they were, added: "Yes, yes, I see now why you are all such good bombers." Haig's visit was reported back home, prompting *The Incinerator* to clarify that it wasn't just the YCVs who met the general:

The men became experts at building up defences with row upon row of sandbags. Here they are attempting to make a corrugated iron hut more secure. *(George Hackney)*

"It was nice to see Sir Douglas Haig amongst us the other day, and what's more, it was very inspiriting. One remark heard when he had gone expresses the feeling felt by all of us: 'A great man. He makes you feel that you'd follow him to Hell'. Sir Douglas said some very nice things to the CO about the battalion, although we did not tell the 'Belfast News Letter' all about it. Now, if he had said to the GOC: 'I specially want to see the 14th to congratulate them on capturing five miles of the German line,' sure, that would have found its way to all the papers without someone having to write an 'open letter' to some kind friend at home. Sir Douglas went to see every battalion in the Division and said a few appropriate words to each CO, which he wished conveyed to the men themselves. Jolly nice things he said, too. Some units are apt to lose their perspective. We hope the Commander-in-Chief will come again before long."

Brigadier General Shuter, newly-arrived commanding officer of the 109th Brigade – he had replaced Brigadier General Hickman, who had been the last remaining infantry brigadier who had accompanied the Ulster Division to France – complimented the Young Citizens on their past record and encouraged them to keep up their good name when he carried out an inspection. He also presented the 14th Rifles with their prize as winners of the brigade bombing competition, leaving the Inniskilling battalions in the shade.

The clerical staff was given an additional task: compiling a list of all those entitled to service or proficiency pay as the records held at the Dublin pay office had been destroyed during the Easter Rising. The uprising also prompted a piece of commentary in *The Incinerator* that left no doubt as to the unionist sentiment that existed in the battalion:

> "What about the Sinn Feiner business? Soldiers are not allowed to talk politics, otherwise much might be said. Speaking for ourselves, we'd rather have seen a little less mercy to some of the rebels. If a man out here plays any old tricks he is given short shrift – shot at daybreak. Remember this man may have fought long and sturdily for his Empire – but still he'd be shot. Then what kind of death do those insurgent dogs deserve – those swine who seize upon the fact that the soldiery is away, fighting and dying to save Sinn Feiner worthless skins – to rifle and riot and murder a whole host of innocent people. Ugh! Doesn't it make your blood boil, lads? Perhaps it's as well that we – being the Press – are muzzled."

The working parties had been engaged in a range of tasks, from relocating officers' huts to digging trenches. The moving of logs from railway wagons was treated by Mullin, with his usual enthusiasm, as some sort of game. "We imagine ourselves lumber men in the NW of Canada. Jack Gibson[9] and I pick the largest logs, put one on our shoulders and run with it to the wood pile we are making."

Harrison and a sergeant were detached from their company at the beginning of June and sent to join other men who were priming hand grenades. "The bombs I had been helping to prepare are presents for Fritz, and by all appearances he is to receive them at no distant date," he recorded as he noted the other preparations going on around him:

> "A tremendous number of new batteries have arrived, mostly large calibre guns. The infantry gave a hand to dig pits for these. We have practised the advance over an elaborate system of 'dummy trenches' for weeks on end, and everybody is fed up. As the time draws nigh scenes of great activity are taking place daily. Engineers are working on the roads, ammunition lorries are going up to the different dumps loaded with shell, and working parties have a job getting through the endless streams of traffic running back and forward to the line. French artillery went through this morning, some batteries of the famous '75' calibre, along with a couple of tremendous big fellows."

On 13 June, the battalion was ordered to Aveluy Wood near the line at Thiepval, leaving Lealvillers at 2.00 pm in the rain and passing through Martinsart at 5.30 pm. Accommodation was to be tents for officers and shelters for the men but they didn't arrive until that evening and then it was discovered that only one of the tents was habitable. Now they were closer to the front, the men were put on iron rations that arrived up in sandbags and consisted of

These makeshift shelters offered some protection against shrapnel and the elements but were death traps in the event of a direct hit. *(George Hackney)*

bully beef, rock hard biscuits and an assortment of oddities. *The Incinerator* carried an article, written by "A Victim" around this time, which showed the contempt felt for such fare:

"The members of the 'Dugout des rats' sat silently around and gazed with horror-stricken eyes at the motley collection of articles just arrived in the daily lucky bag. With many shudders the Lce-Cpl enumerated them, something after the manner of an auctioneer. 'Two du pains – that's a quarter each to-day chaps' – many groans arose, and everyone tight-tightened his belt in anticipation.

'One tin of marmaduke.' This had arrived day and daily for months past so, for the next ten minutes the 'des ratities' chanted softly their jam strafe. Mac cut another notch in his rifle when he saw that it was made by a new firm. He named the notches lovingly: Tickler's, Pinkies, Paxton's, and his manner was like unto the manner of a Sioux numbering his scalps. 'Apres la guerre finit' holds out much hope to the men of the BEF.

'Two tins of brick beef –' 'Combien?' queried Bags sarcastically. The Lce-Cpl wiped the sweat from his manly brow and threatened a blanket court-martial toute suite if order wasn't kept.

'Next we have one 'boojee' – that disappeared under the Lce-Cpl's waterproof sheet – 'Six packets of matches' – one of these also made its way thither just in time, for eight dirty paws shot out like greased lightning for the matches.

'One tin of Macon –' but the Lce-Cpl was here shouted down. Eight eager Tommies fell on the offending dainty and it was heaved into the trench and over the parapet. Mac stood up waving his hand and wiping his eyes. Then he went sadly back and cut No 4 notch deeper, swearing many hefty swears to himself.

Nervously the Lce-Cpl waited till it was quiet again. The strain was beginning to tell on him. He went on weakly: 'Also some best biscuits.' These were dinged back into the sand bag and taken down the trench to be used as bullet proof screens and also for the muddier places of the trench.

The Lce-Cpl bent down again and lifted a lump of cheese. He looked at it, and tears gathered in his eyes. The others were surreptitiously feeling for their gas helmets. Words for once failed the Lce-Cpl. He weakly laid it down again and swooned away.

Mac took down his rifle and lifted up a jack-knife, two more went for the SB's, while the others led it away on a string and only finished it off with the help of a Mills' No 5. And the papers still say: 'Nothing to report on the Western Front.'"

The battalion suffered its second officer casualty when Second Lieutenant Frank Corscadden, who was sitting in a wicker chair outside his tent catching up on his correspondence, was wounded on 17 June, dying the following day. Injuries in the wood, were thousands of men were sheltering, were not unusual as German machine gun bullets whizzed through the trees at night and shells exploded overhead. Hope, however, speculated that a stray bullet from an aeroplane had caused the "mysterious happening".[10]

The emphasis for the Young Citizens was now the shifting to the front of the explosives, ammunition and materials required for the coming battle. On the day the rest of the battalion moved to the wood, Mullin, on a working party with C Company, reported 8,000 bombs being moved from Paisley dump to Gordon Castle, close to Elgin Avenue; the next two days it was hand grenades and stokes mortars that were transported; then for three days the men carried up box after box of .303 ammunition. On 19 June, they began to empty the stores from Gordon Castle up to the front line, with some 150,000 bullets moved that day alone. A party of YCVs also finished constructing the dugouts from which the divisional general staff were to direct the battle. "The pace of events seems to be quickening now. There is excitement in the air we breathe," reported Mullin. Hope found himself sneaking about in the dark so as not to alert the enemy:

Officers were allowed considerably more 'luggage' at the front which afforded them the opportunity to indulge in a few home comforts when out of the line. *(Courtesy of the Somme Museum)*

"We unload wagons at Lancashire dump in the wood, so near the line that everything is muffled, so near that even the neighing of a mule will bring the 'circus' on our track. The dump is a living mass of humanity at night all working overtime in the great preparations for what we now call the 'big do'. We fill sandbags by the thousand in the wood during the day and at night carry them forward to the great causeway which is being built to take us over to Thiepval. The causeway contains millions of bags and the work is being directed by the RE."

Berry was similarly working day and night, and was particularly unhappy at having to carry up poison gas cylinders. "Our last job was carrying up the scaling ladders and fitting them into position in the assembly trenches," he added.

Chapter 12

THE SUPREME TEST

Before you get this we shall have put the value of the Ulster Division to the supreme test. I have no fears of the result. I am certain no General in the armies out here has a finer Division, fitter and keener. I am certain they will be magnificent in attack, and we could hardly have a date better calculated to inspire every national tradition amongst our men of the North. It makes me very sad to think what the price may be; but I am sure the officers and men think nothing of that. They only want to be let go.

Divisional commander Lieutenant General Oliver Nugent to Sir George Richardson, head of UVF, on the eve of battle

SHORTLY AFTER 1.00 AM on 1 July 1916, Major Alan Mulholland, adjutant of the 14th Rifles, made his way up Paisley Avenue, one of the main thoroughfares in the Thiepval Wood trench system, to tell Brigade headquarters that the battalion was in the assembly trenches. There he was given 'zero time' for the attack and got to set and check his watch. Making his way back to his own command post, a task made more difficult by the need to wear his goggles as the air was thick with tear gas, he passed on this additional information to his fellow officers and ensured that their watches were in agreement with his own. All was ready for the opening of the gates of hell and, as he recorded in the *War Diary*, even the earth itself seemed to know:

> "At this time a lull seemed to settle over all the earth as if it were a mutual tightening up for the great struggle shortly to commence. A water hen called to its mate 'midst the reedy swamp and a courageous nightingale made bold to treat us with a song."

The last few days had been ones of mixed emotions, compounded by false starts and uncertainty. On 19 June the preliminary attack orders had been received and read over to all officers. The 109th Brigade, to the right of the divisional front, was to attack over a front of 500 yards, with the 9th and 10th Royal Inniskilling Fusiliers, to the right and left respectively, in the first wave, with the 14th Rifles on the left and the 11th Inniskillings on the right in the second wave. They were but a small part of a battle front that ran for almost 14 miles from Serre in the north to Maricourt in the south. At Gommecourt, another two miles further north, a diversionary attack was planned in the hope of confusing the Germans. The battle had been conceived late in 1915 as a joint British-French offensive, but the contribution of the latter had to be scaled back because of the pressure being asserted by the German army at Verdun, further to the south. In addition to the biggest concentration of artillery so far

Part of a hand drawn map of the trench system in Thiepval Wood prior to the Battle of the Somme. It was from these trenches that the 14th Rifles attacked on 1 July 1916. *(Author's collection)*

amassed on the Western Front, mines had been planted in tunnels constructed under key German defences, with their detonation scheduled for just minutes ahead of the 7.30 am zero-hour.

The non-commissioned officers had, on 21 June, been given an opportunity to view the enemy trenches from the few ridges of high ground that overlooked them from the British side. On the same day seven new officers joined the battalion, "none having been out before and with very short training," according to the *War Diary*. Final attack orders were issued the following day and all tools and stores moved into assembly trenches.

The final days in the lead up to the attack were to be known as V, W, X, Y and Z (later extended when the attack was delayed by two days). The YCVs had struck camp to move to Hédauville, near Forceville, on the evening of 23 June, only to be halted at Martinsart and ordered to carry ammunition to the front line trenches. More than 600 men, in an extended line that snaked from Lancashire dump to the jump-off points, worked in the pouring rain throughout the night. "We left our equipment on the roadside," recorded Mullin. "We proceeded up to the trenches and formed a working party. The battalion worked hard in heavy rain throughout the night. The men stood about one yard apart and passed from one to the other trench mortar bombs." It was 8.00 am on the morning of the 24th that the last of them, "wet and dead beat" according to the *War Diary*, arrived in camp.

As the British guns began what was expected to be a four-day bombardment to soften up the enemy trenches, the men did their best to dry their clothes while snatching some rest amid the din. The next day was a Sunday, with Church parades held in the afternoon. The Rev John Jackson Wright, recalled James Fitzsimons, preached a sermon in which he warned that many of the men in his congregation would not be returning from the forthcoming battle despite having the support of some 300 artillery guns positioned between Martinsart and Thiepval. Battle orders were passed on to every man via the platoon commanders, sergeants and corporals. "We have practiced the attack over similar trenches many times. We all have a good idea of the lay-out. I am perfectly fit and feel on top of the world," noted Mullin. That evening the battalion moved up to billets at Martinsart. Berry was keen to be on the move again:

"Most of us have never been in an attack, but we hoped to avenge our pals who had been wiped out. I won't forget that march up to the assembly trenches – we sang our favourite song 'Pack up your troubles in your old kit bag'. All roads are being shelled by Jerry, so we are compelled to go across country to Martinsart. Pretty heavy marching. We are very interested in the big fireworks display of guns on both sides. The whole sky is bright with bursting shells which give peculiar light – some blue and then orange flashes. We finally arrived at Martinsart at 11.30 pm and are billeted for the night in barns and outhouses. We are very tired but can't get to sleep for Jerry shelling."

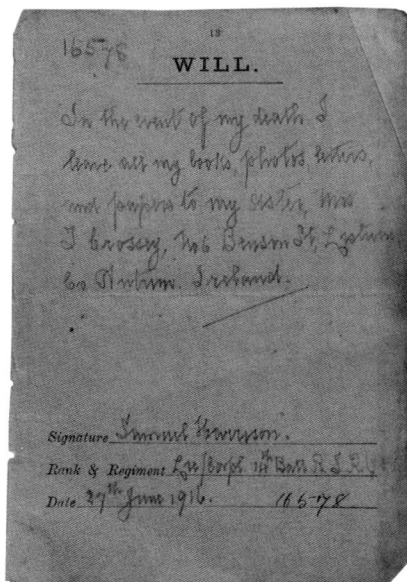

The men were encouraged to draw up their Wills ahead of the battle using a page specifically for the purpose inside their pay books. Lance Corporal Samuel Harrison left all his worldly goods to his sister. *(Courtesy of Alastair Harrison)*

The next few days were spent killing time until at 10.00 pm on Wednesday 28 June orders arrived sending the battalion back to Forceville, as the attack had been put back due to the persistent rain. "We are all surprised and bewildered at orders being changed so suddenly," noted Mullin. Berry was even more frustrated: "We weren't at all pleased as all our work preparing for it seems to have been wasted – such is life in the army." He added two days later: "About fed-up with these countermanded orders. Wish they would settle on something definite." At Forceville the men had neither blankets nor great coats, as they had been stored ahead of the battle, but were at least well back from the front lines.

On 30 June, Major General Oliver Nugent issued a Special Order that was read to the men. It stated:

"On the eve of the offensive for which the Ulster Division has trained and waited for so many months, I wish that every officer and man of the Division should know how absolutely confident I feel that the honour of the British Army and the honour of Ulster are in safe-keeping in their hands. It has been my privilege to command the Division in France during the past nine months, during which time I have had various opportunities of seeing that it has been steadfast in defence and gallant in minor offensives. The time has now come to show to the world the qualities which fit it for the great offensive about to open. Much is expected of the Ulster Division and I am certain that the expectation will be fulfilled. Resolution, self-reliance, and the spirit which knows no surrender and no defeat are present in full measure, and will bear fruit on the battlefield that will resound to the credit of our country. Nine months ago the King, after his inspection of the Division, desired me to write and tell him how it bore itself in its first great encounter with the enemy. I hope that I shall be able to write and tell him how the men of the Ulster Division bore themselves like men in the day of battle, and did all that was expected of them. To every officer and man of the Division I wish success and honour."

John Berryhill Meehan,[1] in a newspaper article published on 12 July 1919, recalled how Captain Slacke had gathered the men of A Company together that evening for a final briefing:

> "Eagerly every man crowded into the long, dark hut, at the far end of which jovial Captain Slacke stood talking to lieutenants Robb (killed), Gracey (wounded), and Carson (missing). The captain raised his hand and instantly all clamour ceased. 'Men,' he began hoarsely, 'men, you all know what tomorrow means to us; we have been given the honour of leading this great offensive, which, please God, will be successful. We have also been given one of the hardest nuts to crack on the British Front; it will take some cracking, boys – we'll crack it! Remember, boys, that old slogan of ours, 'No Surrender,' that must be our watchword tomorrow and, men, mark my words, there's to be no going back; shoot the coward who wavers but – but I know that in A Company, my company, there'll be no cowards. Tomorrow's the 1st of July, the glorious 1st; think what it means to those at home, and just before I go, one word – no quarter. I know I can trust A Company to a man to die fighting rather than be vanquished. God bless you boys. No Surrender!"

Shortly afterwards, at 9.30 pm, the battalion was paraded and, led by A company, marched off by platoons at 100 yards intervals. The rain had at last stopped and the evening was fine and bright with the stars clearly visible. A halt was called to allow the men a rest and give the officers time to part with their horses. According to Hope, the A Company commander bid his horse goodbye with what sounded like a premonition of impending death: "Captain Slacke, who has ridden his horse 'Father' all the way, dismounts, calls his orderly and says 'Beattie, take Father away. I shall never ride him again.'" Meehan draws attention to another horseman equally as glum:

> "As we reached Martinsart Wood we notice a solitary, great-coated figure standing with bared head beside his horse. He was Colonel Bowen, the 14th YCV's commander. As each little party marched by he muttered a hoarse, barely distinguishable, 'God bless you lads,' and wistfully watched them disappear out of sight. A batch of Inniskillings, out in front, commenced to sing and wafted to those behind on the evening breeze came the homely strains of 'Dolly's Brae'. Instinctively each man quickened his pace to this stirring tune and soon the whole long, struggling line began to sing. As we neared the trenches someone commenced the Ulster Division song, Captain Wake's favourite, crude in metre, but right in sentiment, it was handed down from long past Finner days:
>
> Ulstermen, Ulstermen, march, march, march, all together;
> By your right, by your might, we'll be conquered never
> Though the day be dark and long
> Let this be your sunshine ray
> As your forefathers fought in the days gone by,
> Ulstermen will do the same today."

George Hackney risked a sniper's bullet to take this photograph of the German trenches, which can be clearly distinguished in the distance by the tell-tale white lines of excavated chalky clay, ahead of the Battle of the Somme. *(Photograph © National Museums Northern Ireland, Collection Ulster Museum, BELUM.Y15553)*

This photograph, the only 'portrait' in the Hyndman collection, is presumably of the man himself. He was to be severely wounded in the 1 July fighting and subsequently died from his wounds. *(Courtesy of the Somme Museum)*

The men pressed on through the village and over the light railway into Aveluy Wood until they found the main rail line near Authuille, which helped guide the leading platoon across the South Causeway by the River Ancre. Here a "watchful Hun from his lair above Caterpillar Wood endeavoured to spray our path with a machine gun, but fortunately his aim was high and we only had one casualty," recorded Major Mulholland, who personally ensured every man made it into the assembly trenches off Elgin Avenue. Mullin noted in his diary: "There is no rain. The guns are all firing. The din is terrific. As Company runner I am with Captain Val Hyndman. He, of course, is not used to much marching and he is not good on his feet. C Company eventually reaches the line and get into their correct assembly trenches without a hitch of any sort." For many, the waiting is worse than the actual fighting to follow. Hope recorded: "The feeling one has about it all is anything but pleasant. Some seem to realise the seriousness of going to certain death and others laugh at it." He added: "I have no fear of death. No fear at the moment. I do not yet know what it is like to face death – not yet – it is only a matter of hours and then!" For Charles Sheridan, the way he felt was virtually indescribable:

"Our shells were passing over in thousands and the Germans were sending a great many over also, and the din was dreadful, however, I managed to sleep for a few hours on the bottom of the trench and as a result I was almost frozen and there was no prospect of any breakfast for a few days as far as I knew. Well, an officer came around with an issue of rum which we were very glad of as we were all very cold."

The noise was so great that holding a conversation with the man nearest to you was all but impossible with the waiting apparently never ending. Maultsaid recalled: "The wood is a mass of flame; shells are bursting; trees are crashing, all is confusion and din. To talk to your nearest chum is out of consideration. We stagger on then turn right into the assembly trench… to await the dawn. We cannot rest. You cannot sit or lie down – just stand up and wait." With his Bible tucked into his tunic pocket, next to his heart, his thoughts turned to home and loved ones, and the possibility of meeting his dead mother again in the afterlife or, more dreaded than death, being maimed: "God save me from the loss of my sight. How I dreaded blindness – anything but that."

The bombers, who would play a prominent role in clearing the German trenches, were working their way through the boxes of grenades that had been carried up to the front in the days previous when an act of courage that was to win the Ulster Division's first, and the 14th Rifles' only, Victoria Cross took place. One box fell into the assembly trench, spilling out its contents and in the process dislodging some of the safety pins. William McFadzean threw himself on top of the grenades, dying instantly in the explosion but saving the lives of his comrades, though two others were injured, one losing a leg.[2]

Captain James McKee, writing to McFadzean's father, also William, at his home, Rubicon, in the Cregagh area of east Belfast, said: "He saved the lives of a number of his comrades by his action, and we are proud of him. His name has been sent forward to higher authority, with recommendation for a decoration." Corporal Dave Marshall was standing nearby when McFadzean sacrificed his life. He told his brother, Second Lieutenant James Marshall, who wrote to the family: "Willie fell just beside him, and by his heroic self-sacrifice saved the lives of his comrades around him, earning their admiration and gratitude which will never be forgotten by them". Berry, a member of the bombing section, recorded how he and his comrades were standing shoulder-to-shoulder in a trench of their own. "Billy McFadzean was killed in this trench. Some bombs fell off the parapet and sheared the pins but McFadzean threw himself on top of the lot and was blown to pieces. One or two others were wounded with splinters. Don't know yet how I escaped." (See Appendix 5)

The Germans shelled the woods on and off throughout the early hours. By 6.00 am the bombardment was so intense that the candles in the battalion headquarters were constantly blowing out. It was nothing, however, compared to what the enemy trenches had to endure. "Our intense bombardment has opened and shells of all sizes, including the big trench mortars, are raining upon the Hun lines which are covered with smoke and dust. It is marvellous how anything can live under such a hail of shells," noted the *War Diary*, with an addition at 7.00 am reading: "Enemy returns our artillery fire and the Wood is getting uncomfortable." It was through this intensifying fire that the battalion, along with the rest of the division, moved to the jump-off points. The 14th Rifles was now in touch with the 10th Inniskillings.

The German lines opposite had been given labels, with the front line A, the immediate support A1, then the B line, C line, etc, with key points named after Ulster towns and villages to make them easier to recall. It was up to the first wave battalions to press on to the final objective, with the YCVs and the 11th Skins holding the A and B lines, with instructions to turn round the fortifications at the Crucifix, a German strongpoint, while pushing forward 'liaison patrols' to keep contact with the two leading Inniskilling battalions. So confident of victory were the British commanders that the troops, many of them in volunteer units

William McFadzean, a bomber with the Young Citizens, won the 36th (Ulster) Division's first Victoria Cross of the war when he threw himself on top of spilled grenades to save his comrades. *(Courtesy of Andrew Totten)*

like the Ulster Division, had been ordered to form up in No-Man's-Land to advance at a slow steady pace to their objectives. The blunder allowed the German machine-gunners, sheltering in their deep underground shelters, time to emerge when the British guns fell silent to set up their weapons again. The ensuing slaughter contributed much to the almost 60,000 casualties suffered by the British on the opening day of the battle. The German artillery concentrated its guns on the Allied front line and assembly trenches, adding to the human tragedy unfolding in No-Man's-Land. Major Mulholland, who had received what was to prove the last message from Captain Slacke[3] to the affect that he and his men were advancing, recorded: "The Brigade moved off as if on parade – nothing finer in the way of an advance has ever been seen, but alas, no sooner were they clear of our own wire when the slow tat tat of the Hun machine guns from Thiepval village and Beaumont-Hamel caught the advance under a deadly cross fire."

Falls, in the official divisional history, tells of how the leading waves, moving as if on parade, reached the German front line trench and on across it without heavy loss. "Hardly were they across, however, when the German barrage fell upon 'No Man's Land,' upon the rear companies of the first line battalions, and upon those of the second line. And immediately the barrage left it, flanking machine-gun fire burst out from the dominating position of Thiepval cemetery. The 11th Inniskillings and 14th Rifles, as they emerged from the wood, were literally mown down, and 'No Man's Land' became a ghastly spectacle of dead and wounded." The men pushed on despite the heavy toll being taken of friends, comrades and even family. Samuel McIlroy was among the first to fall but his brother Frank was forbidden to stop to help him, being ordered on by Sergeant Powell.[4]

Lieutenant Fred Barker climbed out of his trench with hatred in his heart. An original member of the YCVs, he had joined the Black Watch at the outbreak of war, rising to the rank of sergeant. Only recently commission into the 14th Rifles, his blood was up for the impending battle. "For three long hours we had stood there, listening to the hum of our shells spreading and waiting for the moment when the whistles would blow and we would go 'over the top'," he wrote days later from a hospital bed.

All fear left Belfast man Fred Barker, an original member of the YCVs, as he climbed out of the trenches determined on seeking revenge for the fatalities already inflicted on his platoon. *(Royal Ulster Rifles Museum)*

"Daylight brought its own new misery. Yesterday morning we had assembled in a cosy camp far behind the lines. How clearly we had learnt the plan of today's attack! How jovially we had sat down to lunch; how smartly we marched away over the clear white road – for it was summer – and how we sang! Now as we froze in our narrow trench, yesterday was buried in a world that we had left a long time ago. The dull burst of each shell echoed through the brain like the clang of a hammer. To each of us, I think, came that feeling of utter weariness that only a soldier knows. What was the use of it all? With a sudden crash, a shell exploded some yards away and still trying to keep a cool head I made my way to the spot, for the shell had burst among my platoon. Four men were dead and a corporal lay at the bottom of the trench with both legs gone and a great hole in his side. As I bent over him his eyes opened and looked in mine. Their mute appeal of unfairness, their patient wonder haunt me still. Tears rolled down his cheeks slowly and then with the sigh of a tired child he was gone. I glanced at my watch; only a few more minutes now and the artillery barrage would lift, the first wave of men would 'go over'. Even now the firing seemed to die away as the gunners altered their fuses. For the fraction of a second there seemed to be quietness and in that space of time my senses and reasoning powers returned. The whistles blew, the first wave climbed out of the trenches and with the swish of the shells there rushed through my mind a thousand and one things – thoughts of home and all that was dear to me – a feeling of fear, especially fear of showing that I felt it. It was the greatest moment in the greatest war of all time. Thoughts crowded in and filled my mind – thoughts that are more deadly than the venomous guns spitting their fire a few hundred yards away. Quickly we took our places. Machine guns from the enemy opened fire and the heavy shells plumped around us. 'Nearly time isn't it, sir?' yelled my sergeant. I looked at my watch. I yelled back and put my whistle to my mouth. One blast and we climbed the trench, but that blast blew from me all thoughts, except the memory of my dead corporal and before my eyes there was only the inferno opposite, where we were slowly making our way and where I would find the beasts who had killed the boys – our boys."

B Company's Lieutenant Monard yelled "Come on, boys," before going over the parapet. "We follow him and over the rough trench ladders into the shell-shattered wood," recalled Maultsaid.

"Across a wooden gangway over our front line trench – and we are out into No-Man's-Land. A wall of flame meets us. We stagger and gasp from shock. My very hair seems to scorch under the impact. The air is full of hissing, burning metal and the ground rocks beneath our feet as we tear our way through our own wire defences. At last we are attacking! The bullets sing past…"

German tear gas, the shells exploding amid the black smoke that drifted across the battlefield, was sweet smelling but made his eyes smart and water.

"We surge forward. Bayonets sparkle and glint. Cries and curses rent the air. Chums fall, some without a sound – and others… oh, my God! May I never hear such cries again! There goes the YCV flag tied to the muzzle of a rifle. That man had nerve! Through the road just ahead of us we had crossed the Sunken Road. We could see khaki figures rushing the German front line. The Inniskillings had got at them. Wild Irish yells floated to our ears. We quickened our pace. Here comes Jerry, out to meet us. Yes, but – hands held high above their heads! Shell-shocked and battered, what they suffered during our hurricane bombardment the Lord only knows. Line after line of brown figures press on and on. Gaps are filled. The enemy had now set up a terrible barrage of shell fire and machine guns were hammering out a deadly stream of death… Big gaps appeared but nothing on this earth could have stopped those Ulster boys, their Irish blood aflame, thirsting to get 'close-in' We cannot stop to help the wounded. The order is forward! T'is said that some of the 'Skins' wore Orange sashes, rushing the Germans shouting. 'No surrender!' It's true, too. A finer lot of men never lived. How they fought!"

Maultsaid's own contribution to the battle was to be short-lived, however, as he was soon to suffer a bullet wound that shattered his collarbone.

Hope, like most of the men, was weighed down with materials to help consolidate the new forward line they were expected to create. He was soon persuaded, however, that they were more an impediment to him surviving rather than a benefit:

"I am saddled with a shovel down my back and an enormous coil of wire over my shoulder. Alex – the tallest man in the regiment – is my consoling companion over the front line. A big 5.9 high explosive greets us as we emerge over the top. Alex and I walk right into it. When we recover we decide that spades and wire won't be needed. We can move better without this donkey load. The Hun barrage is concentrated on our front line and the bullets fall all round like a hail storm. We set forward and into the Hun line and feel quite safe when we have clay walls to cover us, even in enemy territory."

The Sunken Road, photographed by the 14th Rifles veterans in 1927, was dubbed the Bloody Road after the battle because it is said to have flowed red with all the blood spilled by the dead and wounded lying out in No-Man's-Land. *(Courtesy of the Somme Museum)*

For Berry "hell broke loose" from the moment he pushed off amid the storm of shells and machine-gun bullets: "Before we had cleared the wood most of my platoon were killed or wounded. The air seemed to be filled with mighty rushing noise, as indeed it was, and the noise of explosions were like gigantic doors being slammed." Making it into the enemy line, he saw something which, years later, was still tickling his sense of humour. "He was a big black bearded fellow of the 99th Bavarian Regiment," he wrote about a German prisoner who had been sent towards the British lines. "I laughed because he had no trousers on and the tail of his white shirt was sticking out below his tunic."

James Fitzsimons had spent the best part of the week leading up to the attack in Thiepval Wood after being detailed along with Rifleman Harkness to stand guard over the battalion's stores of picks, shovels, sandbags and quicklime. He had all but become immune to the tear gas and acted as a guide for working parties left blinded by the chemical. He rejoined the YCVs on their arrival in the wood and went over the top with them despite having orders to report to a casualty clearing station on the down slope by the river that had hitherto escaped being shelled. "Thank goodness I did not go as the morning of the attack they wiped it out," he remembered. His platoon followed the 10th Inniskillings so closely that they avoided the worst of the bombardment, falling into the German lines before most of the enemy had had time to emerge from their dugouts.

As the first German prisoners were scuttling along Elgin Avenue, a runner arrived at battalion headquarters with a message from Company Sergeant Major Lowry[5] of C Company reporting he had reached the Sunken Road, with the corpses piled high there. It was followed by a report from Captain Willis that D Company was consolidating in front of the German B line.

Mullin had crossed over No-Man's-Land at Captain Hyndman's side and was relieved to arrive in the German front trench, where there was already confusion. He heard the

This photograph is believed to have been taken by George Hackney on the morning of 1 July 1916 from the captured German lines. In the foreground can be seen Ulster troops, most likely men of the 14th Rifles, dug in to makeshift defensive positions while on the horizon German prisoners, holding up their hands, are being marshalled together to be taken back across No-Man's-Land. *(Photograph © National Museums Northern Ireland, Collection Ulster Museum, BELUM.Y15555)*

B Company captain order the arrest of a corporal, though he gave no reason for the action. In any event, no one moved to obey him and instead Hyndman sought cover in a nearby shell hole. Scribbling out a message, he tore out the page and handed it to Mullin to take to the battalion headquarters:

> "I took his message and went off as fast as I could and never stopped until I reached our battalion HQ in Elgin Avenue, which was the long communication trench from our front line to the rear… I handed Captain Hyndman's message to the Adjutant. On my way back to HQ I had no time to consider the risk involved. I could hear the machine-gun bullets passing high above my head. The high trajectory undoubtedly saved my life. All around were clouds of black smoke from the enemy shells."

An enemy heavy shell struck the 14th Rifles' headquarters: "Direct hit on our dugout – still alive!" noted a relieved Mulholland. By now it was evident that the 32nd Division, attacking Thiepval village to the right of the Ulster Division, had been beaten back despite repeated attempts to advance. Its failure left the German gunners free to turn their weapons on the flanks of the Ulstermen. Hope, however, was still finding the going comparatively easy:

> "There is little opposition at this point so what is left of our company operates up the line and we find many Huns who are afraid to come out of their deep dugouts. One big dugout houses many of the enemy but they won't come up. They fire a shot up the stairs and down goes a mortar shell which tells its own tale. We get well into the fray and I get curious. The excitement takes me on the prowl on my own. I seem to be alone somewhere, I take a look over the top and to my surprise I see a Hun officer standing on the parapet some distance away."

By 10.30 am Major Mulholland was ordering up more ammunition from the Gordon Castle dump and had filed a request for reinforcements, though they did not arrive until late afternoon. In the meantime, Lieutenant Lack, the "cheeriest and best of the intelligence officers" arrived back in the British lines with 25 enemy prisoners, while word arrived of the death of Lieutenant Wedgwood who, according to Mulholland, was "only a child but had the heart of a lion". Padre Canon King, quoting his source as a wounded officer, claimed the teenager was killed by a German whose life he had spared: "He was in the German trenches and was taking prisoners in the dugouts. He and his party had bombs with them, and the Germans were at their mercy. He came to a dugout where there were some 20 Germans. He might have killed these, but, instead, offered them their lives if they would come out and surrender. They did so, and all came out. He turned his back for a moment, and one of them treacherously shot him dead."[6]

Shortly after 10.30 am the Germans were hitting the front of the wood so hard that trees were being felled and splinters flying in all directions. The enemy artillery and trench mortars were also blasting their former lines in the hope of pushing the Ulstermen out. Major Mulholland could hear the 5.9 inch shells landing before he received the message from C Company, who were on the receiving end, reporting their predicament at noon. Some 45 minutes later the same company appealed for reinforcements.

Rifleman James McRoberts, part of the 'permanent patrol,' spent most of the early hours of 1 July in the comparative safety of an old mineshaft close to the battalion headquarters, the men laughing and singing while some over-indulged in the rum ration. He did have a lucky escape, though, when several high explosive shells landed nearby as he was taking a message along Elgin Avenue, the heat scorching his face. As the conflicting reports began trickling back it was decided to call the scouts into action under Lieutenant Lack to get a better picture of the situation:

"We made our way slowly up to the front line, meeting streams of wounded and tramping over many dead bodies both of our own men and the enemy. After a mad race across the open, I dropped into a shell hole to get my wind and see where I was. Lifting my head over the edge, I could discern no one alive. There were lots of dead about while the shrapnel was sweeping the ground and bursting into a thousand, angry, hissing, flying pieces. The machine guns were ever tinkling… Another rush and another friendly shell hole, again a rush and I was through the German wire, there was little but the posts left, and into the German first line. I found I had arrived, not among my own fellows, but among a mixed lot of the 108th Brigade. The Germans were being bombed out of their dugouts and certain trenches where they had taken refuge. They were wonderfully game, considering what they must have come through, and caused a lot of casualties among our men."

McRoberts made his way to his right to make contact with his own battalion, finding elements in the German second, or B, line:

"There seemed to be nobody who had any authority and groups of men were sitting in clusters everywhere, doing nothing at about 12 noon. I now met Jack Armstrong who had found a German officer's valise, full of maps and the both of us determined to go back with it and report ourselves to Headquarters. The way we went was quite short this time and I reached our trenches safely. I was going down Elgin Avenue when a whiz-bang burst over my head. I felt a burning sensation on the left side of my neck and saw the red blood pouring down my tunic in a gushing flow. I took out my first-aid bandage from a special pocket in my tunic, and Jack Armstrong tied it round my neck."

He made his way to the rear for further treatment. By 1.00 pm an enemy counter-attack on the C line appeared imminent with a mixed force holding it despite flank fire from Thiepval. The danger further increased around 2.00 pm when a train was spotted arriving at Grandcourt full of German reinforcements. Lieutenant Hogg reported back to headquarters that he was digging a line between C and D lines with all available men but was expecting to be attacked at any moment and in desperate need of additional forces.

Fitzsimons had been among a group of men who dug in between the German second and third lines after coming under increasing artillery and machine-gun fire. They were joined by Inniskillings who were determined to press on regardless: "They yelled 'we can go any place the Chocolate Soldiers can.'" A Lewis gun team took up position in the "funk hole" dug by Fitzsimons so he moved another 150 yards further along to his left and dug in again but was growing increasingly concerned about their predicament and decided to take matters into his own hands. "Our artillery had ceased to fire and we could see the Germans in increasing numbers gathering in front of us. I made my way to battalion HQ from shell hole to shell hole and after refusing a drink from the Colonel, demanded he produce a map and get artillery fire where it was needed," he recalled. Lance Corporal Chas B McComb became a casualty close to the German third line, being struck in the neck by a bullet but was fortunate to come across one of the outstanding heroes of the day, Second Lieutenant Reginald Lack. According to Sergeant Major Carson, who was later to be commissioned, Lack was destined to either win the Victoria Cross on 1 July or die in the attempt. In the event it was the latter. Lance Corporal McComb, writing to the officer's parents to express his condolence, told them:

James Fitzsimons survived the battle but his brother Jack was killed in the trenches at Thiepval. *(Courtesy of the Somme Museum)*

> "I was hit when just at the enemy's third line by a bullet which went right through my neck, and I became unconscious for some time, but when I came to again my object was to get my wound stopped bleeding, so I started in a half-stupid way for our own lines. I got almost to our own lines when I met Mr Lack, and when he saw my condition he helped me into our own trenches, got me some water, and took me a long distance down the trench, where he handed me over to a sergeant major telling him to see that I was dressed at once, as I was suffering from haemorrhage from the wound."

Around midday Second Lieutenant Lack was escorting a group of prisoners back to the British lines when he came across his brother-in-law, Second Lieutenant George Radcliffe,[7] who had been badly wounded. Pushing the earth up round him as a shield against the machine-gun fire sweeping the battlefield, he continued across No-Man's-Land to deposit

Matthew Wright, killed attempting to rescue a wounded officer, has no known grave. A 'headstone' placed by his family in Thiepval Wood is now held In the Ulster Tower for safekeeping. *(Courtesy of Lester Morrow)*

Captain Samuel Willis, pictured here in his YCV uniform, was among those killed on the first day at the Battle of the Somme. *(Belfast Telegraph)*

his prisoners and seek help to mount a rescue. Accompanied by Second Lieutenant Matthew Wright[8] and four men with a stretcher, he returned to the German lines.

Within minutes, however, they too had become casualties. Wright, along with some of the men, are believed to have been killed when a trench mortar exploded close by, while Lack was struck in the spine by a bullet, a wound that most probably would have left him paralysed had he survived. Scouts Corporal Brian Boyd and Sergeant Jack Armstrong carried Lack back to their own lines using the stretcher that had been taken out for Radcliffe. Though he lingered on for 17 days, he died of his wounds as he was carried down the gangplank from the hospital ship at Dover.[9]

Throughout most of the day Captain Samuel Willis,[10] of D Company, accompanied by Lieutenant Monard, had held on to the ground won but by 4.00 pm were coming under increasing pressure. Major Mulholland promised reinforcements as soon as they arrived and instructed him to "hold on for all he was worth. He did this right gallantly, ably supported by his second in command Lt Monard, another very tenacious officer". It wasn't until two hours later, however, and only by chance, that the Major found the extra troops promised. "Met a company of a territorial battalion going down along the top of Elgin Avenue. On enquiries being made I found they were my long lost and much sought after reinforcements going the wrong way. The boy in command did not know in what direction he was to go so I put him right and gave him orders that he was to reinforce the remnants of the 109th Brigade in B 7 C lines and to hang on to the S end of Fort Schwaben at all costs."

Hope, meanwhile, was considering "if it wouldn't be better to be captured in a crowd" when he came across Lieutenant Gracey of A Company, who asked him to deliver a message to headquarters. "Before he can say you go, I'm gone, but not with his message. I don't want to face that barrage again. I wheel round the Hun trenches and link up with an assortment of Inniskillings and Rifles. We appear to be in a very advanced position and are warned to get ready to meet a counter attack," he remembered. He saw the Germans gathering in the distance then disappearing into the trenches:

"The attack is surely coming but exactly where or when we are going to meet it we can't tell as the Hun disappears into cover of his trenches away in front.

There is nothing doing so we wait developments. He is not coming over the open. He is going to try picking us off, one by one, at a distance. A 9th Inniskilling lying at the top has got a bullet through his steel hat. He rolls over into the trenches at my feet. He is an awful sight. His brain is oozing out of the side of his head, and he is calling for his pal. An occasional cry of 'Billy Gray, Billy Gray, will you not come to me'. In a short time all is quiet, he is dead. He's the servant to an officer who is lying

in the trench with a fractured thigh, and won't let anyone touch him, and is bleeding badly. They die together."

Berry also found himself well in advance of the British line, close to the 4th German trench line, from which he could see the village of St Pierre-Divion and German field batteries firing over open sights. Using grenades, his group forced the enemy out of the trench immediately facing them. "I was so excited that I forget to pull the safety pin out of my first bomb, but I had plenty and they went off OK," he recalled. "Our bombing section were now five hands. I had a look round and it appeared to me as if I had advanced too far." The group held on until late into the evening when, virtually surrounded and in danger of being taken prisoner, they withdrew.

Mullin had returned to the spot where he had last saw Captain Hyndman[11] but found the trenches round about empty. He was now isolated and alone, without a map or compass, but was much happier that way. Taking shelter in a shell hole he suddenly realised he would have to move again as the Germans were methodically shelling the area. "Now I experienced the disadvantage of a runner's job. I wished that I could find a senior officer as I had a good idea that he would have messages to send back to our CO. I was determined to keep my status as a runner, the red bands on the sleeves of my tunic were there for that purpose." After exploring the German front line, Mullin worked his way forward until he met up with a mixed group of Inniskillings and Rifles in the enemy B line. "There was much running about and excitement," he noted. "The German reserves were seen coming up some distance away and then they disappeared into a communication trench. Our position is exposed and untenable; a NCO of the 10th Inniskillings says 'We better move back while we can'. It is of course every man for himself. Many were left and would be taken prisoners if alive. It is difficult getting through barb-wire entanglement and across deep trenches. We do all that men can do." Together with his chum Bob Douglas, Mullin worked his way back to his own lines.

Rifleman John Boyd had made good progress across the German lines, though the flank fire caused huge casualties as his detachment made its way from the second German line to the third:

> "We pushed on to the fourth trench; time was getting on and we were very hungry. I remember asking our corporal the time (he was the only one with a watch); he said it was 7.30 pm and we would be getting relieved soon (some hope!). I got hit in the left arm by a machine gun bullet shortly after that, about 8.00 pm. The corporal bandaged my arm and told me to go back to the third trench. I got back safely, but was told to go further back as they were full up with stretcher cases. That meant I had to cross 'No-Man's-Land' three times to get to my own lines; all the communication lines were destroyed and I had to make a dash out in the open."

Along the way he came across a friend who was wounded in the thigh and helped him back to the lines, with his mate being wounded a second time as they crossed No-Man's-Land. Boyd eventually reached the safety of an aid station where a Canadian nurse attended to him, though not before she made him throw a grenade he had still in his pocket into a nearby river. "I returned to a cup of tea and a round of bread and jam; absolutely the best meal I have ever eaten, especially after months of hard biscuits and bully beef."

By now it was becoming evident that German pressure was beginning to tell, with the makeshift lines dug by the division giving way. Elgin Avenue was full of men who had been forced to withdraw and there arose the real possibility that the Germans might not only take back their own lines but advance into Thiepval Wood. The men of the 14th Rifles, along with all stragglers that could be rounded up, were ordered to form the centre of a line of defence at Whitchurch Street under the command of the young inexperienced officers who had just joined the battalion days before. To their left was the remnant of the 10th Inniskillings, with the 9th Skins on the right. With nightfall the tension increased. "Such a night of tumult in which the telephone took a prominent part," noted Major Mulholland.

Dusk found Hope with a mixed group of men, many of whom had become casualties. He decided to try his luck elsewhere and began working his way along the trench until, by accident, he came across his own company. "I have walked right into where the counter attack is coming. The Hun heavies have registered on our trench and we get an awful drenching of 5.9 shrapnel – big black coal boxes burst about 25 feet above us. High velocity shells plug the earth all round. We are in a death trap. A man is pushed up onto the parapet to spot events and rolls back into the trench again. He is absolutely peppered with shrapnel." As midnight approached Hope moved another 50 yards down the line to escape the worst of the shelling and in doing so escaped a German raid on the trenches he had just vacated:

"The situation is a peculiar one. I miss the Hun attackers by a hair's breath. They jump into the trench from both sides, overwhelming numbers take a toll of the party but a few escape. At this moment the officer in command of the Inniskillings, Major Peacock, appears. He weighs up the position and says: 'Boys we better go.' Peacock dives through a gap in the trench and I dive after him. I run a few yards –

German prisoners pass along a communication trench at the Somme, many just pleased to escape the constant bombardment they had been subjected to for more than a week prior to the Ulster Division going over the top. *(Courtesy of Lester Morrow)*

run right bang into a huge barb wire entanglement. When I extricate myself, I look round and am – well I don't know where I am. The Hun is in the trenches some yards away and up goes a night light. I flop and observe the ground. A red signal light is lying out in front of another trench. I am in a predicament. If the Hun is in the trench I am to cross I'm for it. I move cautiously and decide to take a run and jump over the next line and over I go. I don't wait for a challenge but there is nobody there as far as I can see. Between the next lines I run across a party who are lying in a huge crater."

The group was still under the command of an officer, who ordered a withdrawal to what Hope assumed was the second German line. Along with other men, he is sent to an outpost under the command of a sergeant who, after a while, leaves them to check the situation with the main party. When he failed to return, Hope went looking for him only to discover that he and the other men had been abandoned. "I advise the post of this breach of faith and we decide to slope too. We guess our position and run down the hill as fast as our legs will take us, over the Hun front line; over the famous Sunken Road and jump into our front line at the top of Elgin Avenue. Not even a challenge from the sentry on duty." Relieved to have reached the comparative safety of his own line again, Hope joins the other defenders in Whitchurch Street. "The wood is still being crushed to bits by heavy 'Krupp' shells and we finish the night sitting waiting for one of these fellows to drop amongst us and put the finishing touch to what has been an exciting adventure."

Berry, likewise, made it back to his own line unscathed, gathering a few German prisoners along the way. Fitzsimons,[12] after his outburst to the colonel over the lack of artillery support, returned to the German lines only to find all was in confusion with the men around him retreating. Remaining in the enemy first line until dusk, he re-crossed No-Man's-Land again where he assisted at a first-aid post. "Threw one soldier out for kicking up such a row. He only had three or four little wounds in his back as if someone had taken a teaspoon and scooped a few spoonfuls out. We had several very badly wounded to attend to. Then helped organise a line of defence in our second line trenches. Difficult to keep the men awake. Batch of new young bewildered officers arrived to take over (not fair to them)."

At dawn the "few bare poles of trees looking out on the morning, that were once a wood, bore eloquent testimony to the severity of the fire," according to Major Mulholland. He set about organising parties to remove the dead and wounded from the trenches to the rear of the front line. "Our battalion musters only a few in the morning when we assemble in the lower reaches of Thiepval," recalls Hope. "The place is reeking with tear gas and Jack Wilson and I move down into the valley. We light a fire and make tea. I have a tin of Pilchards and we have 'fish' for breakfast. The 49th Division are trickling through. They were expected yesterday to hold what we took and we wonder why they are 18 hours late.

The once fine Thiepval Wood and surrounding area was left devastated by the constant bombardments throughout the summer and early autumn of 1916. This photograph, from a collection used by Jim Maultsaid in lantern slide form to illustrate a talk he liked to give on his war experiences, shows a trench with a sandbag barrier constructed across its width. Such defences were thrown up in captured trenches to halt counter-attacks. (Photograph © National Museums Northern Ireland, Collection Ulster Museum, BELUM. Y26402.96)

Expect it is all in keeping with the bungling which is going on. One of their companies halts beside us. An officer asks where he can get water to wash his feet. He is in a state of exhaustion and must be blind as there is a valley and a swamp beside him." Around noon the battalion, amounting to just 120 men and only two of the original officers who went into battle – Monard and Hogg,[13] both slightly wounded but soldiering on – moved into their former assembly trenches as a reserve.

Later that day they were finally withdrawn to Martinsart Wood, where the men spent a restless night amid the constantly firing guns. "We left the line at dawn in penny numbers, passed through Aveluy Wood," remembered Berry.

> "The dead seemed to be piled up here. I met Edgar Byrne of 9 Platoon and I was glad to see him. We walked to Martinsart. He had some dry tea in his pocket and then we 'scrounged' for something to eat. We lit a fire and made tea and forgot yesterday. We were so tired that we slept by the side of a ruined house all day, and were rudely awakened by a sergeant shouting 'All 36 Division parade at once. I was swearing then, as I thought that we had to go into action again, but were relieved when we heard a rumour that we were going out to rest and refit."

Mullin had spent a very uncomfortable night back in the original British front line in Thiepval Wood with no food or sleep and the constant rumours that the remnants of the division along with the now present reinforcements were to launch a fresh attack. When the order came through for the YCVs to withdraw he made his way to Martinsart, where he found field post-cards were being distributed so the men could let their families at home know they were alive. "A gleam of hope now penetrates the gloom," he noted. "I am disappointed but my conscience is clear. I have no regrets concerning my own conduct. I get a welcome cup of tea from the Royal Army Medical Corps." The survivors' slow trickle back to safety was watched by Hope who, believing the gathering of the men in the assembly trenches was in preparation of another attack, had crossed the swamp with Wilson into Aveluy Wood where he unrolled his ground sheet and slept. "Our exhausted nerves are in better trim when we waken late in the evening and go down to the roadway where we see 'what is left of them' crawling in the direction of Martinsart where the battalion is to be sorted out," he recorded.

> "The Martinsart roll call is a wonderful sight. The remnants are trickling into camp. They are arriving, sometimes one, sometimes two or three, and they all get a great cheer, a cheer which brings new life to them. But it is a remnant which returns. Where is Shannon,[14] where is Cousins, where is the wee Jew or Scotty Wilson, where are a host of others – they are missing from the Roll Call. The company is but a shadow, where are the officers, Slacke, Gracey, Carson, Renwick, Robb.[15] Gone! Gone to the place where there is no chin wagging, no kit inspections, no dirty rifles, no unshaven chins."

Lance Corporal William A Greer, writing home to his father at Annavale, Stranmillis Road, Belfast, on 3 July tried to be positive:

"Our Division has made a name for itself these past few days. We knew that something big was coming off soon, and on the 1st July we got the order to attack, and take, if possible, four lines of German trenches opposite the line we had been holding since we came out. The German lines were bombarded for almost a week before we went over the parapet. On 1st July the boys were all very cool about matters, but we had to face a very heavy fire from machine guns, though our artillery had accounted for a big lot of them in the bombardment. We reached the first line of the trenches alright and pushed on to the second and third without meeting very much resistance, as any Germans who survived the preliminary bombardment were almost demoralised by the shell fire. We held on to the four lines of trenches until nightfall, we had to temporarily fall back to our own lines owing to our right and left flanks not being able to push forward with our Division at the time. However, they were regained later, and as I write, we still hold them – not our Division, of course, but another relieving one. The bombardment just before we attacked was terrible. It developed in intensity an hour before the infantry started operations, and how any living being in the German lines could survive it is a mystery. Certainly, they were very glad to be taken as prisoners, and were all very much shaken. We took a big lot of prisoners during the day – some of them big, strong-looking chaps, but a good lot of them young and middle-aged. We ourselves, unfortunately, lost fairly heavily, as you will see for yourself later on. It was only Providence, I think, pulled me through; I had several narrow shaves. My steel helmet saved my life."

The Ulster Division as a whole had suffered 5,500 casualties – dead, wounded and missing – with almost 90 Young Citizens alone killed on 1 July (see Appendix 7). The Battle of the Somme was to drag on until November, with the Schwaben Redoubt, held briefly by the Ulster Division on 1 July, not finally taken until the end of September. For the Young Citizens, however, the battle was over.

Sergeant John Reid Moore was among those killed at the Somme on 1 July 1916. Initially buried in one of the smaller graveyards dotted across the battlefield, his remains were later interred at Connaught Cemetery, close to the Ulster Tower. *(Author)*

Chapter 13

PICKING UP THE PIECES

Of all the inhuman regulations the worst was that all men must wear their equipment, at all times, in the trenches. There was no necessity for such a command; I never saw a German in the front line with his equipment on and I had seen dozens of them.

Rifleman James McRoberts

SHORTLY AFTER DARK, ON the evening of 4 July 1916, medical officer Lieutenant Noel John Hay Gavin slipped over the parapet of the front line trench in Thiepval Wood and into the affections of the men. Accompanied by a small party of volunteers, he made his way from shell hole to shell hole, and through the gaps in the barbed wire to the Sunken Road, now dubbed Bloody Road, in search of survivors. There he found dozens upon dozens of the dead and dying. After treating wounds under the noses of the enemy, the group managed to bring a dozen men back to the safety of their own lines. "He reports that the Sunken Road is full of corpses and that the Wood has been knocked to pieces," noted the *War Diary*. The doctor, however, who had only arrived with the battalion a short time before, had shown his mettle and earned the admiration of fellow officers and men alike. The day previous, what remained of the YCVs had moved out of Martinsart Wood, where the firing of the heavy guns had made sleep virtually impossible, back to nearby Hédauville, the advance troops arriving about 5.00 pm. The next day, the battalion paraded with the rest of the 109th Brigade to be addressed by General Oliver Nugent, commanding the 36th (Ulster) Division, who famously told them that, in his opinion, nothing finer had been done in the war to date:

> "The leading of the company officers, the discipline and courage shown by all ranks of the Division will stand out in the future history of the war as an example of what good troops, well led, are capable of accomplishing. None but troops of the best quality could have faced the fire which was brought to bear on them, and the losses suffered during the advance."

The battalion commander, Lieutenant Colonel Bowen, added his own words of praise:

> "The Commanding Officer wishes to place in everlasting record his high appreciation of all ranks of the battalion during the great attack on 1st July 1916. The advance,

the dash and manner in which the battalion closed with the enemy has never been surpassed and has added fresh lustre to the Army of Ulster and the old and distinguished regiment to which the battalion belongs. The Commanding Officer mourns the loss of so many of his gallant comrades, who made the greatest sacrifice of all and laid down their lives for their King and Country."

The newspapers back home were full of reports of the fighting, with the war correspondents of the nationals warm in their praise for the Ulster troops. Sir Edward Carson, the unionist leader, penned his own words of support in the knowledge that the losses had been severe and that black-edged telegrams were arriving at thousands of homes throughout the province:

"I desire to express on my own behalf, and that of my colleagues from Ulster, the pride and admiration with which we have learnt of the unparalleled acts of heroism and bravery which were carried out by the Ulster Division in the great offensive movement on the 1st of July. From all accounts that we have received, they have made the supreme sacrifice for the Empire of which they were as proud with a courage, coolness, and determination, in the face of the most trying difficulties, which have upheld the greatest traditions of the British Army."

"Everyone was pleased," noted the *War Diary* of the praise heaped upon the battalion, but they were undoubtedly even happier to receive orders shortly before noon on 5 July to move further away from the front, to billets at Herrissart with the divisional headquarters at Rubempré. The Rev John Wright,[1] who had been appointed chaplain to the battalion, joined them there. It was a true baptism of fire for him, though he "gave a good address" at his service on 9 July, according to Mulholland.

The few days spent here were anxious ones as the battalion, like the rest of the division, was on notice to move back to the trenches at an hour's notice. In such circumstances, rumours abounded about the progress of the battle, most of them dark, and it was evident relief that greeted the news that the battalion was to be moved north to the St Omer sector. The journey was completed by stages – to Candas on July 10, through Fienvillers, Domleber to Conteville the following day, where they then entrained, arriving at Berguette shortly after 7.00 pm from where they faced a 15 km slog to Blaringhem, which was reached in the early hours of 12 July. After a night spent in farmhouses, the men paraded again, and set off for Serques. Despite everything they had been through, the significance of the date was not lost on the Orangemen within the battalion. That evening they gathered to hold a meeting of the Young Citizens LOL 871 with Sergeant Thomas Murphy, the Worshipful Master, presiding. Among those in attendance were Lieutenant Thomas Mayes, Quartermaster Sergeant Kenning and Sergeant Foy. A resolution, later published in the Belfast newspapers, called on those at home to volunteer for service while expressing regret at the losses sustained. It read:

"That this meeting of brethren representing the Young Citizens LOL 871 do hereby reaffirm their loyalty to the Crown and Constitution of Great Britain and Ireland,

The Rev John Wright had the difficult task of holding the first drumhead service attended by the 14th Rifles after coming out of the trenches following the Battle of the Somme. *(Belfast Telegraph)*

being Protestant, and calls on all loyal men of Ulster who have not joined the colours to come forward and replenish the ranks of the Ulster Division in order that the Division may remain truly representative, and at the same time help to prosecute the war with vigour and bring it to a victorious termination. The brethren also deplore the heavy losses sustained by the Ulster Division on the date of the 1st July, 1916, and do hereby convey their deepest sympathy to the relatives of their gallant comrades who fell on the field of battle."

RECRUITING SERGEANT (to religious youth): "Young man, you'd look well in khaki."
RELIGIOUS YOUTH: "Sir, I am in the Army of the Lord!"
SERGEANT: "Well, you're a d—— long way off t' barracks."

As the war went on, the men at the front became less forgiving of those at home who refused to sign up, as this cartoon from *The Incinerator* indicates. *(Courtesy of the Somme Museum)*

On 13 July the battalion arrived at Boisdinghem, "a very nice little village" according to the *War Diary*, where they were to spend the next week reorganising, training and effectively recovering from the ordeal of their first major battle. The division was on the move again on 21 July, with the 14th Rifles leading the way through Moulle to Bollezeele, where they spent the night, and then it was on to Romarin, on the France/Belgium border in a fleet of motorbuses. After a quick tea in the transport field, the boys marched up to Red Lodge, "a one-time porters lodge" according to Berry, as support for the 9th Royal Irish Fusiliers and 12th Royal Irish Rifles. "It is marvellous," reported the *War Diary* of the arrival at another "filthy" camp, "after all the sanitation orders issued, some units seem to do as they like." The men were set about cleaning up yet again.

There was also time to reflect on their battle losses, with everyone having lost close comrades. Adjutant Alan Mulholland, writing to the family of fellow officer Matthew Wright at the end of July 1916, felt the change in the battalion. "I feel the loss of all my friends terribly as we were all a happy family and things will never be the same again, they are not producing officers like what we had and never will again." On 28 July, as the men prepared to march for the line, a 12-inch gun close to battalion headquarters exploded, killing four and wounding several more, including two YCVs. "A piece six feet long and weighing a ton was hurled 150 yards through the roof of a house," recorded the *War Diary*. Berry, though a fair distance away, was lucky to escape injury. He recorded:

"One afternoon about 2.00 pm we heard a most awful explosion and a few seconds later the wall of the Red Lodge caved in. We were all upstairs in the loft at this time, so we were got down to ground level in a hurry. One of our heavy guns had burst owing to a premature shell fuse. It killed most of the gun crew and the piece which struck our billet weighed about half-a-ton. The gun emplacement was 400 yards from our billet, so the explosion couldn't be described. Two of our chaps got wounded – Holmes and McAteer. It was fortunate that it struck the wall a glancing blow or there would have been some killed."

At the time the 109th Brigade was in the process of relieving another division of a stretch of the front running from Neuve Eglise to the Warneton Road, known as Anton's Farm to Boyle's Farm on the Wulverghem–Messines road. Although only 3,000 yards as the crow flies, there was more than 2½ miles of trench to be manned. The handover at Ploegsteert continued as planned, with the 14th Rifles taking over a stretch of trench opposite Messines. It was to prove a very quiet spell, with mosquitoes, brought out by the exceptionally hot weather, and visits by senior officers, including General Shuter and General Nugent in successive days, all the men had to trouble them. There was a bit of excitement when an artillery GS Wagon took a wrong turn, heading for the enemy line. It was spotted by friend and foe alike and quickly turned round and into cover, though that didn't stop the Germans shelling the lines in search of it. It was removed early next morning. Berry had a lucky escape while on a working party fixing 'A frames' – structures that lifted the trench duckboards off the ground, allowing for a drainage ditch underneath – when they were spotted by a German Minenwerfer crew. "We could hear the 'pop' of the gun and a few seconds later down it came, but fell into a communication trench a few yards from us. The explosion was terrific and we were drenched in mud and filth. He didn't fire anymore – perhaps they thought they had bagged us."

The Battle of the Somme had taken a heavy toll of the battalion scouts, which were made up of an officer, two NCOs and two men from each company. They had lost their officer, Mr Lack, who was replaced by Second Lieutenant Robert Victor Drought who, with the help of Sergeant Jack Armstrong and Corporal Brian Boyd, set about training replacements. One of these was Mullin, who was delighted to be asked to join what he saw as an elite unit within the battalion. At midnight on 30 July, carrying a bucket of grenades and rolls of white tape to lay a path to lead the party back to safety, he climbed out of his own trench behind Captain James McKee to take part in his first raid. It turned out to be a "tame affair", however, as the gas released from the 14th's lines as a prelude blew harmlessly away, leaving McKee no option but to turn back without a shot being fired.

Relieved on 3 August by the 10th Inniskillings, the battalion moved into new billets at La Grande Munque Farm, where the process of integrating the first of the new replacements that had arrived in recent days began in earnest. There was another casualty sustained on the night of 5–6 August when Private Joseph Sloan, of B Company, was killed while with a working party. Born in Lisburn, the 25-year-old lived with his mother at Malone Avenue in Belfast.

The men lived with the constant threat of gas attack and an incident on 8 August heightened concerns further. A "large paper balloon coming from a south-easterly direction alighted in the field at the back of La Grande Munque Farm. Evidently sent by the enemy to test the wind. All ranks warned to be particularly on the alert for gas attack," recorded the *War Diary*.

The battalion re-entered the same trenches as before on 9 August, with again only visits by Generals Shuter and Nugent and the Brigadier of interest. Away from the line, two YCVs, Corporal Brian Boyd and Rifleman Heasley, were among a group of NCOs and men sent to Bailleul to be reviewed by the King. As the weather broke on 15 August, the 14th Rifles again swapped positions with the 10th Inniskillings, this time going to billets at Red Lodge. "Enemy artillery very active. This billet much 'warmer' than the last, almost

Sport played an important part in the men's lives away from the front line, with football tournaments and boxing bouts regular distractions, as pointed out in this cartoon from *The Incinerator. (Courtesy of the Somme Museum)*

uncomfortably so," noted the *War Diary* on the 16th. A boxing tournament was arranged at short notice on 19 August, with the CO presenting the prizes after two hours of competition. The day before, the battalion had lost another man, Charles King, who "came through the whole business without a scratch" only to be killed accidentally "something the same as Billy Calvert,[2] so that is really hard lines on his people," according to Company Quartermaster Sergeant William Moore.

Back home, a recruiting party, consisting of an officer and three men from each of the Ulster Division's 13 battalions, had arrived in Belfast on 10 August. Adjutant Captain Mulholland led the YCV group, which included Sergeant Jack Armstrong and Lance Corporal Tommy Crothers, both members of the battalion scouts. General Nugent had set the context of their mission in a letter to the Press:

"The officers and men were all through the furious fighting on the 1st–2nd July, and took part in the original attack, in which the Ulster Division made such a name for itself. Naturally, we are all anxious to fill up the gaps with Ulstermen, especially after we have seen how they can fight. It would be a pity for the Division now to have to make up its numbers from English or Scotch recruits."

Nonetheless, the group's arrival was less than auspicious. A letter, signed "Disgusted," appeared in the *Belfast News Letter*:

"I saw a small company of war-worn soldiers marching through Donegall Place today and on asking who they were I was surprised to hear that they were just back from the trenches to start a recruiting campaign for the Ulster Division. They were followed by a small crowd of girls and boys, who were doing their best to raise a cheer, but with small success. The authorities did not think it worthwhile to send a band to meet them, and this small party of gallant men, representing the thousands of heroes who gave their lives for their country on the glorious 1st of July, marched through our city, attracting as little attention as a few recruits marching to barracks. Had the citizens known, they would have turned out in their thousands, and the flags would have been floating from all the business and private homes."

The party had in fact marched to Victoria Barracks, where they were given a meal before being allowed home on leave until the following Monday. In a statement issuing the times and places of the recruiting party's talks, was an assurance that anyone joining the YCVs was guaranteed to be retained in the battalion. The first Belfast meeting was held outside the City Hall at 1.30 pm on Wednesday 16 August, with a second at Carlisle Circus at 8.00 pm. Speaking at the latter, Captain Mulholland referred back to the formation of the Young Citizen Volunteers "to teach young men what their duty was to their country, and that end was attained with most satisfactory success," reported the *Belfast News Letter* .

"At the outbreak of the war the Young Citizen Volunteers offered their services to the Government and were refused, but eventually the Government found that it could not do without them. (Applause) So they were taken into the army, and since joining they had proved themselves an excellent fighting force. There were no finer troops than those of the Ulster Division, and no finer men in it than the Young Citizen Volunteers (applause). He had come to ask the people of Belfast to fill up the gaps made in that battalion, and he was sure he would not be disappointed."

Major Gunning and Sergeant Major Elphick,[3] both members of the battalion but then based at home, spoke at some of the subsequent recruiting meetings, with the former urging the women of Ulster to shun any man not in uniform.

On 17 August an advertisement was published in the same newspaper that made plain the difficulties the 14th Rifles were facing on account of the shortage of recruits from home. Appealing directly to the members of the original YCVs who had not enlisted, it stated:

"Your Comrades in the Trenches are calling to YOU. They want your HELP to uphold the great name they have made for YOU. Each one of them is doing TWO MEN'S WORK, and want you to go out and do YOUR share too. If you join now you will be with your Pals at Home and go out to your Pals Abroad. Join at once and prevent the YCVs being filled with DERBY Recruits. The YOUNG CITIZENS from the Trenches will BE AT ALL MEETINGS."[4]

In contrast to their arrival, the recruiting party got a warm send off when it marched from Victoria Barracks to the station to catch a train to Dublin on the afternoon of Thursday 24 August. Women in the black of mourning were among the crowds. William Moore, in a letter home to his parents in which he attempted to offer words of condolences for the loss of his brother John on 1 July, gives an indication of the pressures the recruiting party were under from distraught families back home. The note, dated 19 August, said:

The Belfast Technical College was a ripe recruiting ground for the army in general and particularly the 14th (Young Citizen Volunteers) Royal Irish Rifles. Among the staff members who joined the YCVs were (l–r) Corporal Edward Courtney, Lance Corporal CC Menary and Lance Corporal F Ballantine. *(Courtesy of the Belfast Met)*

William Moore, in his letters and postcards back home, attempted to console his family on the loss of his brother John by pointing out the tragedy of those whose loved ones were 'missing' yet known to be dead. (*Author*)

"I am sure every other one you meet in Belfast is in mourning. They could hardly miss. Some of the cases are very sad. A father of a sergeant pal of mine met the recruiting party on arrival at Belfast to enquire about or get some little ray of hope about his son who is reported missing but who I know has been killed and there are dozens of very sad cases, so that poor John is far better where he is than here."

Back in Belgium, the battalion had returned to its old trenches on the evening of 21 August, the first few days passing quietly though the British artillery remained very busy. The enemy's machine guns were very active at night but it was its artillery that, on 26 August, dropped two shells into the British front line with effect, resulting in the deaths of two men and leaving a third suffering from shell shock. Those killed were privates John O'Hara, from a Sligo family, and Samuel Athay.

The 10th Inniskillings relieved the battalion on 28 August, with the men returning to Red Lodge. They awoke next morning to a dismal day, with thunder and lightning accompanied by heavy rain. "Red Lodge a very miserable place in bad weather. The roofs of the huts which are canvas and liberally perforated with bullet and shrapnel holes cannot keep out the incessant downpour," noted the *War Diary*. The men were detailed to the usual working parties, with an unfortunate Berry landing himself in hospital after an accident on the Messines road. "I am carrying sheets of corrugated iron on my head. Fell into a deep trench and injured my back. I was paralysed and couldn't walk. I shouted and a sergeant came up and put me on a trolley which he wheeled down to Hyde Park Corner. Another two pals got a stretcher and carried me into a First Aid Station and stayed here one night."

The next evening the weather improved as a raiding party, led by Captain James McKee, prepared to go up to the front. In preparation, gas shells were fired into the German lines for some 35 minutes but the party found the high explosive shelling carried out earlier in the day in an attempt to cut the German wire had failed. When the patrol detonated wire-cutting Bangalore torpedoes to complete the job the enemy opened up with machine-gun fire and rifle grenades. The party was forced "much to their disgust" to return to their own trenches at 4.10 am, some 90 minutes after climbing over the parapet. Two men, Sergeant John Hunter and Private James Murdock, were reported killed on 1 September and may have been part of the raiding party. Neither has a known grave.

The 14th went back up the line at Ploegsteert on 3 September, relieving the 10th Inniskillings. The rain was relentless and, at times, so was the British shelling, with mortar pits having been constructed in concealed spots and reserves of ammunition now available after the shortages of 1915. "Our artillery practically ceaseless all day and night. Periods of heavy bombardments lasting two hours at a time. Very little reply from the Germans," the *War Diary* recorded. Hope recalls an incidence when the British front lines were emptied ahead of the regular afternoon shelling by the enemy so the artillery could deliver a sharp lesson, firing some 1,200 shells in return without the danger of accidentally inflicting friendly fire casualties: "It is the best medicine he has got for weeks. The dose is increased occasionally and we have at last got the upper hand," he wrote.

Relieved on the 6th, the YCVs returned to Red Lodge for the night, leaving the next day for rest billets in Wakefield huts, half a mile from Dranoutre where even the weather picked up a little for them. On 12 September the battalion was back in the line, relieving the 10th Inniskillings. The trenches on this occasion were in need of repair, though such work was difficult as in places the respective front lines were very close. Hope hated it, describing it variously as a "damnable place", a "death trap" and "the hottest spot outside hell". Snipers were at work throughout the night, with trench mortars also active at times and the machine-gunners on both sides sweeping No-Man's-Land.[5]

Lance Corporal Albert Le Bas, a 23-year-old from Dublin, was killed shortly after arriving in the trenches. Hope again:

> "We are told there is to be no monkeying as 'he' is only twenty eight yards away at the nearest point. Our sentries go in first in front of the famous RE Farm. One of these posts has a secret sentry post just outside the parapet which is reached by a small tunnel through the trench. Le Bas is the first sentry to take over and instead of following the 'hole' through the parapet he takes over the top. He doesn't reach the post. A bullet gets him immediately he goes over the parapet. It's a great send off and a warning to all of us..."[6]

The 9th Rifles and 11th Inniskillings launched raids from the trenches on either side of the YCV's position, with the British artillery keeping up a hectic fire rate. Mullin reported: "The enemy sends over some Minenwerfer, his heaviest trench mortar. Our flying pigs and 60 lb mortars open up in retaliation. The 'Minnies' make a very large crater. There is a chorus when all join in, including stokes and artillery at the rear." Despite the absence of dugouts, with sand bagged shelters providing the only cover, Mullin was determined to show no fear. "Even if one was quivering with fear internally, externally one had to appear quite cool and brave to his comrades," he noted in his diary. On 17 September a German trench mortar shell punctured a gas cylinder in the 14th's trenches, causing a stretch of line to be evacuated for several hours. McRoberts recalled: "The fumes at first were strangely sweet but soon the tears where rolling down my cheeks and I was glad to don my goggles. These were a separate article from the respirator and consisted of a wad of flannel with eyepieces held in position by an elastic band round the head," he wrote, adding:

> "The troops up in the front trenches, however, had a filthy spell. The German trenches were only a matter of forty to eighty yards away and there was hardly any wire between us. We occupied the top of a long ridge and the Germans were on the eastern slope of it, so that our movements above the parapet, both by day and night had to be very carefully conducted as they showed up against the skyline."

The battalion handed the sector over to the 10th Inniskillings again the following day and went into the brigade reserve at Aircraft Farm. "Everything a sea of mud and the maximum of discomfort," reported the *War Diary*. It wasn't the only annoyance to be dealt with. Mullin was among a group of Young Citizens attending a concert in the YMCA hut in Dranoutre on the evening of 22 September when the Germans began dropping shells into the town.

Dranoutre, as James McRoberts scribbled on the front of this postcard home, "isn't Larne" but at least it was away from the firing line. *(Courtesy of the McRoberts family)*

Two exploded close by, with a number of men wounded by shrapnel that tore through the wooden walls, and brought the evening to an early end. "The incident created a scare for a short time, though it was quickly forgotten," he recorded.

The next stint in the trenches brought more of the same, with two further casualties, privates Thomas Newell and James Keery. Mullin was again out in No-Man's-Land on 25 September with Second Lieutenant Drought, Corporal Brian Boyd, Sergeant Tommy Crothers and Private Alex Harrison.

> "Word is passed left and right – patrol going out. We have to wait until this message is passed from post to post. Mr Drought and Brian Boyd lead, the rest follow. We must move without making any noise. When we stop we form like the spokes of a wheel. Crothers faces left, Harrison right and I face the rear. We all have revolvers at the ready in our right hands. Silence is golden. Usually we go as close to the Boche line as we can. There are many craters where some of the enemy may be lurking. We then move parallel with the line for some distance and then return. We are intelligence scouts and we must justify our existence by getting useful information."

Mullin found the men were in a "state of tension" as he spent time in the front line the following day and with good cause: "There is a terrific explosion behind the line and to our right. This is only the beginning. Very soon a strafe develops with trench mortars on both sides creating havoc. We do not remain longer than necessary. An order was received at 9.30 pm to cancel patrol. We are not sorry." There was one unusual incident that acted as light relief for the boys. British aircraft had, when weather permitted, been particularly active in this sector and the boys watched in awe as one set fire with its machine guns to an enemy observation balloon that had broken loose from its moorings. It came down to earth in the YCVs sector, with the officer on board being swiftly taken prisoner. The Royal Flying Corps commander in the area was Captain DO Mulholland, who only discovered his brother, the 14th Battalion's adjutant, Captain Mulholland, was in the area when he visited the scene a few days later.

The YCVs left the line again on 30 September, being relieved early by the 10th Inniskillings as it was to raid the enemy trenches that evening. Back at the huts, where the open ground had been turned into a sea of mud by the wet weather, the officers held a dinner marking the anniversary of the battalion's arrival in France. The following day the celebrations continued with the divisional brass band leading the YCVs on a march to Bailleul, where the men were entertained to tea by the 110th Field Ambulance and attended a performance by the Divisional Follies at the cinema. "The scouts rightly have the place of honour at the head of the battalion," recalled Mullin.

"Practically everyone has enjoyed the experience of marching to the music of a brass band. We had a very enjoyable tea which was provided by our field ambulance. After tea we were given our liberty for two hours. We are free to roam about Bailleul as we please. It is a small town, population 13,570. After sporting ourselves in our own way, the time of departure soon (so it seemed) arrived. The regimental call and the 'fall in' sounded at 7.00 pm and at 7.15 the 'homeward' march began. To crown the day tea was ready for us on arrival."

The battalion relieved the 10th Inniskillings on 6 October. This time, however, their spell in the trenches was to be more eventful. Trench mortar shells rained down on the YCVs on their first full day. One man, Private Samuel Major, was killed, another was badly wounded and five others were left suffering from shell shock. The two front lines were so close that the click of the 'Minnies' being fired could be heard and the mortar watched the whole way. "The force of the impact and awful explosion makes a hole that a horse and cart would be lost in," remembered Hope. "There is another and another – we follow the speck as it rises and hold our breath as the missile comes bang to earth. The morale effect is terrible and we are in nerves. A big strapping fellow is crying. Alex and I are sitting on the top of a mine shaft, we can look no longer. We expect the next one will send us sky high." He added: "A sentry is found dead on his post – there is not a scratch on him. He has been killed by the impact caused by the displacement of air. These things will burst a heart at yards – just the terrible impact of the explosion." McRoberts was also feeling the tension and hated the thought that the Germans might be mining below his feet:

"It was most trying on the nerves holding this front line – it was enough to drive the sentry mad. There was the appearance of the trench, which was merely a sandbag breast-work, and most of the bays showed signs of having newly been blown in or just recently repaired. Everywhere there were great shell holes, smashed in dugouts, broken-up rifles, torn clothes and bits of equipment half buried in the sides of the trench. Then no-one could ever know when the trench mortars or rifle grenades might start, when their awful 'swish-swish' might be heard, calling up all kinds of horrible feelings. One stood there, stuck to his position, and looked at his neighbour who also was apparently stuck there. Then the ground underneath was probably mined and there was always the danger of gas, if the wind blew our way. Oh it was more than flesh, blood and reason could stand, and there was no leave, nor sympathy, only cold and hunger, with an awful end and unknown burial place! Look how many have gone the whole dreadful way, one by one; some day it was almost certain to be my turn, and I did not want to be killed now, once I did not mind particularly."

On 9 October at 1.30 am, gas was released from the 14th Rifles' trenches and almost immediately sparked a response from the Germans, resulting in the deaths of six men, of which two were Royal Engineers operating the cylinders. The YCV casualties[7] were Lance Corporal Samuel Ferris and Privates Fred Greer, William McIvor and James Robinson. Two days later, another man, Private George Paysden, died from his wounds.[8]

George Paysden died from wounds inflicted during a German artillery strike in response to an attempt to release poisonous gas from the 14th Rifles' lines. He is buried at Bailleul Communal Cemetery extension in France. *(Courtesy of Andrew Totten)*

At 2.45 am a patrol of 10 men, led by Second Lieutenant Drought, climbed out into No-Man's-Land to make an assessment of the damage caused by the gas release but were fired upon, causing one injury. On 11 October, Adjutant Captain Mulholland was slightly injured during shelling, but remained on duty. Another man, Private James McDowell Bell, of McTear Street, Belfast, was killed the same day. The battalion returned to Aircraft Farm and brigade reserve the next night, though was to sustain further casualties four days later when Privates Francis Hazlett and John Staples were killed by a sniper while on a working party. Another period in the trenches followed the usual pattern, with one man, Private Alfred Wynne, of Lepper Street, Belfast, killed. Another member of the battalion, Lance Corporal David James Sloan, died of his wounds on 24 October. From Belfast, he was 26-years-old and married.

The battalion was again accommodated in the Wakefield huts after its relief towards the end of October. The frequent rain had ensured the camp remained a quagmire. On the 26th of the month the divisional band made the march to Bailleul seem easier, with the battalion having tea with the 110th Field Ambulance and treated to another Divisional Follies show at the local cinema.

The YCVs once more relieved the 10th Inniskillings on 30 October. A raid was planned with the men selected, including McRoberts, Mullin and their fellow scouts, practising for days beforehand the use of ammonal tubes to destroy barbed wire. The raiding party had remained behind when the rest of the battalion had gone to the front. The next day Brigadier General Shuter wished them luck at a special parade. The men were then granted free time, though they weren't in a mood to enjoy it. "The scouts, myself included, all attend concert in YMCA hut, but our thoughts keep wandering from things present to things future," mused Mullin. "The concert is over. The motor buses are waiting to take us as close as they can go to the front line. We leave the buses and proceed in small groups to the front line. My leader and officer is Mr Drought. Much depends on him." The raid, however, launched in the early hours of 1 November, was to prove to be a disaster. The *War Diary* recorded: "A party of 82 divided into two sections under Second Lieutenant JD O'Brien and Second Lieutenant RV Drought respectively attempted a raid on the Bosche trenches. It was unsuccessful, only Second Lieutenant O'Brien and two men getting into the trenches. Our casualties were one man killed and Second Lieutenant O'Brien and 11 men wounded." In Mullin's opinion, the enemy had been expecting the raid and was fully prepared. He noted:

> "The ammonal tubes are pushed through the wire and exploded. The German front line troops were evidently waiting patiently for their prey. They simply let us have showers of grenades. Discretion is the better part of valour. We fire a green parachute flare from a very pistol, and our artillery answer by a strafe of the Boche trenches as arranged. After some time Mr Drought decided it would be futile and reckless to attempt to proceed further with the raid, so that he ordered a retirement. This was carried out slowly in good order."

For Rifleman McRoberts the raid was to prove to be his last. As he had crawled round a huge shell-hole:

> "There was a flash and shot from the German parapet high up in front. I knew we were suspected and rushed up to the wire – there was no creeping any longer. I pushed in the first tube and the other chap helped me with the second. We drove the first two home through the wire right up against the parapet; we did not require the third. My companion, who was a Royal Engineer, quietly fitted the detonator to the fuse and set off the patent lighter. I scrambled back, about fifteen yards and lay down, fingers in ears and mouth open. There was silence for a few seconds, then a terrific explosion, the flame dazzling our eyes.
>
> Our first party rushed the place but I stood by, for I was to enter the trench with the last or search party. Our chaps, however, their eyes dazed by the bright flame and now in complete darkness again, did not rush exactly at the right place and came up against some wire. Bombs were flung and shots fired from the German parapet.
>
> I saw our chaps kneeling and feeling their way. 'Rush them, rush them!' I shouted. 'Show us the way,' said someone. I ran forward to the German parapet, the others beside me, and I tried to fire my revolver but it wouldn't work, it had fallen in the mud when I was laying the tube. I drew out a bomb, and was just about to pull the pin when there was a great flare of light in my eyes and I must have fallen back, although I do not remember doing so.
>
> I next found myself in one of the shell-holes, up to the neck in water. There were still shots and the bright explosion of bombs. The water was red and there were bits of flesh floating in it. My mouth was full of blood and shattered flesh, the right side of my head seemed a blank and there were painful places in my right leg. I thought of my first aid bandage but realised it was useless and that the only thing for me to do was to hurry back to my trenches while I could. I scrambled out of the hole and turning my back to the firing and bomb explosions, I ran across No-Man's-Land, got through some wire and scrambled into the trench."[9]

James McRoberts was badly wounded during a raid on the German lines and never returned to the fighting. *(Courtesy of the McRoberts family)*

The remaining men, bitterly disappointed, were taken back to Dranoutre in buses. The drama wasn't over for the raiding party, however. After arriving back in their huts they began unloading their revolvers when Private William Roy accidentally discharged a shot. Mullin recorded: "Billy Oliver was shot in the left groin. Fortunately he was sitting at the time. Billy Roy was very sorry. He was unable to explain how it happened. The accident was more trouble for our Scout Officer as the CO had to be informed. Oliver was sent to hospital. Mr Drought had to make a report stating what happened. Billy Oliver recovered. There was no inquiry."[10]

The body of the man killed had been left in a shell hole and that evening a party of 10 men, led by Second Lieutenant Ledlie, attempted to bring it in but came under machine-gun fire, with two men killed – Lance Corporal WF Forbes, from Dunadry, County Antrim, but with a family home at Kingsmere Avenue, Belfast, and Private Matthew Allsopp.

Four nights later, on 5 November, Second Lieutenant Drought, accompanied by three men – Sergeants Armstrong and Yeates and Private HG Camlin – slipped out into No-Man's-Land, returning a short time later with the body of Private Herbert Lynch, the man who had been killed during the 1 November raid.[11]

Later that day the battalion was relieved by the 10th Inniskillings and proceeded to Derry Camp. The Germans shelled their route along Kingsway but there were no casualties and the men were able to enjoy another short 'rest' interrupted by working parties.[12]

A particularly sad death occurred on 11 November when Private William Hughes, a 20-year-old from Ballyholme, Bangor, County Down, was killed in action. At the time his parents, Hugh and Elizabeth, were still trying to come to terms with the news that another son, Bertie, just 18, was missing after the Battle of the Somme. It wasn't until April 1917 that his death was confirmed. The battalion was back in the trenches on 24 November, when its front line and communication trenches were showered with Minenwerfers, causing considerable damage and wounding several soldiers. One man, Private William McMinn, was killed outright, becoming the last fatality suffered by the YCVs in 1916. The bombardment caught out in No-Man's-Land a patrol of Young Citizens, Mullin included. He recorded:

"When we are out about half-an-hour and not far from the Boche wire their artillery and TM start a strafe. Their machine guns join in the medley. The Boche are shelling our front and reserve lines. After a time our artillery are compelled to open up in reply. We remain where we are using available cover. The artillery duel continues – ½ hour, 1 hour. I am expecting an enemy raiding party any moment now. There is no escape, we must remain where we are and take whatever comes. After 1½ hours the artillery fire gradually quieted…"

Despite the strafe, the enemy was generally fairly quiet, prompting the *War Diary* to record "This is the quietest tour the battalion has had since coming to this part of the line." After another spell at Derry Camp, the battalion marched to Red Lodge, where it spent the night of 4 December, relieving the 8th Border Regiment in the trenches at Ploegsteert the following day, with the cold more a problem than the enemy. Relieved by the 9th Royal Irish Fusiliers on the afternoon of 13 December, the YCVs moved into divisional reserve at

Kortepyp Camp. On 16 December, the band of the Royal Engineers played in the camp, the programme reportedly much appreciated by the men.

The YCVs celebrated Christmas on 19 December in anticipation of being back at the front on the 25th. CSM William Moore had made his preparations much earlier. In a letter home, in which he mentioned how "we get the *Sketch*, *Mirror* and *Times* out here, but it's the Belfast papers I like to have a good read at every night," he requested cloths for making plum puddings be sent out in the next parcel. "I want to have four good ones, one for each platoon of say one square yard each. You can't get them here. Let me know what it costs as the Company is paying for them." Their arrival was acknowledged in a later postcard. All the men were given the day off and the 14th Rifles' 'Christmas Day' saw the usual programme of football matches held during the morning, with the Follies entertaining the troops during the afternoon. It was back to reality the following day, however, with the battalion temporarily relieving the 11th Skins at the front to allow them to be inspected by Sir Douglas Haig, and the next day beginning their own stint at the front, replacing the 9th Inniskillings in the line. Christmas Day dawned "miserably dull" and wet with half-hearted firing by both sides. "Just an ordinary morning to us," mused Hope. "The crew of a machine gun post are relieved beside us. Some of them never get out – they are wiped out by a few shells which the Hun has dropped in the line to herald the 25th. A day of peace and goodwill – but not for long."[13]

Even Mullin was feeling sorry for himself. He had spent a couple of days in hospital and had returned to the battalion just in time to be sent back to the front but too late for the early Christmas celebrations and dinner. "I will always remember 1916 as the year I was cheated out of Christmas celebrations," he moaned, though Mr Power, his new scout officer, took some of the sting out of the occasion by distributing chocolates, cigarettes and tobacco to his men.[14]

This Christmas card from the "north front" was sent by CSM Willie Moore to his family in Belfast. *(Author)*

That evening the 14th staged a feint attack as a diversion for a raid by the neighbouring 25th Division but the Germans failed to rise to the bait. The battalion's final stint in the trenches for 1916 concluded around 6.00 pm on 29 December when it was relieved by units of both the 9th and 10th Inniskillings.

Chapter 14

WE ARE MERRY AND BRIGHT

Anon, the boom of heavy guns,
With bursting shells from angry Huns,
The firestep's vigil every night,
The fight we waged against frostbite.
The flooded trench and dugouts too,
All added to that hellish brew.

From a poem by Samuel Harrison, 14th Royal Irish Rifles

A SHOW OF 'HATE', in the form of a concentrated artillery barrage, greeted the arrival of 1917. From the comparative safety of Stafford House, the headquarters staff watched the fireworks with approval: "We greeted the opening of the New Year by briskly shelling the enemy. His retaliation was slight. At 7.30 am enemy TMs were active and throughout the day both his and our artillery were busy. Night was quiet," the *War Diary* noted. On 6 January the battalion moved back to the line, taking over from the 9th Royal Inniskilling Fusiliers. Continuing artillery duels and miserably wet weather marked their week in the trenches. "There seems to be no drainage through this ground at all," noted the diary. "Trench boards floating all over the trenches and everybody wet and miserable. One consolation is that the Hun is as bad as ourselves. Everything very quiet as a result." For Rifleman George Mullin the year had got off to a peculiar start. A "desperate calamity has overtaken our army" as a shortage of men resulted in the scouts and bombers being temporarily returned to their respective companies. "I am nevertheless honoured," he noted in his journal, "as Captain Lewis and I go up to the line together in advance of company… The trenches are in a wretched condition. Water, water everywhere as the poet said. Pumping will have to be started at once, or else we will have to wear divers' boots to keep us down." When he wasn't on sentry duty or attempting to catch up on his sleep in a "miserable place" of a dugout named '2d Tube', he took his turn manning the pumps on two hour stints. There was a little excitement three days into the tour when a German patrol was spotted close to the British lines, with the sentries opening fire. Two Germans were reportedly wounded, with Captain Lewis and Rifleman Smith crawling out into No-Man's-Land to capture one and bring him back.[1]

On 12 January Lieutenant Colonel Lloyd, now in command of the battalion, left to attend hospital, leaving Captain Mulholland in charge, himself only having returned four days previously from sick leave, with Captain Hanna his second in command. The battalion, relieved on 14 January and enjoying the comfort of withdrawing in the cover of a heavy fog, was now back in Red Lodge camp. The signallers had a cellar to themselves, shared by seven men with a brazier kept burning day and night. "Sometimes we send into Bailleul for tinned sausages and cook them on our fire," recorded Berry. "I awoke one morning to find a big rat sitting on the end of my bunk. He wouldn't budge until I fired at him with my rifle and got him. Of course the noise awoke the other members of our band who promptly started swearing."

The officers were not faring so well. An order for the transfer of several to other units clearly rankled with the headquarters staff as they struggled to maintain standards:

> "All good officers, thereby depleting the battalion to such an extent that we entered the trenches next tour with eight officers. All 2/Lts in charge of Coys. But will face the music should I be left to command the line myself. The battalion is in such a weak condition in numbers that we can only man the line every 20 yards with very few supports or reserves, which means double work for everyone. Adj acting as CO, 2nd in Command and Adjutant all in one. Captain Lewis brought in to HQ to relieve work."

Colonel Lloyd returned on 26 January but after less than a week again reported sick. The battalion returned to the line on 22 January, taking over from the 9th Skins under "rather heavy fire" that continued throughout the day. All roads to the rear were being shelled, halting the relief for a spell, and though the 25th Division to the battalion's right – which was mounting a raid – took most of the battering, one of the shells falling on the YCV's front went through the roof of a dugout, killing Company Sergeant Major James Scott. The first fatality of 1917, he was a 35-year-old married man from Belfast. He lies in La Plus Douve Farm Cemetery.

Speculation was ripe that a German attack was imminent and preparations to defend Hill 63 were stepped up, particularly after a heavy bombardment began south of Ploegsteert. The YCVs were withdrawn from the line on the 29 January as the threat was downgraded which, according to the *War Diary*, was just as well:

Company Sergeant Major James Scott, pictured here while at Seaford two years previously, became the first 14th Royal Irish Rifles fatality of 1917 when a German shell crashed through the roof of his dugout. *((George Hackney)*

> "Everyone from the higher command down seems to be settling down to the ordinary routine again. I firmly believe the Germans thought we were going to attack and both sides got anxious about things, but it did us quite a good turn. We saw our weakness and that at least was something. Had they attacked we could never have stopped them."

Praising the efforts of the over-stretched officers, and particularly those recently arrived with the battalion, it added: "Great credit is due to these boys for the excellent manner in which they carried on in their command of their companies, as their responsibilities were greatly increased, especially during the night in the line, as we fully expected an attack on our front." The battalion found itself even more at risk on the last day of the month as the artillery batteries close to the rest camp came in for heavy bombardment with shells falling among the accommodation blocks. One man, Rifleman Samuel Boyd, was killed and two others were wounded.[2]

The battalion was back in the front line on 7 February, the week passing without major incident though the men were put on alert a couple of times as the Germans raided the 13th Rifles' trenches to their left. The big event, as far as the headquarters staff was concerned, was the arrival of fresh drafts of men. "Good class of men – cavalry, London Irish, Buffs and others. A fair proportion of NCOs and seemed a competent lot on first inspection," was the assessment of the men who reported for duty on the 7 January. A further batch arrived on the 11 January, prompting the comment: "This makes 285 within less than a week. The battalion is now a battalion in reality, instead of the skeleton it has been for the last six months." On 17 February further shells fell at Red Lodge, one striking a tree beside the headquarters cookhouse killing riflemen John Cleland Baird and Malcolm McColl, who had been servants to Captains Gavin and James McKee respectively.[3] Major OR Vivian[4] arrived on the 20 February as second-in-command and acting commanding officer.

A three-night spell in the trenches, 22–25 February, passed without incident, helped by the fact that conditions were fairly foggy and so hindering the artillery observers. After a final night in Red Lodge, the battalion marched to Méteren outside Bailleul, some eight miles away, where it was to spend the next three weeks resting and undergoing training with the rest of the 109th Brigade. The pattern was quickly established of 'ordinary' training in the mornings and 'recreational' training in the afternoons. Time was also set aside for a little competitive sport, with the YCVs taking on the 11th Skins at football twice and emerging victorious on both occasions, while the YMCA hut was well frequented.

The arrival of a new commanding officer, Lieutenant Colonel Cheape,[5] of the 1st Dragoon Guards, who had formerly commanded the 7th Black Watch, and the return of

The 14th Rifles spent three weeks in camp close to Méteren, where it underwent brigade training. The men were also allowed some down time to rest. *(Courtesy of Alastair Harrison)*

half-a-dozen officers to the battalion added to the general rise in morale. "From having one or two officers per company (our condition some time ago) each company now has eight or nine," recorded the *War Diary*. It is unlikely the adjutant would have been so upbeat had he realised the 14th Rifles was under severe scrutiny. Divisional Commander Oliver Nugent was far from satisfied with attitudes within the battalion, considering it lacked "military spirit". The recent arrival of English reinforcements and the appointment of the highly experienced Cheape, a firm disciplinarian, was at his request and was an attempt to booster battlefield aggression.

The battalion's Orange Order lodge, the Young Citizens' LOL No 871, also took the opportunity of meeting on 16 March, with Brother G Uprichard, the Worshipful Master, in the chair. The first order of business was the election of new officers to replace those injured or killed since its last meeting. CQMS J Kenning was Deputy Master, Lieutenant TH Mayes, an accountant in civilian life, was Secretary, and Sergeant Minnis was returned as the lodge Treasurer. The committee included Lance Corporal Burns, W Condell and CSM J Nevin.[6] Votes of condolence were passed on the deaths of CSM J Scott and Rifleman S Boyd, killed in action and both members of the lodge. On the day the meeting took place the battalion suffered a further casualty with the death of Lance Corporal Roland Henry Darling.

On 20 March the battalion set out on a three-day march to its next destination. After stopovers at Morbecque and Wizernes, it arrived at Nortbécourt on the afternoon of 22 March, where great difficulty was found in securing sufficient accommodation, claimed the diary:

> "It is a village of farms, no shops. Billets for officers very scarce and in some companies as many as six had to sleep on the floor of the mess rooms. The people are not very agreeable and the barns in many cases are anything but weather-proof. Quite the worst place in which the battalion has been billeted since it came on service."

On the Sunday after its arrival the battalion attended a Brigade Church parade at Acquin, where the Rev Henry Montgomery, from Belfast, on a visit to the division, gave the sermon. Much of the time at this period was devoted to instruction in platoon and company attacks, a clear sign that another major offensive was afoot. "We are to attack dummy trenches with 'D' company. These trenches are a replica of the German trenches at Messines. By this training we know that we are to be in it soon again," recorded Berry on 27 March. The weather was unpredictable, with snow, hail and sunshine all in one day. On 29 March the rain was so heavy that all working parties were suspended and the battalion, marching to a range some five miles from the village, was drenched, spending the rest of the day in billets attempting to dry out.

The last day of the month was given over to brigade competitions at Acquin, with the 14th coming away as winners in the platoon drill, signalling, and compass competitions, champions in two of the boxing events, and runners-up in a range of other activities. In the football final the YCVs lost 4-0 to a team from the 9th Inniskillings.

On 4 April, the YCVs retraced their steps to Méteren, where the HQ and A company were billeted from Good Friday, 6 April, the remainder of the men being accommodated in tents amid the mud of a camp near Kemmel Hill. "We are in tents without floorboards. Mud up to the ankles," moaned Mullin. Two days later, on Easter Sunday, they returned to the front line, relieving the 8th Rifles in the Spanbroek sector, just north of Messines. The trench system, from Piccadilly to Stretcher Lane, included three mineshafts that the Germans had already shown a keenness to destroy during previous raids. The trenches themselves had been severely bombarded prior to the Young Citizens' arrival, with much of the wire in front destroyed and parts of the line so low as to expose anyone passing along certain sections. Mullin was posted to Frenchman's Farm, an observation post, and felt more at home: "We are now back in the old familiar surroundings; Fort Edward, Kingsway, Fort Victoria, Regent Street, Piccadilly, etc," he recorded. The Kingsway trench, in particular, was "rotten, all parapet but no back to any extent," according to Hope, who added: "To the left a board describes the trench Happy Moments. Some yards past this place one has to double up when passing a spot marked 'Beware of Snipers'." With heavy fighting going on elsewhere, however, it remained comparatively quiet during the first few days, though Rifleman David Lynch was killed on the 12 April by machine-gun fire as he sat next to the driver of a GS Wagon unloading at RE Farm.

On 14 April, a day of active German artillery fire, a shell fell at Piccadilly, killing three NCOs of the 9th Skins during the relief and wounding D Company's Sergeant Major and another man. The YCVs marched back to Derry Camp and found it "decidedly unhealthy" since the battalion had last occupied it some four months before. "Gun positions behind and on the flanks with accompanying activity of the guns have caused the enemy to strafe the camp, on many occasions with some resultant casualties," recorded the *War Diary*. "It is thought we shall have to vacate the camp and go under canvas and into bivouacs on the hill above." Almost as if to prove the point, the Germans shelled the camp the following day, forcing the HQ staff to move to the flanks for cover. The battalion moved back to the line on 20 April, a day on which the artillery to the rear of Derry Camp had been firing virtually without halt from 6.30 am after German prisoners had reported that a relief was to take place in the enemy lines. Another young German, who had given himself up just as the 14th moved up the communication trenches, said many of his comrades, like himself, were willing to surrender for want of food. Attempts to have him return to the German lines to enlist such wayward men failed as he turned back after only a few steps into No-Man's-Land. The POW passed Mullin in the close confinements of the trench as he was escorted to the rear. The prospect of a similar fate befalling him was clearly disturbing: "As I was going into the line a German prisoner passed me in the trench. That is a prospect I have always dreaded. I think I would resist if humanly possible," he concluded.

Aside from continuous artillery and trench mortar firing by both sides, it was a comparatively quiet spell though there was one somewhat bizarre incident. The *War Diary* reports on 24 April, without further explanation: "One man, Pte Dawson 'C' Coy which is holding the left front of our line, proceeded alone across to the German trenches at 5.45 am. It was broad daylight. He spent close on an hour in the trenches and walked back with his hands in his pockets and his rifle slung over his shoulder. He reported that he had not seen a single Bosche, that the trenches were in bad condition and that there was nothing in them but empty verey light boxes." A patrol sent out the following evening brought in the body of a British soldier who had earlier been spotted in No-Man's-Land. The operation, involving six men, lasted four hours, from 9.00 pm until 1.00 am and was a "difficult stunt" according to Mullin. His papers identified him as a private of 7/8th Royal Irish Fusiliers, part of the

16th (Irish) Division, which was serving immediately to the left of the Ulster Division.

Coming out of the line on the evening of 26 April, two companies were billeted at Aircraft Farm and two under canvas in open fields. The distinctly rural surroundings clearly struck home with Adjutant Mulholland, the regular author of the *War Diary*. On 1 May he recorded: "Another beautiful day with a smiling country stretching out as far as one can see, with the birds keeping up perpetual song, the woods and hedges springing into life, and it saddens one to think that the sun beams down on a world at war; death and destruction wrestling with building up and life!"

The following day the battalion relieved the 10th Inniskillings in the right sub sector. The sustained British artillery firing continued, with occasional German Minenwerfers coming back in response. On the morning of 5 May, around 9.30 am, an officer and two men slipped over the parapet into No-Man's-Land. Lieutenant JD O'Brien, accompanied by Corporal G Topp and Rifleman S Hogg made their way across to the enemy trenches. Spotting a German officer and four men sitting talking, they tossed in a grenade, wounding two and forcing the others to flee for the safety of a dugout. They attempted to take one of the wounded Germans prisoner but more enemy troops arrived on the scene and a firefight developed, though the Young Citizens were still able to withdraw with their captive. General Nugent, the divisional commander, sent a message of congratulation on the success of the raid.

In what was likely to have been a direct response to the 14th's action, the Germans attempted to raid the British lines, storming the sector to the battalion's right, which was held by a New Zealand unit. It was a failure, in that only one enemy soldier got into the British trenches, where he was taken prisoner, though the artillery and trench mortars fired by both sides in support resulted in YCV casualties. Throughout the day and into the next night the British artillery 'punished' the enemy for its actions, but received the same in reply as the Germans shelled the rear areas. Mullin, who was fortunate to witness events from a distant observation post, noted:

"Much excitement. Our 60 pounders opened a heavy strafe on Boche second line at 2.00 pm. Enemy replied immediately with 3" TMs (trench mortars) and rocket bombs. Our Stokes mortars joined in the melee. All quiet at 5.00 pm. Slight strafe between 10.00 pm and midnight. Their 'heavies' shell our reserve line. Our artillery reply."

A ration party making its way through Lindenhoek crossroads was hit, killing one man, wounding several others, and destroying the supplies. The artillery duels continued over the next few days, with all the guns on the Second Army front firing in five minute bursts at intervals throughout the day and night with the German response being the raking of the back area. John Kennedy Hope, during one bout of heavy shelling, found himself sharing a trench with a German escapee. He grumbled: "A small dog, apparently Hun property, crawls in at my feet, shivering with fear. When the strafe is over I pitch the pup out into No-Man's-Land. There is enough vermin in the line." As the battalion made its way to the rear after being relieved by the 9th Inniskillings, the Germans opened an intense 30-minute barrage. "Thus concluded the worst tour of the trenches as regards number of casualties, since November," noted the *War Diary*.[7]

Back under canvas, the battalion enjoyed the spring sunshine with only the occasional

German shell, in search of the railway and artillery guns nearby, disturbing their peace. The 'runners' changed into shorts because of the soaring temperatures, and immediately regretted it as the mosquitoes became more active.

In early Spring the division reorganised so as to allow a brigade at a time to be taken away for training. The 36th's front was also narrowed, allowing one brigade to hold it with the second in reserve. On 14 May, the Young Citizens moved into divisional reserve at Newmarket Camp near Locre. There was only accommodation for two companies, with the other two setting up bivouacs in the nearby fields. Not that those who found places in the huts were particularly better off: "On our arrival we found the huts were absolutely devoid of furniture, and for hours the pioneers were busily engaged in making forms, tables, etc, out of whatever old pieces of wood they could find," recorded the adjutant. Mullin seemed more than happy not to be under canvas: "We are now accommodated in huts situated on the Bailleul road. This is a change from bivouacs." What men weren't engaged in working parties in the back areas were put through their drills time and again in rapid loading, rapid firing, fire discipline and use of their respirators in the belief that they had become too dependent on the use of grenades and the bayonet. Nonetheless, the armoury sergeant was kept fully occupied in the last weeks of May putting a sharp edge on the battalion's bayonets. The Bailleul–Locre road, which ran past the 14th's camp, was a "scene of activity from early morning until far into the night, troops passing, motor lorries and motor cars and motor bicycles rushing along, and guns of all calibres pursuing their steady onward way, all suggesting that the 'Push' against the Wytschaete–Messines ridge is imminent," said the *War Diary*. A model of the German trench system had been prepared and Mullin accompanied Scout Officer Wood to view it on 20 May, noting that its "horizontal and vertical scales were 1/350 and 1/25 approximately". As before, the replica was used to give the men an idea of the terrain they were to attack over.

In between training and carrying out battle preparations, the battalion mounted one of its most successful raids on the enemy. On the evening of 22 May a party of 18 NCOs and men, led by Lieutenant Hogg, climbed aboard lorries which took them to the Lindenhoek crossroads, where they dismounted and proceeded on foot into the front line held by the 13th Rifles. At 1.40 am the next morning they climbed over the parapet into No-Man's-Land and rapidly crossed to the German lines, where they were able to gleam evidence that the enemy was reinforcing. When some 15 yards away they spotted five Germans who were evidently startled to see British troops so close. Lieutenant Hogg and his party charged forward to be met by a shower of grenades tossed by the fleeing Germans. The officer, despite being slightly wounded by fragments from the bombs, and accompanied by Corporal Allan Montgomery, gave chase along the parapet for about 50 yards before jumping into the trench to capture a wounded German who had been abandoned by his comrades as he had been unable to keep up. The group then returned to the British lines with their prize without a single shot fired after them. The success of the raid was hailed throughout the division, with General Nugent phoning the adjutant to offer his congratulations. The battalion commander, taking advantage of the situation, asked for four extra leave places for the men and received them. Lieutenant Hogg's name was forwarded with a recommendation and he received a bar to his Military Cross, and Corporal Montgomery[8] and Private J McGee were nominated for Military Medals.

There was plenty of entertainment on offer for those in reserve, with the band of the 16th (Irish) Division performing every day close to the camp, and the Pierrots of the 11th Rifles putting on performances in the natural amphitheatre close to Kemmel Hill. While the men could still hear the sounds of war from their camp, they were rarely bothered by direct shelling though, on 27 May, the enemy guns sought out a dump on the Locre–Bailleul road that evidently had been spotted by its aerial observers. As a result the battalion's horses, along with those of other units, had to be temporarily evacuated from their lines. That evening the officers of the YCVs who had been present at the Battle of the Somme dined together at Bailleul. In the early hours of the following day the German artillery again shelled the area, apparently searching out a 'conspicuous' large wooden structure built as a repair shop for the guns. The building was close to the A and D companies' bivouacs, with 19 men, including Second Lieutenant JP Sayles, wounded and one man, Lance Corporal George Burns, killed outright. That evening, when the shelling started up again, the CO ordered the men to abandon their tents and sleep out in the open in a valley nearby. They repeated the operation the next night and, sure enough, the German shells began to drop – forcing the adjutant, regimental sergeant major, the guard, and the few officers who remained in camp to make a prompt exit.

On 1 June, without warning, the battalion was ordered to move to a new site. Because of the short notice, only the headquarters staff and two companies marched out that evening, the remaining two companies following the next morning after rounding up the working parties. Their new base was a bare field close to Berthen, where the evening was spent setting up tents and bivouacs and digging latrines. The 3 June, apart from a short parade service, was free with the *War Diary* waxing lyrical:

> "The sky was a brilliant blue; the sun shone all day, its heat tempered by a soft wind. Under the leafy trees which fringe the camp field, the men sat writing letters and reading and talking, or lay sleeping. In the afternoon the Divisional Band came and gave us a concert lasting an hour and a half. Everyone seemed absolutely happy and oblivious of the fact that the Day is almost here."

Everybody, it noted, was optimistic and enthusiastic. The next two days were similarly relaxed, with a "quiet day's training" followed by a two-hour open-air concert performed by a party from the 4th Manchester Regiment. The Divisional Band and Follies also took their turn entertaining the men following an afternoon spent rehearsing for the coming attack.

On the eve of the battle the battalion received a boost with news that the popular medical officer Captain NJH Gavin had been awarded the Military Cross in the King's Birthday Honours for his courage under fire while helping the Somme wounded the previous year. It was a good omen as the men made their final preparations for battle.[9]

After marching to Newmarket Camp, they rested a few hours before collecting their equipment. At 9.00 pm the battalion – minus 14 officers and 200 other ranks out of a fighting strength of 45 officers and 939 men – left the camp for the front lines with D company leading the way. The headquarters staff, headed by Lieutenant Colonel GHR Cheape and Adjutant JA Mulholland, arrived at their battle HQ at 11.30 pm, with the first D Company platoon, under Second Lieutenant Brian Boyd, reporting there 15 minutes later before continuing on to the assembly trenches. At 1.30 am Captain McKee reported the company was in position, with all other company commanders able to make similar claims within the hour. The 14th Rifles had filed into the trenches to the right of the 109th Brigade front, with the 107th Brigade further to the right. Both had attachments of the 108th Brigade as mopping up troops. About this time a low-flying plane passing over the lines was fired on for, although no-one was sure whether it was friend or foe, "he had no business there at that hour" according to the *War Diary*. It was only after it was brought down was it discovered to be British. John Kennedy Hope, professing no fear and great hopes of success, claimed half the men of the battalion were new recruits who were about to experience their first taste of going over the top. He reported:

> "Morrow comes round with the rum, a square face for each platoon. I am the end man on the left flank and when the bottle arrives it is scarcely touched – nobody wants it. Morrow throws the bottle over the parapet."

Throughout this preparation period, with the exception of the odd German shell, it was one-way traffic as the British guns relentlessly bombarded the trenches opposite. Then, with just a few minutes to go, a ghostly silence fell over the lines.

At the stroke of 3.10 am all hell broke loose as the Battle for Messines Ridge began. "The button is pressed at the end of the cable and a million pounds of ammonal goes up below the Hun line," recorded Hope. "The greatest explosion the world has ever known throws us back into the trench. There is a wall of fire, a storm of fine dust and over we go." Berry had been awaiting the beginning of the battle sheltering inside a pill-box, which "just bounced up and down and we couldn't keep our instruments steady." Captain Mulholland wrote in the *War Diary*: "On the second, terrific explosions took place all along our front and guns innumerable opened up. The noise is too terrible to describe. Even in this deep dugout we cannot hear each other speaking." Mullin, as a company scout, had led C Company into the front lines before returning to battalion headquarters in Regent Street. He had climbed on

One of the Messines mine craters photographed in 1927 by the 14th Rifles old comrades on a tour of the battlefields. *(Courtesy of the Somme Museum)*

top of the scout dugout for a better view. "And then the mines go up and the barrage starts and the companies follow up. Not many yards away a battery of howitzers is firing over my head. I get the blast and the din is terrific."[10]

For more than two hours the headquarters staff could do nothing but sit and wait, with the only information received coming from the wounded as they passed down the line. It was the same for those left behind, who spent the night in a field above the camp "No-one slept much as everyone's thoughts were with those who were about to fight. They heard the bombardment open and mines go off," the *War Diary* noted. The mine at Spanbroekmolen hadn't detonated as expected and, obeying their instructions, the men had not waited but had left their trenches and were advancing when it exploded. The divisional history says a "few of the leading men of the 14th Rifles, out in No Man's Land were thrown off their feet by the force of the explosion… but there were no casualties and the men quickly closed in to the barrage." The eagerness of some of the men to push on resulted in the leading troops being injured by the British creeping barrage, according to Hope. "We let the barrage creep on. A sniper is at work near us. One of my section drops. We dive into a shell hole and wait. The SB (stretcher bearers) pick up my man and place him on a stretcher. The sniper gets the SB – dead. We go on."

At 5.30 am the first message arrived back at headquarters from Second Lieutenant Treanor – brought in by Rifleman Gault, who had taken some 40 minutes to get there, an illustration of how far the battalion had advanced – reporting his map reference and that he was gathering his 11th Platoon, of C Company, to assault the next trench. After another short delay, similarly upbeat messages began to flood in: a machine-gun nest at Scott Farm had been taken, the gunners killed and the weapon packed off with the carriers; other members of the battalion, along with soldiers from the 9th Rifles, took out a machine-gun post with the bayonet at Skip Point. Captain Cansdale and Second Lieutenants Kennedy, Morrow and McHugh all individually reported reaching Jump Point, the strongest enemy position, linking up with the units on their flanks. Hope was among the troops now occupying what had been expected to be the most difficult obstacle. "There is little opposition and very soon we place the yellow flag on Jump Point, our objective," he recorded with a touch of understatement.

> "The attack is brilliantly successful. Reserves come through like clockwork and are soon pushing ahead. We are consolidating our objective which is close to the track used by the pack mules bringing up the corkscrew stakes, barb wire and ammunition."

Brigadier General Ricardo, the Brigade commander, was among the first to be told of the 14th Rifles' success. The 109th's intelligence officer, observing from high ground, had reported by telephone seeing a yellow flag within the strongpoint. "Yellow be damned!" he bellowed down the line as officially the YCV's flag was (a presumably indistinct) orange. He informed the division accordingly, which in turn was able to notify the Corps headquarters that Jump Point had fallen on schedule.

Captain Hanna, meanwhile, was in Ocean Trench by 5.07 am (though it was 6.50 am

Second Lieutenant Sydney Treanor sent the first message received by headquarters reporting just how far the 14th Rifles had advanced within hours of the opening of the Battle of Messines. *(Courtesy of Andrew Totten)*

Brigadier General Ambrose Ricardo was delighted to receive a message from the Young Citizens reporting their successes. *(Courtesy of the Somme Museum)*

The YCV flag is proudly held aloft by the victors at the Battle of Messines. It was brought home to Belfast at the end of the war and today is stored at Belfast City Hall. *(Photograph © National Museums Northern Ireland, Collection Ulster Museum, BELUM.Y15430)*

before the message got back to HQ) but reporting heavy casualties. Lieutenant O'Brian was particularly upbeat. He was, he reported at 6.00 am, consolidating on the crest of Jump Point, having made contact with the 9th Rifles on his right, who were doing the same.

> "I have remnants from B, C and D Coys. I am gaining trench on my left. I have placed outposts on my front. Everything A1. We are merry and bright. If you could send up shovels I should be obliged. God Save The King."[11]

Others were requesting water, ammunition and bombs, along with wire and stakes to help secure their positions. At 7.15 am Captain Hanna had 200 men and four Lewis guns in action. He set 120 to work, covered by two of the Lewis teams, consolidating the line and sent the remainder back to Ocean Trench. A little later, at 8.10 am, he sent a fresh despatch: "If there are any stragglers send them up to me to help in work of consolidation. Things are OK. Troops in front of me and on right and left have apparently taken Green Lane with comparative ease, the enemy surrendering at once when cornered. Snipers in front are bothering us at present." About the same time Second Lieutenant Kennedy was to the right of Jump Point with two platoons and stragglers from other battalions; Second Lieutenant Treanor was also digging in with A Company. From his advantage point Berry had witnessed more than most of the battle as it unfolded, including the German counterattacks being repulsed. He noted:

> "Our tanks are now in action and nothing seems to be an obstacle to them. We could see fairly well – we had to keep a sharp look-out; then the messages came in and we are kept very busy. Some artillery officers have just come in to us. They look quite pleased with the situation. We can see hundreds of prisoners marching down the Locre Road under escort."

Mullin had moved forward behind the YCVs along with his officer, Mr Wood, who was looking for a suitable dugout in the Red Line as an advanced battalion headquarters, selecting a position near Scott Farm, the strong point overrun by the battalion hours earlier. The pair then moved further forward, to the Blue Line before Mullin was ordered back, around 8.00 am, to accompany the commanding officer, Lieutenant Colonel Cheape, on a reconnaissance of the ground taken.

> "He is tall and takes long strides. He walks quickly. Between the Red and Blue lines he stopped and made a sketch and report which he handed to me with instruction to take it to our Brigade HQ. This I did. On my arrival there I was shown into the Brigadier's office. He was comfortably seated with his elbows on the army table speaking on the telephone. I simply stood about one yard from his table and waited. Brigadier General Ricardo was in a happy mood, talking gaily to General Nugent. The brigadier held out his hand and I handed him Colonel Cheape's message. The brigadier opened the message and I had the pleasure of hearing him say to General Nugent 'I have just got a message from Colonel Cheape' and then he read the message out. The Brigadier was obviously delighted. I will remember this incident as long as I live. It gave me as much joy to deliver the message as it did to the Brigadier to pass it on to General Nugent."

Colonel Cheape, meanwhile, had joined Second Lieutenants Wood and Allen, also shown the way by Mullin, and a gunnery officer at the dugout at Scott Farm, with Captain Mulholland, who had the Royal Engineers begin making a nearby dugout serviceable again, arriving later. Long before noon the big guns were being brought up into forward positions to support the men, who were pushing on. At 12.30 pm the *War Diary* summed up the situation as the battalion consolidating on the Blue Line with the 10th Skins pushing on to the Black Line. "The whole day has been a huge success. Our artillery could not do more and the battalions taking part in the advance went for their objectives without hesitation. It was a splendid sight."

It was fortunate for Samuel Harrison that everything had gone so well, as he had missed the battle after returning late from leave. He had delayed his departure from Belfast so he could met up with his brother, then based in Dublin as he recovered from wounds. "I volunteered to go up the line, but the Adjutant wouldn't hear of it. At first he took a serious view of my case, but after I had explained about Albert, he didn't seem so bad. Anyway, I didn't hear anything more about it!" At around 3.00 pm the soldiers of the 11th Division began passing through the 14th's positions to prepare for the next thrust, accompanied by cavalry and horse artillery. Around the same time "one solitary tank can be seen moving slowly across the shell-pitted ground wandering aimlessly, but presume it has a certain job to do," noted Mulholland. In the late afternoon the remainder of the headquarters staff moved to Scott Farm, making communication with the rear HQ, already difficult because enough wire couldn't be found to reach, even more troublesome. The *War Diary* recorded:

Samuel Harrison arrived back late from leave and missed the start of the battle. Fortunately, with such good news coming from the front, the officers were in a good mood and nothing further came of it. *(Courtesy of Alastair Harrison)*

"It is strange to think that last night we sat in the front line in fear and trembling that the Bosche would spot us assembling in our trenches, and tonight we are three miles behind his lines and some of his big guns are in our possession and we now see the dugouts and roads, woods and railway lines we have watched so carefully on the map."

Mullin, meanwhile, was still on his feet. After leaving the brigade HQ he had returned to Lieutenant Colonel Cheape's side for a time and was employed on a number of tasks, including carrying water up for the officers and delivering messages to the company commanders. About 11.00 pm he accompanied Mr Wood in an unsuccessful attempt to contact the CO of the 12th Rifles, who were mopping up and consolidating the rear area. He spent the remainder of the night at the battalion HQ, snatching what sleep he could.

Second Lieutenant Brian Boyd, who had started in the ranks of the Young Citizens, went over the top at Messines carrying the YCV flag and was among the first to fall. He is pictured here with his young brother, Denis, a member of the 10th Belfast Scouts group. *(Courtesy of Andrew Totten)*

The battalion had received word to prepare to pull back to the support lines shortly before midnight, with the 12th Rifles to relieve them. However they failed to show and at 7.00 am the YCVs were allowed to pull out and fall back to the trenches from which they started their attack, a move largely completed by 10.00 am. Mullin and his great mate Tommy Crothers made breakfast from their emergency rations, heated over a tin of solidified methylated spirits, before leaving. "The black tea was delicious. This snack was the first food that we had since Wednesday night," he noted. The scouts arrived back at their camp around 1.00 pm where, like the rest of the battalion, they were delighted to find bottles of stout waiting for them courtesy of the CO. Colonel Cheape had arrived with the Young Citizens from a battalion of the Black Watch still wearing his Glengarry with its two long streamers. Unsure initially of the quality of his Irish battalion, he was seen throwing his Glengarry in the air with delight during the Battle of Messines, such was his pleasure at its performance. The battalion's casualties, while light in comparison to the Somme, were still considerable. They included Second Lieutenants SHL Downey of D Company, and Brian Boyd of B Company, killed along with more than 40 other ranks.[12] (See Appendix 8)

The wounded, numbering less than 140, included Second Lieutenant LH McCaw, Second Lieutenant HS Kennedy, and Captain McKee.[13]

Those left out of the battle rejoined the survivors and that evening, fearing a German counterattack, the YCVs were ordered to 'stand to' for close to two hours until the danger passed. At 9.00 am on 9 June, the 33rd Brigade provided the relief and the men marched back to Newmarket Camp, weary but elated.

Chapter 15

THE HELL THAT WAS PASSCHENDAELE

I don't think we grew callous about things but when Sergeant Jimmie Scott had just returned from cleaning up after a mortar bombardment and we were having something to eat and talking about it, he picked up a small piece of bread and said they were blown into pieces as small as this and popped it into his mouth. It was taken as a matter of course.

Rifleman Jim Fitzsimon, 14th Royal Irish Rifles

LIFE IN THE BATTALION returned to 'normal' very quickly after Messines. On 9 June Commanding Officer Colonel Cheape paraded his troops at Newmarket camp to congratulate them. The former CO of the 7th Black Watch told the men he had never commanded a better battalion and would not leave the YCVs for any other. The following day a service of thanksgiving was held and attended by Brigade commander General Ricardo and the battalion COs. A few lazy days followed, allowing the Young Citizens a chance to recharge their batteries before, on 13 June, the battalion moved again, this time to an open site near Westoutre, where the accommodation was in tents. "The camp is nicely situated with plenty of water convenient for washing," commented Mullin. Training recommenced the following day in the belief that the Brigade – with Colonel Cheape now acting brigadier while Ricardo was on leave – was being sent further back for intensive instruction.

It turned out, however, that there was more heavy work to be undertaken. On 16 June the YCVs, minus a small group under the adjutant, were moved to a camp near Kemmel for convenience, as they were to provide large scale working parties for the Wytschaete area. The next day A and B companies left camp at 3.15 am to help build a new road, followed some 12 hours later by C and D companies. The task was scheduled to last four days but order and counter-orders caused confusion and delay.

On 18 June the battalion again moved, this time to Doncaster Huts outside Locre on the Bailleul road, which had just been vacated by a unit of the 16th (Irish) Division and were "in a filthy condition" according to the *War Diary*. After just one night they marched on to Onraet Wood and into newly won German dugouts in the support lines of the new front where they endured a restless night under enemy shellfire. The next few days were spent clearing the battlefield, salvaging what was good and repairing and reinstating dugouts and defences, largely under the guidance of Major Vivian. In addition, each evening eight platoons of men were sent up to the front lines to work on repairs and the strengthening of the lines. It was dangerous and unpleasant work, especially as the German artillery continually probed the back areas looking for British batteries. On 20 June three men were killed and two wounded by a shell exploding in the C Company area. They were Sergeant James McGinty, an Englishman who had been transferred into the YCVs from the 10th Reserve Cavalry Regiment; Corporal John Boyd, from Carrickfergus; and Rifleman John Watson, from Belfast. There were further casualties three days later, when Sergeant John James McCoubrey, from Belfast, and Sergeant David English were killed and a number of others injured by enemy shelling of a gun just 100 yards from the battalion's headquarters on the edge of Onraet Wood.[1]

Overall, there were many more German guns in operation, with additional pieces suspected of having arrived from the Eastern Front, while aeroplanes from both sides tussled for superiority, with 17 reported in the skies above the YCV positions on one occasion. "I watched two enemy planes over our lines shoot down two of our aeroplanes, though a squadron of our 'fighters' were not far off," Mullin noted in his diary.

The battalion moved into the front line late on 24 June, relieving the 9th Skins, and establishing the advanced HQ in a "palatial German dugout". At this point the line consisted of a number of strong points and posts, with efforts being made to construct a trench linking them and dig a new communication trench. Everything had to be accomplished at night as the entire front was under enemy observation and it was impossible to move about in daylight. The Germans, of course, were aware of the nocturnal activities, and shelled constantly causing many casualties. "The so-called trenches are in a very bad condition," reported Mullin, based with other scouts at Sonen Farm, some 1,200 yards south-east of Wytschaete hospice. Conditions weren't helped by a "heavy Boche strafe" that began around midnight on 25 June and continued with varying intensity over the coming days.

Mullin, accompanied by Second Lieutenant Wood, escorted battalion doctor Gavin up to the front line at 1.00 am on 27 June to attend the injured. Among the casualties was Sergeant Arthur Patton, originally from the Shankill area of Belfast, and Rifleman John Philip Stride, a Londoner who had been living in Middlesex at the time of enlistment. The 9th Skins working party, toiling in the front line, had suffered likewise. There was a further death, also of an English recruit, on the 28 June when Rifleman Alexander Leadbetter, from Birmingham, who had initially enlisted in the London Regiment, died. Another man, Rifleman James Berry, from Linton, Kent, passed away from wounds the following day. The geographical spread of the casualties reflected the fact that the YCVs were no longer an overwhelmingly Belfast, or even Irish, battalion with many of the latest replacements coming from the south of England in particular. "The battalion is getting quite an English flavour about it," noted James Kennedy Hope:

> "We are brought up to strength again with a huge draft of conscripts, mostly 'gawd blimey gentlemen'. We also have a lot of newcomers in disbanded cavalrymen. Quite a motley and some very funny artists too."

The battalion, after being relieved by the 10th York and Lancaster Regiment, part of the 37th Division, pulled back to Curragh Camp, near Canada Corner on the Westoutre Road, close to Locre, and described by the *War Diary* as "the finest we have struck".

1 July, the first anniversary of the opening day of the Battle of the Somme, was marked by a 10.00 am service of remembrance and dedication during which the men presented arms in memory of those who had fallen 12 months previously. That afternoon the battalion was again on the move, this time to Strazeele, being led out of camp on the 10-mile march by Major Vivian as Lieutenant Colonel Cheape was on leave. Some of the men were able to stop en route to enjoy a bath though the benefit was likely to have been rapidly lost that evening as the farmhouses and cottages used for accommodation were "not over-clean". Mullin, who had initially been left behind, caught up with his 12th platoon comrades at the estaminet they were billeted in where he found "the boys were drinking beer or whatever else they fancied".

The rest of the brigade was within three miles and the two other brigades close by as the Division was being withdrawn for the promised two weeks of training. The next few days passed comfortably as the YCVs took in almost 80 reinforcements, mostly men from the Army Service Corps, and enjoyed some relaxation. On 4 July the battalion bugles and band, formed only three weeks previously, played the general salute as Brigadier General Ricardo visited the battalion for an inspection. Later in the afternoon the Divisional Follies performed in an open field, with the YCV band playing during the interval. It received a qualified review: "It played extremely well for the time they had for practice," remarked the *War Diary*.

Reveille was at 4.00 am the next morning so an early start could be made on the five-mile march to Hondeghem, with the band leading the way. The men, who were billeted in farms in the surrounding area, were given the remainder of the day off for rest and sightseeing. Arriving at 8.30 am, Mullin and his fellow scouts went to an estaminet where they enjoyed a second breakfast "served in good style, white tablecloth, etc". Later he enjoyed afternoon tea in the Café de Paris

76 SAINT-OMER. — L'Hôpital Militaire. — LL.

The town of Saint Omer was a major administrative centre for the British Army in France during the First World War. *(Courtesy of Alastair Harrison)*

before exploring the village. The evening ended with the band playing the 'Retreat'. The next day was more of the same, the battalion being on the march from 5.30 am and arriving at Arques, after almost a 10-mile hike, shortly before noon. Mullin, likely with tongue firmly in cheek given the animosity of the past, noted how the battalion's path crossed with their Belfast comrades during a halt for breakfast: "We were delighted to see our friends the 107th Brigade marching past. It was nice to see them. The usual salutes were exchanged. They, like us, are heading west in the direction of St Omer." After dinner most of the men headed for bed in preparation for the 1.00 am start for an area south-west of Foret Nationale de Tournehem, with A Company billeted at Haute Pannee – a "very small village (three estaminets and a windmill)" according to Charles Sheridan – and the other three companies at Le Buisson. The first of the men, after a stop for breakfast, arrived shortly before 10.00 am. This was their final destination where they would spend the best part of three weeks and which would be, for many, one of their finest periods with the army. Certainly Mullin and the rest of the battalion scouts were determined to get their stay off to an enjoyable start. One of their number, Tommy Crothers, had been awarded the Military Medal and the men could celebrate in style as their officer Mr Wood had generously provided 20 francs so they could retire to the nearby watering hole to toast his health. "And so we had a happy party in the estaminet," he noted in his diary. The following day the scouts marched to the St Louis River, close to Bonningues, where they spent the day swimming and relaxing on its banks, only returning in time for dinner. The rest of the day was free, with Mullin choosing to help a farmer in the evening to stack hayricks. A sports day was organised for 12 July, traditionally marked as a holiday for the anniversary of the Battle of the Boyne, with the men served their main meal at the sports ground.

In general mornings were largely given over to training, usually starting at 6.30 am and ending by 11.00 am, with the remainder of the day free. On 13 July a divisional night exercise was conducted, consisting of a 'raid' by the scouts during a mock relieving of the line. The following week the battalion split into attackers and defenders. "The enemy send out patrols at 9.30 am. The main attack begins at 10.00 am. I am on outpost duty and try to keep concealed," wrote Mullin "Later the enemy approach rather cautiously. I retire and alert strong point, which I help to defend. There is no retirement. I am either captured or killed there. The battle ends about 1.00 pm." The programme of training was also designed to help the drafts of fresh men, many coming from disbanded units and others conscripts, fit into the battalion. Bringing the YCVs back up to strength, however, also contributed to the further diluting of the Belfast hue of the battalion. Mullin noted: "We also have a number of newcomers from the disbanded cavalry regiments. We now hear many unfamiliar accents such as boys from Larne, Derry and Dublin."

For many, however, the most important 'battle' at this period was on the football pitch. The YCVs played their first match in the Brigade Association Football Cup on 14 July, winning through in a tough game against No 4 Company ASC, 36th Divisional Train, by one goal to nil. It had an easier run against the Machine Gun Company, running out 5-1 victors. Ultimately the battalion made it through to the final where it met the 11th Skins on Saturday 21 July. Mullin noted with glee:

"The match began at 6.00 pm at the ground of the 9th Battalion Inniskillings. During the first half the teams were evenly balanced, neither being able to score. Kelly for the YCV battalion scored the only goal of the match six minutes before the whistle went for full time."

The cup was presented by Brigadier General Ricardo, GOC, 109th Brigade, to 'Boggie' Martin, the captain of the YCV team. A victory parade was held as the newly-won silverware was carried back to Haute Pannee. However, the horse fraternity was less fortunate. A gymkhana, scheduled to take place at Aquin, had to be abandoned because of heavy rain.

There were also plenty of VIP visitors to the training area during this period. General Nugent, commanding the Division, arrived on 13 July to watch the men training and "appeared pleased". The following day Lieutenant General

General Oliver Nugent, commanding the 36th (Ulster) Division, visited the 14th Rifles while they were in the Saint Omer sector. Although full of praise for the Young Citizens publicly, he was more forthright with his views in private. *(Courtesy of the Somme Museum)*

HE Watts, commanding the XIX Corps of the Fifth Army, spent time with the men. On 15 July, following a Brigade service conducted by Bishop Llewellyn Gwynne, Assistant Chaplain General, General Nugent presented medals for gallantry and devotion to duty won by men and officers of the battalion. Brigadier Ricardo visited the training area on 19 July to watch the battalion practice company attacks.

On 26 July, the battalion marched out of Haute Pannee "much to their own regret and that of the inhabitants" and back to the reality of war. At Boisdinghem they boarded buses that carried them the 25 miles to the Winnezeele area: "We move east for some time and then turn north. The days of Sunday school excursions are long past. We know the way," noted Mullin. A further mile on foot brought them to their new camp of tents. The battalion was now much closer to the front and there was no doubt in anyone's mind why they were there: "All through the night we could hear the guns thundering on the front about 16 or 17 miles away," noted the *War Diary*. "All round are troops. They are assembling for the next 'Push.'" After four days the battalion relocated to a camp in the Watou area, about five miles from Poperinghe, with the move unable to be completed until dark because of enemy activity. They were now in reserve with the opening of the Battle of Ypres just hours away.

Passchendaele, wrote Siegfried Sassoon, was "hell". In more than three months of fighting, much of it in a quagmire of mud, some half-a-million men died. Officially known as the Third Battle of Ypres, the intention had been to break through the German lines, forcing a retreat from the coastal bases from which the enemy was waging the submarine war that was so badly hindering Britain's war effort. Some 3,000 guns fired 4.5 million shells during the preliminary bombardment but the damage caused, combined with the heaviest rainfall in 30 years, merely succeeded in turning the Flanders battlefield into a sea of mud that sucked men to their deaths. The initial attack was launched on 31 July 1917, with a second attempt to renew the offensive on 16 August. There were further gains in September and by November Passchendaele itself finally fell. In total the Allies had moved forward five miles.

From the outset the omens had not been good. As the YCVs readied themselves to enter the fray, the news from the battle lines was far from encouraging. After the early

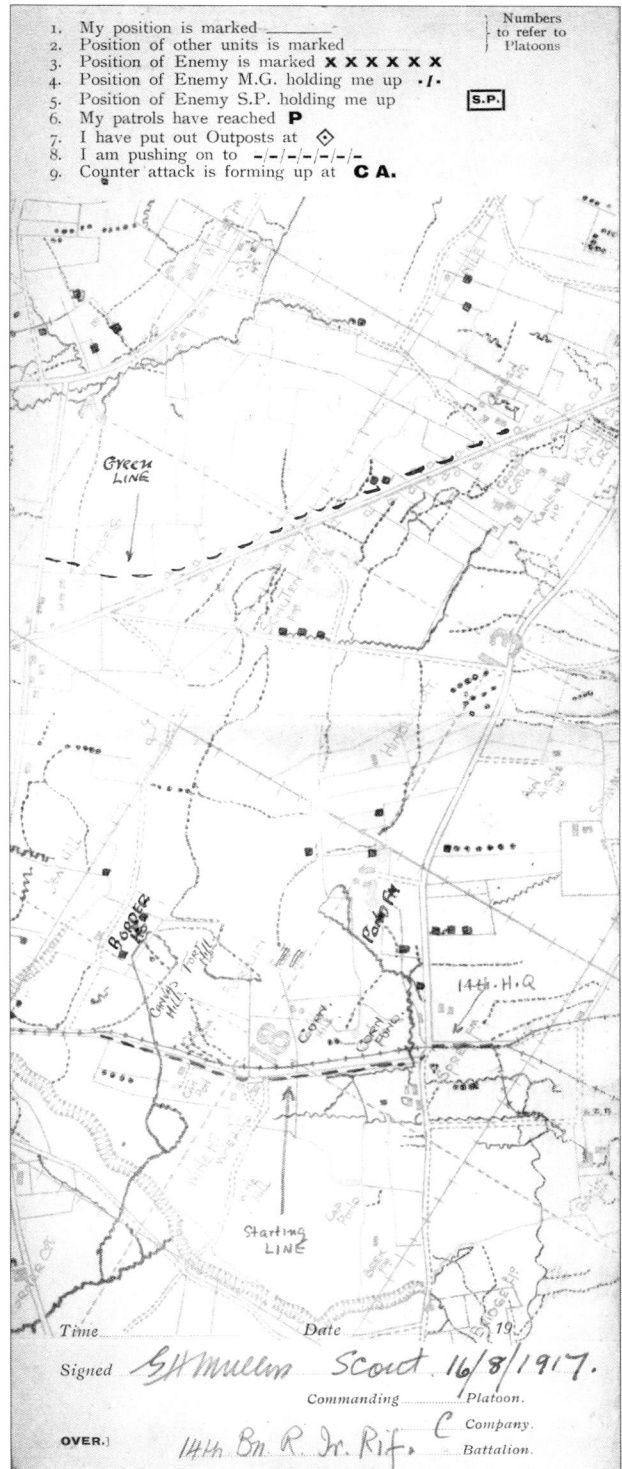

This map of the Passchendaele front was retained by George Mullin. Note it shows the position of the 14th Rifles headquarters. *(Courtesy of the Somme Museum)*

upbeat claims of great success, the heavy rain and German resistance brought the advance to a virtual halt and even caused some units to fall back. "Reports from the line are rather depressing. Everywhere is a sea of mud and there is very little shelter for the troops," noted the *War Diary* on 2 August. The following day the battalion left camp to move into a forward position. The 109th Brigade was to the left of the divisional front, taking the place of the 166th Brigade of the 55th Division. The 9th and 10th Royal Inniskillings were in front, the 11th Skins in support and the 14th held in reserve. The handover was a shambles, according to the *War Diary*:

> "The whole place is just a picture of desolation. The arrangements about relief and information of this locality are at present nil, and Coys must just ferret round and find water, shelters and everything else they require – one cannot help comparing the handing over of the 36th Division after the capture of Messines Ridge with this handing over."

Casualties quickly mounted, with six men killed – riflemen Henry William Bird, Robert McGimpsey, Joseph McCracken, Charles Fowler, William Whiteside and Thomas Taggart.[2] A number of these died and several others were wounded in one particularly bloody incident after being caught in the open on 3 August.

Accommodation in the reserve trenches was very limited and in a very poor condition but were "heaven compared to what the poor fellows in the trenches have to put up with," noted the adjutant.[3]

On 5 August the 11th Skins were moved back west of Ypres, with the 14th sending two platoons to hold the line the Inniskillings had vacated. The remainder of the battalion was in support of the 107th Brigade, which was holding the line. German shelling of the rear areas caused casualties, particularly amongst the carrying and working parties. Early on 6 August the YCVs were withdrawn to a canvas camp a few miles back. "Everyone delighted to get out of the line. Opinion is unanimous that it was the worst bit of line the battalion

Both the battles of Messines and Passchendaele were undertaken to relieve the pressure on Ypres, which had effectively been under siege since the early months of the war, suffering huge devastation. *(Courtesy of Alastair Harrison)*

La Guerre 1914-15
L. C. H. Paris

220. YPRES. — Intérieur des Halles après le bombardement.
YPRES. — Interior of the Markets after the bombardment.

was ever in. The enemy never stopped shelling," said the *War Diary*. Their new position was only an improvement in comparative terms, as enemy shells continued to scream overhead throughout the night in search of the railway line and main road nearby. The men were moved to one side of the camp the next evening, though this was no safe haven either. With little sleep over the two nights, an order was issued to take down the tents and move elsewhere. This was accomplished in a thunderstorm, with everyone soaked to the skin as they marched along roads resembling rivers such was the flow of water running along them. The new camp was established at Vlamertinge where, away from the shells, sleep was at last possible. Aerial activity, when the weather permitted, was brisk as each side attempted to bring down the other's observation balloons. German planes also bombed the back areas and constantly buzzed the YCV's camp.

Shortly after 6.00 pm on 14 August the battalion moved out for the trenches in front of Hill 60, stopping at a dump along the way to collect extra equipment and ammunition. It was raining heavily and the Germans were shelling the road, with one landing at the rear of A Company, killing a number of men and wounding several others. Headquarters was established nearby, with heavy shells falling all around and a number of direct hits reported.[4]

At 1.00 am on the 16th, after being relieved by the 9th Inniskillings, the YCVs moved further forward to their jump-off points. The *War Diary* recorded things were "very hot". The trench was so full of men the HQ staff couldn't get to its allocated dugout and instead took shelter until things quietened down. Mullin and the other scouts had established their own post in a captured dugout, from which his officer, Lieutenant Wood, had summoned him on the 15th, after the artillery liaison officer had reported to the battalion headquarters.

George Mullin was escorting an artillery observer in No-Man's-Land when he was wounded and had to find his way initially to a first aid post then further back in search of an ambulance. *(Courtesy of Andrew Totten)*

"He is handed over to Mr Wood. Mr Wood sends for me and explains that I have to take our new friend from the artillery with me when we advance tomorrow morning at zero hour 4.45 am. I am to be his guide and companion during the battle. I have maps, field-glasses and know most of the officers, whereas he is a complete stranger in our brigade."

A final briefing for company commanding officers was held shortly before 3.00 am on 16 August, with them leaving immediately afterwards to move the men into position. A direct hit on the HQ dugout near Spree Farm shortly afterwards killed at least six and wounded many more. However, it did not collapse, bearing testimony to the strength of the German concrete and skill of their engineers. "Dugout full of wounded, can only bandage a few of them as we have no more dressings. Their sufferings are terrible and we cannot move," Mulholland wrote in the *War Diary*. The slaughter was only beginning. At 4.45 am the 14th climbed out of the trenches and into a storm of machine-gun and artillery fire. For Mullin, however, the battle was already over. He recorded:

"My liaison artillery officer and I now proceed to our attack position on battalion starting line. Movement is slow for the ground is a quagmire with all shell holes full of water. The artillery officer and I are lying close together, quite flat, waiting on the word to go and the start of our creeping barrage. I am

Lance Corporal John Dixon, a member of B Company from the Ormeau Road in Belfast, was 25 when killed at Passchendaele. He is commemorated on the Tyne Cot Memorial. *(Central Presbyterian Association Magazine)*

lying flat with my arms extended in front of my body, the officer is on my right. He is talking about bringing his battery up. A Boche shell explodes on the officer's right, a piece comes my way and my upper arm is shattered close to the shoulder. My new friend did not need to be told. I owe much to that artillery officer. He was my guide now. He at once took off all my equipment. He gave me good advice. I was inclined to linger. He told me to get back as quickly as I could, while I could. Up to now it had always been the other fellow, but it was my turn now. I felt I was letting the artillery down. I kept my haversack and field-glasses. I said goodbye to my officer and he in turn wished me good luck. We then parted."[5]

What little news filtered back to the battalion headquarters over the next couple of hours was all negative: Lieutenant Wood and Regimental Sergeant Major Jacquest[6] wounded; Lieutenant Ledlie, of D Company, held up by machine-gun fire from Pond Farm and calling for support which had "melted into the 'blue' somewhere, but certainly not out in front"; reports from the wounded that other officers had fallen.

Cyril Falls, author of the *History of the 36th (Ulster) Division*, summed it up:

"On the right of the 109th Brigade, the 14th Rifles had to cross ground far worse even than the ordinary, completely under water, in fact. In their passage they came under withering machine-gun fire from Pond Farm. Lieutenant Ledlie made a fine attempt to capture this place, surrounding it on three sides with the few men remaining to him when he reached it, and killing any Germans who showed themselves. With his numbers so greatly depleted, he waited for support before making an attempt to rush it, sending back two messages. But no support came; the men could not face the machine-gun fire. They had already suffered greatly from the artillery barrage, which the leading waves had avoided. At eight o'clock, seeing that his position was hopeless, he withdrew his men a hundred and fifty yards, covering his retirement by Lewis-gun fire."

Contact with the 13th Rifles on the right flank had been lost and shortly after 6.00 am it became clear that the advance was held up with men falling back. Charles Sheridan blamed

The 36th (Ulster) Division's ambulances, a number of them purchased with money raised in the province, were worked hard at Passchendaele. *(Belfast Telegraph)*

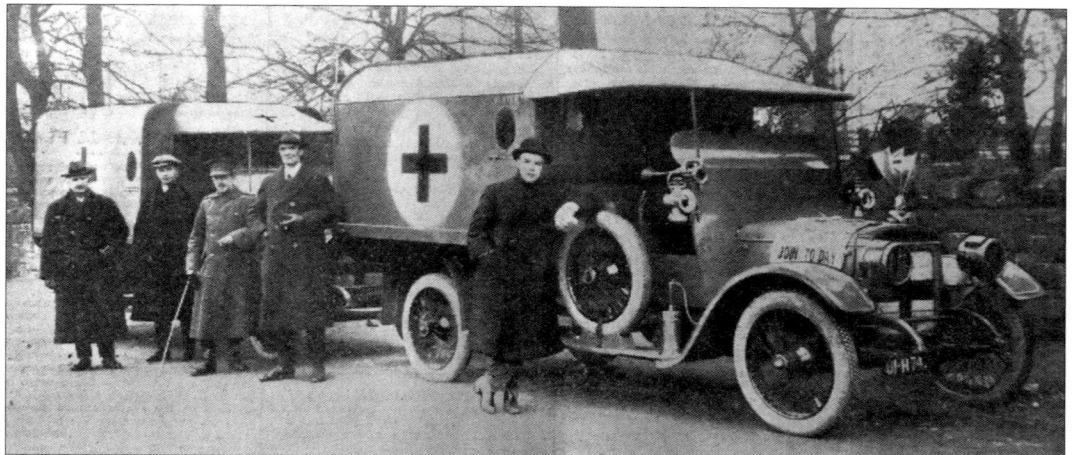

the lack of reinforcements for the failure of the attack. "We reached the top of the ridge but we lost so many in getting there that we were unable to hold on to what we had gained, and as usual there were no reinforcements, as the British army always expect one division to do the work of six," he wrote years afterwards.

Major Vivian rallied about 30 men and led them forward to take a German strong point, which he rapidly turned round into a defensive position. Adjutant Mulholland, concerned about a German counterattack, organised the men milling around the vicinity of his headquarters into a defensive line, strengthening it with the addition of a Lewis gun. Major Vivian returned to arrange supplies of rockets, ammunition and water for the new line, sending Second Lieutenant Reddy out to take charge of the new outpost and using Lieutenant Duncan and his carriers as reinforcements. The German bombardment was relentless, forcing the HQ staff to relocate. Lieutenant Ledlie established a forward post in front of a segment of line being held by the 11th Inniskillings, with all available supplies sent to him. About 9.00 am he sent up the SOS rocket to warn that the Germans were massing to counterattack, with everyone standing to in their trenches but the assault failed to materialise. The forward line, noted the *War Diary*, was the safest place to be at that time. With virtually all the advanced first aid posts having been knocked out, casualties had to be carried long distances to receive medical treatment, with a number of men risking their own lives time and again to get comrades to safety. Nor, when they did get to a first aid post, were they necessarily safe. The divisional history noted: "Captain Gavin, RAMC, attached to the 14th Rifles, did splendid work at Rat Farm, where two other medical officers were killed." This gallant medical officer was awarded a bar to the Military Cross he already possessed for continuing to treat the wounded despite the dangers.

Corporal Thomas Henry, aged just 20, was on attachment to the 109th Trench Mortar Battery when killed at Passchendaele. The Belfast man is commemorated on the Tyne Cot Memorial. *(Courtesy of Andrew Totten)*

In the early hours of 17 August a company of the 8th Rifles took over the battalion's forward positions, allowing the YCVs to withdraw to the old British line. More than 100 men had been killed outright on 16 August with another 216 wounded, of which a number subsequently died.[7]

Of the 19 officers who went into the battle, more than half had become casualties. Among those killed were Second Lieutenants Hugh Victor Strain Kennedy, Samuel Hugh Walker, James McBurney and Francis Warren Coffee, and Lieutenant Herbert Finlay Rea, while Lieutenant John Dwyer O'Brien died of his wounds on 17 August.[8] (See Appendix 9)

Later that day the battalion moved further back to join the cadre kept out of the battle, arriving "weary and tired out, everyone downhearted," according to the *War Diary*, "but time will make us forget the horrors and leave only the memory of our brave comrades and their valiant deeds in the face of certain death". About 6.00 pm that evening the men were herded on board a series of buses and driven back to their old camp at Winnezeele. "Everyone glad to be out of the sound of the guns again. Still even back here the Boche is active, bombing camps and railway stations from aeroplanes," the diary noted. The following day, 18 August, Lieutenant Colonel

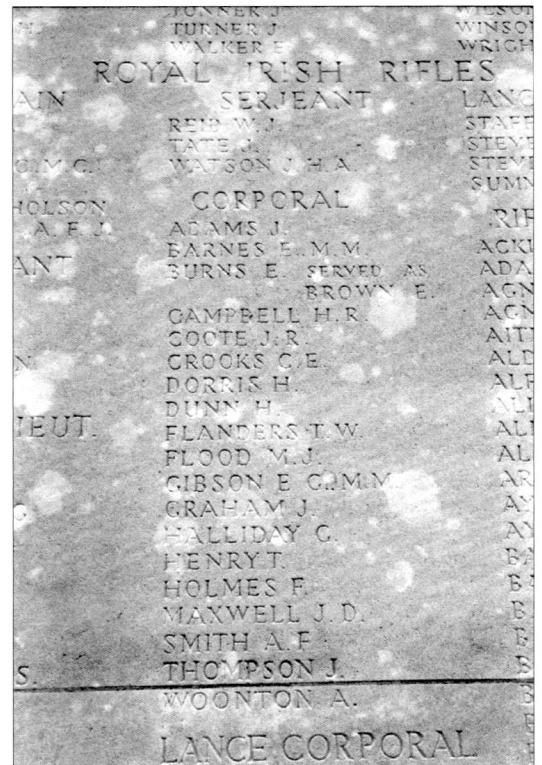

Cheape said goodbye to the battalion, leaving the next day to take over command of the 86th Brigade. He had been the YCV's ninth commanding officer. That same day Brigadier General Ricardo addressed a brigade church parade, stressing that the 109th Brigade had not been responsible for the failure of the push. Present at the parade was the 1st Battalion of the Royal Irish Fusiliers, who had been transferred to the Ulster Division. It brought to the surface concerns within the battalion about its future. "This is significant. Does it mean that our battalion is going to another brigade? Or does it mean that it is to be disbanded and the officers and men scattered over other battalions?" the adjutant confided to the *War Diary*.

News of the extent of the casualties was filtering back to Belfast and beyond. The *Belfast News Letter* commented:

"Thursday, 16th August, will long be remembered in the annals of the Imperial Province as the date of a difficult and trying action in which the volunteer Division was again called upon to make heavy sacrifices, the losses on the present occasion being comparable with those inflicted before Thiepval on the 1st July, 1916. The Division has for the third time upheld the highest traditions of the Province, and every county in Ulster is once more facing tragic bereavement. The dark days which followed the opening of the Battle of the Somme are still fresh in the public mind. Gallant officers and men fell in the victorious advance on the Messines-Wytschaete Ridge on the 7th June last, when, in the words of Sir Hubert Gough, the Division 'displayed the greatest courage and dash, as well as the greatest discipline and training,' and now as a result of the fierce struggle north-east of Ypres another long list of casualties has again cast the province into mourning."

The *War Diary* was strikingly direct about the failings of the operation. It recorded:

"The whole thing has been a miserable failure for reasons which are obvious to us all; our men did all that was asked of them, but the peculiar attitude of the enemy and his methods, were not properly appreciated by the powers that be. Our divisional staff and brigade staff did everything that was humanly possible, as we know from past experiences how well they look ahead and the splendid system they work upon, even with all our losses and failure our confidence is not shaken in our Division, and the aim and object of us all will be to bring back to our men the splendid fighting spirit which we have always had. We went into this battle knowing that things were not right and that spirit is fatal, but all round us the signs were very clear and no one could blame either officers or men – they did their best and from our point of view could have done no more."

Even years later Sheridan still had strong feelings on the failure of the attack, though he was too much of a gentleman to do more on paper than give a nod toward his anger: "I think I remember one of the papers describing it as a 'Glorious Failure,'" he recalled, "however they were not there. I would describe it in quite another way only I don't know who may read this book after I've finished with it and if any person who had not been to

Ypres happened to read it with things like that in it they possibly would not understand." He added:

> "When the division came out of the stunt I was told off to a party for searching and burying the dead, a d-----d awful job when one knows that some of the poor chaps are lying all over the place in pieces, we were to go up in the light railway but as 'Jerry' was shelling the railway there like h--- the driver dared not go up, so the party was a wash-out for which I was very thankful."

After four days of rest the battalion was put on a train heading south. It was going to need time to rebuild and that task was to be carried out in the Cambrai sector.

Saint George's Church in Ypres is effectively a memorial to all those who died in defence of the town. *(Author)*

Chapter 16

CURSED IN THE WORST COCKNEY IRISH EVER

The men will be lost without an estaminet to visit, a farmhouse at which to purchase milk and eggs, a girl to philander with, but none of these are to be found within a radius of many miles. The nearest brewery is 18 kilometres away so the troops must become willy-nilly teetotallers to a man. Warfare under these conditions is 'no bon'.

Battalion *War Diary*

THE JOURNEY SOUTH BEGAN at 5.30 am with the YCVs marching from their camp to the village of Caestre, some seven miles away, where they boarded rail carriages. The train left about 10.00 am, arriving in Bapaume some eight hours later. A further march of five miles remained, ending at a camp in the Barastre area where the accommodation was tents and bivouacs. The battalion's *War Diary*, however, was more concerned at the lack of liquid refreshments: "There isn't a farm house or village for miles occupied by civilians. As far as the eye can see one observes grass dotted over with camps, ruined farmsteads, villages and towns." Life in such desolation was going to be difficult, it concluded.

On the evening of 28 August 1917 the battalion moved closer to the line, sleeping in old and dirty Nissen huts. The following evening it took over a section of front in the Hermies sector from units of the 9th (Scottish) Division, the relief not being completed until after 1.00 am owing to delays in moving the men along the light railway as the trucks were regularly stopped to allow empty wagons to pass. According to divisional historian Cyril Falls, there were "practically no defences at all, save a shadowy front line and some trenches round the village". A heavy programme of trench-digging and wiring was drawn up, keeping the men busy throughout a week that passed relatively quietly apart from occasional bursts of activity by the enemy artillery. The British, conserving stores, limited its response to some 30 shells per gun each day. Only one soldier, Rifleman Rodrick Emile Leadbetter MacKenzie, a Londoner, was killed in action during this period, losing his life on 2 September.[1]

The headquarters staff had to temporarily abandon its huts after shells fell close to where the adjutant and runners were quartered, though the interruption to sleep was short lived. Relieved by the 10th Skins on the evening of 6 September, the men returned to billets where training and reorganisation both got underway, though there was no shortages of distractions. On 9 September most of the men enjoyed a somewhat different sporting entertainment – a baseball game between teams from American and Canadian units stationed nearby. The following day their new Corps commander, Lieutenant General CL Woollcounte, inspected the battalion, while on the 11th the YCVs put on a concert in the YMCA tent. On the 14th they were back in the line, the week again passing fairly uneventfully, though the German guns did pay some attention to communication trenches. At the church parade on the first day back in billets at Bertincourt, the brigadier presided, praising the men of the battalion who had received awards for the 16 August fighting.

The same pattern continued over the coming weeks, the time in the trenches spent on repairs and improvements. "The front doesn't suit us," mused Hope. "So we are digging a continuous front line. The trenches have been linked up and we are fitting in dugouts for the winter. We have a great time installing elephant back shelters."[2]

Alastair Harrison has faithfully kept all his father Samuel's papers, letters and mementoes of the war so he can pass them on to the next generation, including his identity tags, cap badge and battalion identification. (Author)

Likewise, the spells in billets were occupied building huts and making life more comfortable. The normal working day was from 8.00 am to 2.00 pm, with the men free to organise sport or attend concerts or other entertainments in the afternoons and evenings. The battalion also absorbed considerable numbers of replacements, some of them returning YCVs wounded earlier and now fit again for duty, others coming from the amalgamated 8/9th Rifles, while some were newly-trained conscripts. James Kennedy Hope, with his usual cynicism, noted: "The battalion is filled up with more canon fodder, nearly all greenhorns."

At the start of November the *War Diary* reported the death of the Medical Officer, Dr Noel John Hay Gavin,[3] who had been with the battalion for some 20 months. He was thrown from his horse on 2 November, suffering a fractured skull, and died a few hours later without recovering consciousness. "He was a man of charming personality and as brave as a lion. To know him was to love him. We shall miss him greatly, both officers and men," it noted. He was buried from No 21 Casualty Clearing Station, with a large number of officers from the Division attending the funeral at Rocquigny–Equancourt Road British Cemetery, Manancourt.

After two months of having it comparatively easy, the men began noticing the tell-tale signs that another 'Push' was coming. The battalion was being called upon to provide unloading and working parties, while the traffic on the roads was increasing day on day. Artillery guns began to mass in the sector, their movement made more comfortable by the heavy fog that hung around for days at a time.

On 16 November the YCVs took over the entire brigade front line, allowing the other battalions of the 109th to train for the impending attack over a scale mock-up of the German front created by a plough. When relieved again by the 9th and 10th Inniskillings, the 14th Rifles dropped back into the support line without casualties despite the Germans shelling the Hermies–Demicourt road throughout the relief.

Shortly after 1.00 am on 20 November the enemy heavily shelled the YCV lines, both front and support trenches being pounded by heavy explosives and shrapnel. The

The Battle of Cambrai was the first time in the First World War when tanks were employed in large numbers and helped prove their worth to the many doubters. *(Illustrated History of the Great War, 1917)*

bombardment was repeated several times in the next few hours, but became perfectly quiet as Zero hour approached. The Battle of Cambrai was to see the first major use of the tank in warfare. No preliminary artillery bombardment was employed, with some 476 tanks advancing along a 10 km front at dawn on 20 November 1917, supported by six infantry and two cavalry divisions and backed up by 1,000 guns and 14 squadrons of the Royal Flying Corps. At 6.20 am, "the barking boys let loose – lights green, red and white and star shells going up at different places" and the machine guns and artillery opening fire. A company of the 14th Rifles, attached to the 10th Inniskillings, helped clear the communication trenches on the Demicourt–Flesquieres road but most of the battalion remained in support.

At 8.30 am confirmation of success was received when a message sent by Second Lieutenant Treanor, via a runner, reported the advance as going well on the right with troops passing through Havrincourt meeting only slight opposition. A further message, timed at 7.40 am and taking almost an hour to arrive with headquarters, said Havrincourt had fallen but the enemy was bombarding the forward trenches. An hour later it was reported to HQ, where dozens of prisoners were now filing past, that the Slag Heap had been taken without opposition. Second Lieutenant Knox sent a runner to headquarters, arriving about 10.00 am, to say he had taken all his objectives. The good news continued all day, with casualties reported to be slight across the entire brigade line. In total, the British had captured some 8,000 prisoners and 100 heavy guns by the end of that first day alone. Rifleman Sydney Chapman, from Great Yarmouth, Norfolk, was the 14th Rifles' only fatality on 20 November, while Rifleman Samuel McConnell, from Ballymacarrett, east Belfast, died from wounds the next day and Second Lieutenant Henry Edward Kyte passed away from his injuries on the 22nd.

The British generals were elated with their success and attempted to push on. At 8.00 am on 21 November the company commanders held a conference on the plans for fresh attacks, with headquarters staff moving forward later in the morning. The 14th Rifles and 10th Inniskillings penetrated to the outskirts of Moeuvres but this time the resistance was much tougher. B Company was held up by machine-gun fire east of Moeuvres but managed to link up with the 9th Inniskillings, who were in turn being pinned down by the machine-gunners. By 3.00 pm A Company was working its way to the right, along a trench by the canal, in an attempt to meet up with B Company but had to work round an enemy outpost. D Company had found Moeuvres heavily held and urgently requested artillery support. Coming under heavy fire from the village and the German flank trenches to the west, the battalion's positions at Moeuvres had to be surrendered. As the men from both C and D companies fell back Second Lieutenant Reddy rallied them, reporting to HQ that the enemy appeared to be preparing a counterattack. With all hope of a further advance gone, and the risk of ground being lost again, runners were despatched by headquarters at 5.40 pm with messages for all companies to form a defence line.

The battle had not gone to plan for James Kennedy Hope, whose relief at being in reserve was shattered when his new officer, again christened 'Snowball', decided to join the battle. After apparently leading the men up the wrong trench and opening fire with whizzbangs on an abandoned trench, "Snowball wakes to find he had taken the wrong turn," according to Hope.

> "We are out of our depth. We get out of this mess quicker than we got into it. We move into our proper area and find another beauty spot. There is a railway line in front. We cross it under a hail of bullets and reach another Hun system, seemingly the rear of the line. We are in a shallow trench about 20 yards from the village of Moeuvres. We cannot move from here. The Hun is clipping the grass of the parapet. We are well in front. 'We the reserve company of the support battalion of the attacking Brigade'. The Hun is keeping up a continuous sweeping of bullets. He knows we are here. It is impossible to put a hand above the trench. We are warned to prepare to take the hornets nest Moeuvres at 4.00 pm. It is a fond farewell to everybody this time. We know we won't even get as far as the parapet not to speak of Moeuvres. The wonderful order is cancelled to our great relief and we sit tight and await developments. At night we shift from this 'mouth of death.'"

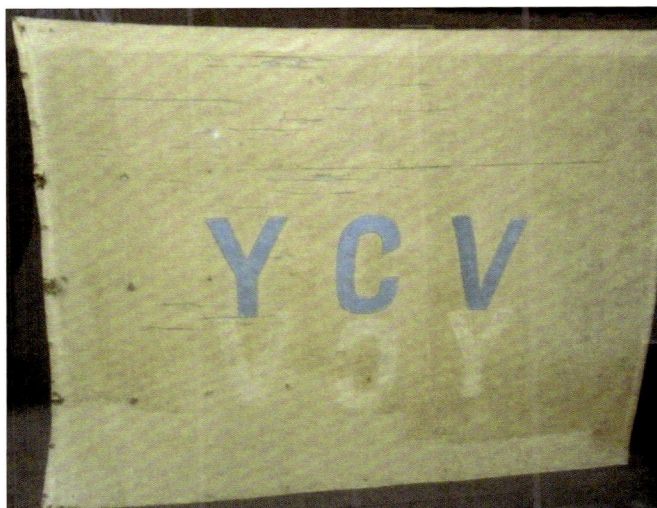

This YCV flag was carried into battle and saw plenty of action before being returned to Belfast. Today it is in the safe custody of Belfast City Hall. *(Author)*

Hope's section, with the support of a Lewis gun, was ordered to take up positions in No-Man's-Land as an early warning of a German counter-attack.

> "We are sitting in a big shell hole on a roadside. It is a most illuminating sight. Trench warfare in our own line is 'jam' compared with sitting in a shell hole in the enemy's quarter and at the most advanced point of the attack by our division, a little to our left lies Moeuvres. There seems to be a gradual dip in the country immediately in front. In the distance we see the lights of Cambrai. It is a wonderful situation. With the nose of our Lewis gun sneaking over the top of the hole we are in, we lie and take in a great movement. The Hun machine

is getting warmed up. We can see line after line of transport headlights swinging round the roads bringing up the stuff to stop the advance. We get palpitations of the heart as we listen to the limbers and carts rattling along on the road in front. If we give them a burst we will 'bring down the house'…"

The following morning, the battalion – with the temporary exception of those holding the front line – was ordered to withdraw to the original front line as men of the 12th Rifles relieved them. The next day the battalion was moved back to Hermies, taking over the old support line only to be moved forward again on the 24th as an attempt was made to retake Moeuvres, which had fallen the previous day. It wasn't until the 27th that the battalion was pulled out entirely, marching to Beaulencourt to camp about two miles from Bapaume. Hope recalled coming out of the line "in a hell of a snowstorm" and trudging for hours "more dead than alive" only to discover that no accommodation had been prepared for them. "We stand out in the snow all night. There is almost a mutiny. It is damnable treatment. A tot of rum doesn't quell the anger prevailing. We are all sick. It is a made up affair as a protest. The medical officer's hut is besieged. Any old grouse. All back to duty. The incident is smoothed over. We are told the billeting officer is drunk and is sent back to Boulogne for court martial. Perhaps, perhaps not. He is cursed in about 10 different dialects." Billeting was found and after two days of rest, during which attempts were made to clean both men and clothes, they were marched into Bapaume and entrained for Riviere, finally ending in a camp at Gouyen-Artois, close to Arras.

On 30 November orders were received that the battalion was to be withdrawn to the rear for three weeks of rest and training – but within hours was back on the road to the front line after word arrived that the Germans had broken through. The YCVs marched 14 miles to Achiet-le-Petit, sleeping in tents, then the next day on to Bancourt, where they were issued with tents and bivouacs that had to be erected in the bitter cold and rain. On 2 December the men made their way to Bertincourt, finding accommodation in their old billets despite the presence of other troops. The next day was spent awaiting orders to move into the front line but none came. Hope recalled: "We march as we never marched before… Haig stands at the entrance to big headquarters and watches us march past. He is cursed in the worst Cockney Irish ever I heard."

On the 4th they marched to Hayincourt Wood where they were issued with ammunition and grenades, being moved into trenches in the early evening. Those not deployed in the lines were sent to the divisional reinforcement camp at Etricourt while others were attached to the transport lines at Sorel-le-Grand. After dark on the 5th the 14th Rifles moved further forward to take over trenches north of Vacquerie as support to the 9th and 10th Inniskillings. Early on the 6th B Company suffered a number of casualties in a bombing fight with a party of Germans, while men from A Company were reported missing after being cut off. Hope, whose section was led by Second Lieutenant Whiteside, an officer who was taking part in his first battle since being commissioned from being a sergeant, takes up the story:

"The Skins are somewhere in front and we are supporting. I don't know the position but expect the officer in charge does. Into the Hun area we go. We are well away

Field Marshal Sir Douglas Haig was not too popular a sight for lads of the 14th Royal Irish Rifles as they hurried towards the battle at Cambrai. *(Courtesy of the Somme Museum)*

'somewhere' when the Hun barrage drops on the trench. On we go, there is no intercommunication. I am in charge of the bombers – 'dirty dog'. Whiteside the officer brings me up to lead the platoon. Temporary luck – I arrive at the front of the platoon when we are attacked from the rear, and cut off. The Hun has come in from a side trench and is bombing. Some of the boys are hit. There is a scurry. We jump about eight feet of high trench into the open."

Hope found himself in a trench occupied by seven Germans who put up no resistance when he dropped in to make them prisoners, though it took him to demonstrate that his rifle was loaded to convince them to begin moving.

"Another gesture and I'm pushing them all into our line at the end of a bayonet. I take the lot as far as Brigade HQ, one of them can speak good English. I get a 'bite' and some tea at HQ and up again I go. On my way I stop a company runner. He has good news. I read his message which says: 'The situation is becoming serious and will require the supervision of a senior officer'. Morrow our company commander."

Hope rejoined his section in time to take part in an exchange of grenades with the attacking Germans until a sortie over the top brings it to an end. During the fighting Second Lieutenant James Samuel Emerson, a 22-year-old from Collon, County Louth, serving with the 9th Royal Inniskilling Fusiliers, won the Victoria Cross. His citation gives a flavour of the nature of the fighting:

"For repeated acts of most conspicuous bravery. He led his company in an attack and cleared 400 yards of trench. Though wounded, when the enemy attacked in superior numbers, he sprung out of the trench with eight men and met the attack in the open, killing many and taking six prisoners. For three hours after this, all other officers having become casualties, he remained with his company, refusing to go to the dressing station, and repeatedly repelled bombing attacks. Later, when the enemy again attacked in superior numbers, he led his men to repel the attack and was mortally wounded. His heroism, when worn out and exhausted from loss of blood, inspired his men to hold out, though almost surrounded, till reinforcements arrived and dislodged the enemy."

On 8 December, in pouring rain and awful mud, and with the enemy shelling hard, the battalion was relieved by the 15th Rifles, and spent the night in tents in Havrincourt Wood. They were, according to the *War Diary*, "miserable, tired, dirty men who had done splendid work". The Germans shelled the wood on the morning of the 9th, causing no casualties but making life difficult. It was with relief, therefore, that the battalion marched out about 6.00 pm to more comfortable billets at Metz-en-Couture, the journey being completed in heavy rain and "almost up to the knees in mud". Shells falling close to the battalion's headquarters were recorded in the diary entry for the next day, along with the strafing of nearby roads by enemy aircraft. The health of the battalion, after weeks spent exposed to the elements with little rest or sleep, was causing concern to all. On 11 December, for example, some 118 men reported on the sick parade, while a request for 160 men for a working party fell short, the medical officer deeming that only 75 were fit to go. With orders to return to the front the next day, the battalion made representations for a change of orders to allow for a period out of the line. "The men are cold in billets and their clothes are still wet. It is small wonder that there is much sickness," noted the diary. The request was taken on board, with the brigade spared further fighting. "Evidently it has at last been realised that until the men have had a complete rest they cannot be considered an efficient fighting unit," penned the adjacent.

It was a hollow victory for the battalion, as it only served to confirm to General Nugent, the Divisional Commander, that his earlier attempts to stiffen the 14th Rifles' fighting resolve had failed. His opinion of the YCV would not have been helped by the fact that Cambrai, after the initial success, had ultimately proved a failure. Typically the British had failed to move reinforcements up quickly enough to exploit their early gains and the momentum was lost. A series of German counter-attacks, employing huge numbers of men, began to reverse the tide and within a week all the ground lost had been regained. Both sides lost heavily, with the Germans sustaining 50,000 casualties and the British 45,000. (See Appendix 10)

Hope records how the battalion was paraded in a square at Metz-en-Couture with "the boys who were misbehaving themselves in the Cambrai battle lined up in the middle. Our misdeeds are read out and we each receive personal congratulations from the Brigadier." In fact, Hope ultimately received the Military Medal for his gallantry and his officer, Lieutenant Morrow, the Military Cross.[4]

YCV old comrades walk along the rows of graves at a cemetery on the Cambrai battlefield looking for the final resting places of friends. (*Courtesy of the Somme Museum*)

Chapter 17

THERE WASN'T A SHOT TO BE HEARD

Many of them were the best we had, many of them I know so well. I loved to grasp their strong Protestant hands when I came here. Many of them you and I will never see again. We mourn their loss. May the great God let them know that on this 12th of July we do not forget one of them. We know they are sleeping their last sleep in France and Flanders, and another thing we know, they have left behind them an example which we will try to follow.

Sir Edward Carson, 12 July 1918

CAMBRAI HAD BEEN THE last major battle that the 14th Royal Irish Rifles was to be involved in as a battalion, though its men, both under a different guise and as individuals, had much more fighting to conclude. On 13 December, after spending most of the day on standby on the Cambrai front because a German prisoner had claimed that a large scale enemy attack was imminent, the battalion marched three miles to Sorel-le-Grand where it was housed in huts with the rest of the brigade. After two days the men were on the road again, arriving in Rocquigny where they were accommodated in Nissen huts in "quite the best camp we have been in for a long period". The next day the men were marched to Etricourt, where they boarded trains for what turned out to be a "very tedious and chilly" journey in cattle trucks, arriving at 11.00 pm in the village of Mondicourt, a few miles from Doullens, in driving snow. A further march of four miles remained to Grouches-Luchoel where the men, being housed in barns, settled down quickly. The officers, however, deprived of their kits and mess boxes due to the Transport getting stuck in the snow, spent a miserable night "beside whatever kind of fire they could procure through the hospitality of the French inhabitants". With the locals having their fuel, sugar and bread rationed, they were disinclined to be generous.

Also in great demand, but in short supply, was fuel for the burners. In the run-up to Christmas 1917, the great complaint was the cold and scarcity of wood, coal and coke. "The men are frozen in their billets," the *War Diary* recorded on the 18th. Working parties, some 200 strong, were called for to clear snow off the roads while every day more and more men were reporting on sick parades suffering from flu-like ailments. Each day a quarter of the strength was allowed into Doullens in the afternoon, making their way back for lights out in the evening. Amiens, the only city in the Somme region, was 15 kms away and could be reached by rail, on an "actual passenger train" as noted by a happy Hope, at a cost of nine pence. Back pay had come through and the men were trying to "drown

George Holmes with a couple of unnamed mates from the 14th Royal Irish Rifles. *(Courtesy of the Somme Museum)*

the past in champagne and beer while the money lasts," he added. Christmas Day was celebrated in traditional style, with snow covering everything with a fresh fall in the evening. "The battalion had a splendid feed – prime turkey with plenty of vegetables, followed by plum pudding and washed down with beer," said the diary.

On the morning of the 29th the YCVs marched out of camp to Mondicourt, where they boarded trains to Moreuil, some 14 miles south east of Amiens, where the accommodation was better than expected and the welcome warm though costly: "It is understood that British soldiers have not been billeted in the town for nine months. Prices advanced 50 per cent within an hour of our arrival," commented the *War Diary*.

The New Year was marked by church services and further free time to spend in Amiens, with 10 per cent allowed into the city each day. The stay in Moreuil was short, however, though half the population turned out on 7 January to see the boys as they trudged off on a four mile trek to Mezieres along roads which were under deep snow in places. However, their welcome in the neighbouring village was much cooler than the one they had just left. "Our reception was nearly as frigid as the weather, none of the people wishing to have us," recorded the adjutant. "Locked doors or irate women met us at every turn." To further complicate matters, the 9th Inniskillings and 109th Field Ambulance were billeted in the same village, with more than one unit being allocated the same accommodation in places. After two nights the battalion moved on to Rethonvillers, with none of the men dropping out despite a sharp pace being kept up over the 18-mile route. "We passed through miles of country which had been devastated, a melancholy waste of barren fields and wrecked villages," said the diary. The battalion was now in the French sector and marvelled at the live-and-let-live attitude they witnessed.

"Passing through a fairly large town named Roye we saw a singular sight, viz, an unaccompanied German entering a shop to make purchases. A large number of Bosches were working in the streets cleaning them of snow. They were guarded by two or three elderly French soldiers and looked happy and well-fed."

Rethonvillers had until recently been held by the Germans and, though it had suffered some damage, was largely intact, providing the men with good accommodation during their brief stay. On 11 January, the battalion moved closer to the front, another march of 19 miles bringing them within hearing distance again of the guns. The battalion was split between the villages of Artemps and Grand Seraucourt, taking over billets from French troops.

On the 13 January the YCVs moved into the support trenches, with the 9th and 10th Skins in the front line and the 11th Inniskillings in reserve. The trenches and dugouts met their approval but there were too few of them for the officers, who were in larger numbers in the British Army than in the French. A thaw, however, told a different story: "After the long spell of frost, the rapid thaw has caused the sides of the trenches to fall in and the sandbags of the dugouts have become loosened. Conditions above ground are very miserable," reported the *War Diary*. German shelling and frequent rain showers added to the shambles. The 14th moved into the front line on the night of the 17 January, relieving the 10th Inniskillings. At 6.00 am the following day the Germans heavily shelled the French battalion on the YCV's right flank, with some falling among the men of C Company, killing one man, Rifleman Edward Gain,[1] and knocking out a Lewis gun position.

Later in the day enemy machine-gun fire caused a couple of casualties. There was more excitement the following evening when the Germans heavily shelled an outpost known as the Sphinx post, following up with a raid in force, though there were no casualties in the battalion lines. The men came out of the front line again on 20 January, going into Brigade reserve in place of the 9th Inniskillings. Because they were constantly under observation, the men couldn't train or enjoy any form of recreation, and so had largely to be content with cleaning up themselves, their surroundings and equipment. The battalion went back into the front line on 27 January for two of the quietest nights it had ever experienced, the enemy apparently content after having snatched several men in raids days earlier. Relieved by the 9th (North Irish Horse) Battalion of the Royal Irish Fusiliers, the men marched back to billets in Grand Seraucourt.

A considerable amount of work went into creating this cover for the YCV drum. It was photographed during an exhibition at Belfast City Hall themed on trench art. *(Author)*

Although they did not know it, the 14th Royal Irish Rifles had served its last spell in the trenches. Rumours had been rife for weeks but on 30 January word was received from the War Office that divisions were to be reorganised with brigades reduced from four to three battalions with the excess units merged or disbanded. "It is almost certain that the 14th RI Rifles will be one. It will be hard after nearly 3½ years existence, almost 2½ of which have been spent on active service, to be merged in another battalion or be broken up. C'est la guerre," wrote the adjutant. On 3 February the diary reported that the reorganisation of the three brigades of the 36th (Ulster) Division was underway but no word on the fate of the YCVs had been received though "an appeal is being made that this unit should not be broken up, but whether it will get through in time or have any effect is doubtful. Things are moving rapidly." On 8 February the battalion said goodbye to the disbanded 11th Inniskillings, officers and the band marching more than two miles to play as 400 men of the Skins marched past on their way to join the 9th Inniskillings. "The 11th and 14th Rifles have always been good friends, have met in friendly rivalry on the football field, and have fought shoulder to shoulder in many fights. These are depressing days for the Ulster Division," noted the *War Diary*. The following day the YCVs finally received word they were to move out of the 109th Brigade, which was now to consist of the 1st, 2nd and 9th Royal Inniskilling Fusiliers.[2]

In fact, despite publicly expressing regret at the demise of the 14th Rifles, the Ulster Division's commanding officer Major General Oliver

194

Nugent had recommended the battalion's disbandment and launched a scathing attack on its record in a confidential letter written to the adjutant general in December 1917. It read:

"The 14th Royal Irish Rifles now in the 109th Brigade to be broken up and used to make up casualties in the Royal Irish Rifles battalions in the Division. This battalion should in my opinion be broken up in any case. About a year ago, I reported them as totally wanting in military spirit and asked for a CO and a large draft of Englishmen to try and create a fighting spirit in them. You gave me both, and while Cheape was in command they certainly improved, but since he left they have been tried and found wanting. It is significant that their present CO told me two days ago that most of the English draft sent to them a year ago have become casualties. The Brigadier says he cannot trust them and I know that he is right. They are poor stuff, either as workers or fighters and have been a constant source of anxiety during the past three weeks."

An order creating Entrenching Battalions was issued by the adjutant general on 10 February 1918. These new units were to be under Army or Corps control rather than divisional commanders, were not to be split up, had to work on defences only and were not allowed any further forward than the 'Rearward Zone'. In total, some 25 Entrenching Battalions were formed across the Western Front. Three were made up from the men displaced from the 36th (Ulster) Division. The 21st Entrenching Battalion was created from the 8/9th and 10th Royal Irish Rifles, and 10th Royal Inniskillings Fusiliers; the 22nd Entrenching Battalion consisted of the 11/13th Rifles; and the 23rd Entrenching Battalion was formed from the men of 14th Rifles and 11th Inniskillings. That same day the YCVs handed over their billets at Grand Seraucourt to the 1st Skins with the four companies marching to Marteville, some eight miles away, where they took over huts alongside a railway embankment. The headquarters staff and another 130 men were sent to Douvieux,

Rifleman TE Bruce was one of a number of staff members from the Belfast Technical College who joined the 14th Rifles. *(Courtesy of Belfast Met)*

17 miles away from the main body. Major Mulholland, who had inherited command of the battalion, along with his second-in-command, were posted to XVIII Corps HQ.

Since coming out of the line, the 14th had been providing huge working parties to dig trenches and prepare defences for the anticipated German attack. Now they were allocated the task of digging channels for cables. A final diary entry for 17 February 1918, blandly records the inevitable: "We are almost immediately to become an entrenching battalion under the name of No 23 Entrenching Battalion. Our work will be digging trenches in the rear zone." Some 200 members of the 11th Inniskillings, accompanied by seven junior officers, joined the new battalion but kept their own identity.

The long anticipated German attack was launched on 21 March 1918, with the Ulster Division among the units feeling its full might. Three German armies pushed forward in the early morning mist, bypassing strong points and rapidly taking ground. The British army was thrown into disarray, with orders for withdrawal being issued that evening. The following day the retreat continued piecemeal with the real possibility arising of the British

Now in the safekeeping of Belfast City Hall, this flag, featuring the 14th Rifles' battle honours, was not completed until after the battalion had been disbanded. *(Author)*

Fifth Army's defences collapsing and a potential 49-mile gap opening up between it and the British Third Army. On 23 March, all available troops were thrown into the battle in a bid to halt the German advance, with the YCVs of the 23rd Entrenching Battalion coming under the orders of the 30th Division, which was attempting to hold the line of the Somme canal around Offoy. The men held trenches along the waterway and part of the railway line towards Canizy in what was now effectively the front line. About 6.00 pm the commanding officers of the 182nd Brigade, the 23rd Entrenching Battalion, the 11th South Lancashire Regiment and a composite battalion that had been rapidly organised to the left of the line met up in an unsuccessful attempt to reorganise so that they would have the one consecutive line.

The YCVs were now in front of Verlaines, which they continued to hold until forced to retire about 7.00 am on 24 March. As part of mixed companies, they fell back in the direction of Ramecourt to the south-west. In total, some 26 YCVs were killed during the month of March, most during the fighting on the 23rd and 24th (see Appendix 11). There were further deaths in April: Rifleman Thomas Booth, from the Shankill area of Belfast, and Rifleman Edward George Youngman, from Lowestoft, Suffolk, both being killed in fighting on the 20th; Sergeant David Marshall, a Scot who on 1 July 1916, had escaped unscathed despite being in the trench with Billy McFadzean when the box of grenades had spilled, died of wounds on the 24th; and Rifleman William Wilson, from Carlisle, was killed in action on the 27th.

By the end of April, however, the German offensive on the Somme had been brought to a halt at Villers-Bretonneux, just short of the city of Amiens. Other enemy actions along the Western Front in the coming months likewise failed to produce a breakthrough but exhausted German resources and men. In August 1918, the British began a series of attacks that would ultimately take them to victory. The 23rd Entrenching Battalion had ceased to exist and the remaining YCVs, like so many of their comrades before and at disbandment, were transferred to other fighting units. Three men still listed as belonging to the 14th Rifles passed away in June, the 'died' next to their names indicating natural causes: Rifleman Charles Henry Adams, from Peckham, Surrey, on 19 June; Rifleman Peter Reilly, a Dubliner, on 20 June; and Rifleman Maxwell Davis, from Belfast, at home on 30 June.

First World War death records tend to be arbitrary at times and indicate that the last members of 14th Royal Irish Rifles to be killed in action were riflemen John Patterson and Robert Walker, who died on 16 and 22 July respectively – some five months after the battalion had been officially disbanded. The former was from Barrow-in-Furness, Lancashire, and the latter Port Glasgow. Others, severely wounded earlier in the war, also died as YCVs, such as Sergeant George Brankin on 2 October 1918; Rifleman Robert Currie three days later; and Lance Corporal James Riddell Taylor who lies in Riseberga Churchyard, Sweden, where he was laid to rest following his death from pneumonia. The 31-year-old, who died just three days before Christmas 1918, had been awaiting repatriation to his home in South Parade, Belfast, after his release from a prisoner-of-war camp in Germany.[3]

However, men who had formerly served in the battalion were fighting in units across the Western Front, with the deaths or service recorded under their new units. Captain John McMinn, for example, an original officer with the pre-war Young Citizens and a founding member of the battalion, was killed in action on 27 May 1918, while attached to the 5th Durham Light Infantry. The 32-year-old, who lived in north Belfast with his wife Isabella, had perhaps been living on borrowed time. He had served in the home corps for a spell after an accident in France and had also been wounded the previous August and again in December 1917. Hope, who had left the battalion for what he hoped would be a cushy job working with a town major, was quickly thrown back into the fighting and saw a former YCV comrade similarly engaged. He wrote:

Rifleman Maxwell Davis died at home on 30 June 1918, and is buried in the graveyard of Drumbo Presbyterian Church. *(Author)*

"We are divided into platoons and find ourselves in Villeselve. To my surprise I see the officer in charge is Foy, the first sergeant of our platoon in the 14th. He is getting some dirty work as an officer – probably his 'first job' and last. We take over a post from the French in front of Villeselve and are led to believe troops of ours are in front and will pass through us later in the day. I have my doubts. My one dread is being captured. I don't want to be captured and I take jolly good care I'm not. Two hours pass and I weigh up the situation in spite of Foy. He has taught me a lot earlier in the war no doubt but he can show me nothing in a fix like this."

Not for the first time, Hope makes his own call on the best strategy – fleeing the line along with another soldier. "We are not a minute too soon," he records. "The trap is set. The village is lifted sky high with ferrous high velocity shells of big calibre. Foy and the platoon are left and pass through into the prison camp." Hope eventually ended up in No 12 platoon of A Company of the 1st Royal Irish Rifles, where "most of the boys are old 14th".

Charles Sheridan, who was on leave when the battalion was disbanded, was posted to the Machine Gun Corps as a signaller just two days before the German attack and saw plenty of action.

Rifleman W Heasley, who though wounded in four places at the Somme had continued to carry out his job as a battalion runner, was one of a number of men who transferred to the Heavy Branch Machine Gun Corps, later to be renamed the Tank Corps. From Manor Drive in Belfast, he had formerly worked as an apprentice fitter at the Belfast engineering firm Mackies. Quartermaster Sergeant Harrison McCloy, who had played for Cliftonville football club and had been honorary secretary of the Irish Football League, was killed by shell fire on 21 August 1917, while serving in a tank. Lance Corporal Jack Stuart was awarded a Vellum certificate for his courage in a tank at the Battle of Arras. Former YCV Company Sergeant Major William McIlveen, who before the war had worked as a clerk in Harland and Wolff's shipyard, was killed by a sniper on 6 May 1918, his 26th birthday, while serving with the 15th Rifles. He had won the Distinguished Conduct Medal at Messines the year before and later added a bar to his medal. His brother, Sergeant John McIlveen, also of the 14th Rifles, won the Military Medal in 1917. An upholsterer at Anderson and McAuley's store in Belfast before the war, he was commissioned in 1918 and survived the war. Second Lieutenant Dalton Prenter, who served 16 months in the ranks with the YCVs before being commissioned, was killed in the German offensive of 21 March 1918, while serving with the 9th (North Irish Horse) Royal Irish Fusiliers. The 27-year-old from Fitzroy Avenue in Belfast had formerly worked for Moore and Weinberg in Linenhall Street in the city. He is remembered on the Pozieres Memorial.

Berry, another old member of the 14th, ended up in the 1st Rifles and finished the war in a barracks at Soldatenheim, Belgium. He recorded:

"We have just retired for the night when in came an officer (Captain Bill Bell) who informed us that an armistice had been signed by the enemy. I can't describe how I felt when I heard the glad news but suffice to say that we didn't stay in bed. We

James Russell, who joined up with George Mullin only to be released for war work, later re-enlisted in the Royal Engineers and saw action throughout 1918. *(Courtesy of Andrew Totten)*

marched out into the square any how (no discipline) and started dancing and singing and holding hands, officers and men alike. We were about two miles behind the line. There wasn't a shot to be heard – but plenty of verey lights were going up. We came in to our billets in the early hours of the following morning happy with the knowledge that we were finished with the job."

LOOKING EAGERLY FOR WHITE FLAG.

MEMORABLE DAY AT FRONT.

ONE QUESTION ON ALL SIDES.

(By Percival Phillips.)

WITH THE BRITISH ARMIES IN THE FIELD, Friday Night.—For the first time since they came into being the three British Armies advancing on Mons and Maubeuge went forward yesterday fighting—but on the look-out for a flag of truce.

The German plenipotentiaries on their way to hear Marshal Foch's terms of armistice were drawing near the Allied lines. Our troops heard during the afternoon that they might cross the front between Le Cateau and Guise.

Explicit orders were issued regarding the procedure to be adopted if they appeared opposite the British zone. The vanguard of our advancing armies was warned to keep watch, and if a White Flag appeared it was to be recognised immediately, and the armistice delegates were to be brought in and taken to the nearest Divisional Headquarters, who would examine their credentials, and arrange for their safe conduct to the designed rendezvous.

Naturally, the German delegates chose the most direct route to Marshal Foch—through the lines of the French 1st Army, which adjoins the British 4th Army, south-east of Le Cateau.

But the mere possibility of being the first to sight their flag, and witness such an historic event, fairly electrified our troops, and kept them eagerly alert all the way from the flooded fields beside the Mons canal southward along the front of the 1st, 3rd and 4th Armies. This has been one of the memorable days of the war.

The advance towards Mons and Maubeuge continues with little opposition, but the question is on the lips of every man: "Have they agreed to the armistice?"

The news that the German envoys were delayed by the congestion of traffic within their own lines evoked grim amusement It is easy for our gunners to picture the disorder approaching chaos which prevails on the crowded roads. They have kept the German forward areas under constant fire. The roads to Mons and those beyond Maubeuge which are being utilised for the removal of material have been rendered well-nigh useless.

Last night there were great sheets of flame reflected at intervals against the eastern sky, and the rumble of distant explosions as of munition dumps blown up by the enemy. His artillery indulged in unusual outburst of shelling useless, and for the most part, perfectly reckless, as though other ammunition was being simply got rid of.

The infantry resistance in front of Mons

For some the end of the war came as an anti-climax, while for others it was cause for the biggest celebration ever. (Belfast Telegraph)

Chapter 18

THE LAST POST

Dare we grudge their quiet sleeping
Who have fought such odds?
Envy them, the day completed,
Facing death, yet undefeated,
Their honour in good keeping
And their hand in God's

Poem recited at the unveiling of the 14th Rifles
statue at City Hall on 1 July 1924

DAVID LOWRY, A PRE-WAR YCV officer, sat down at his desk in his Donegall Place office on 23 May 1919, some six-months after the end of hostilities, to compose a letter on which the future of the organisation would hinge. Addressing it to Sir Edward Carson at his London residence in Eaton Place, he wrote of how "a large number of men who took a good deal to do with the Young Citizen Volunteers of Belfast are anxious to have the Battalion re-established in the city". He went on:

> "The Lord Mayor is also in favour of the project, but, before putting it to him in a
> formal way and asking him to move in the matter, as an old Company Commander
> I thought it better to write and ask your opinion as to what would be the outcome.
> We do not wish to agitate and after proceeding to a certain point have to abandon
> the attempt through opposition on the other side. Do you think there is a possibility
> of Young Citizens such as we had in Belfast before the War being promoted under
> present political conditions? Your opinion will be the main factor in deciding us as
> to what to do in this matter."

The reply, just three days later, was friendly enough but just as effective as a death warrant in sealing the fate of the YCVs. "I should of course be glad to see the Young Citizen Volunteers Battalion re-established in the City but I doubt whether it is feasible to do this at the present moment, except with the consent of the Irish Government…"

The formation of the 14th Royal Irish Rifles in 1914 had not meant that the Young Citizens Volunteers of Belfast had ceased to exist. Those who remained at home were a self-contained unit within the Ulster Volunteer Force and continued to meet for drill at Ormiston on a regular basis and to recruit new members with the intention of getting back up to battalion strength. Part of their training was marksmanship, and the YCVs held a number of competition events throughout 1915 with UVF units and local shooting clubs as their opponents, and finished the year undefeated. However, in May 1916 the UVF, and so the YCV, was effectively stood down though still existed on paper. Three years later, on 1 May 1919 – barely three weeks before the Lowry letter to Sir Edward – the Ulster Volunteer Force was officially demobilised with its commanding officer, Sir George Richardson, standing down.

The "political conditions" referred to were the Anglo-Irish War or War of Independence, then in its early stages and set to sweep northwards into Ulster, where it would be simply known as 'The Troubles'. The violence sparked talk of reviving the UVF and in places former members, together with fresh volunteers, came together unofficially to protect their communities against the threat of raids by the Irish Republican Army. Elsewhere, a number of other 'civilian forces' had been formed. These included two, one at Castledawson and another at Maghera, raised by Colonel Chichester, the commanding officer of the YCVs.

Fred T Geddes, the man who had first proposed the formation of the YCVs, had also found a new paramilitary interest during the war years, becoming secretary of the Belfast Defence Corps, formed in February 1915 at a meeting at the Ye Olde Restaurant in the city. It recruited men between the ages of 18 and 60 for the duration of the war, though was later disbanded having failed to receive official sanction. Former temperance members of the Young Citizens also founded the Belfast Volunteer Training Corps, which used St George's Market twice a week for rifle practice. It mounted guards on the docks and shipyards and assisted the Harbour Police marshal passengers alighting from the steamers. It, too, was disbanded for want of official sanction.

In August 1919, the YCVs flags were laid up, being presented to Lord French, the former British Expeditionary Force commander, who accepted them on behalf of the city corporation. The *Belfast News Letter* reported:

> "One of these had been carried by these gallant boys through a great deal of terrible fighting at Messines Ridge. It was fitting that these flags should be handed to his excellency by Mrs Spencer Chichester, OBE (Moyola Park, Castledawson), whose husband, Lieut-Colonel RPDS Chichester, raised and commanded the battalion known as the 14th Royal Irish Rifles (YCV)."

Julia McMordie, widow of the former Belfast Lord Mayor, attends a remembrance service along with officials and members of the 10th Boy Scout group at the City Hall on 7 June 1920, the third anniversary of the death of member Brian Boyd. Note the YCV flags hanging above the table. *(Courtesy of Andrew Totten)*

Mrs Chichester, it noted, took the deepest interest in the battalion and had been responsible for many of the comforts sent out to the Front. Lord French told the gathering in the Great Hall of Belfast's City Hall: "I have great pleasure, and I consider it a great honour, to present this flag. It was carried by the Young Citizen Volunteers of Belfast in a great deal of terrible fighting at Messines Ridge, and I am quite sure it is a trophy which Belfast will value and always keep." The second flag had been made by the women of the Ulster Ladies' Work Society, based at 11 Chichester Street in Belfast, at the request of Mrs Chichester but had never been presented to the battalion. Today they are stored in the basement of the City Hall, only being displayed on 1 July each year.

Lord French was in Belfast to take the salute at the Peace Day parade of 9 August 1919. While London had held its march on 19 July, the date had been deemed too close to the traditional Orange Order day of 12 July, hence the delay. Belfast Corporation contributed £12,000 to the cost of the parade, which began in the north of the city, wound its way past the front of the City Hall where the saluting dais was set up, and finished in Ormeau Park. A guard of honour stood stalk still by a temporary cenotaph erected in the grounds of the City Hall. It took the parade, which included many of the surviving members of the 14th Rifles, three hours to pass any given point.

The City Hall, where the Young Citizens were first conceived, also became the home of a permanent memorial to the 14th Royal Irish Rifles, though it took nearly a decade of planning and fund-raising to achieve. In July 1916, following the slaughter on the Somme, a shrine of flowers was created outside the City Hall. Among the tributes was a wreath, finished in the blue and grey ribbons of the YCVs, laid by David Adams and W Calvert and bearing a message from the Young Citizen Memorial Committee: "In affectionate remembrance of the dear boys". Mr Adams, a Justice of the Peace, lost a nephew who was serving with the battalion. Along with Miss May Gibson, sister of a YCV soldier and a tireless supporter who had visited the wounded, the families of the dead and dispatched aid parcels, Mr Adams organised a meeting in the Kinghan Memorial Hall to explore the possibilities of creating a monument to the Young Citizens. Among those who spoke on the need to provide a worthy tribute to the dead was William McFadzean, father of the 1 July Victoria Cross hero. A motion, proposed by RJ Ross and seconded by Mr Calvert, approved the project and the formation of a committee to take it forward. Eight years later, on 1 July 1924, the fruits of their labour were finally revealed. Colonel Chichester's widow, Dehra, was given the honour of unveiling the bronze statue of a soldier upon a pedestal of Portland stone, referred to affectionately by the veterans as 'Wee Joey'. Her voice trembling with emotion as she performed the ceremony on the East Staircase, Mrs Chichester paid tribute to the "very best of the young manhood" of Belfast. The *Northern Whig* reported:

The Belfast City Hall memorial to the 14th Royal Irish Rifles, affectionately known as 'Wee Joey', was unveiled by Dehra Chichester, the widow of the Young Citizens' first commanding officer. *(Author)*

"It was (proceeded Mrs Chichester) only fitting that that memorial should find its place within the walls of the building with which they were so closely associated – a building which was the concrete embodiment of the spirit of the great city of which those men were proud to be Young Citizen Volunteers (Hear, hear). It was an honour and privilege for her to be asked to unveil that memorial. As they had heard

from the Lord Mayor, her husband raised the battalion, he commanded it until his health gave way, he looked upon the members of it as his children, he glorified in their glory, he suffered with them in their losses, and she (the speaker) had shared those feelings with him. (Hear, hear). She saw them go out in their vigour and pride of manhood, and saw what was left of them marching past that City Hall on their return. She was proud, though sad, that it fell to her lot that day, to write the end to the last chapter of the book of their life. But let the pages of that book be turned over and read tenderly and proudly, and let them all glory in its story. Belfast had every right to be proud of its Young Citizen Volunteers, who wrote their names in imperishable letters of gold in the annals of the brilliant 36th Ulster Division. (Hear, hear)."

Mrs Chichester said Thiepval was written in blood on the hearts of many wives, mothers, sisters and sweethearts, and the statue would be a reminder to future generations of the brave deeds of the YCV who had fallen for King and country. The ceremony concluded with the playing of the 'Last Post'.

The 'Wee Joey' statue became the centre of remembrance for the veterans of the 14th Rifles. In addition to having representatives lay wreaths at the Cenotaph in the grounds of the City Hall each 1 July and Armistice Day, it became a tradition for surviving members to hold their own ceremony inside, laying a wreath at the base of the figure in memory of lost friends. Between the wars, and again for a number of years after the Second World War, the regimental flag was displayed above 'Wee Joey'. In addition, the men met annually for dinner in November to renew friendships and recall old times. Organised by the YCV Reunion Committee, later named the YCV Old Comrades Association, the chairman used the old battalion bell, which had once hung outside the guardroom at Finner, Randalstown, Seaford and Bramshott camps, after being presented by Workman Clark & Co shipyard, to call for silence. The evening always concluded with a toast to "Our Fallen Comrades".

The remains of Colonel Chichester leave his home, Moyola Park, Castledawson, escorted by members of the Chichester Masonic Lodge 506. *(Belfast Telegraph)*

While once hundreds had attended the reunion evenings, the numbers naturally decreased over the years as old soldiers 'faded away.' Colonel Chichester, whose military career had been blighted by medical problems, passed away in December 1921 after a short illness. He had only months before been elected as Westminster MP for South Londonderry. Mrs Chichester, who had been elected MP at the first Northern Ireland elections in 1921, married Admiral Henry Parker in 1928 and stood down from parliament the following year. In 1933 she again stood for election for South Londonderry, a vacancy created by the death of her son-in-law Captain Chichester-Clark. With her resignation in June 1960, she became the final original member of the first Northern Ireland Parliament to withdraw from active politics. She had been the first woman to reach a Junior Ministerial position; first to be appointed a member of the Stormont Cabinet when she became Minister of Health and Local Government in 1949; and the first female to move the Address in reply to the King's speech and to propose the election of a Speaker. She was succeeded at Stormont by her grandson, James Chichester-Clark, who went on to become the leader of the Ulster Unionist Party and Prime Minister of Northern Ireland between 1969–71, while another grandson, Robin Chichester-Clark, was MP for Londonderry at Westminster from 1955 until 1974 and served as Minister of State for Employment in the Conservative administration. In 1957 she was created a Dame Grand Cross, following the award of the DBE in 1949. Dame Dehra passed away on 28 November 1963 at her home, Shanemullagh House, Castledawson.

William Moore moved to England after the war and lived to a ripe old age. He is seen here on holiday in Scarborough with his wife. *(Author)*

The death of former Regimental Quartermaster-Sergeant George Uprichard was lamented at the 1926 battalion Armistice dinner, when he was described as "one of the most gifted and most popular members of the battalion – a good comrade and a gallant soldier". Captain James McKee, who had lost a leg at Messines, found a job as secretary to the principal of his old school, Campbell College, and lived at Stormont Park, east Belfast. He died in hospital on 14 July 1934, following major surgery and was buried at Dundonald Cemetery, with the 'Last Post' sounded by a bugle party of the Campbell College Officers Training Corps.

Alan Mulholland, who as adjutant and later commanding officer, had been the bedrock of the battalion, continued his military career as well as entering politics. The Donaghadee man and former Campbell College pupil had been mobilised in 1914 with the 6th Black Watch, transferring to the 14th Rifles three months later, remaining with the Young Citizens until disbandment. He commanded the 1st Royal Irish Rifles briefly in 1918 before joining the War Office staff. He earned the Military Cross, two mentions in despatches and the French Croix-de-Guerre with Palm leaves during his service. Between the wars he commanded a Territorial Army battalion of the London Irish Rifles and in 1939 joined the staff of the Western Command, where he remained until 1946. Colonel Mulholland, who

Sergeant Hugh Neely, pictured enjoying a drink with a couple of former comrades during their 1927 tour of the battlefields, went on to serve in the Home Guard during the Second World War and celebrated his 100th birthday in the Somme Nursing Home in east Belfast. *(Courtesy of the Somme Museum)*

had initially followed his father and grandfather into the linen business in Belfast, ran his own advertising business in London. A Conservative, he was a member of the Westminster City Council for 31 years, serving as Mayor in 1949–50. A leading member of the London Ulster Association and a Justice of the Peace, he was made an MBE for his services during the Second World War. He passed away at his London home in 1966.

Like Colonel Mulholland, Sergeant Hugh Woods Neely was a regular at battalion reunions. Originally from Swatragh, County Londonderry, but living in the Shankill Road area of Belfast, he had been badly wounded on 1 July but still managed to carry an injured comrade to the dressing station, for which he was awarded the DCM. Recommended for a commission, he was discharged from the Army after being injured in an accidental

The Ulster Tower, standing on ground once occupied by the German front line trenches, commemorates the men of the 36 (Ulster) Division's sacrifice on the Somme. *(Author)*

mortar explosion during training. He returned to his former job in the Civil Service and, while working for the Ministry of Pensions in County Cavan, was ambushed by the IRA but only lost his car. Sergeant Neely, who served in the Ulster Home Guard during the Second World War and was a leading Orangeman, later became a deputy principle in the Civil Service and was awarded the MBE in 1949. He retired in 1956 and spent his last years in the Somme Hospital, where he marked his 100th birthday. He had continued to lay a wreath at the YCV memorial in the City Hall up until late in life.

Another soldier to reach his 100th birthday was Thomas Bones Stephenson. He had enlisted seeking vengeance for the death of his brother, William, killed with the 14th Rifles in April 1916. Thomas, as an acting captain, won the Military Cross in 1918 for organising bombing parties to drive the raiding Germans out of the British lines but was badly injured, being invalided home. He married Christina Kennedy, sister of Young Citizen William, who had been killed at Messines in 1917, while his sister, Essie, married William's brother, Chancellor Kennedy, an officer in the Ulster Division.

Donald Clark, great uncle of UTV presenter Paul Clark, had

been a member of the YCV before the war. Afterwards he lived on the Crawsfordburn Road, Bangor, with his wife Mary. They had no children and he died in 1980. The Clark family had been involved in the manufacture of military uniforms during the war. Thomas McAuley, one of the original 1912 YCVs, served as a Lewis gunner. After the war he entered the family building business in Belfast and joined up again in 1942, aged 45, serving as a captain in the Pioneer Corps, mainly in Africa. He retired at 85 and lived until he was 92, dying in 1988. Samuel McAvoy, of the 14th Rifles, was one of three brothers, the others serving in the 2nd and 15th Rifles. He was severely gassed and suffered circulation problems the rest of his life, resulting in the loss of both legs, though he could still make his way from his east Belfast home to the nearby public house.

John Wallace Corry, a keen musician, was also an original YCV and likewise suffered lung damage as the result of breathing in mustard gas. He was unfit to return to his job as an iron pounder in Harland and Wolff and suffered symptoms for the remainder of his life. Captain Cecil Victor Smylie, who had served with the YCVs, passed away at his home in Deramore Park, Belfast, on 7 August 1960. He had been a fellow of the Institute of Chartered Accountants in Ireland, senior partner in the firm of Messrs Hugh Smylie and Sons, honorary treasurer of the Belfast Cathedral and the Ulster branch of the Irish Rugby Football Union, of which he had been a past president. He had been one of the founders, and a past president, of the Methodist College Old Boys' Association, a former captain and president of Collegians rugby club, honorary treasurer of the Belfast branch of the British Legion, and secretary of the fund for the building of the Northern Ireland War Memorial Building in Belfast.

Veteran D McCoubrey, addressing his comrades at the reunion dinner of 1946, as the world recovered from a second global conflict, told them:

> "God forgive any man who glories in war, for it is the work of the very devil himself. Yet it is a remarkable thing that out of that very evil has come good – that banding together of pals of other years, cementing a friendship that only death can sever."

APPENDIX 1

The YCV Constitution and Bye-Laws

The Young Citizen Volunteers of Ireland.

CONSTITUTION AND BYE-LAWS.

NAME.

1.—The organization shall be called "THE YOUNG CITIZEN VOLUNTEERS OF IRELAND." It shall be strictly non-sectarian and non-political.

OBJECTS.

2.—The objects of the Corps shall be—

(a) To develop a spirit of responsible citizenship and municipal patriotism by means of lectures and discussions on civic matters.

(b) To cultivate, by means of modified military and police drill, a manly physique, with habits of self control, self respect, and chivalry.

(c) To assist as an organization, when called upon, the civil power in the maintenance of the peace.

MEMBERSHIP.

3.—Membership shall be confined to males between the ages of 18 and 35; but a member attaining 35 years during the currency of any session may remain a member until the end of that session. Provided that (1) this age limit shall not apply to officers or honorary officials; (2) the Volunteer Council may establish a reserve corps of members over 35 years. Members shall be not less than five feet in height, and shall present credentials of good character.

4.—Application for membership shall be made only on the form annexed to this Constitution.

ORGANIZATION.

5.—The members shall be distributed into Companies. Each Company shall number at least 30 members, and no Company shall exceed a strength of 50.

6.—Each Company shall be under the command of a Captain. Where the Company forms part of a Battalion, the Battalion Council shall appoint the Captain; when the Company does not form part of a Battalion, the Captain shall be appointed by the Volunteer Executive.

7.—Each Company shall also have at least one Lieutenant to every 25 members, and one Staff Sergeant to every ten members. Each Lieutenant shall be nominated by the Captain, subject to the approval of the Battalion Council where the Company forms part of a Battalion, and in other cases subject to the approval of the Volunteer Executive Council. Each Sergeant shall, after the first year, be appointed from the ranks by the Captain.

8.—Each Company shall annually, in the month of October, appoint a Treasurer, Secretary, and a Committee of three members, and may at the same time appoint a President and Vice-Presidents, and the persons so appointed shall, with the Captain and Lieutenants, form the Company's Executive for the year.

9.—Six or more Companies in any City or Urban District may be formed into a Battalion by the Volunteer Council. The Volunteer Council may attach to any Battalion any Company formed in any district in which no Battalion is for the time being existing. The Battalion shall cease to exist if the number of Companies on its strength falls below four.

10.—The Executives of the Companies in a Battalion shall form the Battalion Council, and they shall, not later than the 15th of November in each year, appoint a President, Surgeons, Treasurer, and Secretary, who, if not already members, shall be ex-officio members of the Battalion Council. The Lord Mayor, Mayor, or Chairman of the Urban Council for the time being of the area of the Battalion shall, if willing to act, be elected President.

11.—The duties of the Battalion Council shall be to admit new Companies, to appoint or approve of the appointment of Officers of Companies, to make rules for the effective management of the Battalion, to arrange for addresses and instruction on civic matters, to make an annual report to the Volunteer Council on the affairs of the Battalion, and generally to take such steps as may be necessary to promote the objects of the Corps. A Battalion Council may appoint such Committees, and with such powers, as they may think necessary.

12.—The Young Citizen Volunteer Council (herein called the Volunteer Council) shall consist of the Councils of each Battalion, the Captains of Companies not forming parts of a Battalion, together with representatives of the Council of any City or Urban District in which a Battalion exists, and such persons as the Volunteer Council may annually co-opt. Such representatives shall, in any City or Urban District divided into wards, be one representative for each ward, nominated by his colleagues in the representation of such ward in the City or Urban Council, and shall, in any Urban District not divided into wards, be two members of the District Council nominated by their colleagues in that Council.

13.—The Volunteer Council shall meet annually, on some date to be fixed by the Volunteer Executive, and being not earlier than the 15th of November, and not later than the 15th of December in each year. At such annual meeting the Volunteer Council shall co-opt new members, receive and consider the reports of the Battalion Councils, a report from the Volunteer Executive, and a report from the Council's Treasurer; they shall elect a President and Vice-Presidents of the Corps, the Volunteer Executive, a Secretary or Secretaries, and Treasurer, and transact such other business as may be brought before them. The Volunteer Council shall meet at such other times as they may determine, or upon receipt of summons issued by direction of the Volunteer Executive.

14.—The Volunteer Executive shall consist of a President, three Vice-Presidents, one representative from each Battalion for every six Companies in such Battalion, and the Secretary or Secretaries and Treasurer of the Volunteer Council; provided that any Battalion comprising a number of Companies greater by a fraction than any multiple of six shall be entitled to one representative for such fraction. Such representatives shall be nominated by the Battalion Councils respectively.

15.—The duties of the Volunteer Executive shall be—

(a) To admit new Companies formed in areas in which no Battalion exists.

(b) To superintend the management of Companies not forming part of a Battalion.

(c) To superintend the issue of uniforms.

(d) To manage the general funds of the Corps, and solicit subscriptions and donations, and generally to do all acts which might be done by the Volunteer Council, except those specified in Articles 13 and 21 hereof.

16.—Each member shall, on enrolment,, pay to the Treasurer of his Company, 2/6, and likewise pay 6d at the beginning of each month succeeding that in which he is enrolled.

17.—Each Company shall contribute to the general fund of the Corps 5/- affiliation fee on enrolment, and an annual contribution of not less than 1/- per member.

18.—Each annual contributor of £5 and upwards shall be eligible for election as a Vice-President, and each annual contributor of £2 and upwards shall be eligible for co-option as a member of the Volunteer Council.

DRILLS.

19.—Members shall attend drills once a week from October to April, and once a month from May to September for the first year, and once a month after that.

20.—Each Company shall hold its annual inspection in April, and each Battalion its annual review and sports in May or June.

ALTERATION.

21.—This Constitution and the Bye-Laws hereto annexed shall not be altered except at a meeting of the Volunteer Council. Such alteration shall only be made by a two-thirds majority of those present and voting. Notice of any proposed alteration must be sent to each member of the Council at leas tone week previous to the meeting.

BYE-LAWS.

1.—Members missing more than three drills in succession from October to April, or two drills in succession from May to September, without leave, shall be fined 6d for each absence, unless such fines be remitted by the Company's Executive on cause shown.

2.—Members not attending punctually at drills shall be fined at such rate as the Company's Executive shall fix.

3.—Drill shall consist of modified military and police drill, single-stick, rifle, and baton exercises, signalling, knot-tying, and such other exercises as the Company's Executive may select, or as may be directed by the Volunteer Executive.

4.—Life-saving and ambulance work shall be taught where possible. Route marches shall take place at intervals.

5.—Strict discipline and obedience shall be enforced by and shown towards all Officers.

6.—Members shall not, as such, take part in any political meeting or demonstration; nor shall they wear the uniform of the Corps if attending any political meeting.

7.—Any member guilty of serious or continuous breach of the Constitution, Bye-Laws, or Rules of the Corps, or of any Battalion or Company, shall be liable to expulsion. Sentence of expulsion shall be pronounced only by the Volunteer Executive, and only on a report of the Battalion Council or the Captain commanding the Company to which the expelled member belongs, and only after an opportunity shall have been given to such member to be heard in his own defence.

8.—Uniforms shall be issued only on such terms as may be directed by the Volunteer Executive, and members shall only receive uniforms upon giving such security for the cost of the same as the Volunteer Executive may require.

9.—No member shall part with his uniform under any circumstances without the consent of the Volunteer Council.

YOUNG CITIZEN VOLUNTEERS OF IRELAND.

Form of Application.

I, ...

of ....

occupation, ...

being now of the age of .... years, hereby apply for enrolment in the Young Citizen Volunteers of Ireland, and I agree to abide loyally by the Constitution, Bye-Laws and the Rules of the Corps, and of any Company or Battalion to which at any time I may belong.

Dated this .... day of .... 191......

The Young Citizen Volunteers' Constitution and Bye-Laws set out its rules and regulations, including the need to be seen as non-political and non-sectarian. *(Courtesy of Andrew Totten)*

APPENDIX 2
An Irish Corps d'Elite

THE YOUNG CITIZEN VOLUNTEERS
An Organisation with Possibilities

ITS OBJECTS AND AMBITIONS
(By 'An Old Fogey')

With the Lord Mayor as its patron and president, with the City Hall as its rallying place, with all that is best in local commerce, industry, and enlightenment in hearty sympathy with the aims, the Young Citizen Volunteers of Ireland will be formally inaugurated as an organisation this evening. The plant bids fair to grow like Jonah's gourd; let us hope that it will prove as powerful and permanent as a young cedar of Lebanon.

What to do with our boys is a complex problem which daily presents new difficulties, and daily is the subject of new solutions. An equally tough and many-sided problem is what to do with our youths.

Boys' organisations for the inculcation of discipline and duty, for the cultivation of moral and religious sentiment, for the improvement of physique are legion. Boys' Brigade, Church Lads' Brigade, Boy Scouts, Boy Bluejackets – all these are admirable in their character and their work. But the day comes when the trousered youth quits the knickerbockered battalion. Boys leave the Brigade at sixteen, the Scouts are superannuated at seventeen, the Church Lads at nineteen. Youths who have belonged to either of these organisations and have come to regard as essentials the comradeship, the exercise, the emulation, and the esprit de corps which all of them supply feel the pinch sorely when they are unceremoniously thrust outside by that bald sexton Time. True, there are the young men's societies waiting to receive them, rich in all their attractions of gymnasia, classes, functions, and entertainments. Still the societies cannot quiet rekindle the old warm feeling of comradeship that existed in the ranks. They cannot supply the healthful discipline of the 'company' nor compensate the 'hobbledehoy' for the lost 'Kalon' of his boyhood. It is a critical period; the need of the continuation school is felt in the physical as in the mental education. And thus too often the smart set-up of the 'company boy' degenerates into the slouch of the disbanded soldier. And too often the promising lad becomes a drifting aimless youth just for the lack of that warm comradeship and healthful discipline. As a great poet sang,

> "The magnet of his course is gone, or only points in vain
> The shore to which he shivered sail can never stretch again."

Here proposes to come in the Young Citizens' Corps. It will take hold of ex-brigadier, ex-scout, and ex-bluejacket, and put them in the position of again enjoying the warm comradeship of the ranks, the healthful discipline of the company. It will take, too, the raw youth who has never known these influences, and assist in shaping him into a well-set-up, self-respecting, moral citizen, able to assist intelligently when called upon in the government of his city, to assist patriotically should the need arise in the defence of his country.

'Non-sectarian and non-political.' It is the ambition of the organisers to make these qualities in the corps real, not nominal merely. They would like the Young Citizen Volunteers to be a body in which 'some are for a party, but all are for the State.' Is it impracticable? I remember asking Mr William Jennings Bryan (of 'free silver' and oratorical fame) how he explained the intense patriotism of the citizens of the United States, seeing that they were recruited from the four winds of heaven. "Well," he replied, "they come to live there, you know, and the securer and better they make the country the securer and better will be their own particular lot." It is a pity that this broad philosophy cannot be applied unadulterated in our little patch of earth here just as it is in the broad expanse of the great Republic. But surely it might be applied to the extent of a united effort towards the making of healthful useful citizens.

'To teach the young idea how to shoot' – at least in the soldierly sense of the term – is not part of the programme of the organisation, yet drill is an important feature, and it is contemplated in spite of War Office suspicions to make the members familiar at least with the mechanism of the death-dealing rifle. Militarism is not to be carried too far, though militarism is undoubtedly a great power with the young. We don't want enthusiasm in that direction to get beyond the review stage. Our national physique and stamina need improving; the Olympic games and various other recent lessons have taught us that truth. There is nothing so potent in working this improvement as drill. Let a young fellow practise keeping his chest in the right place until he is twenty-five, and Nature will usually take care that it holds its right place afterwards. Life in cities is less strenuous, more hygienic than it was thirty years ago, and our youth have both more time and more opportunity for the patriotic duty of improving their physique and developing their muscles than they need to have. But they want an intelligent lead, and this the Young Citizens' Corps designs to give them.

Local companies of between thirty and fifty are to be formed each under a captain and honorary major, with a lieutenant and staff sergeant to every ten members. The liberal proportion of officers, commissioned and non-commissioned, may convey a faint suggestion of General Bombastes' army or of Artemus Ward's projected corps, in which everybody was to rank as brigadier general. Still this characteristic will serve to fire the ambition of rank and file, every member of which may carry a captain's badge in his haversack. Six or more companies in any centre are to form a battalion, and the officers of such companies a battalion council, who will annually appoint a battalion president, vice-presidents, honorary chaplains, treasurer, and executive. Then there is to be a general council, consisting of the captains of companies and members of each battalion executive associated with a number of prominent citizens interested in the organisation. It will be gathered that it is not intended to confine the organisation to Belfast. As a fact, arrangements have already been made to form a battalion in Derry, and probably there will eventually be companies in most of the Ulster towns.

The finished production of the movement is the responsible citizen; to the goal of responsible citizenship every effort will be directed. Lectures and discussions on civic matters are to be some of the milestones on this road; 'the cultivation of habits of self-control, self-respect, and chivalry' – a comprehensive curriculum – is to be associated with a weekly military and police drill, athletics, and ambulance work. Members are eligible for enrolment between the ages of 18 and 35, but only those able to present credentials of good character will be accepted, while each applicant must give an undertaking to comply strictly with the rules and to set an example of gentlemanly conduct to his comrades. The entrance fee is 2s 6d, and the subsequent subscription 6d per month.

A distinctive uniform will be worn, and it is quite possible this uniform may in due course come to be recognised as a hallmark of reliability and trustworthiness among the youth of the city. We can imagine it figuring in deputations to the City Council. We can picture the company of YCC marching into the Council Chamber, deploying to the right of the Mayoral chair, advancing two guns, and opening a telling fire upon some Corporation blunder or muddle. We can fancy the uniform in a street fracas implying effective assistance to the police and the vindication of the sovereignty of the law. And we can picture it in the event of a threatened foreign invasion guarding the shores of Belfast Lough, and bringing to that duty the discipline of Landwehr and the enthusiasm of arms of the empire.

It is undoubtedly good for young men to band themselves in this way for mutual improvement, and with the worthy ambition of doing the city if not the State some service. Man in his highest development is essentially a gregarious animal. His solitary virtues are not those which make much for civilisation and progress. Where youth burns the midnight oil, and for the rest of his time is engaged in laboriously trimming his solitary lamp, the possible result may be sage or inspired writer, the probable result is a narrow-souled feeble-bodied recluse.

The captain of a thirty-strong company of the YCC will have a public reputation to sustain. The staff sergeant having a 'file of men' at his command, besides the ambition of becoming a captain, will feel himself like the centurion of old, who can say to either of that file 'go', and he goeth. 'Come', and he cometh, 'Do this thing', and he doeth it. A great deal of course will depend upon the officers, but capital material is to be found in many of the 'Old Boys' of the city. There is equally good material for the rank and file of an organisation which does not seek to interfere with any existing body. The raw recruit often makes the finest soldier. Marshal Suvarov took a body of Russian peasants and drilled them in the course of a few months into the splendid infantry that captured Fort Ismail. And thus we may reasonably look for healthy emulation in the ranks between the 'Old Boys' and the raw levies.

 The movement seems to possess great possibilities both in dimensions and in results. Our esteemed Lord Mayor, who will preside at to-night's meeting, and who has accepted the presidency of the corps, has high hopes of its moral influence and civic value. Many leading citizens have expressed their warm sympathy with the idea, and have promised to give it their practical support. One of the rules is as follows:- "This organisation being of a civic character shall be strictly non-political and non-sectarian, and members shall not as such take part in any political demonstration, nor shall they wear the uniform if attending any meeting of a political nature." That means that there is no restriction upon members as to joining any political body or taking part in any political demonstration, but they must not do so as members of the YCC or in the uniform of that organisation. Even though one may be whimsically reminded of Maitre Jacques in 'L'Avare', who, when receiving orders as cook, declined to listen to any interpolated instructions as coachman until he had changed his coat, the rule seems a fair enough one formulated to meet a position which the organisers of the movement cannot ignore. After to-night's meeting the Hon Secretaries, Messrs FT Geddes and HG Stevenson, will probably be kept busy enrolling members of the Young Citizens' Corps.

Report from the *Northern Whig*, September 1912

APPENDIX 3
Units of the 36th (Ulster) Division

107th Brigade[1]

8th Battalion (East Belfast), the Royal Irish Rifles *(merged with 9th Battalion RIR to form the 8/9th Battalion August 1917, moved to 21st Entrenching Battalion February 1918)*

9th Battalion (West Belfast), the Royal Irish Rifles *(merged with 8th Battalion RIR to form the 8/9th Battalion August 1917, moved to 21st Entrenching Battalion February 1918)*

10th Battalion (South Belfast), the Royal Irish Rifles *(moved to 21st Entrenching Battalion February 1918)*

15th Battalion (North Belfast), the Royal Irish Rifles

107th Machine Gun Company *(joined December 1915, moved to 36th Battalion MGC March 1918)*

107th Trench Mortar Battery *(joined April 1916)*

1st Battalion, the Royal Irish Fusiliers *(joined August 1917 moved to 108th Brigade February 1918)*

1st Battalion, the Royal Irish Rifles *(joined February 1918)*

2nd Battalion, the Royal Irish Rifles *(joined from 108th Brigade February 1918)*

108th Brigade

11th Battalion (South Antrim), the Royal Irish Rifles *(merged with 13th Battalion RIR to form the 11/13th Battalion August 1917, moved to 22nd Entrenching Battalion February 1918)*

12th Battalion (Central Antrim), the Royal Irish Rifles

13th Battalion (County Down), the Royal Irish Rifles *(merged with 11th Battalion RIR to form the 11/13th Battalion August 1917, moved to 22nd Entrenching Battalion February 1918)*

9th Battalion, the Royal Irish Fusiliers

108th Machine Gun Company *(joined January 1916, moved to 36th Battalion MGC March 1918)*

108th Trench Mortar Battery *(joined April 1916)*

7th Battalion, the Royal Irish Rifles *(joined October 1917 merged with 2nd Battalion November 1917)*

2nd Battalion, the Royal Irish Rifles *(joined November 1917 moved to 107th Brigade February 1918)*

1st Battalion, the Royal Irish Fusiliers *(joined from 107th Brigade February 1918)*

109th Brigade

9th Battalion (Tyrone), the Royal Inniskilling Fusiliers

10th Battalion (Londonderry), the Royal Inniskilling Fusiliers *(moved to 21st Entrenching Battalion Feb 1918)*

11th Battalion (Donegal and Fermanagh), the Royal Inniskilling Fusiliers *(moved to 23rd Entrenching Battalion February 1918)*

14th Battalion (Young Citizens), the Royal Irish Rifles *(moved to 23rd Entrenching Battalion February 1918)*

109th Machine Gun Company *(joined January 1916, moved to 36th Battalion MGC March 1918)*

109th Trench Mortar Battery *(joined April 1916)*

1st Battalion, the Royal Inniskilling Fusiliers *(joined February 1918)*

2nd Battalion, the Royal Inniskilling Fusiliers *(joined February 1918)*

---

1 Between November 1915 – February 1916 107th Brigade was exchanged with 12th Brigade from the 4th Division for instructional purposes.

APPENDIX 4
Armchair Generals and Afternoon Frocks

Try our famous stew… If you are pleased, keep it dark. If not, curb your language. Quality warranted. Quantity guaranteed – when water is plentiful.

An 'advertisement' in *The Incinerator*

The battalion magazine was *The Incinerator*, which was only to be published twice, in May and June 1916. The loss of wonder and innocence that accompanied the horrendous casualties at the Battle of the Somme and the subsequent move north to Belgium probably contributed to its further publication being curtailed though the deaths and injuries sustained by many of its former contributors and subjects might have been the major cause of its demise. *The Incinerator* had a distinctive sense of humour, heavy with 'private' jokes and asides that presupposed you were already aware of what was being alluded to but purposely not being explicitly detailed due to the censorship applied from above. Even though at this distance it is sometimes hard to appreciate or even understand on occasions, it provides an invaluable window into the characters and thinking of the YCV soldiers of 1916.

The magazine was edited by Lieutenant SH Monard, who appealed to others to contribute and not leave it to a "few chaps who have sympathised with the Editor". He went on in typically flippant *Incinerator* form: "Although we say it as shouldn't, the 14th, within its fold, has genius and talent of every description. Men who can make bath-houses out of bully-beef tins, and Christmas cards from Maconochie labels, should have no difficulty in putting a few impressions on paper."

The title *The Incinerator* came from an obsession headquarters had at the time about the disposal of rubbish. Lieutenant Monard told his readers:

> "It may be remembered that a notice was put in Battalion Orders a few weeks ago asking for suggestions as to a name for the journal. A period of grave anxiety ensued, for not one of the many titles suggested seemed to hit the point squarely. A 'Bullets' staff would have been inadequate to give the consideration to such names as 'The Religious Rock', the 'Pull-Through', 'Indirect Fire', 'Active Service Pink 'Un', etc, etc, etc. It fell to the lot of Divisional Headquarters to supply the needful. This elegant organisation decided to get fretful about rubbish, and the need for numerous incinerators was freely discussed. Company commanders wandered around wearing worried looks, forgotten text books were unearthed and searched for models and details – the Battalion journal obtained its name. 'Twas all quite simple. The officer commanding _ Coy. absent-mindedly greeted us one morning. He wanted to be friendly, and presently asked: 'Well, what about the incinerator?' He meant 'What about the magazine', of course. And now either appellation would be correct."

The 'advertisements' emphasised the Tommies' favourite themes – the shirkers back home, the desire to return to Ireland, poking fun at the Germans, and criticism of the rations. Under the banner line of Sales and Exchanges, for example, one reads: "A good bargain – The following articles will be given in exchange for one ticket to Ireland: 1 rifle and bayonet in good working order; 1 set of straps, comprising 2 good pouches, 1 water bottle and 1 entrenching tool; 1 good valise, capable of holding anything you have been able to pinch – For particulars apply to any Private in the battalion." Another went: "Great Sale – Owing to our inability to use same, we offer a large number of first class vessels, including dreadnoughts, cruisers, torpedo boats, etc. On view any day in Kiel Harbour, Kaiser Bill & Coy, (late Von Tirpitz Ltd.)"; and again: "Clothing for men. We have a choice selection of the proper wearing apparel for young slackers for the season. Khaki tunics and trousers, first class boots, grey backs and drawers, splendid value. If the above does not appeal to you we will give you in lieu a set of delightful lingerie. A charming afternoon frock in chiffon, velvet and ninon. Costume to match. Dainty pair of shoes, fine glace kid. Britain's Clothing Establishment. Branches all over the world."

Soldiers weren't allowed to openly discuss politics and rarely did anything resembling party-political comment make it into print. One notable exception, however, appeared in the June 1916 edition of *The Incinerator* referring back to the Easter Rising of a few months previous:

> "What about the Sinn Feiner business? Soldiers are not allowed to talk politics, otherwise much might be said. Speaking for ourselves, we'd rather have seen a little less mercy to some of the rebels. If a man out here plays any old tricks he is given short shrift – shot at daybreak. Remember this man may have fought long and sturdily for his Empire – but still he'd be shot. Then what kind of death do those insurgent dogs deserve – those swine who seize upon the fact that the soldiery is away, fighting and dying to save Sinn Feiner worthless skins – to rifle and riot and murder a whole host of innocent people. Ugh! Doesn't it make your blood boil, lads? Perhaps it's as well that we – being the Press – are muzzled."

The same edition took a similarly scathing view of the armchair generals back home in Britain whose impatience with the apparent lack of activity on the Western Front galled the men at least as much as the republican insurgency. "By the way, it is rumoured that the war will be over by August," it reported. "Various people in England, from their comfortable armchairs and after their good meals, have come to this conclusion, and are even betting about it. Couldn't we all imagine the same kind of thing after a ten-course dinner and 'several' liqueurs and whiskies? Such delusions are easy for some people, especially when they happen to be a few hundred miles from the firing line." It went on:

> "Some idiot was speaking to one of the 14th when the latter was home on leave. 'I can't see,' said he, 'what you chaps are doing out there. When are you going to make 'the push'? Why, even your casualties have decreased fifty per cent!' A pig-sticking death would be too merciful a death for such as he."

The Incinerator, through its tongue-in-cheek descriptions of everyday life, gives a down-to-earth view of what it was like to be a soldier. The edition of May 1916 gave a particularly pointed blow-by-blow account of a typical day:

"The fun begins at reveille, at the first notes of the joyous bugle, when the sergeant in charge breaks forth into that pleasant song of Solomon's, "Rise up, my loves, my fair ones, and come away." At least, this is his text, though the sermon is somewhat irrelevant, as sermons usually are; and his expressions have not that sublimity and poetry so evident in the Biblical expression. "Come on, now, get up there, ye parcel of ----. Are ye going to lie there the whole ---- day? What the ---- are ye lying there for, scratching yourselves. You there, in the corner, do ye not hear me spaking till ye?" Such is a sergeant's general method of awakening the sleeping beauties, and the pity is that so much fine language is lavished on unappreciative ears.

Parade and breakfast: After an instructive early morning parade, when he is shown the most scientific methods of cleaning a road so as to leave a nice tidy path for his shiny boots, he gets his breakfast. In the old days this was a very casual business, but what a difference in the Army! There is more sport in getting one's breakfast than in a whole season of football. Breakfast means a Dixie of tea and a bit of fried bacon with some dip. 'Dip' is a small word, but it is on this small, insignificant word that the British Army depends. For it is the mainstay and the only hope of a soldier's breakfast. No dip, no breakfast; no breakfast, no parade; no parade, no trained men; no trained men, no British Army … However, the fun begins when there is a scarcity of 'dip'. Have you ever seen a Rugger scrum, or a street riot, or a meeting of the General Assembly? Well, combine all three, and you have a platoon fighting for 'dip'. As recruits, all may have joined to fight for King and Country, but their one aim in life, as veterans of 17 months' service, is 'dip'. And, unsophisticated reader, you might be guilty of saying 'What a dip!' But think! What do we all fight for; what do we all yearn after and strive to hold? Is it not life? And 'dip' is life to the British soldier.

Kit inspection: This inspection is generally held on Sundays, and naturally so, for cleanliness is next to godliness, so 'tis said, and a kit inspection is cleanliness in concrete form. So for any who may be surprised at the selection of Sunday as the day for kit inspections we hope this simple explanation will suffice. What is the object of these inspections? They must have some object, as nothing is ever done in the Army without an object. (Oh! I know that sometimes the object is very hard to find.) If a company wished to go to a range for firing practice, and if instead of securing the services of one who knew its whereabouts they trampled on unguided till they were far past the range, many would think that history had repeated itself and that someone had blundered. Not so; this company would be taken far out of its way in order that it might find its way back, in order that it might have a chance of using that deciding factor in warfare, its own initiative. That is the object – somewhat obscure to some, but nevertheless always there. So in a kit inspection, though here the object is even more obscure. At first glance one might imagine that the object was to prevent the sergeant's hand from losing its literary skill, or perhaps to teach him the necessity of always carrying a notebook and pencil. Or indeed, you might think that it was to turn one's thoughts back to dear old Belfast; back to old familiar haunts – to dear old Smithfield or Maggie Moore's blest abode. But in all these conjectures you would be mistaken, for the object of a kit inspection is to find out whether you have a complete kit and whether you think you need any article replaced. In future, then, my comrades, have this object in view when you lay out your kit for a kit inspection. There is no use for me to say in what order or in what quantity you should lay out your belongings, for that would be attempting the impossible. In the words of an English poet: 'The old order changeth, giving place to new'."

An article apparently about the factious characters of Smith and Wilson, selected for night guard in the front line trenches, was also published in the June edition. Despite making light of the experience, it gives the reader a feeling of the physical discomfort and cold terror faced by men staring into the unknown:

"In the dark hours of the night, Wilson, who has been trying to persuade himself that he has been sleeping for the last two hours, is seriously contemplating getting up and going out for a rest, when the gruff voice of the NCO on duty warns him and his partner to turn out. Giving Smith a vicious kick, he dons somebody else's muffler, and likewise 'acquires' a pair of trench gloves. All being ready, the two unfortunates, rifle in hand, follow the NCO to their post of duty, where the weary sentries, glad to be relieved, mutter something about a wiring party being out and a patrol that was to have gone out, and disappear into the darkness. The worthy NCO, with a parting 'Bonne nuit,' leaves his victims to their fate and paddles off down the trench.

Silence reigns supreme. Each sentry strains his eyes to see No-Man's-Land in front of him. A short distance opposite they know that the enemies' lines are situated, with the Promised Land further beyond. At present all that can be seen is our wire and that only indistinctly. Suddenly there is a noise, a stone falls off the parapet. 'What's that?' 'Only a rat, you fool; nothing to get the wind up for,' answers Smith. Our sentries continue their vigil uninterrupted. To their gaze those posts at our wire seem to move. They appear to take form. Yes, surely they are moving along slowly and noiselessly in single file. Wilson's eyes grow dim. He closes them for a second and nervously fingers his safety catch. There are the figures still moving past. Now one stops. He is bending over to talk to his neighbour. Suddenly a flare light goes up and breaks out into all its glory and brilliance. One is dazed for the moment, but ere the light dies out our sentries satisfy themselves that the wire posts are posts after all and not the fantastic objects they appeared a short time before. Wilson grasps this fact with a sigh of relief and mops the sweat on his brow with the oily rag kept for the purpose of preparing for rifle inspections.

The silence becoming monotonous, he whispers to his companion: 'Are you cold?' Now by this time Smith has a feeling of complete 'fedupness'. He is cold, sleepy and wretched. His feet, well he wonders if they are still there! Not being able to feel or see them in the darkness, he becomes uneasy. A horrible feeling overtakes him. Supposing the feet had fallen off, without acquainting him of the fact? Feet, he considers, are as heartless as NCOs. He had read of such things happening before in cases of frostbite. Upon his musings breaks this rude query: 'Are you cold?' from his neighbour. Smith considers it beneath his dignity to reply to such a ridiculous question, and remarks about the night being oppressively hot. Then edging up to Wilson, says in a most dismal tone: 'I say, mate, what a blooming life!' An expression borrowed from our old friends, the Warwicks, and only used in moments of great dejection.

Relief up! The voice startles them, and they find that the next sentries have arrived to relieve them. Wishing our new arrivals a pleasant time of it, our cheerful Tommies stagger off in the direction of their funk hole."

APPENDIX 5

The Soldier Boy of the McFadzeans

Let me tell you a story of honour and glory,
Of a young Belfast soldier Billy McFadzean by name,
For King and for Country Young Bill died bravely,
And won the VC on the fields of the Somme.

From a song written in his honour

William Frederick McFadzean was the first member of the 36th (Ulster) Division to win the Victoria Cross and the only soldier of the Young Citizen Volunteers to earn the award. His act of courage was summed up by King George V when, presenting the medal to his father, William McFadzean senior, he told him: "Nothing finer has been done in this war for which I have given a Victoria Cross than the act committed by your son to save many lives in giving his own so heroically."

Born at Lurgan, County Armagh, on 9 October 1895, his family moved to Belfast when he was a child, living at Rubicon in the Cregagh district. He was educated at Mountpottinger Boys School and the Trade Preparatory School at the Municipal Technology Institute on College Square. Described as being "13 stones and six feet tall, a fine healthy young Ulsterman," he had proved himself a useful player with Collegians rugby club in the city and was a member of the Central Presbyterian Association and 1st Ballynafeigh and Newtownbreda East Belfast Regiment of the Ulster Volunteer Force. He had been serving his time as an apprentice in the linen business of Spence, Bryson and Company on Great Victoria Street when war was declared and joined up at the Old Town Hall in Belfast on 22 September 1914. In a letter to his parents he wrote: "You people at home make me quite proud when you tell me I am the soldier boy of the McFadzeans. I hope to play the game and if I don't add much lustre to it, I certainly will not tarnish it."

Trained as a 'bomber,' the 20-year-old and his comrades were in a trench in Thiepval Wood in the early hours of 1 July 1916, priming their grenades for the battle ahead, when a box was spilled and the pins fell from several. Without hesitation Rifleman McFadzean threw himself onto the grenades, dying instantly in the explosion but saving the lives of those around him. Two men were reported injured, one of whom subsequently had to have a leg amputated. His VC citation, gazetted in September, 1916, read:

"For most conspicuous bravery. While in a concentration trench and opening a box of bombs for distribution prior to an attack, the box slipped down into the trench, which was crowded with men, and two of the safety pins fell out. Private McFadzean, instantly realising the danger to his comrades, with heroic courage, threw himself on top of the bombs. The bombs exploded, blowing him to pieces, but only one other man was injured. He well knew his danger, being himself a bomber; but without a moment's hesitation he gave his life for his comrades."

His C Company officer, Captain James McKee, wrote to Mr McFadzean:

"You will have great satisfaction in knowing that he died a hero's death. Our men were in the assembly trenches, and bombs were being distributed. Your son had a box passed to him, and in the passing some bombs dropped out. In falling, the safety pins fell out; and your son, realising the danger to his comrades, flung himself on top of the bombs. He was killed, and two others were slightly wounded. He saved the lives of a number of his comrades by his action, and we are proud of him. His name has been sent forward to higher authority, with recommendation for a decoration."

Second Lieutenant James Marshall, of the 11th Rifles, in a letter of sympathy, says his brother, Corporal Dave Marshall, of the YCVs, "told me to say that Willie fell just beside him, and by his heroic self-sacrifice saved the lives of his comrades around him, earning their admiration and gratitude which will never be forgotten by them." Lieutenant Colonel Chichester, his original commanding officer, wrote to the family in September 1916:

"I feel that I must write to express to you my feelings of admiration for your son's splendid bravery. I was greatly grieved to hear of his death at the time that I heard of his magnificent and heroic deed. I did not write to you then as I knew he was recommended for the Victoria Cross, and I waited to do so till it should have been definitely conferred on him. You must indeed be proud of such a son, and the thought of what he did must be a great consolation to you in your grief. I want to let you know that I am very proud of the fact that he served under me, and that he has added to the honour which his battalion has already won. It is not only his battalion which has every right to be proud of him, but the whole of the Ulster Division. No man could have died a nobler death."

Lieutenant Colonel Bowen, then the CO, wrote similarly:

"It was with feelings of deep pride that I read the announcement of the granting of the VC to your gallant son, and my only regret is that he was not spared to wear his well-earned decoration. It was one of the very finest deeds of a war that is so full of

Billy McFadzean standing on the steps of his home, Rubicon, in the Cregagh district. *(Courtesy of Andrew Totten)*

William McFadzean is photographed with his section. He is standing to the rear, second from the left. *(Courtesy of Andrew Totten)*

big things, and I can assure you that the whole battalion rejoiced when they heard of it. Your gallant boy is gone from us, but his deeds will for ever live in our memories, and the record will go down for all time in the regimental history, which he has added fresh and great lustre to."

Mr McFadzean travelled to Buckingham Palace, on a third class rail ticket provided by the government, in February 1917, to receive his son's medal from the King. At a special service on Sunday 1 July 1917, a brass memorial to Rifleman McFadzean was unveiled at Newtownbreda Presbyterian Church by Lieutenant Colonel CW Barlow, General Staff Officer of the Northern District. The tablet, mounted on teak, took the form of a shield and was placed in the left transept of the church. It reads:

"In memory of Rifleman William Frederick McFadzean, VC, 14th Battalion, Royal Irish Rifles, YCV (Ulster Division) who was born at Lurgan on the 9th October, 1895, and who, to save the lives of his comrades, gave his own life on the 1st July, 1916, at Thiepval Wood, France. When in the trenches in which the men of his Battalion were massed for attack, the fuses of some bombs having been accidentally ignited, he threw himself on these bombs, so covering them with his body that by their explosion he alone was killed. 'Greater love hath no man than this, that a man lay down his life for his friends' – St John XV 13. In such a death there is no sting, in such a grave there is everlasting victory. This tablet is erected by his fellow members of the 1st Battalion, East Belfast Regiment, UVF, and Ballynafeigh and Newtownbreda Unionist Club."

The service was led by the church minister, the Rev Robert Workman, with six other clergy taking part and with a detachment of 14th Battalion soldiers from Newcastle in attendance. A number of wounded men from the UVF Hospital's limbless branch were also in the congregation, including Rifleman George Gillespie, who had been beside Rifleman McFadzean when the grenades exploded. The *Belfast News Letter* reported that the church was full to overflowing. It went on:

> "Amongst the officers present were:- Lieutenant Colonel RPD Spencer Chichester, late officer commanding the Young Citizen Volunteers; Major JW Harper, Young Citizen Volunteers; Captain EV Longworth, Headquarters Staff, Northern District; Captain EH Nelson, District Musketry Officer, Northern District; Captain SH Monard, Young Citizen Volunteers; Captain Fras C Forth, 18th Battalion Royal Irish Rifles (Principal of the Municipal Technical Institute, at which Private McFadzean was a pupil in the Trades Preparatory School); Captain RJ Buchanan, 15th Battalion Royal Irish Rifles (North Belfast Volunteers); Second-Lieutenant PW Frew, 20th Battalion Royal Irish Rifles; Second Lieutenant NK Rea, 9th–10th Battalion Royal Irish Fusiliers; Second-Lieutenant James Marshall, 11–18th Battalion Royal Irish Rifles; Dr WR MacKenzie, late captain Royal Army Medical Corps, and medical officer of the Young Citizen Volunteers. Others present were – The High Sheriff (Mr William Tougher, JP); Sir Robert J McConnell, Bart, DL; Mr Lloyd Campbell, representing Lieutenant General Sir George Richardson, KCB, General Officer Commanding the Ulster Volunteer Force; Messrs JB Niblock, Hugh Hobson, and Charles Neill, representing the 1st Battalion East Belfast Regiment UVF; and RI Calwell (president), FW Woods (honorary secretary) and Thomas McKinty, representing the Ballynafeigh and Newtownbreda Unionist Club. Mr William McFadzean, Rubicon, Cregagh, father of Private McFadzean, who was accompanied by Mr RP Bowden and other relatives, was accommodated in a front seat."

A cigarette card carrying an image of the Victoria Cross hero was a popular collector's piece. *(Courtesy of Andrew Totten)*

Pte. WILLIAM F. McFADZEAN, V.C.

Colonel Barlow unveiled the tablet, beside which was a photograph of Private McFadzean with the Victoria Cross suspended from a rosette formed by green and black ribbons, the regimental colours of the Royal Irish Rifles. The Rev Workman concluded his lesson by reading a telegram from Captain JA Mulholland, adjutant of the Young Citizen Volunteers: "YCVs salute the memory of their fallen hero, Willie McFadzean." The Last Post was played and the service ended with the singing of the National Anthem.

In addition to the memorial at Newtownbreda Presbyterian Church, Rifleman William McFadzean is commemorated at the Thiepval Memorial to the Missing on the Somme, within Thiepval Wood, First Lurgan Presbyterian Church, Collegians RFC, by Castlereagh Borough Council, at Old Lurgan Town Hall and on the Lurgan War Memorial.

APPENDIX 6
Late Lieutenant Victor H Robb
Impressive Funeral in Belfast

The first funeral in Belfast of an officer belonging to the Ulster Division took place yesterday and was a result of the great British advance which began on the 1st of July. The deceased was the late Lieutenant Victor H Robb, who proved himself as gallant as a soldier as he was keen as a sportsman, and his remains, which had been brought over from London, were he succumbed to his wounds, were interred in the City Cemetery with full military honours.

The attendance bore striking testimony to his popularity in both civil and military life, for rarely has a larger number of people of all classes in the community turned out, especially in a time like the present, to pay a last farewell tribute to one who was not only a fellow citizen, but, in the best sense of the word, a national hero. In addition to hundreds on foot were many who drove in a long line of vehicles, and at every stage in the journey from the house, Kirk Bruighean, Fortwilliam Park, to the grave, groups of mourners assembled to show their sorrow and regret. Behind the gun carriage, on which rested the coffin covered with a Union Jack, was an open landau laden with wreaths of beautiful design, forwarded by bereaved friends and sympathisers.

The chief mourners were – Lieutenant RC Robb, Royal Naval Air Service (brother); Rev RM McCheyne Gilmour, and Messrs Charles Pearson, James Beck, Kennedy Robb, Thomas Robb, and DA Fee (uncles); Rev R Cooke, Rev Hugh Kirker, Messrs Wm Cooke, Wm Robb, Wm Beck, and JA Beck (cousins), and other relatives. Amongst the officers present were Colonel WEC McCammond, OC 3rd Battalion RIR; Colonel Chichester, and Captain Bentley. There were also in attendance a number of non-commissioned officers and men of the Young Citizen Volunteers, some of whom had not quite recovered from wounds received in action. The band of the 3rd Battalion Royal Irish Rifles, who also supplied the firing party under Lieutenant McAreavy, headed the mournful procession.

Impressive services were conducted at the deceased's residence and at the grave, the officiating clergymen being Revs Dr Maconachie, RM McC Gilmour, and Lyle Harrison. Messrs Melville & Co Ltd, Belfast and Lisburn, had charge of the funeral arrangements, which were carried out in a most satisfactory manner.[1]

Report from the *Belfast News Letter*, 26 July 1916

---

1 On 1 January 1915, the Secretary of the War Office issued a statement that made such funerals possible. It said: "Cases have occurred in which relatives of soldiers dying in the United Kingdom have expressed a desire that the soldiers should be buried near their homes. As the cost of this would in many cases be prohibitive to relatives it has been arranged that in the case of a soldier where death is attributable to active service, and whose relatives especially desire the funeral to take place at his home, the cost of the conveyance of the body may be met from public funds. It will be understood that any further expense involved apart from railway charges and the cash allowance for burial expenses will be defrayed by the relatives."

APPENDIX 7
The 14th (YCV) Royal Irish Rifles dead of July 1916

1 JULY 1916

Charles ADAMS, Rifleman, 19, was born and raised in Belfast. Commemorated on the Thiepval Memorial.

William AGNEW, Rifleman, born in Liverpool and enlisted in Belfast. Commemorated on the Thiepval Memorial.

Hugh ANDERSON, Rifleman, was originally from Larne but had been living in Belfast at the time of his enlistment. He was 20 years old. Commemorated on the Thiepval Memorial.

John BELL, Rifleman, born at Workington, Cumberland, but living in Lisburn 1914. Commemorated on the Thiepval Memorial.

Alexander BENNETT, Rifleman, aged 19, was the son of Henry Bennett, 18 Grampian Street, Belfast, and had been an apprentice painter in Queen's Island when war was declared. Commemorated on the Thiepval Memorial.

Joseph BLACK, Rifleman, from Portadown, enlisted in Belfast. Commemorated on the Thiepval Memorial.

Thomas BLAIR, Rifleman, from the Shankill area of Belfast. Buried at Connaught Cemetery.

Samuel BOND, Sergeant, aged 23, born at Baltimore, County Cork, was the youngest son of William Bond, Royal Navy. His mother lived at 6 Manor Drive, Belfast. He was a member of A Company. Commemorated on the Thiepval Memorial.

Hudson BOOTH, Rifleman, aged 21, had been born at New Jersey, United States. His mother was living at Wimbledon Street, Belfast.

Robert BOTHWELL, Lance Corporal, aged 20, originally from St Louis, New York, had been living in London in 1914 and came to Belfast to enlist. He had formerly worked at Warnocks store in Royal Avenue in the city and had been a member of the YCV pre-war. A Presbyterian who listed his nearest next of kin as an uncle, served in A Company. Buried in Connaught Cemetery.

Robert BURROWS, Lance Corporal, was from the Shankill area of Belfast. Commemorated on the Thiepval Memorial.

John BURTON, Sergeant, from Belfast. Commemorated on the Thiepval Memorial.

Joseph BUSTARD, Lance Corporal, was a married man from the Shankill area of Belfast. Commemorated on the Thiepval Memorial.

William Ewart BUSTARD, Lance Corporal, from Belfast. Buried at Connaught Cemetery.

William CAMPBELL, Rifleman, aged 23. Eldest son of William Campbell, 101 Ogilvie Street, Belfast. He had a brother serving with the Seaforth Highlanders. William, who had been born at Ballymacarrett, had worked as a bookbinder in the firm of McCaw, Stevenson and Orr. Commemorated on the Thiepval Memorial.

William John White CARSON, Second Lieutenant, aged 29, was the only son of William McRobert Carson and Sarah Carson of Tareen House, Old Cavehill Road, Belfast. Commemorated on the Thiepval Memorial.

Duncan DARROCH, Sergeant, aged 24, from Belfast. Commemorated on the Thiepval Memorial.

Alfred DEARDEN, Lance Corporal, aged 29, from Belfast. Commemorated on the Thiepval Memorial.

Robert DEMPSTER, Rifleman, aged 35, was born in Moneyrea, County Down. He left behind a wife, Mary, and seven children at Dover Street, Belfast. He had worked for the city Corporation for 20 years before enlistment.

William DEVLIN, Lance Corporal, from the Shankill area of Belfast. Buried at Connaught Cemetery.

James DOBBIN, Rifleman, from Kilwaughter, County Antrim, enlisted at Larne. Commemorated on the Divion Wood Cemetery Memorial, Connaught Cemetery.

Samuel DONALDSON, Rifleman, aged 22, from Belfast. Commemorated at the Thiepval Memorial.

James ELLIOTT, Rifleman, aged 26, was originally from Londonderry but living in Belfast in 1914. Commemorated on the Thiepval Memorial.

John FAULKNER, Rifleman, aged 19, from Derryloran, Cookstown, County Tyrone. Commemorated on the Thiepval Memorial.

John Henry FITZSIMONS, Corporal, from Coagh, County Tyrone. Buried at Connaught Cemetery.

David FOY, Lance Corporal, a married man from the Shankill area of Belfast who had worked for Hanna & Brown before the war. Buried at Mill Road Cemetery. He was initially reported as 'missing' and not confirmed dead until almost a year after the battle. His father, also David, was the worshipful master of the Sandy Row Orange Order

Lodge in Belfast and the honorary secretary of the Irish Football Association. Another brother, Charles, was badly wounded at the Somme and invalided out of the army, and a third brother George, also YCVs, was later commissioned.

John FULTON, Lance Corporal, born Dungannon, County Tyrone. Buried at Mill Road Cemetery.

David GIBSON, Rifleman, born and lived Killswater and enlisted at Ballymena. Commemorated on the Thiepval Memorial and at First Ballymena Presbyterian Church.

Joseph GREGG, Rifleman, born at Gilford, County Down. Commemorated on the Thiepval Memorial.

John HAFFERN, Rifleman, from the Shankill area of Belfast. Commemorated on the Thiepval Memorial.

William HANNA, Rifleman, aged 21, from the Shankill area of Belfast. Buried at Mill Road Cemetery.

Benjamin Chapman HARLEY, Second Lieutenant, aged 22, was the battalion intelligence officer and a member of B Company. From Watford, Herts. Commemorated on the Thiepval Memorial.

John HART, Rifleman, aged 18, from the Shankill area of Belfast. Commemorated on the Thiepval Memorial.

John HENDERSON, Rifleman, aged 24, was the second son of John Henderson, 13 Collyer Street, Belfast. He had worked at Messrs Slacke and Co, Ashton Street, Belfast, and served under the head of that firm, Captain Owen Slacke, also killed on 1 July 1916.

Alexander HILDERSLEY, Lance Corporal, aged 21, was awarded the Military Medal four months after his death for repairing telephone wires despite being buried twice by falling debris from German shells. Initially reported missing. He had been the eldest son of Alex Hildersley, plumber and heating engineer from the Oldpark Road, Belfast, and had worked alongside his father before enlisting. Commemorated on the Thiepval Memorial.

Samuel HILLAND, Rifleman, from Ballyward, County Down. Commemorated on the Thiepval Memorial.

Robert HUGHES, Rifleman, aged 18, was born in Belfast though his parents, Hugh and Elizabeth, later moved to Bangor, County Down. Commemorated on the Thiepval Memorial.

William JACKSON, Rifleman, was born at Ballymacarrett, east Belfast, Son of John Jackson, The Mount, Mountpottinger, he was initially reported missing. A brother, Corporal John Jackson, was wounded at the Battle of Cambrai in 1917. Commemorated on the Thiepval Memorial.

Robert JAMISON, Rifleman, from the Shankill, Belfast. Buried at the AIF Burial Ground, Flers.

John JEFFS, Rifleman, aged 21, was born at Ballymacarrett, east Belfast. He was the youngest son of the late Richard Jeffs, The Mount, Belfast, and his mother Margaret who died three weeks after the Somme battle. John had been on the office staff of the Belfast Ropeworks and had played for the Inglewood football club. He is commemorated on the Thiepval Memorial.

Robert John JOHNSTON, Rifleman, aged 24, was the son of Thomas Johnston of Century Street, Belfast. Commemorated on the Thiepval Memorial.

William JOHNSTON, Rifleman, aged 20, served with A Company. Commemorated on the Thiepval Memorial.

Francis KEENAN, Rifleman, was born at Downpatrick, County Down. He was the second son of Colour Sergeant W Keenan, of the 5th Royal Irish Rifles, to die in the war. A brother, Lance Corporal Patrick Joseph Keenan, 21, of the 1st Rifles, had been killed in March 1915. The family was originally from Fermoy, County Cork, though was living at Sussex Place, Belfast, in 1914. Commemorated on the Thiepval Memorial.

James KENNEDY, Rifleman, aged 26, was from Glenavy, County Antrim. Commemorated on the Thiepval Memorial.

William KING, Lance Corporal, aged 33, was born at Ballymacarrett, east Belfast. Reported missing, he was officially presumed dead on the first anniversary of the Battle of the Somme. Son of the late James King, of Bentinck Street, Belfast, he had been educated at the Royal Belfast Academical Institution. Formerly a journalist, he is commemorated on the Thiepval Memorial.

Joseph KYLE, Rifleman, from the Shankill area of Belfast, had worked as a designer for Richardson, Sons & Owden, having served as an apprentice in the firm. He contributed artwork to the battalion's magazine, The Incinerator. Joseph was one of three soldier sons of John Kyle, 10 Belgravia Avenue, Belfast.

George LARMOUR, Rifleman, aged 25, was from east Belfast. Commemorated on the Thiepval Memorial.

Albert LAUGHLIN, Rifleman, aged 20, from the Shankill area of Belfast, was the fourth son of William Laughlin, 110 Battenberg Street, Belfast. Had been a member of the West Belfast UVF and worked at engineers James Mackie and Son's Albert Foundry.

Griffith LEWIS, Rifleman, was from the Shankill area of Belfast. Buried in Mill Road Cemetery.

Samuel MAGOWAN, Rifleman, from Belfast. Commemorated on the Thiepval Memorial.

William MAJURY, Rifleman, from Belfast. Commemorated on the Thiepval Memorial.

Samuel McCALL, Rifleman, from Belfast. Commemorated on the Thiepval Memorial.

Henry McCASHIN, Rifleman, born in County Galway but enlisted in Belfast. Commemorated on the Thiepval memorial.

Austin McCLEERY, Rifleman, from Belfast, was the third son of Hugh McCleery, 41 Arkwright Street, Belfast. He had worked as an apprentice cabinet-maker before the war. Buried at Connaught Cemetery.

Joseph McCLUNE, Lance Corporal, from Belfast. Commemorated on the Thiepval Memorial.

James McCUNE, Lance Corporal, from the Shankill area of Belfast. Commemorated on the Thiepval Memorial.

Robert McILROY, Rifleman, aged 25, from Belfast. Commemorated on the Thiepval Memorial.

Samuel McILROY, Rifleman, aged 26, was born in Belfast but had been living in Blackstock, South Carolina, America, prior to the war. Attached to the 109th Light Trench Mortar Battery. Buried in Connaught Cemetery.

Frederick McINTYRE, Rifleman, aged 19, was from Belfast. Known by the uncomplimentary nickname of 'Fat' McIntyre, he was a signaller and served alongside Charles Sheridan, with both being attached to the Royal Engineers' signal section at brigade headquarters briefly.

William McKEOWN, Lance Corporal, aged 24, from east Belfast. Commemorated on the Thiepval Memorial.

Joseph McMURTRY, Lance Corporal, from Ballyvaugh, County Antrim. Commemorated on the Thiepval Memorial.

Samuel MERCER, Lance Corporal, from Belfast. Commemorated on the Thiepval Memorial.

George MOLYNEUX, Rifleman, born at Ligoniel, north Belfast, was the son of George Molyneux, who played for Everton Football Club and was an English international. A second son, Ellis Molyneux, served with the 20th The King's (Liverpool Regiment) and was killed in October 1916. Both are commemorated on the Thiepval Memorial.

John Reid MOORE, Sergeant, aged 22, from Belfast. Son of Thomas Gourley and Susan Moore, of 19 Baltic Avenue, Belfast, and great uncle of the author. He was attached to the 109th Light Trench Mortar Battery. Buried at Connaught Cemetery.

Arthur MORROW, Rifleman, aged 19, from Belfast. Buried at Connaught Cemetery.

Albert Ernest NELSON, Lance Corporal, aged 21, from Belfast. Holder of the Military Medal. Buried at Connaught Cemetery.

Frederick NELSON, Rifleman, aged 23, from Belfast. Buried at Tincourt New British Cemetery.

James Patterson PARKES, Rifleman, from Belfast. Commemorated on the Thiepval Memorial.

Paul G POLLOCK, Lance Corporal, aged 21, was born in Glasgow. He was the son of the Rev John Pollock of St Enoch's Church, Belfast. A notice that appeared in the *Belfast News Letter* on 27 July 1916, read: "Rev John Pollock (St Enoch's Church), 7 Glendore Park, Antrim Road, will be glad to receive any information regarding his son, Lance Corporal Paul G Pollock, Scout, B Company, 14th Battalion Royal Irish Rifles (YCV), who was engaged in the advance of the Ulster Division on 1st July last, and has been 'missing since that date.'" He is commemorated on the Thiepval Memorial.

James Hamilton PURDY, Rifleman, from east Belfast. Commemorated on the Thiepval Memorial.

William RIDGWAY, Lance Sergeant, aged 20, from Belfast. Buried at AIF Burial Ground, Flers.

James RITCHIE, Rifleman, from Belfast. Buried at the Thiepval Anglo-French Cemetery to the rear of the Thiepval Memorial.

William RODDY, Rifleman, aged 26, from Keady, County Armagh. Commemorated on the Thiepval Memorial.

Robert RODGERS, Rifleman, aged 27, was born at Carrickfergus but was living in the Bloomfield area of east Belfast in 1914. A member of A Company, he is buried at Connaught Cemetery.

Peter ROGERS, Rifleman, from Drogheda, County Lough. He is buried at Mill Road Cemetery.

Peter ROONEY, Rifleman, aged 20, from Kilkeel, County Down, but living in Belfast before the war. A member of A Company, he is commemorated on the Thiepval Memorial.

Francis Robert SAMPSON, Rifleman, 19, was the son of Captain H Sampson, holder of the Military Medal, and Mary Sampson, of Willowbank Gardens, Belfast. Commemorated on the Thiepval Memorial.

Edgar SAVAGE, Rifleman, aged 18, was from east Belfast and a member of D Company. He was the eldest son of JH Savage, Ardoyne Fire Station, Belfast. Commemorated on the Thiepval Memorial.

William John SCOTT, Sergeant, aged 27, from Belfast. He was a member of A Company and left behind a wife, Charlotte, at Sunnyside Street, Belfast. Commemorated on the Thiepval Memorial.

John James SHANKS, Rifleman, aged 19, from Belfast. He was a member of C Company and the son of John and Elizabeth Shanks of Hillview Street, Belfast. Commemorated on the Thiepval Memorial.

Robert SHANNON, Rifleman, aged 22, from Belfast. The son of Alexander and Sarah Shannon of Cliftonville Road, Belfast, he was a member of C Company. Commemorated on the Thiepval Memorial.

Charles Owen SLACKE, Captain, aged 44, left a widow, Catherine Anne Slacke. He is buried at Connaught Cemetery.

Aubrey STEVENSON, Sergeant, from east Belfast. Commemorated on the Thiepval Memorial.

Samuel WELLS, Rifleman, from Lougheran, Lisburn. Commemorated on the Thiepval Memorial.

Thomas WELLS, Rifleman, born at Magheralin, County Down. He was living at Lougheran, Lisburn, in 1914. Commemorated on the Thiepval Memorial.

David WILLIAMSON, Rifleman, aged 26, from Tandragee, County Armagh. Lieutenant SH Monard, writing to his father at Market Street, Tandragee, said: "During the battle he never left my side, and he was with me in the fourth line of the German defences." Commemorated on the Thiepval Memorial.

Frederick WILLIAMSON, Rifleman, from Lisburn but was living at Muckamore, County Antrim, when he enlisted. Commemorated on the Thiepval Memorial.

Samuel WILLIS, Captain, aged 43, left a wife at home in Coleraine, County Londonderry. Commemorated on the Thiepval Memorial.

Matthew John WRIGHT, Second Lieutenant, aged 28. The C Company officer was the son of the Rev William Wright of Newtownards, County Down. Commemorated on the Thiepval Memorial.

Robert James WRIGHT, Rifleman, aged 20, was born at Ballinderry, County Down, and was living at Moneymore, County Antrim, when he enlisted at Randalstown. Commemorated on the Thiepval Memorial.

2 JULY 1916

Joseph Maxwell COCHRANE, Rifleman, aged 32, from Belfast. He was the son of former Sergeant Cochrane, Royal Irish Constabulary, of Rugby Avenue, Belfast. Joseph had formerly worked in the moulding shop at the Harland and Wolff shipyard. He died of wounds and was buried at Puchevillers British Cemetery.

3 JULY 1916

Victor Harold ROBB, Lieutenant, died of wounds. Buried at Belfast City Cemetery.

5 JULY 1916

Wallace McMullan WOODSIDE, Corporal, aged 26, from Holywood, County Down. The son of a doctor, he died of wounds and is buried at Puchevillers British Cemetery.

7 JULY 1916

James Valentine HYNDMAN, Captain, aged 29, was the son of James Hyndman, Antrim Road, Belfast. Buried at Wimereux Communal Cemetery. Died of wounds.

8 JULY 1916

Walter FERGUSON, Lance Corporal, aged 24, from Belfast. Died of wounds. Buried at Caudry Old Communal Cemetery.

11 JULY 1916

Alexander SMITH, Rifleman, aged 22, from Belfast. He was one of the battalion's star footballers. Buried at Etaples Military Cemetery.

18 JULY 1916

Reg Lambert LACK, Second Lieutenant. Died of wounds. Buried at St Nicholas Churchyard, Thames Ditton.

Compiled largely, but not exclusively, from the records of the Commonwealth War Graves Commission (CWGC) and the Soldiers Died in the Great War database, the list above should be considered as indicative rather than exhaustive. While every attempt has been made to name all those of the 14th (YCV) Battalion killed between these dates, the records are at times contradictory and sometimes contain the wrong information leading to the possibility that some names have been omitted.

APPENDIX 8
The 14th (YCV) Royal Irish Rifles dead of early June 1917

7 JUNE 1917

Stanley ANDERSON, Rifleman, aged 20, born at Larne, County Antrim. Son of Charles and Agnes Anderson, Tottenham, London. Buried at Lone Tree Cemetery.

William ARMSTRONG, Rifleman, aged 27, from Belfast. Buried at Spanbroekmolen British Cemetery.

Harold AUSTIN, Sergeant, aged 22, from Tonbridge, Kent. Buried at Spanbroekmolen British Cemetery.

Henry Robert BLAIR, Rifleman, from Clonaslee, Queen's County. Commemorated on a special memorial at Spanbroekmolen British Cemetery.

James BLAIR, Rifleman, aged 38, from Barony, Lanark. He had worked 25 years for the General Post Office in Glasgow before the war. Buried at Spanbroekmolen British Cemetery.

Charles BLAKE, Rifleman, from Belfast. Buried at Spanbroekmolen British Cemetery.

Frank Thomas BOULDING, Rifleman, aged 27, from Ashford, Kent. Buried at Lone Tree Cemetery.

Brian BOYD, Second Lieutenant, aged 19, from Belfast. Holder of the Military Medal. Buried at Bailleul Communal Cemetery.

Thomas BRADY, Sergeant, aged 21, born at Longford but was living at Limerick in 1914. Buried at Dranoutre Military Cemetery.

Patrick BROOKS, Rifleman, from Enniscorthy, County Wexford. Buried at Lone Tree Cemetery.

Robert BURT, Rifleman, aged 19, from Kent. Buried at Spanbroekmolen British Cemetery.

Cecil Charles COOPER, Rifleman, aged 20, from Maidstone, Kent. Buried at Spanbroekmolen British Cemetery.

Thomas CRAIG, Rifleman, aged 23, from Belfast. Buried at Lone Tree Cemetery.

Sydney James Livingstone DOWNEY, Second Lieutenant, aged 21 from Belfast. Buried at Spanbroekmolen British Cemetery.

Archibald DRYLAND, Rifleman, from Kent. He had formerly served with the East Kent Regiment. Buried at Lone Tree Cemetery.

Robert FLEMING, Lance Corporal, aged 22, from Antrim. Buried at Spanbroekmolen British Cemetery.

Thomas GIBNEY, Corporal, enlisted in Dublin. Buried at Spanbroekmoken British Cemetery.

Frederick GILBERT, Rifleman, from Kent. Buried at Bailleul Communal Cemetery.

Henry GRIDLEY, Rifleman, from Clapham, Surrey. Commemorated on a special memorial in Spanbroekmolen British Cemetery.

Robert HARVEY, Rifleman, from Belfast. Buried at Lone Tree Cemetery.

Edward HAYTER, Rifleman, from Bristol. Buried at Bailleul Communal Cemetery.

Albert Ernest HERAPATH, Rifleman, aged 22, from Abergainthy, Wales. Buried at Spanbroekmolen British Cemetery.

William George HILL, Corporal, from Cookstown, County Tyrone. Buried at Spanbroekmolen British Cemetery.

William KENNEDY, Rifleman, from Wishaw, Lanark, but living in Belfast in 1914. The son of the Rev Dr SG Kennedy, of Cromwell House, Cromwell Road, Belfast, he had attended Methody College, Belfast, and the Royal Belfast Academical Institution. He had worked in the Shaftesbury Square branch of the Northern Bank prior to enlistment. William was awarded the Military Medal for his actions at the Battle of the Somme, where despite being wounded himself he carried a comrade to safety in spite of heavy fire. Buried at Spanbroekmolen British Cemetery. His younger brother, Josiah Alexander Chancellor Kennedy (Jack), 1896–1957, enlisted in the Canadian army but later transferred to the Royal Irish Rifles. His wife Essie Stephenson had previously been engaged to William. Another brother, James Kennedy, was killed on 21 March 1918, while on attachment to the 1st Rifles from the 8th Rifles.

James Leonard KNIGHT, Rifleman, aged 20, from Cardiff, Wales. Commemorated on the Menin Gate Memorial.

Francis LAVERTY, Corporal, from Belfast. Buried at Lone Tree Cemetery.

Samuel MACAULAY, Corporal, aged 24, from Birkenhead, Cheshire, but living in Belfast before the war. Buried at Spanbroekmolen British Cemetery.

Thomas Henry MARSON, Rifleman, from Stratford, Essex. Buried at Spanbroekmolen British Cemetery.

Alfred MASSEY, Rifleman, from Dromore, County Down. Buried at Spanbroekmolen British Cemetery.

Frederick McKEE, Rifleman, aged 29, from Carrowdore, County Down. Buried at Spanbroekmolen British Cemetery.

Francis McNALLY, Rifleman, from Sligo. Buried at Wytschaete Military Cemetery.

William John MINTY, Rifleman, from Bristol. Buried at Irish House Cemetery.

William NISBET, Rifleman, from Irvine, Ayrshire. Buried at Irish House Cemetery.

Robert Campbell, ROSS, Rifleman, aged 19, from Belfast. He was the third son, and one of 12 children, of teacher RJ Ross, an elder in Great Victoria Street Presbyterian Church. He was a pre-war member of the YCVs, the Central Presbyterian Association, and the Boys' Brigade. He had been operating as a stretcher-bearer bringing in the wounded when killed.

James Herbert SCOTT, Rifleman, aged 21, from Hillsborough, County Down. Buried at Spanbroekmolen British Cemetery.

Ambrose SHEARING, Rifleman, from Dorset. Buried at Lone Tree Cemetery.

Johnston Hill SIMPSON, Rifleman, aged 27, from Ballynahinch, County Down. Commemorated on a special memorial in Spanbroekmolen British Cemetery.

William SPENCE, Rifleman, aged 20, from Belfast. He was the second son of Samuel Spence, Albertbridge Road, a well-known city missionary. Buried at Lone Tree Cemetery.

Charles Herbert WESTBROOK, Rifleman, from Middlesex. Buried at Spanbroekmolen British Cemetery.

Frank WILLIAMS, Rifleman, aged 34, from Kempsford, Glos. Buried at Lone Tree Cemetery.

Arthur WILLIS, Rifleman, from Yorkshire. Buried at Spanbroekmolen British Cemetery.

Thomas George WORTLEY, Sergeant, aged 33, from Belfast. Buried at Spanbroekmolen British Cemetery.

8 JUNE 1917

Frederick MAIR, Rifleman, from Newcastle-on-Tyne. Buried at Bailleul Communal Cemetery.

9 JUNE 1917

Edward MURRAY, Rifleman, from Southampton. Buried at Bailleul Communal Cemetery.

11 JUNE 1917

David Ernest CUMMINGS, Rifleman, aged 25, from Belfast. Buried at Bailleul Communal Cemetery.

Compiled largely, but not exclusively, from the records of the Commonwealth War Graves Commission (CWGC) and the Soldiers Died in the Great War database, the list above should be considered as indicative rather than exhaustive. While every attempt has been made to name all those of the 14th (YCV) Battalion killed between these dates, the records are at times contradictory and sometimes contain the wrong information leading to the possibility that some names have been omitted.

APPENDIX 9

The 14th (YCV) Royal Irish Rifles dead from 16–31 August 1917

16 AUGUST 1917

James AGNEW, Rifleman, aged 19, from Belfast. Commemorated on the Tyne Cot Memorial.

Alfred ALDWORTH, Rifleman, aged 22, enlisted at Tralee, County Kerry. Family lived at Tahilla, Kenmare, County Kerry. Commemorated on the Tyne Cot Memorial.

David ANDREWS, Lance Corporal, from Belfast. Commemorated on the Tyne Cot Memorial.

Robert ANDREWS, Rifleman, from Belfast. Buried at New Irish Farm Cemetery.

John Leslie ARMSTRONG, CSM, aged 24, from Belfast. Commemorated on the Tyne Cot Memorial.

William BAIRD, Rifleman, from Wigan, Lancs. Buried at Dranoutre Military Cemetery.

Walter BAKER, Rifleman, from Lisburn, County Antrim. Buried at Bridge House Cemetery.

John BIGGART, Rifleman, aged 19, from Ballymoney, County Antrim. Commemorated on the Tyne Cot Memorial.

John Kirkwood BLAIR, Rifleman, aged 23, from Holywood, County Down but with a family home in Belfast. Buried at New Irish Farm Cemetery.

Frank Edwin BRABY, Rifleman, from Camberwell, Surrey. Commemorated on the Tyne Cot Memorial.

Robert John BROOKS, Rifleman, aged 19, from London. Buried at New Irish Farm Cemetery.

Sydney Herbert Arthur BROWN, Rifleman, aged 20, from Middlesex. Commemorated on the Tyne Cot Memorial.

William BROWN, Rifleman, aged 25, from Belfast. Buried at Brandhoek New Military Cemetery No 3.

George David BRYAN, Rifleman, aged 29, from Reading, Berks, though he had been residing in London. He left behind a widow, Dora. Buried at Bedford House Cemetery.

William CARLISLE, Rifleman, aged 19, from Belfast. Commemorated on the Tyne Cot Memorial.

Joseph CASSELLS, Rifleman, aged 20, from Tandragee, County Armagh, though the family later moved to Whiteabbey, County Antrim. Commemorated on the Tyne Cot Memorial.

James CLARKE, Rifleman, from Knockbracken, County Down. Commemorated on the Tyne Cot Memorial.

James Alexander CORRY, Rifleman, aged 26, from Belfast. A member of C Company, he is commemorated on the Tyne Cot Memorial.

James COUGHTREY, Rifleman, aged 19, from Middlesex with a family address at Kilburn, London. A member of C Company, he is commemorated on the Tyne Cot Memorial.

John COUSINS, Rifleman, aged 21, from Belfast. Commemorated on the Tyne Cot Memorial.

Theophilus Arthur COX, Rifleman, aged 26, from Middlesex. Commemorated on the Tyne Cot Memorial.

Kenneth James Bishop CROWDER, Rifleman, aged 21, from London. Commemorated on the Tyne Cot Memorial.

Agnew CROWE, Lance Corporal, aged 19, from Glenwherry, County Antrim. Son of Patrick and Margaret Rowney Crowe, of Glenhead, Glenwherry. Commemorated on the Tyne Cot Memorial and at Glenwherry Presbyterian Church.

James Herbert CULL, Lance Corporal, from Belfast. Commemorated on the Tyne Cot Memorial.

Alfred CULLIS, Rifleman, from Middlesex. Commemorated on the Tyne Cot Memorial.

William DARLINGTON, Lance Corporal, from Hanley Green, Lancs. Commemorated on the Tyne Cot Memorial.

Duncan DAVIDSON, Rifleman, aged 26, from Belfast. He had been attached to the 109th Trench Mortar Battery and is commemorated on the Tyne Cot Memorial.

John Harvey DIXON, Lance Corporal, aged 25, from Magherafelt, County Londonderry originally but living in Belfast prior to enlistment. A member of the Central Presbyterian Association in Belfast, and a pre-war Young Citizen Volunteer, he was a member of B Company and had been in charge of a Lewis Gun Section during the battle. He had previously fought at both the Somme and Messines. The Rev John Knowles, Presbyterian Chaplain, wrote to his father: "We are all deeply grieved for the loss of your son. He was a good soldier, faithful in his duty, and has been faithful unto death." Commemorated on the Tyne Cot Memorial.

Henry DORRIS, Corporal, aged 21, from Belfast. Commemorated on the Tyne Cot Memorial.

Richard DOUGLAS, Rifleman, aged 22, from Belfast. Commemorated on the Tyne Cot Memorial.

Arthur James DUCK, Rifleman, born at Portsmouth, Hants, but enlisted at Fulham, London. Commemorated on the Tyne Cot Memorial.

Albert Edward ELLIS, Rifleman, aged 19, from London. Commemorated on the Tyne Cot Memorial.

Walter FISKE, Rifleman, aged 34, from Norfolk but living in Kent prior to the war. A member of C Company, he is commemorated on the Tyne Cot Memorial.

Frank FITZER, Rifleman, aged 18, from Middlesex. Commemorated on the Tyne Cot Memorial.

Thomas McNiece FLEMING, Rifleman, aged 21, originally from Crumlin but living in Belfast pre-war. Buried at New Irish Farm Cemetery.

Frederick FOOTE, Rifleman, aged 23, from Middlesex. An only son, he is commemorated on the Tyne Cot Memorial.

James Wesley FOSTER, Rifleman, aged 19, from Bedford. Commemorated on the Tyne Cot Memorial.

Alexander John FREEMAN, Sergeant, from Essex. Commemorated on the Tyne Cot Memorial.

John FULLERTON, Rifleman, aged 34, from Kircubbin, County Down. Commemorated on the Tyne Cot Memorial.

Joseph George GAVIGINE, Rifleman, from London. Commemorated on the Tyne Cot Memorial.

William GIHON, Lance Corporal, aged 24, from Belfast. A member of B Company, he lies in Tyne Cot Cemetery.

William James GINGER, Rifleman, from Dunstable, Beds. Buried at New Irish Farm Cemetery.

Gildo GREGORY, Rifleman, aged 19, from London. Commemorated on the Tyne Cot Memorial.

George Wasson HALL, Rifleman, aged 19, from Belfast. The son of a Royal Irish Constabulary officer, he lies in Potijze Chateau Grounds Cemetery.

George HAMPTON, Rifleman, from Surrey. Commemorated on the Tyne Cot Memorial.

David HANLEY, Lance Corporal, aged 26, from Belfast. He left behind a widow, Lilias, of Rosapenna Street, Belfast. Commemorated on the Tyne Cot Memorial.

Frederick Howard HARMAN, Rifleman, aged 33, a married man from Southampton who enlisted at Watford, Herts. Commemorated on the Tyne Cot Memorial.

James HARPER, Rifleman, from Belfast. Commemorated on the Tyne Cot Memorial.

Joseph HARRIS, Rifleman, aged 25, from London. Married to Dora, he was serving as a runner during the battle and reportedly was struck by a piece of shrapnel in the chest as he moved forward as part of the advanced headquarters. Commemorated on the Tyne Cot Memorial.

Joseph HASLEY, Rifleman, from Belfast. Commemorated on the Tyne Cot Memorial.

Thomas HENRY, Corporal, aged 20, from Derryloran, Cookstown, County Tyrone, though with a family address in Belfast. A member of the 10th Belfast Scouts before the war, he was attached to the 109th Trench Mortar Battery. A brother, AW Henry, formerly with the YCVs, was wounded on 1 July 1916, while serving with the 8th Royal Irish Rifles. Commemorated on the Tyne Cot Memorial.

William Quintus Ewart HILL, Rifleman, aged 25, from Belfast. The eldest son of John and Catherine Hill, of Chadwick Street, Belfast, he was a member of the Young Citizen Volunteers prior to the war and had worked in the offices of the Corporation Gas Works. Rifleman Hill had been awarded the Military Medal for his bravery during the Battle of Messines in June, 1917. Commemorated on the Tyne Cot Memorial.

George HILLIER, Rifleman, aged 36, from Surrey but living in Middlesex prior to the war. A married man, he is commemorated on the Tyne Cot Memorial.

Charles Henry HITCH, Rifleman, aged 18, from Kent. Commemorated on the Tyne Cot Memorial.

William HOGGETT, Rifleman, aged 39, from Norfolk. He left behind a widow, Susannah. Commemorated on the Tyne Cot Memorial.

William HOWSER, Rifleman, from Middlesex. Buried at New Irish Farm Cemetery.

Edward James HUMPHREYS, Rifleman, aged 19, from London. Commemorated on the Tyne Cot Memorial.

David JAMISON, Rifleman, from Ballymena, County Antrim. Commemorated on the Tyne Cot Memorial.

William KEENAN, Lance Corporal, from Belfast, died of wounds. Buried at Brandhoek New Military Cemetery No 3.

Joseph KELLY, Rifleman, enlisted in Belfast. Buried at New Irish Farm Cemetery.

Hugh Victor Strain KENNEDY, Second Lieutenant. Commemorated on the Tyne Cot Memorial.

William KERR, Rifleman, aged 22, from Belfast. Buried at Lijssenthoek Military Cemetery.

Edward KETTLE, Rifleman, aged 19, from London. Commemorated on the Tyne Cot Memorial.

Alexander LAIDLAW, Rifleman, aged 39, born in Edinburgh though enlisted in Glasgow. Buried at New Irish Farm Cemetery.

James LOWRY, Rifleman, aged 19, he was born at Ahoghill but living at Fenagh, Cullybackey, before enlistment. Commemorated on the Tyne Cot Memorial.

Robert Ernest LOWRY, Rifleman, aged 19, from Belfast. Commemorated on the Tyne Cot Memorial.

Patrick LYNCH, Rifleman, aged 20, from Phillipstown, King's County (Offaly). He was originally listed by both the CWGC and the Soldiers Died in the Great War database as having been killed on 13 April 1916. However, following representations made to the CWGC, and the presentation of evidence to the contrary, his date of death was altered on the records to 16 August 1917, though the Commission still insists on commemorating him on the Thiepval Memorial at the Somme, rather than at the more appropriate Tyne Cot Memorial.

Horace Dunster MARTIN, Lance Corporal, aged 29, from Kent. Commemorated on the Tyne Cot Memorial.

John McATEER, Rifleman, aged 23, from Belfast. A member of C Company, he is buried at New Irish Farm Cemetery.

James Wilson McBURNEY, Second Lieutenant, aged 19,

with the family home at Moatville, Comber, County Down. Commemorated on the Tyne Cot Memorial.

Robert McCORMICK, Rifleman, from Donegore, County Antrim, though living at Holywood, County Down, prior to enlistment at Belfast. Commemorated on the Tyne Cot Memorial.

David McCULLOUGH, Rifleman, aged 36, from Belfast. Commemorated on the Tyne Cot Memorial.

Hugh McDONALD, Rifleman, aged 23, from Dromore, County Down. He is listed by Soldiers Died in the Great War as serving with the 14th Royal Irish Rifles but by the CWGC as being a member of the 13th Rifles. He is buried at Tyne Cot Cemetery.

Joseph McKIBBEN, Rifleman, from Holywood. Commemorated on the Tyne Cot Memorial.

David MILLS, Rifleman, from Ballymarlow, County Antrim. Commemorated on the Tyne Cot Memorial.

Allan MONTGOMERY, Lance Corporal, aged 24, from Antrim though living in Ballymena at time of enlistment. Commemorated on the Tyne Cot Memorial.

Robert MORROW, Rifleman, aged 20, from Ballywilliam, Crossgar, County Down, though the family later moved to Belfast. Commemorated on the Tyne Cot Memorial.

Oliver Joseph MURKIN, Rifleman, aged 19, from Norfolk. Holder of the Military Medal for bravery, he is commemorated on the Tyne Cot Memorial.

Samuel MURRAY, Rifleman, aged 23, from Ballyblack, County Antrim, though the family later relocated to Newtownards, County Down. Commemorated on the Tyne Cot Memorial.

William NEVIN, Company Sergeant Major, aged 22, from Ballymena, County Antrim, but with a family address at Finaghy Park, Belfast. Commemorated on the Tyne Cot Memorial.

James Goldie NOBLE, Rifleman, aged 19, from Ayr, Scotland. Commemorated on the Tyne Cot Memorial.

George PAISLEY, Lance Corporal, aged 21, from Belfast. Commemorated on the Tyne Cot Memorial.

Harold Jamison PATTERSON, Lance Corporal, aged 19, from Belfast. Commemorated on the Tyne Cot Memorial.

Herbert Finlay REA, Lieutenant. Commemorated on the Tyne Cot Memorial.

William John REID, Sergeant, aged 21, from Belfast. Commemorated on the Tyne Cot Memorial.

Charles Edward ROGERS, Rifleman, from Middlesex. Commemorated on the Tyne Cot Memorial.

John Albert RUDKIN, Rifleman, aged 30, from London. A married man, he is commemorated on the Tyne Cot Memorial.

John SHARKEY, Rifleman, aged 23, from Dublin. Commemorated on the Tyne Cot Memorial.

William Francis SHIPHAM (spelt SHIPHAN in CWGC records), from London. Commemorated on the Tyne Cot Memorial.

Albert SMITH, Rifleman, aged 22, was born in Partick, Lanark, Scotland, but living in Hamilton Road, Bangor, County Down, in 1914. Commemorated on the Tyne Cot Memorial.

Thomas James SMYTH, Rifleman, aged 19, from Drumbeg, County Antrim though living at Dunmurry at the time of enlistment. Buried at Potijze Chateau Grounds Cemetery.

James Arnold SPLADING, Rifleman, aged 24, from Kent. A married man, he is commemorated on the Tyne Cot Memorial. His wife later remarried.

Arthur Richard SPENCLEY (spelt SPENCELY in CWGC records), from London, was married. He is commemorated on the Tyne Cot Memorial.

George SPRATT, Rifleman, aged 24, was born in Brooklyn, New York, and enlisted at Belfast. The married man served in B Company and is commemorated on the Tyne Cot Memorial.

George STAFFORD, Lance Corporal, was from Gorey, County Wexford but living in Belfast when the war began. He was wounded at the Somme on 1 July 1916, receiving treatment at a hospital in Sheffield, England. Commemorated on the Tyne Cot Memorial.

John STEWART, Rifleman, from Templepatrick but living in Larne, County Antrim, in 1914. Commemorated on the Tyne Cot Memorial.

Henry Albert SUMNER, Rifleman, aged 21, from Somerset but living at Devizes, Wiltshire, at the outbreak of war. Commemorated on the Ploegsteert Memorial.

William TAYLOR, Rifleman, aged 32, from London, was married. Buried at Brandhoek New Military Cemetery No 3.

Edward TULL, Rifleman, from Essex. Buried at Bedford House Cemetery.

Frank WALKER, Rifleman, aged 38, from Kent. He left behind a widow, Christina, and had been employed at the

General Post Office in Tunbridge Wells for 24 years prior to joining the Army. Commemorated on the Tyne Cot Memorial.

Samuel Hugh WALKER, Second Lieutenant, aged 26. His parents lived at Dee Street, Belfast. Commemorated on the Tyne Cot Memorial.

William WITTERICK, Rifleman, from London. Buried at Tyne Cot Cemetery.

George Seymour WOOD, Rifleman, aged 19, from London. Commemorated on the Tyne Cot Memorial.

Andrew YEATES, Sergeant, aged 31, from Downpatrick, County Down, though the family later moved to Belfast. Hope recorded in his journal of his war years: "I have just said goodbye to Andy Yeates, one of our old sergeants, who was wounded earlier in the war. He is going up too. He tells me he has the fear of death – the fear that he won't come out. He is killed a few hours after he 'goes in'." Buried at New Irish Farm Cemetery.

17 AUGUST 1917

Frederick JACQUEST, Regimental Sergeant Major, aged 35, from London. He died of wounds and is buried at Lijssenthoek Military Cemetery.

John Dwyer O'BRIEN, Lieutenant, aged 28, from Skibbereen, County Cork. Holder of the Military Cross, he is buried at Brandhoek New Cemetery No 3.

Lewis James ROBINSON, Rifleman, from London. He was buried at Ypres Reservoir Cemetery after dying from his wounds.

18 AUGUST 1917

William John WRIGHT, Sergeant, aged 27, from Belfast. He left a widow, Catherine Jane Wright, who later moved to Ballycushion, Templepatrick, County Antrim. Sergeant Wright is buried at Brandhoek New Military Cemetery No 3.

19 AUGUST 1917

Frederick FROST, Rifleman, aged 36, from London. A married man who died of his wounds, he is buried at Abbeville Communal Cemetery Extension.

Rubin PILCHER, (H PILCHER, according to CWGC records), Lance Corporal, from Margate, Kent, died of wounds. Buried at Brandhoek New Military Cemetery No 3.

Robert Wilfred WOOD, Rifleman, aged 21, from Southport, Lancs. Buried at Brandhoek New Military Cemetery.

20 AUGUST 1917

Walter David GIBSON, Rifleman, aged 27, from Oldcastle, County Meath, but living at Devonport, County Devon, at time of joining the Army. He was buried at Boulogne Eastern Cemetery after dying from wounds.

29 AUGUST 1917

Arthur Archibald CAFFYN, Rifleman, aged 22, from London. He died of wounds and was buried at Wimereux Communal Cemetery.

Compiled largely, but not exclusively, from the records of the Commonwealth War Graves Commission (CWGC) and the Soldiers Died in the Great War database, the list above should be considered as indicative rather than exhaustive. While every attempt has been made to name all those of the 14th (YCV) Battalion killed between these dates, the records are at times contradictory and sometimes contain the wrong information leading to the possibility that some names have been omitted.

APPENDIX 10

The 14th (YCV) Royal Irish Rifles dead from 6–18 December 1917

6 DECEMBER 1917

Sydney CLAWSON, Rifleman, from Belfast. Commemorated on the Cambrai Memorial, Louverval.

Michael Joseph COUGHLIN, Rifleman, from Cardiff, Wales. Commemorated on the Cambrai Memorial, Louverval.

George HOWSE, Rifleman, from Banbury, Oxford.

Buried at Rocquigny–Equancourt Road British Cemetery, Manancourt.

Martin JENNINGS, Rifleman, from Kilkenny, enlisted in Belfast. Commemorated on the Cambrai Memorial, Louverval.

David JONES, Rifleman, from Ashton in Makerfield, Lancs. Commemorated on the Cambrai Memorial, Louverval.

George SKILLEN, Rifleman, aged 29, from Newcastle, County Down, though living in Banbridge at time of enlistment. Buried at Rocquigny–Equancourt Road British Cemetery, Manancourt.

7 DECEMBER 1917

Bert INGREY, Rifleman, aged 25, from Middlesex. Buried at Rocquigny–Equancourt Road British Cemetery, Manancourt.

William Joseph MASON, Rifleman, aged 21, from Belfast. He had been employed as an apprentice clerk at the Belfast Board of Guardians. His uncle, David Adams, JP, told a board meeting on 11 December 1917, that Rifleman Mason's company had taken its objective, earning the congratulations of the colonel. The Royal Engineers then arrived to repair a bridge, with the YCVs ordered to protect them. As Willie Mason climbed over the parapet he was hit by German machine-gun fire. The day before his death from wounds he told his parents, who had travelled to be at his bedside, that "he did not regret his action in joining the army, and that he would do the same thing over again". Rifleman Mason, a member of A Company, lies in St Sever Cemetery Extension, Rouen.

Walter MILLS, Rifleman, from Kent. Commemorated on the Cambrai Memorial, Louverval.

Thomas SMITH, Rifleman, from Chipperfield, Herts. Commemorated on the Cambrai Memorial, Louverval.

John WHITE, Rifleman, from Belfast. Commemorated on the Cambrai Memorial, Louverval.

13 DECEMBER 1917

Albert James DUNNETT, Rifleman, aged 20, from Kemptson, Beds, died of wounds. Buried at Rocquigny–Equancourt Road British Cemetery, Manancourt.

14 DECEMBER 1917

Joseph GREER, Rifleman, aged 31, from Mallusk, County Antrim. Buried at Etretat Churchyard Extension.

16 DECEMBER 1917

Thomas John GRAHAM, Rifleman, from Pomeroy, County Tyrone. Commemorated at the Thiepval Memorial.

17 DECEMBER 1917

Malcolm McCOLL, Rifleman, aged 21, from Belfast. Buried at Berks Cemetery Extension.

18 DECEMBER 1917

James GAULT, Lance Corporal, from Doagh, County Antrim. Buried at Le Cateau Military Cemetery. The Commonwealth Graves Commission records suggest he died on 8 December 1917.

Compiled largely, but not exclusively, from the records of the Commonwealth War Graves Commission (CWGC) and the Soldiers Died in the Great War database, the list above should be considered as indicative rather than exhaustive. While every attempt has been made to name all those of the 14th (YCV) Battalion killed between these dates, the records are at times contradictory and sometimes contain the wrong information leading to the possibility that some names have been omitted.

APPENDIX 11

The 14th (YCV) Royal Irish Rifles/23rd Entrenching Battalion dead from 21 March–27 April 1918

23 MARCH 1918

George Stirzker BELL, Rifleman, aged 29, from St Anne's-on-Sea, Lincs., and husband of Mary Ellen Bell. Formerly with the Army Cyclist Corps, he is commemorated on the Pozieres Memorial.

John BROWN, Lance Corporal, aged 33, from Dunmore East, County Waterford. Commemorated on the Pozieres Memorial.

Gerard Ebenezer FYSH, Rifleman, aged 23, from King's Lynn, Norfolk. Formerly 1st/18th Battalion London Regiment, he was one of five brothers who served during

the war. Commemorated on the Pozieres Memorial.

Edwin Robert LLOYD, Rifleman, from London. Commemorated on the Pozieres Memorial.

Edward MOONEY, Rifleman, from Newtownards, County Down. Buried at Ham British Cemetery, Muille-Villette.

John O'BRIEN, Lance Corporal, aged 44, from Bailieborough, County Cavan. A member of C Company and holder of the Military Medal, he is buried at Ham British Cemetery, Muille-Villette.

Frederick William PERROTT, Rifleman, aged 21, from

Surrey. Commemorated on the Pozieres Memorial.

Francis John WATKINS, Rifleman, from Birmingham. Commemorated on the Pozieres Memorial.

24 MARCH 1918

Joseph Henry HADDOCK, Second Lieutenant, aged 28, husband of May, of Leigh-on-Sea, Essex. Buried at Ham British Cemetery, Muille-Villette.

Robert Victor LYONS, Second Lieutenant, aged 21, from Belfast. Commemorated on the Pozieres memorial.

Albert BENSON, Rifleman, aged 21, from Middlesex. Formerly of the Middlesex Regiment, he is commemorated on the Pozieres Memorial.

David BROWN, Rifleman, enlisted in Belfast. Commemorated on the Pozieres Memorial.

Joseph COULTER, Corporal, aged 25, from Belfast. A member of C Company, he is commemorated on the Pozieres Memorial.

Thomas DOCHERTY, Lance Corporal, lived at Muff, County Donegal, but enlisted at Berwick-on-Tweed. Buried at Eppeville Old Churchyard.

Alfred Thomas EDWARDS, Rifleman, from Gloucester. Formerly a member of the Rifle Brigade, he is commemorated on the Pozieres Memorial.

David ELLIOTT, Rifleman, aged 29, from Belfast. Husband of Mary Elliott, Hunter Street, Belfast, he is commemorated on the Pozieres Memorial.

Charles Arthur HARVEY, Rifleman, from London. Commemorated on the Pozieres Memorial.

Alexander McCANN, Rifleman, enlisted at Belfast. Commemorated on the Pozieres Memorial.

James McCARROLL, Rifleman, aged 22, from Belfast. According to the additional information on the CWGC record, he was the "youngest son of the late William John and Mary McCarroll. One of three brothers, three Brothers-in-law, two Cousins and four Nephews who served in the Great War, one of whom fell". Commemorated on the Pozieres Memorial.

Harry McGOWAN, Rifleman, aged 29, from Holyford, County Tipperary, though living at Arklow, County Wicklow, before the war. Commemorated on the Pozieres Memorial.

Patrick MULLEADY, Rifleman, aged 29, from Killow, County Longford. Commemorated on the Pozieres Memorial.

Harry PHILLIPS, Rifleman, from Tidal Basin, Essex. Buried at Eppeville Old Churchyard.

26 MARCH 1918

William ANDERSON, Rifleman, from Belfast. He had been attached to the 36th Machine Gun Corps when killed. Commemorated on the Pozieres Memorial.

27 MARCH 1918

Walter Henry CORK, Rifleman, aged 29, from Sussex. Buried at Eppeville Old Churchyard.

Neil HEAVERON, Rifleman, aged 23, had been born in Ireland but was living at Paisley, Renfrew, in 1914. He died of wounds and is commemorated on Villers Saint Christophe Churchyard Memorial 27, Ham British Cemetery, Muille-Villette.

30 MARCH 1918

Harry NICOL, Rifleman, aged 20, from Belfast. He was on attachment to the Fifth Army Infantry School when killed. Commemorated on the Pozieres Memorial.

20 APRIL 1918

Thomas BOOTH, Rifleman, aged 18, from Belfast. He was a member of 14th Rifles according to Soldiers Died but with the 1st Rifles according to the CWGC. Commemorated on the Tyne Cot Memorial.

Edward George YOUNGMAN, aged 20, from Suffolk. He was a member of 14th Rifles according to Soldiers Died but with the 1st Rifles according to the CWGC. Commemorated on the Tyne Cot Memorial.

24 APRIL 1918

William WILSON, Rifleman, from Carlisle, Cumberland. Holder of the Military Medal and Bar, he was buried at Red Farm Military Cemetery.

28 APRIL 1918

David MARSHALL, Sergeant, from Gourock, Renfrewshire, though with a family home in Belfast. He died of wounds in Germany while a prisoner-of-war and was buried at Berlin South-Western Cemetery. Date of death according to Soldiers Died was 24 April 1918, but 28 April 1918 by the CWGC records.

Compiled largely, but not exclusively, from the records of the Commonwealth War Graves Commission (CWGC) and the Soldiers Died in the Great War database, the list above should be considered as indicative rather than exhaustive. While every attempt has been made to name all those of the 14th (YCV) Battalion killed between these dates, the records are at times contradictory and sometimes contain the wrong information leading to the possibility that some names have been omitted.

APPENDIX 12
Young Citizen Volunteers revisit Mesnil

Mesnil, a village in the Somme, near the town of Albert, defended with wonderful gallantry by the 14th Battalion Royal Irish Rifles (the YCVs of the Ulster Division) was the scene of a happy little ceremony yesterday.

Sixty ex-members of the battalion, mostly from Belfast, who are at present doing a tour of the battlefields, visited the village this forenoon and were received by the Mayor (Monsieur A Maguier). Major JA Mulholland, MC, presented his old comrades-in-arms, and the company repaired to the spot where the old church stood, where the ceremony took place.

During the defence of the village the hands of the church clock in some mysterious way moved at very irregular intervals, usually after or previous to the relief of troops. Whether it was the action of a spy or the occasional vibration from the explosion of shells it was never ascertained, but to prevent any mistake about the matter the hands were removed. A short time after the church was demolished by German artillery fire.

The hands have since been in the possession of the officer who gave instructions for their removal, and to-day they were presented to the Mayor in a unique and appropriate form.

The hands are set at Armistice hour – 11.00 am – and on the right are the crossed flags of England and France, having in the centre the Croix-de-Guerre, the Croix-de-Guerre having been presented to the Commune by the French Government. On the left is the badge of the Royal Irish Rifles and the regimental motto underneath. A short history of the clock hands in French and English is printed in ivory on each side of the shield.

These hands were presented to the Mayor by Major Mulholland on behalf of the 14th Battalion Royal Irish Rifles. The Mayor was also presented with a gold-mounted regimental stick by the men of the party. In making the presentation, Major Mulholland said:

Today the shield bearing the clock hands is kept in the Mayor's office in the Hotel de Ville, just across from the rebuilt village church. *(Courtesy of the Somme Museum)*

"It was with feelings of both pleasure and sadness that they as ex-members of the 14th Battalion Royal Irish Rifles visit the village that day, because although they had some happy days in that neighbourhood they had also very sad memories of their sojourn in that area. The majority of us, he continued, lived and fought around here for many months, and whilst we can recall hours of fun and laughter when resting in the surrounding villages, there is ever present with us the memory of many of our comrades who lie buried in the military cemeteries close to Mesnil.

We have returned to-day to do honour to their memory, to walk over the ground which they so nobly defended, to think more deeply of their gallantry and self-sacrifice, and we trust that visits such as this will help, if indeed help is needed, to maintain the friendship which exists between our two countries.

We are taking the opportunity when here to give back to you the hands of your

The hands from the church clock, taken down by the YCVs on the orders of Adjutant Alan Mulholland, are returned to the Mayor in 1927. *(Courtesy of the Somme Museum)*

old church clock, which was destroyed by German artillery when we occupied the village, and we feel that they will be received by you in the spirit in which we restore them. It would be our earnest hope and belief that they will be treasured not alone by the old residents, but by their children, and that they will be a reminder of the part played in the Great War by their village.

Need I explain the import of the words 'C'est fini?' Whilst they, together with the setting of the hands at eleven o'clock indicate the cessation of hostilities, are they not the last words of Him who made the great sacrifice and set the example to all mankind, that it is greater to lay down one's life for one's friend than to gain the whole world?

There is also a Croix-de-Guerre affixed to the shield, and I would here congratulate your commune on that honour which has been conferred upon you by the French Government.

I should refer to the motto of our regiment which you see on the shield. 'Quis Separabit', or 'Who shall separate us.' Is it not appropriate and applicable to our two nations, who fought side by side in the greatest of wars? I have now very great pleasure, Mr Mayor, in handing over to you this shield on behalf of our old battalion."

The Mayor acknowledged the gifts in a brief speech.

(**From the** *Belfast Telegraph*, **14 July 1927**)

How Verdun was saved

A further report of the visit of ex-members of the 14th Royal Irish Rifles (YCV) to the Flanders battlefields shows that this itinerary was an extensive one. It was the first organised tour of the battlefields by members of this unit of the 36th (Ulster) Division.

The party included five of the battalion's officers – Major JA Mulholland, MC; Major

H Clokey, MC; Major JW Harper; Lieut WJ Allen; Lieut E Morrow and about 60 ex-NCOs and men.

The tour commenced in Belgium, the jumping-off point being Ostend, from whence the party proceeded to Ypres, where a day was spent in visiting the various sectors in which the battalion had fought.

Leaving Ypres the party proceeded on a two-day motor tour. Among the places visited were Wytschaete, Dranoutre, Bailleul, Bethune, Vimy Ridge, Arras, Bapaume, the Australian Memorial in Delville Wood, Contalmaison and Albert.

The culminating point of the trip was the visit on Wednesday to Mesnil, a small village in the Somme Department, close to Thiepval, which was held by the 36th Division prior to the attack of 1st July 1916.

While the 14th Royal Irish Rifles held the village the clock on the church was destroyed by German artillery fire, and the hands have since that time been in the possession of Major JA Mulholland, MC, who was second in command of the battalion. Major Mulholland, with the intention of returning the clock hands to the town, had them mounted on a shield, together with a battalion badge and a Croix de Guerre – which honour was conferred upon the town by the French President. Also on the shield is an inscription in English and French and the words 'C'est fini' (it is finished).

On arriving in Mesnil the party formed up in front of the Maire (a wooden hut) and Major Mulholland handed over the shield to the Mayor (M Maovier) in a telling speech published in earlier reports of the ceremony.

The Mayor in his reply thanked Major Mulholland, the officers and men for their gift, which would be much appreciated by the present and future generations. He understood the purpose of their tour and sympathised with them in their great losses and the trials they had passed through.

Referring to the attack of the 1st July, he said that when the French Army was being hard pressed at Verdun and there was great danger of a breakthrough, the Somme Battle was launched. The enemy rushed his reserves to that front and Verdun was saved. They all knew and appreciated the great and glorious part played by the 36th (Ulster) Division of the British Army in the first days of the attack when they lost so heavily.

He wished on behalf of the town and himself to pay tribute to the gallantry of the 14th Battalion of the Royal Irish Rifles and in particular to Major Mulholland.

Major Mulholland was then presented with a bouquet by a schoolboy, and a golf-mounted 'swagger' cane was given to the Mayor by ex-Sergeant James Diamond, the presentation being made by Major Harper.

Subsequently the school children of the village placed flowers on the Cross of Sacrifice in the British War Cemetery.

In the afternoon the party visited the 36th Division Memorial Tower at Thiepval and a wreath was laid in the memorial chamber of the tower by ex-Sergeant R Stewart.

After these ceremonies the tour of the battlefields was continued. The last two days, Thursday and Friday, are being spent in Paris.

(From the *Belfast Telegraph*, 15 July 1927)

END NOTES

Chapter 2

1 HG Stevenson was the north of Ireland representative for the Ministry of Pensions and an associate of the Central Presbyterian Association in Belfast. He was awarded the Order of the British Empire in 1918.

2 The Belfast Citizens' Association was formed in 1905 as a link between the elected representatives of the city council and the public they served. Its influence waned after the outbreak of the First World War and it felt the need, in July 1915, to point out that the reason it was not featuring so much in the Press was that it had dedicated its permanent staff to work for the Soldiers' and Sailors' Families Association. "While this extra work has naturally engrossed a large portion of their time, the officials have not forgotten the original objects of the association, and they hope to show their vitality by renewed energy as soon as happier circumstances allow the public to devote their energy anew to domestic and civic problems."

3 The YCV's steering committee already knew at this stage that it faced an uphill battle to receive official recognition. The Minute Book records of a meeting held on 29 August 1912: "The secretaries reported that the Army Council had refused to supply obsolete rifles for the use of the corps, and a statement was made by Councillor Dr Williamson with reference to the advisability of paying attention to ambulance work."

4 Sergeant Robert Bentley, later a captain and the first adjutant, played a pivotal role in licking into shape the raw recruits of the 14th Royal Irish Rifles during its early months. James Fitzsimons recalled: "Marvellous man who made the battalion what it was. I remember him taking the battalion at drill in Shane's Park. After a run through he gave the order 'Fall out' the officers, the platoon sergeants and NCOs, right and left markers, and put the battalion through its paces just as well without them." He had initially been employed by the YCV as a drill instructor for three nights a week, receiving £1, later increased to 35 shillings a week. He submitted an appeal for a rise in January 1914, resulting in an increase to £2 a week.

5 The Central Presbyterian Association lists 190 members on its role of honour, of which a dozen lost their lives. Some 27 young men and one member of staff joined the 14th (YCV) Battalion of the Royal Irish Rifles, with three killed in action.

6 An English man who had been persuaded to give up his role as vice-principal of Manchester School of Technology to oversee the proposed Belfast Technical College, Francis Charles Forth was an enthusiastic supporter of the YCV and UVF, allowing the latter to use the college's bakery facilities to feed the men. He had arrived in the city at the end of 1900 and set about his task with typical drive and determination, even visiting Germany where similar institutions were widely accepted as the best in Europe. In 1915 he joined the Royal Irish Rifles, being appointed a captain with a reserve battalion. Captain Forth resigned his commission towards the end of 1917 to return to college life. He died in 1919 after contracting Spanish flu.

7 Born in India in 1832 of Irish parents, Field Marshal Earl Frederick Sleigh Roberts was a distinguished soldier and supporter of the unionist cause. He won the Victoria Cross in 1858 while with the British East India Company, transferring to the British Army four years later. A former Commander-in-Chief of the Army in Ireland, he cemented his reputation as a military commander in the Boer War. It was Lord Roberts who recommended Sir George Richardson as commander of the Ulster Volunteer Force. He returned to the colours in 1914 but died of pneumonia at St Omer, France, in November that year while on a visit to Indian troops. Robert Stephenson Smyth Baden-Powell, a national hero after the successful defence of Mafeking during the Boer War, was Chief Scout; the Earl of Rosebery was a former Liberal Foreign Secretary and served as Prime Minister for a short time following the resignation of William Gladstone in 1894.

8 The National Rifle Association, now based at Bisley, was founded in 1859 to provide training in marksmanship to the newly formed corps of volunteers being raised in the wake of the perceived threat of a French invasion. Its role later expanded to take in a wider group of organisations, including the Scouting movement.

9 Born in London in 1868 to a rich family with an estate in County Sligo, Constance Gore-Booth met Polish-born Count Casimir Dunin Markievicz while studying in Paris in 1898. They married in 1901 and moved to Dublin two years later. She became involved in politics, joining Sinn Fein in 1908 and founding Fianna Eireann the following year, along the same lines as the Boy Scouts but with a strong military element. Countess Markievicz was sentenced to death for her part in the 1916 Easter Rising, commuted to life in prison. However, she was released from prison the following year and continued to play an active part in the republican movement. She died in 1927.

Chapter 3

1 Lieutenant Colonel Robert Chichester was the son of Lord Adolphus John Spencer Churchill Chichester and grandson of Edward Chichester, 4th Marques of Donegall. He married Dehra Kerr-Fisher, who later became president of the East Belfast Division of the Ulster Volunteer Medical and Nursing Corps and one of four vice-presidents of the Belfast District, over which Mrs Julia McMordie, wife of Lord Mayor Robert McMordie, sat as president. Mrs Chichester and Mrs McMordie later became the only two women elected to the first Northern Ireland Parliament in 1921. The Colonel and his wife had two children, a son Robert James Spencer Chichester who died in 1920 at the age of 18, and a daughter, Marion Caroline Dehra Chichester, who married James Lenox-Conyngham Clark. They had three children, the eldest of who was James Chichester-Clark, who went on to become the eighth leader of the Ulster Unionist Party and Prime Minister of Northern Ireland from 1 May 1969 until 20 March 1971. His brother, Robin Chichester-Clark, was MP

for Londonderry at Westminster and held a number of positions of prominence in the Conservative governments of Harold Macmillan and Edward Heath.

2 Ormiston, previously owned by shipbuilder Sir Edward Harland until 1887, was afterwards bought by his partner William Pirrie, later chairman of Harland and Wolff. Chichester rented the property. An advertisement in the *Northern Whig* in June 1912, shows the house was then up for let. Placed by Royal Avenue estate agents RJ McConnell & Co, it describes it as a "Gentleman's Residence" at Knock lately occupied by Lord Pirrie, and "standing in own grounds, which are exceptionally well laid out". Before the war, a former butler, sacked by Lieutenant Colonel Chichester, claimed at a court case when he sued for £10 owed in back pay, that rifles had been stored in the wine cellar at Ormiston, a claim that was dismissed as irrelevant to the matter in hand. Harland & Wolff, which held ownership of the property after Lord Pirrie's death in 1924, sold it to Campbell College in 1928. Having passed through the hands of both the Police Authority and the Northern Ireland Assembly, the latter considering it as potential office space for civil servants, it was returned to the private sector in 2015.

3 Colonel Walter Edwin Carson McCammond was commissioned into the 4th Royal Irish Rifles in 1892, later becoming its commander. During the 1916 Rebellion his battalion, renamed the 3rd RIR on the outbreak of the First World War, was in Dublin, being stationed at Portobello Barracks. He attempted to cover up for Captain JC Bowen Colthurst, a member of his battalion, over the shooting of three men at the barracks, including Francis Sheehy Skeffington, in retaliation for the loss of several soldiers killed by the rebels. He later gave evidence at the public inquiry into the killings. McCammond died in August 1923.

4 George FitzRoy Henry Somerset, the 3rd Baron Raglan, was a former Grenadier Guards officer who served as Under-Secretary of State for War from 1900 to 1902 and Lieutenant Governor of the Isle of Man from 1902 to 1918. He died in October 1921.

5 In March 1924, businessman Nelson Leech was shot dead during a robbery at Purdy and Millard's sculptor works at College Square North, Belfast. The gunman, Michael Pratley, a former soldier, was later hanged at Crumlin Road Gaol for the killing.

6 FWL May and William Glass were both pre-war members of the 6th Black Watch Territorial Battalion and were mobilised in August 1914. May, who became a captain, was the son of a Bank of Ireland agent from Newry. He was a member of Malone Rugby Club and had worked in insurance before the war. He had later transferred to the 36th (Ulster) Division and was killed on 8 June 1917, with the 11th Royal Irish Rifles, being buried at Dranoutre Military Cemetery, Belgium. William Glass, a former member of the Central Presbyterian Association who belonged to Fitzroy Avenue church in Belfast, was killed on the Western Front in 1917. An original member of the YCVs, he taught Sunday School, served as a Boys' Brigade officer, and was a drill instructor to several companies of the Ulster Volunteer Force. Second Lieutenant Glass, who had two brothers serving in the Army, was a father of four sons who, in 1917, were living with their mother in her native Isle of Man.

7 Lieutenant Alexander McKee was 35 when killed in action on 22 November 1917, while serving with the 10th Royal Irish Rifles. His body was never found and he is remembered on the Cambrai Memorial at Louverval, France. An only son, his late father, also Alexander, had worked at the Ulster Spinning Company and his mother Agnes was living at Madison Avenue, Belfast, at the time of his death. A member of the original YCV, he had joined the Black Watch before obtaining a commission in the RIR and had been among the troops sent to Dublin during the Easter Rebellion of 1916. Lieutenant McKee had been a member of Ekenhead Presbyterian Church in Belfast, where he served as the Boys' Brigade captain, and of the Ulidia Masonic Lodge No 135.

8 The money aspect became ever more problematic as the months passed, as little of the corporate funding promised in the early days materialised. Ultimately shipbuilder Frank Workman had to fund the organisation out of his personal fortune to keep it afloat.

9 Peter Kerr Kerr-Smiley had formerly served in the 21st Lancers, taking part in the Boer War. He was MP for North Antrim from 1910–22 and rejoined the Colours during the First World War, serving with the 14th Rifles until a stomach infection caused his return to Ireland. In April 1916, he was appointed to the General Staff. Kerr-Smiley died in June 1943.

Chapter 4

1 Usually referred to by his initials, BWD Montgomery was almost 60 years of age in 1913. He was unmarried and lived with several sisters and nieces who were attended to by a number of domestic servants. He had served as Honorary Secretary of the Ulster Club in Royal Avenue, Belfast, for a number of years.

2 The solemn and binding oath to resist Home Rule was based on the Scottish Covenant of 1638 but had been shortened and put into plain English. It was drafted by Thomas Sinclair, leader of Ulster Liberal Unionism and a member of the YCV steering committee.

3 Frank Workman was later to lose his only son during the war. Lieutenant Edward Workman, holder of the Military Cross, was 29 when he died on 26 January 1916, when on attachment to the 2nd Royal Irish Rifles. He had been educated at Charterhouse and Trinity College, Cambridge. Lieutenant Workman lies in Etaples Military Cemetery, France. A nephew of Councillor Workman, Lieutenant Ernest Workman, was commissioned into the 14th Royal Irish Rifles but later transferred to the Army Services Corp where, in December 1917, he earned a mention in despatches. His brother, Lieutenant Charles Workman, also the holder of a Military Cross won while with the Cameronians, died at the age of 20 on 20 July 1917, from wounds received serving in the Royal Flying Corps. Their father was Dr Charles Workman of Glasgow.

Chapter 5

1 Thomas Carnduff went on to become an accomplished poet, author and playwright. Unlike many of his YCV colleagues, he didn't join up in 1914, continuing instead to work at the Workman and Clark shipyard. However, in 1917 he enlisted

in the Royal Engineers, seeing active service in France. On his return to the shipyard he was made redundant, an experience he was to endure many times in the future as he struggled to provide for his young family. Although a unionist, and member of the C1 Special Constabulary for a number of years, his experience of working-class life greatly influenced his later politics, which took on a greater socialist hue. He died in April 1956.

Chapter 6

1 Lieutenant Hanna had the nickname 'Snowball' and evidently was not a callous man. Hope recorded how, when a German mine accidentally exploded under the enemy lines, he declined to call down an artillery barrage: "We want our artillery to splash but 'Snowball' Hanna won't be too severe."

2 Captain Charles St Aubyn Wake was a true old soldier. The son of Admiral Charles Wake, he had served in the Dorsetshire Regiment during the Nile Relief Expedition of 1885 and as a lieutenant in the Zanzibar Protectorate Force, losing a leg in the storming of a stockade. After a spell as vice consul at Mombasa, he rejoined the army in 1896, serving with the East African Rifles during the Uganda mutiny. In 1903 he became a captain in the Devon Militia, retiring in 1907 to take up a post as a recruiting officer. The lure of active service was too much, however, and he joined the Turkish army as an officer to take part in the Libyan War of 1911–12. He was recruited for the Ulster Volunteer Force, commanding the South Belfast Battalion at Balmoral, and through the UVF was commissioned into the 14th Royal Irish Rifles. According to Hope: "There is a general reshuffle of the gentlemen and our mystery man Captain Wake departs with all his belongings on a side-car. He has had a difference of opinion with the CO. We line the road and cheer him as he passes and wonder if he thinks it is sympathy or a soldier's farewell. It is a mixture of both." It was reported in April 1915, that Captain St Aubyn Wake had been temporarily appointed to command the 18th (Reserve) Battalion Royal Irish Rifles at Holywood. He ended the war as a major in the Royal West Kent Regiment. A brother, Major Hugh St Aubyn Wake, of the 2nd Battalion 8th Gurkha Rifles, was killed in action in November 1914, and another brother, Captain D St Aubyn Wake, served in the Royal Navy on board HMS *Jupiter*.

3 Sergeant Ralph Cole was later wounded in the face and right foot at the Somme on 1 July 1916. He was the son of Joseph Cole, a jeweller with a shop on the Shankill Road, Belfast, and had been a member of the pre-war YCVs. The sergeant did a mean impersonation of the silent movie star Charlie Chaplin, winning a prize at a battalion event for giving the best imitation. "Just as well the mule he had was quiet or there might have been unlooked for amusement," noted the battalion magazine, *The Incinerator*.

4 Lieutenant Charles McMaster later transferred to a trench howitzer battery.

5 Lieutenant Johnny Long was from Lisburn and was mentioned in despatches by Haig in December 1917. John Kennedy Hope, with his usual disdain for officers, referred to him as a "wee porkey gent".

Chapter 7

1 The restricted hours apparently did little to prevent the brigade from quenching its thirst for alcohol. At a meeting of the Synod of Belfast at the end of April 1915, the Rev William Martin, whose church was in Randalstown, spoke on "Gospel in the Camps". Although he specifically praised the young men of the YCV who he said "came up to his idea of what soldiers should be," he added: "There was a dark side to the picture, but notwithstanding all that was being done for the soldiers their efforts were absolutely inadequate and the publicans simply laughed at them. The men in the trade seemed to have only one thought – the sale of drink legally or illegally, whether the nation would sink or swim. It was the publicans' harvest day in Randalstown, and they knew it, and were reaping that harvest for all they were worth." He also blamed the military leadership for allowing "wet canteens" to continue.

2 The quality of the huts being erected for the army was questionable. In November 1914, there were 20 new camps under construction across the UK, with between 250 and 400 huts required at each to accommodate 30 men per hut in a space measuring 60 ft by 20 ft by 7 ft 6 ins to the eaves. According to the newspapers, a trade union report published that month complained: "The soldiers' huts are not lined inside, and the flooring is laid on the bare joists, no felt being used. There is a door at each end, and there are three windows on each side. There are no partitions of any kind, simply great bare buildings with one stove in the centre. The men sleep four inches off the floor in little box beds. When the flooring dries plenty of fresh cold air comes up through the joints. The sides and ends of the huts are weather boarded. The roofs of many let in sunshine and rain, and the water lies on the ground for days. When the hut contracts were given out it was understood that the prices ranged from £139 to £150. In order to house the troops quickly some contractors dispensed with the usual construction put into such work. The huts should be handed over to the Government with 25 per cent discount."

3 Company Sergeant Major Stevie Griffith was an old soldier who had formerly served in the Royal Irish Rifles. Trench warfare took its toll on him and he was sent back to Ireland early in 1916 suffering from "the rheumatics" to take up a training role. The June 1916, edition of the battalion magazine, *The Incinerator*, paints a picture of a popular NCO. Described as a "small, but sturdy and robust figure who helped to mould us into something like soldiers", he had made his mark at Finner Camp. "We were unused to Army ways, and our first acquaintance with Sgt-Major Griffith made us inclined to regard him as a 'fair terror,' but by-and-by it was recognised that his gruffness was only on the surface, and that underneath, lay a solid foundation of geniality. He gained the confidence of the men when they quickly recognised in him one who would see fair play, and no one whose cause was just had ever the slightest fear in approaching him." Also known as 'Chancer', he was fond of telling humorous stories of his service in India and South Africa and was always ready with a quip. A comment about the smallness of his feet produced "Sure, sir, they aren't feet at all. They are just turn-ups to keep my legs from ravelling out."

4 Medical Officer MacKenzie went on sick leave himself just days after this first death, with Lieutenant JH O'Neill taking over responsibility for the battalion's health temporarily. John Kennedy Hope, as usual, had something less than complimentary to say about Dr MacKenzie: "He is disliked by all and sundry, and is known as 'No 9 medicine and duty'. A doctor of course, but an old woman. One fellow says he is a maternity doctor so we are all right." In fact, the doctor had been an assistant surgeon at the Samaritan Hospital in Belfast and returned to that post in 1916, after resigning his commission following two years of service. His father was Dr WG MacKenzie of University Square, Belfast.

5 The Antrim Board of Guardians, meeting on 25 February 1915, reported a number of cases of 'spotted fever' in the Randalstown district, including two cases in the military camp. With no room for them at Ballymena Hospital, it was decided to ask the authorities if Purdysburn Fever Hospital could accommodate them. At the same meeting it was said that at least four cases of cerebrospinal meningitis had been notified in the Randalstown district though, as informing the authorities was not compulsory, it was suspected that there were other cases.

6 Corporal Wallace McMullan Woodside was the son of Dr John and Maria Woodside, 3 Princess Terrace, Cregagh, east Belfast. He died of wounds on 5 July 1916, at the age of 26, and is buried at Puchevillers British Cemetery.

7 David Truesdale, in his notes to James McRoberts' memoir *Young Citizen Old Soldier*, suggests the use of "Chocolate Soldiers" dates from this time and was in direct response to the Colonel's decision to organise a special train.

8 Major Hervey Ronald Bruce was the eldest son of Colonel Sir Hervey Bruce, Bart, DL, of Downhill, Coleraine. A JP for County Derry, he saw considerable action during the Boer War with the 1st Highland Light Infantry, which he had joined in 1892, and later the Cavalry Division. He transferred to the Irish Guards in 1900, being made a captain the following year. He was entitled to wear the Queen's Medal with six clasps and the King's Medal with two clasps. Prior to 1914 he had been a prominent member of the North Derry Regiment of the UVF. Too old for front line duties, he was later transferred to the 1st Garrison Battalion of the Royal Irish Rifles.

9 Mullin recalled a further incident concerning the sergeant and the Ould Kinnaird. His close friend, Private James Russell, a fellow battalion scout, was later released from the Army to return to his civilian employment with Robert Craig & Sons Engineers, in Great George's Street, Belfast. "One day, during the dinner hour, Russell was sitting on the footpath in York Street, with other apprentices. They were all wearing overalls. As Russell sat enjoying the warm sun, he saw Sgt Kinnaird approaching on his way to the station. Russell waited until the sergeant passed, and then, at a suitable distance, Russell innocently whistled the three notes of the 'Signallers Call', which the sergeant knew so well. Sgt Kinnaird turned back, but all that he could see was a row of overall clad engineering apprentices. There was nothing the sergeant could do, only resume his journey to the LMS station, with the apparent

mystery of the 'Signallers Call' unsolved."

10 According to Hope, there was far less than 60 lbs of equipment being carried that day: "The people think we are carrying heavy packs – most of these contain a straw pillow."

11 Regimental Sergeant Major Elphick had been a Colour Sergeant in the 5th Battalion of the Royal Irish Rifles and had once been its drum major. He was fundamental in raising the YCVs band and music evidently played a big part in his life. Harrison spoke of route marches led by Elphick, "an old soldier and martinet of the Regular Army," during which "we made the welkin ring as we marched along the roads of Donegal, whilst the pipes, flutes, or bugles gave us the step in turn." He was taken off the strength of the battalion in 1916 and sent home suffering from lumbago. His son also served in the battalion.

12 The Rev George Ryles Wedgwood, of University Road Methodist Church, Belfast, had two sons serving in the 14th Royal Irish Rifles at this time, both of whom were subsequently killed at the Battle of the Somme.

13 Major General Charles H Powell, commanding the Ulster Division, had sent the men home on Christmas leave with something to think about: "The MGC hopes that the men of the division will fully realise that this war is going to be a long drawn out one, and that men, and more men, in thousands, will be wanted, in order to preserve our home, our industries, and our independence from being ruthlessly trampled upon by the enemy. It is incumbent, therefore, on every man who goes to his home this Christmas to seriously discuss the matter with his relations and friends, with a view to getting more men to join the colours. With the New Year, the MGC knows that every effort will be made by officers and men to put their shoulders to the wheel and prepare themselves, and quickly to take their place beside their brothers-in-arms at the front."

14 Shane's Castle later became the Scotch Command Depot convalescents' camp, being filled with Scottish soldiers recovering from wounds. The UVF Motor Corps carried concert parties from Belfast to the camp on a regular basis, gardening was started on a large scale, a band and string orchestra established, a minstrel troop formed, and a golf course created in part of the camp. The Ulster Volunteers appealed for the public to donate a range of items to help the men pass the time until they were fit enough to return to the trenches, including books, sports equipment, plants and sheet music, with the UVF headquarters at the Town Hall acting as a collection point.

Chapter 8

1 Seaford could boast of its own hero. Major Cuthbert Bromley, born in the town, had won a Victoria Cross at Gallipoli in April 1915, while serving with the 1st Lancashire Fusiliers. *The London Gazette* recorded: "On the 25th April 1915 headquarters and three companies of the 1st Battalion, Lancashire Fusiliers, in effecting a landing on the Gallipoli Peninsular to the West of Cape Helles, were met by very deadly fire from hidden machine guns, which caused a great number of casualties. The survivors, however, rushed up to and cut the barbed wire entanglements,

notwithstanding the terrific fire from the enemy, and after overcoming supreme difficulties, the cliffs were gained and the position maintained. Amongst the very many gallant officers and men engaged in this very hazardous undertaking, Captain Bromley, Sergeant Stubbs, and Corporal Grimshaw have been selected by their comrades as having performed the most single acts of bravery and devotion to duty." Major Bromley was killed on 13 August 1915, when a troop ship en route to Egypt was sunk in a U-boat attack.

2 The battalion was certainly not entirely 'Irish'. Timothy Bowman, in *Irish Regiments In The Great War*, estimates from the nominal roll that more than 25 per cent of the volunteers in the Young Citizens were from England, Scotland or Wales, while another 17 per cent were from parts of Ireland other than Belfast. He also points out that during the 1914–15 period there were five officers and 98 other ranks serving in the battalion who were Roman Catholic.

3 The Rev Pollock's choice of holiday destination was no doubt influenced by the fact that his son Paul was with the Young Citizens in Seaford. He next went to the newspapers in July 1916 when a notice appeared in the *Belfast News Letter* : "Rev John Pollock (St Enoch's Church), 7 Glendore Park, Antrim Road, will be glad to receive any information regarding his son, Lance Corporal Paul G Pollock, Scout, B Company, 14th Battalion Royal Irish Rifles (YCV), who was engaged in the advance of the Ulster Division on 1st July last, and has been 'missing' since that date." In fact, Paul, just 21-years-old, had been killed on 1 July 1916. His body was never found and he is remembered on the Thiepval memorial.

4 The origin of the term is uncertain but may lie, accidentally, with Irish playwright and author George Bernard Shaw. One of his works, *Arms and the Man*, is a bitter-sweet story of a Serbian soldier who is content to while away his time in a lady's bedroom eating soft centres from a box of chocolates rather than fight. In 1910 the play was given a fresh lease of life when turned into a 'romantic' comedy, enjoying a run of more than 500 nights following its opening at the Lyric Theatre in London. On 21 October 1912 – just a month after the meeting at the City Hall that had formally brought the YCV into being, the curtain at the Grand Opera House in Belfast was raised on a performance of what was termed an "unauthorised parody". The theatre critic of the *Belfast News Letter* was less than impressed: "One would hardly go so far as to say that the librettists have improved on the original. They have taken daring liberties with the text, but still enough of the sparkling wit and paradoxical style remains to allow of identification. What the librettists have done is to transform the comedy into farce, using that word to express rampant and joyous burlesque, made out of irrelevances of dialogue and grotesque situations." Audiences, however, loved it so much that the production returned to the same venue the following year. Its title was *The Chocolate Soldier*.

5 The two men who drown were Driver Thomas Pollock, a 36-year-old married man from Dromore, County Down, and fellow Driver R Wilson, who died on 18 July 1915. Three other Ulster soldiers died during the division's stay in the area: Private Joseph Topley, of the Royal Irish Fusiliers, a 22-year-old from Laurelvale, Tandragee, County Armagh, died on 18 August 1915; Private Robert Simpson, of the 11th Royal Inniskilling Fusiliers, from Farnamullan, Tamlaght, Enniskillen, County Fermanagh, who was only 19 when he lost his life on 25 August 1915; and another Army Service Corps private, S Maconachie, who died on 2 September 1915. They are among the 253 First World War soldiers buried in Seaford Cemetery, many of them Canadians as the town became one of the main Canadian training centres during the war and was the location for a spell of a Canadian Stationary Hospital.

6 Canon Richard GS King, a son of the cloth, would have been well-known to many of the Ulster Division before the war as he was an outspoken opponent of Home Rule who regularly had articles published in the local newspapers. He had been chaplain to the 2nd (Roe Valley) Battalion, North Londonderry Regiment of the UVF. His eldest son, 19-year-old Lieutenant Robert Andrew Ferguson Smyly King, 2nd Royal Dublin Fusiliers, was severely wounded on 10 May when a 'Jack Johnson' mortar blew in his dugout at La Bassee, smashing both legs and his right hand. Although one leg had to be amputated two days later, the lieutenant showed signs of recovery until tetanus symptoms appeared. With Canon King and his wife by his bedside, the teenager died at No 7 Stationary Hospital, Boulogne, on Whit Sunday, 1915. His funeral service was read by the Rev Lowry Hamilton, Chaplain to the Forces and an old family friend. A nephew, Sub-Lieutenant HS King, Royal Navy, was killed at the Battle of Jutland in May 1916. Canon King resigned his commission as Senior Chaplain of the division in November 1916, earning a mention in the Haig despatch of January 1917. In 1921 he was instituted Dean of Derry in Saint Columba's Cathedral and regularly travelled from Londonderry to Belfast to attend the battalion's reunions until his retirement to England.

7 In James McRoberts' published journal, *Young Citizen Old Soldier*, the passage has the term 'Young Canadians' rather than 'Young Citizens.' After discussion with the book's editor, David Truesdale, it seems this was the result of a typographical error believed to have been made many years ago during an early transcribing of the original manuscript.

8 Major Harper was stationed for a period in the south of Ireland during 1917 but had, according to Hope, returned to the battalion as second-in-command at the start of 1918. He was later appointed Town Major with responsibility for the area in front of St Quentin, followed by a posting to an instruction role at base camp.

Chapter 9

1 Named *Empress Queen* to mark Queen Victoria's Diamond Jubilee, the paddle steamer was chartered by the Admiralty in 1915 as a troop carrier. On 1 February 1916, carrying 1,500 men from Le Havre, she ran aground on the Isle of Wight. No lives were lost but efforts to refloat her failed and she had to be abandoned. After lying on the rocks for a number of years the *Empress Queen* finally slipped under the waves during a gale.

2 Sheridan was invited to come back to the house anytime, and

even to visit after the war, but feared what his fiancée might think of such an offer. Of a second stay in Beauval he recorded seeing a lot of his new friends, feeling the need to add: "I mean as regards visiting them not the other way (this last because I think a great many of the people at home are under the impression that the French maidens have a liking for the mode 'a la Adam et Eve')."

3 William Lorimer's father, also called William, was a member of the battalion but was back in Belfast at the time of his son's death. He survived the war. William junior, in addition to the YCV, was a member of various organisations, including the City Temperance LOL 1197, City Temperance RBP and the William Johnston Memorial Lodge 207. The Rev S Hamilton, in a letter to Mary Lorimer, wrote: "Your poor husband had not the strength to battle with the bad attack of pneumonia, and though the doctors did all in their power he has passed away. It is not possible to help you in this hour of your sorrow and deep distress with any words of sympathy, but I hope you are among relatives and friends who will help you to bear this great and crushing blow. He was always thinking of you, poor lad, and did so want to get round. God has not willed it so, and in God's keeping you must leave him till he brings you together in a world where the parting and sorrows of these awful days can find no place or part."

4 Major JE Gunning, whose home was Manor House, Moneymore, County Londonderry, was a prominent figure in the formation and early training of the Young Citizen Volunteers and subsequently the 14th Royal Irish Rifles. He was treated for his injuries at Campbell Hospital, Cambridge Square, Hyde Park, London, and was back recuperating in Belfast by 26 January 1916. In May 1916, it was reported that he was then attached to the 19th Royal Irish Rifles in Newcastle, County Down. After a spell as a railway transport officer, he joined the Headquarters of the Irish Command in October 1917 on supply duties.

5 Lieutenant Colonel HR Bliss was said by *The Incinerator* to be the strictest of disciplinarians and staunchest upholder of military tradition. "His eye was like unto an eagle's, his manner brusque and pointed, but his heart was soft as a woman's." Described as a "real soldier" to whom everyone looked up, he had a "portly figure" and dry sense of humour, and rode Ally Sloper, the "ugliest horse in the Army".

6 Lieutenant R Renwick, the machine-gun officer, was to be wounded on 1 July. He was later promoted to captain and survived the war to provide musical entertainment at the battalion reunion dinners. Originally from Bothwell, near Glasgow, Scotland.

Chapter 10
1 William Alick Parkinson Willson was the youngest son of a retired member of the Indian Educational Service then living at Mill House, Ballinasloe, County Galway. Injured early in 1916, he was invalided home for a period, being attached to the 19th Royal Irish Rifles. He was later transferred to the 12th Royal Irish Rifles and was serving with the 22nd Entrenching Battalion when killed on 1 April 1918, at the age of 24. Buried at Moreuil Communal Cemetery Allied Extension.

2 Sergeant William Calvert, who had reportedly turned down the offer of a commission in December 1914 in order to stay with his friends in the ranks, had been a company commander in the Cliftonville Battalion of the North Belfast Regiment of the UVF. In civilian life he had worked for jewellers Gibson Limited and was obviously a keen sportsman being a member of Cliftonville Golf Club and serving as captain of Cliftonville-Shamrock Football Club for two years and later a member of Cliftonville FC. His father, WH Calvert, had sat on the committee of the club for 18 years and was a representative on the Irish Football Association. Sergeant Calvert had three brothers in the services, Louis who was with the Canadians, Murrie who had enlisted in the Australian army, and Norman, who had joined the YCVs with him.

3 Harrison, after moving into a "hotter" part of the front, was at pains to point out that the YCVs were keen to take on whatever task they were allocated: "I don't want to give the impression that we want to pick out a soft spot, just because we are the 'Chocolate Soldiers', a nickname we are not particularly fond of, but which has been attached to us by others. The Germans were probably better judges as to whether we should be classed along with the rest of the 'soldiers' out here, than some people whom I have heard about."

4 Francis O Bowen, a regular officer who had served with the Royal Irish Regiment since 1902 until being posted to the Ulster Division in September 1915, came to the YCVs from the 16th Royal Irish Rifles.

5 According to the *Belfast News Letter* of Monday 27 March 1916, the congregation for the memorial service filled the hall to overflowing, with Dr Montgomery delivering the address himself. The paper quotes him as saying: "A beautiful young life had been given up for King and country, and for the great principles which lay behind the present dreadful war – principles for which good and brave men had contended throughout the world's history. Young Carl Penman endeared himself to all who knew him by his kindly, genial manner, his winsome disposition, his manly qualities, and his true Christian character. He set a noble example to the youths and young men of that congregation and in that district. Wherever Carl Penman was known he was esteemed and loved. His intellectual qualities would doubtless have carried him far had he been spared. Into that region they could not enter."

6 Sergeant William Stephenson, a member of D Company, was a 25-year-old from Fitzwilliam Street in Belfast. He had been a member of the Central Presbyterian Association, of the choir of Great Victoria Street Presbyterian Church, of Sydenham Rugby Club, and of the Young Citizen Volunteers pre-war. His brother, Andrew, also served in the battalion and narrowly missed the same fate three months later at the Battle of the Somme. Harrison, a private, and Stephenson had been pals but had been made aware of the Army Regulations that forbid such friendships. "He was a good 'scout' was Billy, who would occasionally strum on my old mandolin of an evening, and could he play! I regret to say he could not!" he recalled years later.

7 A German shell had toppled the statue of the 'Golden Madonna', atop the basilica in Albert, in January 1915, leaving it hanging at

a perilous angle. French engineers wired it up and the soldiers of both sides came to believe the war would only end when it fell. It was a British shell that eventually finished the job during the temporary German occupation of the town during the spring and summer of 1918. A replica of the statue was added to the rebuilt church as the original was never found.

Chapter 11

1 Lieutenant Walker's brother-in-law was Captain Gerald Lowry, who had married his sister Cecilia on 14 August 1915. He had been severely wounded during the Battle of the Aisne, September 1914, resulting in the loss of his sight.

2 Lance Corporal David Hanley, whose parents lived at Mountview Street and widow Lilian at Rosapenna Street, both Belfast, was himself killed on 16 August 1917, and is remembered on the Tyne Cot Memorial in Belgium.

3 Lieutenant Colonel Chichester was reported, in March 1916, to have been admitted to hospital in France suffering from bronchitis. By May he had returned to Ireland but was still enduring lung trouble. Adjutant Alan Mulholland visited him at his new home in Castledawson, and reported: "It was touching to see the Colonel's face flushing with pride when he heard of the behaviour of the men during the recent heavy 'strafe'."

4 Major Llewellyn had joined the 14th Rifles on 14 April 1916, to cover for the 'indisposition' of Colonel Chichester. A veteran of the Boer War, in which he had served with the 1st Royal Inniskilling Fusiliers, he had clearly proved himself a capable and popular commander. The Incinerator reported: "Major Llewellyn, who was with us a very short time, but long enough to prove to us that we were blest with a very skilful and far-seeing commanding officer. He was very cut up at having to leave us, but he was peremptorily ordered to report to the War Office for instructions re proceeding to Africa. The major has had big African experience, and will be invaluable out there during these trying times. He didn't want to leave us, though, and we are extremely sorry to part with him. The 14th wishes him Bon voyage, Bon Fortune, and by jingo, a safe and speedy return."

5 Tom Sloane's brother arrived with the YCVs in May 1916, without knowing he had been killed days before. The Incinerator reported: "A sad incident occurred on our arrival at the haven of 'comparative rest'. In a small draft of men from the base was a smart corporal, who asked to be sent to the same company as his brother. He was up to that minute unaware that his brother had been killed in action. The silent and respectful welcome he received as a member of his brother's old platoon must have assured him that although he had lost a brother, he had found many true friends. We are fortunate in securing a man who bears a name which already is writ prominently in our annals."

6 George Tollerton was employed by the Great Northern Railway Company and left behind a widow and two children living at Coronation Street, Portadown. He had two brothers serving, one of whom, Thomas, 29, was later killed at the opening of the Battle of the Somme on 1 July 1916, with the 9th Royal Irish Rifles. Their father, Private Thomas Tollerton from Magheragall, near Lisburn, was a member of the 11th Royal Irish Rifles. Lieutenant

Renwick, in a letter to Mrs Tollerton, said: "It is my very painful duty to inform you of the death of your husband, Private George Tollerton, of my section. During a very heavy bombardment of our trenches on the evening of the 5th inst, and while he was on duty with his gun team, a trench mortar shell exploded in the trench, killing him instantaneously. During the bombardment he stood by his gun with great courage, and his name has since appeared in battalion orders for gallantry."

7 Rifleman T Gray, one of three brothers in the battalion, was among those wounded on 5 May and was evacuated to England where he died on 23 May. The "news of his death was a great surprise, as it was understood his wound was not serious," according to The Incinerator, which added: "It was a shrapnel case, though, and the ever-to-be-hated Hun apparently poisons this particular weapon. Always be quick with the iodine, boys, if a pal gets a shrapnel splinter. The remaining two Gray boys must see to it that their brother's death is adequately avenged when their chance comes." Rifleman Gray, whose parents lived at Ballycoan, Purdysburn, was buried at Holy Trinity churchyard, Drumbo.

8 Striking a lighter note, and an example of trench humour, is how a wound suffered by Rifleman Harry Lindsay on 5 May was reported by The Incinerator. "It was but a slight wound, but uncomfortably situated. Stretcher-bearer Burns was dressing the 'inconvenience,' in the Coy Sgt-Major's dugout, when a friend endeavoured to cheer Lindsay by remarking: 'Och, cheer up, me ould hero. In a few hours ye'll be havin' a nice girl dressing the shpot for yez!' 'Away to h---! I'm not wanting any blessed girl messing me about. I want to stay with the boys – Ugh! Is that iodine ye're trying to wean me with, Bobby?' We've just got the word about Lindsay being 'off the strength,' and, faith, we feel very weak without him."

9 Lance Corporal Jack Gibson, whose parents lived at Chestnut Gardens, Belfast, was a runner on 1 July, and continued to carry messages back and forth from headquarters throughout the day despite being wounded. He also suffered a serious injury early in 1917 and was reported to be still recovering in May of that year when he received the Ulster Divisional Card for gallantry and good work under fire.

10 The battalion lost another man, Private James Dickson, a 22-year-old of 7 Cadogan Street, Belfast, who was attached to the 109th Trench Mortar Battery, when he died of wounds on 28 June 1916.

Chapter 12

1 According to John Kennedy Hope, John Berryhill Meehan was the son of a solicitor who had been in the Officers' Training Corps at Queen's for years and knew the Army text books from cover to cover. "His one drawback is a slight stammer, and he can't get promotion," he said. Meehan, who apparently had a habit of losing his kit, was particularly fond of his long locks, which he kept in check with 'Anzora Cream'. Hope again: "We are warned that one's hair must have a jail cut by a certain date. My mate takes no notice. He isn't going to do without his Anzora. We have an inspection. The barber runs the clippers over the top of

Berryhill's head and tells him to report at the barber's shop to have it all off. He's like a Hun now and is known in the platoon by the awful nickname of 'bucket-mouth'.

2 Rifleman George Gillespie, who had been standing beside McFadzean in the trench when the grenades spilled, was one of those wounded. A year later he was still being treated at the Limbless Branch of the UVF Hospital in Belfast and was among those who attended a church service in memory of the VC hero.

3 Captain Charles Owen Slacke was 44 when he died. A son of Sir Owen Randal Slacke and grandson of Sir Charles Lanyon, the architect responsible for so many of Belfast's finest buildings, his family owned the Wheatfield area of the city and land at Newcastle, County Down. He married Catherine Anne, daughter of MP and former Belfast Lord Mayor Sir Daniel Dixon, in 1902. A former leader of the UVF's North Belfast Regiment, he had been among the officers at the funeral of Belfast Lord Mayor Robert McMordie in 1914. A memorial service for Captain Slacke was held in St John's Church, Newcastle, on Sunday 13 August 1916, during which it was stated that his other grandfather had been rector of Newcastle. His body could not initially be recovered and his wife applied at Dublin in December 1916 for permission to presume death and apply for probate. Meehan, in his newspaper article of 1919, said: "One report stated that together with a mere handful of men, isolated on the fringe of Thiepval village, the gallant captain held out long into the night, fighting against enormous odds, preferring to die rather than surrender. Another report stated that Captain Slacke was last seen side by side with Captain Willis, also killed, in the midst of a counter-attack, "fighting with his naked fists, being ultimately beaten to the ground under the rifle butts and bayonets of the attacking Hun". Today his body lies in Connaught Cemetery at Thiepval.

4 Sergeant Ernest R Powell survived the war and took an active part on the arrangements committee for the post-war reunions. Mullin recorded: "Sgt Powell was highly thought of, and a favourite of the platoon." An enthusiastic member of the 20th Company of the Boys' Brigade, based at Ormeau Road Methodist Church, he became its Captain after the war."

5 Company Sergeant Major Joseph Lowry, son of Richard Lowry of Glenanne, County Armagh, had been a professional soldier. He had enlisted in the Gordon Highlanders in 1903, spending seven years in India, and was on the Reserve list when war broke out. Formerly an instructor with his local UVF battalion, he was mobilised and sent to the Front, taking part in a succession of battles during October and November 1914, until wounded. He transferred to the 14th Rifles in 1915, and was awarded the Military Cross for his actions at the Somme.

6 Second Lieutenant Philip Wedgwood died on the same day as his brother, Second Lieutenant Gilbert C Wedgwood, who had originally been a member of the YCVs but had transferred to the Machine Gun Corps in January 1916. Their father was the Rev George R Wedgwood, of University Road Methodist Church, Belfast. Another brother, George, was in the Royal Navy. In his letter to the Wedgwood family, Canon King wrote: "I knew your sons well. I saw a great deal more of the younger

because he remained in the battalion, and he and I were warm and intimate friends. He was a most lovable boy, and as brave as a lion. He looked so young that when he was chosen to go to the front with the 14th I felt it deeply. But no-one could have borne himself more courageously during the heaviest fighting than he did."

7 Second Lieutenant George Radcliffe's mother appealed in the newspapers for anyone who had information about her son, who she knew had been severely wounded, to write to her at Kingstown-on-Thames, London.

8 Second Lieutenant Matthew J Wright was one of three sons of the Rev Dr William Wright, a Newtownards clergyman, to join the Colours. A former employee of James P Corry Ltd, in Belfast, he had been injured in May 1916 in an accident while acting as an instructor in a bomb throwing school. Sent home to recuperate, the 28-year-old refused an offer to extend his leave so he could return to 'the boys'. There has long been confusion over when and where he died. His family erected a stone memorial in his memory in Thiepval Wood in the belief he died there. It can still be seen today in the Ulster Tower. His body, however, was never recovered and he is remembered on the Thiepval Memorial. Adjutant Alan Mulholland recalled: "I remember so well in our Finner days advising Matt how to go about getting his commission and recommending him to the CO and I am glad to say I never once regretted it as he was a good officer."

9 Englishman Second Lieutenant Reginald Lambert Lack was born at Streatham Hill in 1891. From an upper middle-class family, he was working as a china manufacturer in America when war was declared and immediately returned home. He joined the 14th Royal Irish Rifles in October 1914 and a month later married Elsie Radcliffe, the sister of fellow officer George Radcliffe. In a letter to his widow, Lieutenant Stanley Monard wrote: "We thought Reggie was going to pull through all right, his constitution being so sturdy; but the Boche seems to poison his shells and shot. You know, of course, that Wright was killed and Reggie wounded in trying to get your brother George in. The feat was an heroically impossible one, owing to the place being quite showered with shells. They knew that, but persisted in the attempt." Sergeant Armstrong, responding to a letter of thanks from the officer's mother, wrote: "For your son I had the deepest feelings of admiration and respect, and I send you my heartfelt sympathy in your bereavement. I had the honour to serve under Mr Lack since January 1915, and I know that I shall never meet a finer soldier or a more perfect gentleman. What I and Corporal Boyd did on July 1st would have been done by any of the scouts, for we all honoured and loved Mr Lack more than I can tell, and my sorrow at his loss is greater than I can express."

10 Captain Samuel Willis was 43-years-old when killed on 1 July 1916. Adjutant of the 3rd Battalion of the North Derry Regiment of the Ulster Volunteer Force, he had been on the teaching staff at Coleraine Academical Institution for almost 20 years. Originally from Mountcharles, County Donegal, he had been living with his wife, Mary Christina, at Portrush before the war. His body was never found and he is remembered on the Thiepval Memorial to the Missing. In November 1916, Private Samuel Cochrane, of the Royal Inniskilling Fusiliers, claimed while back in Coleraine

on home leave that he saw an unwounded Captain Willis being taken prisoner by the Germans. He said he had attempted to rescue him but had been forced to withdraw when more enemy troops arrived. Adjutant Mulholland noted in the *War Diary*: "A most gallant soldier Willis, his coolness and clear-headedness throughout the day tended greatly towards the success of the operations. I regret that he is reported missing, a great loss to the battalion – a born leader of men."

11 The eldest son of James Hyndman, Nevara, Chichester Park, Belfast, who owned a flax merchants at Church Street in the city, Captain James Valentine Hyndman had been seriously wounded. The former UVF member ultimately ended up in No 14 General Hospital, on the French coast, where he died on 7 July. He is buried at Wimereux Communal Cemetery.

12 Jim Fitzsimons had initially been one of three brothers in the 14th Royal Irish Rifles. One, Jack, was killed at the Somme on 1 July 1916. The other, Ernest Fitzsimons, was clearly an exceptional soldier. A member of the OTC at Queen's University, he earned first place in the corps exam and was commissioned into the Rifles, where he was a platoon officer until August 1916. He became the 109th Brigade Intelligence Officer, was appointed to the General Staff, promoted to captain then major. He remained in the army for a period after the war, and accompanied the body of the Unknown Soldier back to London as part of the guard of honour.

13 Stanley Hopkirk Monard was a Londoner, with his father having an address at Regent's Park in the capital. He reportedly came to Belfast initially with Commander Oliver Locker-Lampson, MP, to assist in the organisation and clothing of the Ulster Division before receiving a commission in the 14th Royal Irish Rifles. Lieutenant Monard, editor of the battalion newspaper *The Incinerator*, suffered 25 shrapnel wounds to his head and legs on 1 July 1916, but returned to duty after having them bandaged. He married Miss Kathleen McIlroy, youngest daughter of Mr John McIlroy, Belvedere, Donaghadee, at St Mary Magdelene Church, Belfast, on Thursday 28 December 1916, with Canon King and the Rev GA Stephenson performing the service. The Young Citizens' Adjutant, Alan Mulholland, was the best man with other officers present. Jim Maultsaid, though he didn't always see eye to eye with him, described the captain as "a real active service officer . . . (who) loved his Irish boys." William Frederick Hogg was born in Belfast though his family was living at Ballsbridge, Dublin, by 1916. He was awarded the Military Cross for his actions at the Somme on 1–2 July. On 26 November 1916, the lieutenant was struck off the battalion strength after again being wounded. He had been looking through a trench periscope at Wulvenghem when it had been hit, with a splinter striking him on the head. Lieutenant HH Hooton, of B Company, who was from Nottingham, was severely wounded on 1 July and died more than a month later on 5 August 1916. He is buried at Etaples Military Cemetery.

14 Rifleman Robert HP Shannon, initially reported missing and later confirmed killed at the Somme, was the son of Alex Shannon, Elmgrove Terrace, Belfast. He had been a member of Cliftonville Football Club before the war.

15 Second Lieutenant Robert Gracey, a nephew of Sir William Whitla, was reported missing believed killed on 1 July 1916. However, his father James, at his home at Helen's Bay, County Down, received a postcard from his son on 12 August telling him that he had been wounded and was a prisoner-of-war in Saxony. In December 1916, he was transferred to Switzerland where he remained interned until an agreement between Britain and Germany allowed the now Lieutenant Gracey and several hundred others to return home. Second Lieutenant William John White Carson was 29-years-old and the only son of William McRobert Carson and Sarah Carson, of Tareen House, Old Cavehill Road, Belfast. Educated at Dungannon Royal School, he had taken a degree in surveying at a London college before joining his father's estate agency in Rosemary Street, Belfast. His body was never identified and he is commemorated on Thiepval Memorial. Lieutenant Victor Harold Robb died of wounds on 3 July 1916. John Kennedy Hope had come across the wounded officer "in a trench in the heart of Thiepval with seven bullet wounds in his chest," pausing to give him a drink of water. "He is apparently breathing his last in an atmosphere absolutely polluted with tear gas with which the Hun is now drenching the place," he recorded. An obituary published in the *Belfast News Letter* on 24 July read: "Lieutenant Victor Harold Robb, Young Citizen Volunteers, who has died in a London hospital from wounds received in action on the 1st inst, was a well-known figure in Belfast and particularly in motoring circles. The youngest son of the late Mr Kirker Robb, of Kirk-Brughean, Fortwilliam Park, the deceased officer was educated in England. Deciding on a business career, he served his apprenticeship as a motor engineer with Messrs Chambers & Co Ltd automobile engineers and agents, Chichester Street. Lieutenant Robb was himself a most enthusiastic motorist, and this fact tended to intensify his interest in the progress of the industry." (See Appendix 6)

Chapter 13

1 The Rev John Jackson Wright had been the Presbyterian Minister of Ballyshannon when the battalion was stationed at Finner Camp, Donegal, and was a regular visitor to the tents and hosted many services. "The Volunteers have found him the most sympathetic and brotherly of men, and nowhere is he made more welcome than in the tents of the YCVs," reported the *Belfast Telegraph* in 1914.

2 Billy Calvert was killed in a grenade blast while instructing men.

3 Major JE Gunning was injured late in 1915 when his horse slipped, throwing him to the ground and rolling on top of him, breaking his left leg so severely that he was evacuated to the Campbell Hospital in London for treatment. From Moneymore, County Down, he was well enough to return home by the end of January 1916, but was never to see the Front again. He spent a spell with a reserve battalion, then as a railway transport officer before being attached to the headquarters of the Irish Command in Dublin. Sergeant Major Elphick had been struck off the battalion strength in France in early 1916 suffering from lumbago and sent back to Ireland. A widower since 1909, he had served in the 5th RIR, in which he had been the drum-major and

an acknowledged expert in Swedish drill. The Young Citizens' three bands were his great passion and under his ever-watchful eye he turned them into a credit to the battalion, often taking the bands out on the road to help keep the men in step during route marches. One of his sons and a nephew, Rifleman Jack Flynn, served in the YCVs.

4 Late in 1914 the newspapers had carried a report claiming that a second YCV reserve battalion was to be formed for the purposes of training recruits for the 14th Rifles but this failed to materialise in any recognisable form. As a consequence, the battalion was very conscious that it was going to struggle to find Ulster replacements for its losses. Derby men came from a body of volunteers who had forwarded their names for call up if necessary, with the government promising to delay the enlistment of the married men among them to the end. It was the brainchild of Lord Derby, who had been appointed Director-General of Recruitment in 1915. In August the previous year he had suggested the idea of 'Pals Battalions' where men from particular areas could serve in the same unit as their neighbours. It had proved extremely successful though its down side was evident following the Battle of the Somme when thousands of black-edged telegrams carrying news of a death flooded Belfast and the province within days. The Derby Scheme did not catch the public imagination to the same extent, though an estimated 350,000 men did assent to being called up. It was dropped at the end of 1915 in favour of conscription. Lord Derby later served for a spell as Minister of War.

5 Hope reported how the men would sometimes use the German snipers as a form of amusement: "We dare not look over in the day time. We use small periscopes stuck on the end of a bayonet. I have five of these smashed in one afternoon. We feel amused at this and occasionally put up a dummy head – complete with steel hat, so that he can try his luck."

6 McRoberts described RE Farm as "a ruin about four hundred yards from the German line. We could move about freely in the open here, for the Germans were over the hill and the place was not under observation from any point. There was a row of dry, small dugouts, or rather houses built with sandbags, and these were our billets." However, he later recorded: "We always considered that about RE Farm, a person could not be hit by a German bullet. One night I was helping Sergeant Major JJ Mackey to unload a limber when I heard something coming in contact with his tunic and he said, putting a hand to his stomach, that he had been hit. We led him into the candlelight of our cellar and took off his shirt. There was a German bullet buried about an eight of an inch in his stomach but there was also a hole drilled right through his right arm made by the same bullet."

7 The dead were buried at Pond Farm Cemetery, with Hope one of those ordered to prepare the graves. He recorded: "There has been heavy strafing in the line and we are about to bury six. No coffins. They are just sewn up in a blanket and we lower them into the shallow pit. The wee graveyard is a new plot at a spot known as Pond Farm, about 1,000 yards behind the front and in full view from the ridge where the Hun is. Canon King in full surplice conducts the burial service. We cannot even bury the dead in peace. The Hun is ever watchful and he shells the little party. The Canon is reading a chapter from the Bible and continues to read as the shells drop round."

8 Lance Corporal Samuel Ferris, a married man who was originally from Dromore, County Down, had won the Military Medal at the Battle of the Somme. His widow later remarried. Private Greer's family lived at Lurgan but he was living in Belfast at the outbreak of war, working in the Mountpottinger branch of the Ulster Bank. He had been a member of Collegians rugby club and belonged to Cregagh Presbyterian Church Choir and committee. A brother, who had also worked for the Ulster Bank in Clones, was serving with the Canadian forces and in October 1916 was in hospital in England recovering from shrapnel wounds to the shoulder. Privates McIvor and Robinson were both Belfast men. Private Paysden was also the holder of the Military Medal. His father, Captain J Paysden, of Brookvale House, Connsbrook Avenue, Belfast, was commander of a transport ship. An older brother was an assistant scoutmaster with the 10th Belfast Scouts.

9 Doctor Gavin applied a dressing to James McRobert's face wounds and sent him back down the line for further treatment along with Alec Flynn, another of the walking wounded. He was hospitalised and eventually returned to Britain. In January 1918, he was discharged from the army having been classified as 80 per cent disabled for life. He returned to Queen's University, Belfast, obtained a degree in Civil Engineering and eventually became County Surveyor of Armagh.

10 Second Lieutenant Robert Victor Drought later left the YCVs. While attached to the 7th Royal Irish Rifles he was severely wounded leading a raid on the German lines during which a prisoner was snatched and several of the enemy killed. Awarded the Military Cross for his valour, he died of his injuries on 9 June 1917, at the age of 30. His family was from Blackrock, County Dublin.

11 Before the war Private Herbert Valentine Mitchell Lynch had worked in the North Street shop of William Twaddell, who was later to become a member of the Northern Ireland Parliament and the first MP to be killed by the IRA. A former member of the North Belfast Regiment of the UVF, Lynch was a son of Staff Sergeant Major Denis Lynch, former Barrack Warden of Victoria Barracks, Belfast. A brother, Sergeant Thomas Lynch, was serving with the 9th Royal Irish Rifles.

12 One of the tasks that working parties from the 14th Rifles were given, now they were in Flanders, involved working as labourers to the engineers preparing the series of tunnels being dug towards the German lines. The following year these would be filled with explosives and detonated at the commencement of the Battle of Messines. Hope recorded: "We are introduced to miners who are away in below the surface digging. It is a big long tunnel graded gradually. When we get to the end we are below the Hun line. A dirty, rotten, dangerous and nasty job." He went on: "We get a big candle and a tot of rum after the job is finished for the night. Not a pleasant occupation and we are glad when we move out of that place. The danger of being buried alive if the Hun blows in the galley is not a nice experience by any means. We hold the line for three days at a spell. This is the work we are doing during the three days we are out for a rest."

13 The fatalities may have been members of the Machine Gun Corps. No YCV soldiers died on Christmas Day 1916.

14 Second Lieutenant HR Power had been a noted athletic. He had represented Dublin University in the Irish intervarsity contests held in Belfast in June 1914, winning the high jump competition and that same year had been second in the all-Ireland high jump championships, clearing over six feet. The son of James Power, of Ballydavid House, Thurles, he had transferred out of the YCVs early in 1917 to the Royal Flying Corps and was killed in action on 22 August that year with the 48th Squadron. He is buried at Zuydcoote Military Cemetery, France.

Chapter 14

1 Captain Percy B Lewis was awarded the Military Cross for this action. The citation read: "For conspicuous gallantry in action. Accompanied by one man, he attacked a party of four of the enemy, captured a prisoner, and repelled the remainder. He set a fine example of courage and initiative." Percy Lewis had joined the Young Citizen Volunteers as an officer, having formerly been a member of the Gloucestershire Hussars, some 18 months before the outbreak of war. He had worked as a claims superintendent with the Ocean Accident and Guarantee Corporation in Belfast and had returned home in June 1915, to marry Miss Ethel Simpson Gunning, whose mother lived at Cedar Grove, Cregagh, Belfast. His own widowed mother lived at Eagle House, Cathays, Cardiff. In June 1916, he was appointed transport officer for the 109th Brigade, taking over from Cyril Falls, author of the *History of the 36th (Ulster) Division*, but later returned to his battalion.

2 Rifleman James Andrew Stewart, a 24-year-old from Belfast, who died of wounds on 15 February 1917, may have been among those wounded on the day Samuel Boyd was killed. He had been born at Ballymena but his parents, James and Jane Stewart, had moved to Virginia Street, Belfast. Buried at Bailleul Military Cemetery Extension.

3 John McCleland Baird was 22-years-old and from Belfast; Malcolm McColl, aged 21, had lived with his parents at Finaghy.

4 Lieutenant Colonel OR Vivian was later that year to command the 14th Rifles in his own right. He was the son of the first Lord Swansea and ultimately inherited the title. He had married into an Irish family when, in 1906, he wed a sister of Lord Holmpatrick, Abbotstown, Castleknock, County Dublin. Mullin recorded in his diary: "This morning Mr Wood sends me on an important message. I have to take 'Father's' glasses to the transport lines, for the glasses to be repaired. I must add that 'Father' is Major the Hon Odo Vivian, our venerable second-in-command. He is Lord Swansea's heir. He is much interested in the YCV battalion, especially the scouts. I have also to take in a telescope and to bring back milk for the quartermaster." After the war, during a meeting with Mulholland, he "expressed his love and affection for the 14th as a whole".

5 Captain George Ronald Hamilton Cheape, appointed temporary lieutenant colonel, was a member of an ancient Scottish family and son of the late Lieutenant Colonel George Clerk Cheape, of Wellfield, Gateside, Fifeshire. Formerly a captain in the 11th Hussars and lieutenant colonel of the Fifeshire Light Horse, he had succeeded to the family estate in 1900 at the age of 19. In 1912, he had married Miss Margaret Bruce Ismay of the White Star Line, owners of the *Titanic*. In August 1916, Cheape had been appointed commanding officer of a Territorial battalion of the Black Watch. One of his brothers, Captain Leslie St Calir Cheape, who had been a well-known polo player, was killed in action in 1916.

6 Company Sergeant Major Nevin was himself killed on 16 August 1917, aged 22. A married man from the Clonavon area of Ballymena, he had been living in Belfast before the war and was an original member of the YCV. A tailor by trade, he had latterly been working as a photographer for the Lafayette studio in Donegall Place, Belfast. His body was never identified and he is remembered on the Tyne Cot Memorial.

7 Those killed on 5 May 1917, were Private Charles Richard Aynscomb, a 20-year-old who, though born in England, had been living in east Belfast prior to the war. He had been wounded on 1 July 1916, the opening day of the Somme battle; Lance Corporal Alexander Pollock, just 19, who was Scottish by birth but again had been resident in Belfast in 1914; and Corporal John Snowden, 22, from Carlton Street in Belfast, a member of Canton Street Mission Hall. His brother, Matthew, also serving in the Rifles, survived the war. According to Mullin, Snowden had only recently returned to the battalion in France: "He joined us as a recruit at Randalstown in 1915. He was sent to the reserve battalion and came out a corporal. His luck did not hold!" Two other soldiers died of wounds in subsequent days – Rifleman Henry Charles Shall, who passed away on 6 May; and Thomas Stanley Goodwin, also a rifleman, who died on 8 May. Private W Baird is recorded as having died on 21 May.

8 Corporal Allan Montgomery was killed later that year on 16 August, aged 24, and is remembered on the Tyne Cot Memorial. Born at Antrim, his parents lived at Castle Street, Ballymena. In civilian life he had worked as a traveller for the Belfast firm of Young and Anderson, and had been a member of the Masonic Order. The Rev John Knowles, writing to his parents a few days after his death, told them: "I am very sorry that up to the present, his body has not been recovered but we hope that soon an advance may take place which will render this possible. Your son has seen much service out here and in everything that he did he proved himself a brave and gallant soldier, and we were all sorry to hear that the decoration for which he had been recommended, and which he thoroughly merited, was somehow never bestowed upon him. Now he has won a soldier's higher honour by laying down his life fighting for a glorious cause. He has been faithful unto death and we all mourn his loss and our heartfelt sympathy goes out to you." Corporal Montgomery, who had been wounded at the Somme, had been recommended for recognition three times without success.

9 The Battle of Messines opened on 7 June 1917, and officially closed a week later on 14 June. Seen as a prelude to Third Ypres, which was to follow in August, it had strictly limited objectives of which taking the Messines-Wytschaete ridge was the most significant. The British bombardment began on 21 May and, at precisely 3.10 am, 19 huge mines were detonated under the German front lines. The enemy's forward defence zone was

rapidly overrun and, despite later resistance, the British forces had secured the entire ridge by 9.00 am on the first day. By that night all the principle objectives had been secured and by 14 June the newly-won line had been consolidated.

10 A relentless battle had raged to find and destroy each other's mines in the run-up to the battle. Hope, displaying typical trench humour, found a bungled German attempt at counter-mining very funny: "Peter Gross and I are sitting on the firestep enjoying our 'dip'. Something suddenly pushes up the earth beneath us. Peter exclaimed 'My God Jennifer we're going up'. There is a rumbling noise, somebody is going up. A huge column of earth and smoke over the way. It is a mine, some yards in front of us in the Hun front trenches. Two miners have arrived up our mine shaft and they are deathly pale. The Hun has blown a gallery and sent his own men into the air. We think this a great joke. Over the way the Hun stretcher-bearers are pulling out the casualties. One of our sergeants is looking over the top and having a laugh. His laugh is cut short. A Hun sniper has put a bullet into his mouth and it comes out at the side of his cheek. Then we all laugh too. Some say good old sergeant – we say!!!"

11 In a letter written following the battle, Lieutenant Colonel PJ Woods, commanding officer of the 9th Royal Irish Rifles, said: "I have heard nothing but praise of your Bn and the splendid spirit and dash in the attack, and the cheerful willingness during the consolidation. This made it a pleasure and an honour to fight beside and co-operate with the YCVs. I heartily reciprocate and echo your wish that the 9th and 14th may advance side by side in any future operations. A better Bn to work with, and be certain that their job would be done, and well done, I would not ask for."

12 Second Lieutenant Sydney James Livingston Downey was 21-years-old and from Hampden Terrace, off Rugby Street, Belfast. Second Lieutenant Brian Boyd served in the ranks with the 14th Rifles before being granted a commission. He had been a member of the 10th Belfast Scouts before the war and had hoped to return to it as an officer. He was made a military scout, earning many mentions in Mullin's diary. He won the Military Medal at the Somme for carrying a wounded officer to safety under heavy fire and earned the comparatively rare honour of being allowed to return to his own battalion as an officer upon being commissioned. On 7 June 1917, he went over the top at Messines carrying the battalion flag and was one of the first to fall. Aged just 19, he was the eldest son of William E Boyd, manager for Messrs Manfield & Sons, Donegall Place, and formerly of Ballyferris, County Down, and had been educated at the Royal Belfast Academical Institution.

13 Captain James McKee, a pre-war member of the YCVs, was taken to a base hospital in France. On 10 June, three days after being wounded, surgeons had to amputate his left leg above the knee. By July he was receiving treatment in the military hospital at Victoria Barracks in Belfast and was awarded the Distinguished Service Order the following month for his bravery at Messines. A pre-war member of the YCVs, he was commissioned on 17 September 1914, and promoted to captain on 8 December of that year. His elevation clearly didn't go down well with everyone with John Kennedy Hope complaining: "McKee says 'he's Kimmy no longer by King's this, that and

the other thing.'" He had missed the Battle of the Somme as he had been away on a course of instruction at the time. A gifted footballer who had played centre-forward for Cliftonville, he had been captain of the Belmont Presbyterian Church Boys' Brigade company for a number of years before the war. Captain McKee's father Samuel, of Cyprus Park, Belfast, passed away in December 1916 and his brother, WD McKee, a member of Wandsworth Football Club who had returned from the Argentine to join the army and had been mentioned for distinguished service in Dublin during the 1916 uprising, was killed on 12 August 1917.

Chapter 15

1 Sergeant McCoubrey had been well-known in athletic circles, being the secretary of Ulsterville Harriers Club. His parents lived at Abercorn Street, off the Lisburn Road in Belfast. John McCoubrey had joined the YCVs in September 1914 and had been severely wounded in September 1916, returning to France the following April. In civilian life he had been a branch accountant for the London and Lancashire Fire Insurance Offices. A younger brother also served in the 14th Rifles. Sergeant David English, from Glenarm, County Antrim, had lived on the Ormeau Road, Belfast before the war. He had been a popular figure in junior football and cricket circles, a UVF company commander and a member of Ballynafeigh and Newtownbreda Unionist Club. He is buried at Messines Ridge British Cemetery. Rifleman William James Irwin, from Belfast, one of those injured, died on 23 June 1917.

2 Thomas Taggart and William Whiteside were both north Antrim men. Taggart, a builder by trade, had enlisted late in the war, in September 1916. At the age of 37, he would have been one of the older 'new recruits'. From Alfred Street, Ballymena, he left a widow, Martha, and two children. His parents, John and Hanna, lived at Queen Street, Ballymena. He has no known grave but is remembered on the Menin Gate, Ypres. Whiteside, who had lived at Glenleslie, Clough, is buried in Vlamertinghe Cemetery, Ypres, and is commemorated at Cloughwater Presbyterian Church.

3 Rifleman David Henry Nichols was killed on 4 August 1917; James William Mitchell died on 6 August; Frederick Elliff died the following day from wounds; and Isaac Smyth was killed outright on 11 August.

4 The shelling on 15 August killed three riflemen – John McGuiggan, Hugh Johnston and William Alexander – along with two lance corporals, Robert Yorke and Percy George Amos.

5 Mullin found it difficult making it back to safety "owing to the ground being sticky mud like thick glue. Also it was not yet dawn. I inadvertently go into a shell hole full of water and I had great difficulty in getting out. I reached a small pill-box which was a dressing station. It was full but I managed to squeeze in. I sat on the concrete floor to rest after my exertion. The blood was still pouring from my arm. After sometime someone looked at me and said that I better try and go further back as they could do nothing to help me. There was nothing for it but to continue my journey westward on foot. I reached a point eventually where in the distance I saw three or four motor ambulances parked. When I reached them an orderly escorted me into one.

Very soon I arrived at the 109th field Ambulance near St Jean. From here I went on to Reamy casualty clearing station. I now received medical attention. My uniform was cut off with a large pair of scissors; an anaesthetic put me to sleep, and an operation followed between 8.00 and 9.00 am." He ultimately ended up back in Belfast and was never to see the front line again.

6 Regimental Sergeant Major Frederick Jacquet may have been among those pulled from the headquarters dugout after it suffered a direct hit by German artillery. A former Grenadier Guardsman from Bromley in Kent, he died of wounds on 17 August. James Kennedy Hope appeared to be referring to him when he recorded: "I miss too in many ways our big Regimental Sergeant Major who with 13 others lies buried in a concrete dugout, the result of a direct hit on a captured German pill box. I refused to be his batman." RSM Jacquet is buried at Lijssenthoek Military Cemetery, Belgium.

7 Among the deaths most keenly felt had been that of Company Sergeant Major John Leslie Armstrong. The 24-year-old "gentleman and soldier", according to Hope, was killed taking up rations to the men in the line on 16 August 1917. His body was never identified and his name is recorded on the Tyne Cot Memorial. From the Cliftonpark Avenue area of Belfast, he had come up through the ranks. He earned the Military Medal during the Battle of the Somme and even before the war he had been honoured with the Royal Humane Society for saving a life in Dundrum Bay. A member of Donegall Swimming Club, he had worked in the linen business prior to enlisting.

8 Hugh Kennedy had been a designer in the Belfast company of John Shaw Brown and Sons Limited before the war and a member of both Wandsworth Football Club and Ballynafeigh Cricket Club, captaining the latter. He was commissioned on 4 October 1915, and went to the front in June the following year. The young officer was wounded at least twice while serving with the YCVs, on 21 August 1916, and at Messines on 7 June 1917. James McBurney joined the Army straight from the Royal Belfast Academical Institute, being still two months short of his 17th birthday. The younger son of Thomas McBurney, Moatville, Comber – his older son was a lieutenant in the Transport Service – James had been a member of Queen's University Officer Training Corps. Commissioned in September 1916, he had been posted to the front in December that year from the 20th Rifles at Newtownards. He was just 19 when killed. Second Lieutenant Coffee, a 28-year-old from Rathgar, Dublin, was attached to the battalion from the 5th Royal Irish Rifles. His body was never identified and he is remembered on the Tyne Cot Memorial. Herbert Rea was initially reported missing. The son of John Rea of Ann Street, Belfast, he had been a member of the East Belfast UVF. The former Royal Belfast Academical Institution pupil, who was 25 when killed, had worked as an accountant for the firm of HB Brandon and Co, Belfast. He was commissioned from the Black Watch Territorials and had been wounded in July 1916.

Chapter 16

1 The battalion lost only one other soldier that month. Rifleman Benjamin Fuller, also a Londoner and a former member of the City of London Regiment, died of wounds at home in Peckham, London, on 19 September.

2 The spells in the trenches in October only resulted in one further death, that of Rifleman Samuel Dempsey, from the Shankill Road in Belfast, who was killed in action on 17 October 1917.

3 Captain Noel John Hay Gavin, from Wellington, New Zealand, and a member of the Royal Army Medical Corps, was attached to the YCVs in 1916, succeeding Dr MacKenzie, and was awarded the Military Cross in the King's Birthday Honours List of 1917 and a bar for his conspicuous bravery at Passchendaele in August of the same year when he continued to treat the wounded despite being injured himself and his position being under constant artillery fire. A letter published in the *Belfast News Letter* on 8 November 1917, but sent originally by an unnamed soldier to his mother, read: "As I write, I hear that the battalion is the poorer – and very much poorer – by the loss of one of the best men I have ever met. I mean our doctor, who has done so much for us all. He was thrown from his horse last night, sustaining such severe injuries that he died this morning. We may get the best doctor in the army, but never will we get one to come up to Dr Gavin's standard. He was so gentle always, and paid the greatest attention to the meanest soldier in the battalion, listening to every complaint, no matter how small, and doing his best to fix it up. After telling you so much about him in days gone past, I felt it would not be out of place to write these few words in passing, as I know both you and E looked on him as a sort of personal friend."

4 After the 14th Royal Irish Rifles was disbanded, Hope again met Hugh Gelston Morrow, now a captain serving in the 15th Royal Irish Rifles, as the former was coming out of the line and latter going in. He heard of his death, on 20 October 1918, a short time later. Morrow was 24 and had lived at Avonmore Terrace, south Belfast. He is buried at Harlebeke New British Cemetery in Belgium.

Chapter 17

1 Edward Gain, though born in Glasgow, was living in Downpatrick when he enlisted at Belfast.

2 On the day the battalion learned it was to be disbanded, Rifleman William James Smyth, from Belfast, passed away from natural causes.

3 Lance Corporal Taylor had been wounded in the leg at the Battle of the Somme on 1 July 1916. The *Belfast News Letter* reported on 28 July 1916: "Mr Alex Taylor, Donegall Street, Belfast, yesterday received a postcard from his son, Lance-Corporal JR Taylor (YCV), stating that he is wounded and a prisoner of war in the Festungs Lazaret (Prison Hospital), Kaiserin Augusta School, Cologne. Lance Corporal Taylor was shot in the knee during the advance on the 1st inst, and when his comrades retired they had reluctantly to leave him behind in a dugout – indeed, he insisted on them doing so rather than imperil their own safety. He says that he is well treated, and that there are 'a number of the lads here'. Six weeks is the usual period allowed for receiving news from prisoners of war, and in the case of Lance Corporal Taylor word has come through unusually quickly."

NOTES ON SOURCES

Veterans' journals, diaries and letters form a large proportion of this book: indeed, it is through their writings that the story of the Young Citizen Volunteers and the 14th (YCV) Royal Irish Rifles is told. These include the correspondence between Jim Fitzsimons and his brother Edwin, held by the Somme Museum; the diary of Charles Sheridan; the unpublished journal of Samuel Harrison, 'Tent, Billet and Dugout: The story of a Young Citizen Volunteer of Belfast'; the war diary of Rifleman H Berry; the Volume of Reminiscences left by John Kennedy Hope; extracts from the diary of Jim Maultsaid; the considerable writings of James McRoberts, published as *Young Citizen Old Soldier: The Journal of Rifleman James McRoberts, 14th Battalion Royal Irish Rifles, January 1915–April 1917*; and certainly not least, the extensive diary of George H Mullin. Many others, through letters and reports published in newspapers, contributed to the volume of first-hand testimony so important to getting a sense of what it was like to be a soldier in the Great War. Permission to quote from these has been sought and granted in most cases, though it was not possible in all instances to trace the appropriate copyright holder. In these exceptions your understanding is sought.

Another great source was the 14th Battalion official *War Diary*, much of which was written by long-time adjutant Alan Mulholland, and the battalion's newspaper which, despite only amounting to two editions, is packed with useful information and opinion.

The Public Record Office of Northern Ireland holds the surviving papers of the Young Citizen Volunteers of Ireland, including records of the various committees and accounts, and those of the Ulster Volunteer Force.

Secondary Sources
Books

Bowman, T, *Irish Regiments in the Great War: Discipline and Morale*, Manchester University Press, Manchester, 2003

Bowman, T, *Carson's Army: the Ulster Volunteer Force, 1910–22*, Manchester University Press, Manchester, 2007

Canning, WJ, *A Wheen of Medals: The History of the 9th (Service) Bn. The Royal Inniskilling Fusiliers (The Tyrones) in World War One*, published by the author, 2006

Crozier, FP, *A Brass Hat in No-Man's Land*, Cedric Chivers, Bath, 1968. First published by Cape, London, 1930

Denman, T, *A Lonely Grave: The Life and Death of William Redmond*, Irish Academic Press, Dublin, 1995

Dungan, M, *Irish Voices from the Great War*, Irish Academic Press, Dublin, 1995

Falls, C, *The History of the 36th (Ulster) Division*, Constable, London, 1996. First published by McCaw, Stevenson and Orr, Belfast, 1922

Grayson, RS, *Belfast Boys: How Unionists and Nationalists Fought and Died Together in the First World War*, Continuum, London, 2009

Jeffrey, K, *Ireland and the Great War*, Cambridge University Press, 2000

Johnstone, T, *Orange, Green and Khaki: The Story of the Irish Regiments in the Great War, 1914–18*, Gill and Macmillan, Dublin, 1992

Keegan, J, *The First World War*, Pimlico, London, 1999

Lucy, G, *The Ulster Covenant: An Illustrated History of the 1912 Home Rule Crisis*, Colourpoint Books, Newtownards, 2012

Macdonald, L, *Somme*, Papermac, London, 1983

McRoberts, J, Ed David Truesdale, *Young Citizen Old Soldier: From boyhood in Antrim to hell on the Somme – The Journal of Rifleman James McRoberts, 14th Battalion Royal Irish Rifles, January 1915–April 1917,* Helion & Company Ltd, Solihull

Moore, S, *The Irish On The Somme: A battlefield guide to the Irish regiments in the Great War and the monuments to their memory*, Local Press Ltd, Portadown, 2005

Middlebrook, M, *The First Day on the Somme*, Penguin, London, 1971

Middlebrook, M, *The Kaiser's Battle, 21 March 1918: The First Day of the German Spring Offensive,* Penguin, London, 1978

Mitchell, G, *Three Cheers for the Derrys! A History of the 10th Royal Inniskilling Fusiliers in the 1914–18 War,* Yes! Publications, Derry, 1991

Orr, P, *The Road to the Somme: Men of the Ulster Division Tell Their Story*, Blackstaff Press, Belfast, 1987

Perry, N, *Major General Oliver Nugent and the Ulster Division, 1915–1918*, Sutton Publishing, Stroud, 2007

Shooter, Lt Col WA, *Ulster's Part in the Battle of the Somme: 1st July to 15th November, 1916*, printed by the *Northern Whig*, 1966

Smyth, D, *Journey of Remembering: Belfast Book of Honour*, Johnston Publishing (NI), Portadown, 2009

Stewart, ATQ, *The Ulster Crisis: Resistance to Home Rule, 1912*, Faber and Faber, London, 1967

Taylor, JW, *The 1st Royal Irish Rifles in the Great War*, Four Courts Press, Dublin, 2002

Taylor, JW, *The 2nd Royal Irish Rifles in the Great War*, Four Courts Press, Dublin, 2005

Thompson, R, various volumes, *Coleraine Heroes, Ballymoney Heroes, Ballymena Heroes, etc*

Newspapers

Belfast Evening Telegraph
Belfast News Letter
County Down Spectator
Irish News and Belfast Morning Post
Irish Times
Northern Whig

INDEX

Abbeville 96

Acheux 103, 105, 122

Achiet-le-Petit 188

Acquin 163

Ailly-le-Haut-Clocher 96

Aircraft Farm 153, 156, 165

Albert 116, 233, 235, 241

Amiens 85, 86, 191, 192, 195

Ancre, River 108, 116, 117, 132

Armistice 197–198

Armstrong, Sergeant Jack 138–139, 140, 149, 150, 158, 243

Arras 188, 197, 235

Ashton, Lieutenant Colonel CCG 97, 102

Auchonvillers 104, 105

Aveluy Wood 125, 132, 144

Bailleul 149, 155, 156, 161, 162, 166, 167, 173, 235

Balloon, observation 154, 179

Bangalore torpedo 152

Bapaume 184, 188, 235

Barastre 184

Barker, Lieutenant Fred 47, 134

Baxter, Willie 33

Bayencourt 88

Beaulencourt 188

Beaussart 105

Beauval 86, 87, 95, 101, 241

Belfast Defence Corps 200

Belfast Technical College 21, 27, 45, 55, 151, 194, 219, 236

Belfast Volunteer Training Corps 200

Bentley, Robert 18, 46, 52, 54, 55, 62, 220, 236

Berneuil 101, 102, 103

Berry, H 12, 50, 52, 53, 57, 59, 64, 73, 74, 79, 83, 84, 85, 89, 103, 106, 111, 113, 116, 117, 118, 119, 123, 124, 127, 130, 133, 136, 141, 143, 144, 148, 149, 152, 161, 163, 168, 170, 197, 249

Berteaucourt 102

Bertincourt 185, 188

Bisley 80, 236

Blaringhem 147

Bliss, Major HR 82, 97, 241

Boisdinghem, 148, 177

Bordon 79, 80

Boulogne 83, 188

Bowen, Lieutenant Colonel Francis O 108, 120, 131, 146, 217, 241

Boxing 79, 150, 163

Boy Scouts 9, 11, 15, 16, 18, 21, 22, 23, 29, 64, 200, 208, 236

Boy's Brigade 9, 11, 15, 16, 18, 21, 22, 29, 114, 208, 226, 237, 243, 247

Boyd, Brian 140, 149, 154, 167, 172, 200, 225, 243, 247

Boyd, John 141

Bramshott 79, 83, 202

British Army:

    Infantry Divisions:

        16th (Irish) 47, 165, 167, 173

        36th (Ulster) 5, 12, 14, 33, 76, 83, 102, 108, 133, 146, 166, 176, 178, 180, 193, 194, 202, 211, 216, 234, 235, 237, 246

    Infantry Brigades:

        107th Brigade 51, 67, 76, 86, 95, 107, 168, 175, 178, 211

        108th Brigade 51, 67, 95, 138, 168, 211

        109th Brigade 49, 51, 58, 63, 70, 86, 95, 97, 102, 108, 111, 123, 124, 128, 140, 146, 149, 162, 168, 169, 176, 178, 180, 182, 185, 193, 194, 211

    Infantry Battalions:

        Entrenching Battalions 194, 195, 196, 211, 231

        Royal Inniskilling Fusiliers:

            9th Battalion 51, 64, 66, 69, 72, 140, 142, 159, 160, 161, 163, 164, 165, 174, 176, 178, 179, 185, 187, 188, 189, 192, 193, 211

            10th Battalion 51, 66, 69, 109, 128, 133, 136, 141, 142, 149, 152, 153, 155, 156, 158, 159, 165, 171, 178, 184, 185, 186, 188, 192, 193, 194, 211

11th Battalion 51, 56, 64, 66, 69, 100, 108, 109, 111, 112, 115, 117, 128, 133, 134, 153, 159, 162, 176, 178, 181, 192, 193, 194, 211, 240

Royal Irish Fusiliers:

9th (North Irish Horse) Battalion 51, 88, 115, 128, 148, 158, 193, 197, 211, 219

Royal Irish Rifles:

7th Battalion 47, 211, 245

8th (East Belfast) Battalion 47, 51, 79, 104, 122, 164, 181, 211, 225, 228

9th (West Belfast) Battalion 51, 153, 169, 170, 185, 194, 211, 242, 245, 247

10th (South Belfast) Battalion 47, 51, 104, 107, 194, 211, 237

11th Battalion 29, 47, 51, 95, 167, 211, 217, 237, 242

12th Battalion 13, 47, 51, 148, 172, 188, 211, 241

13th Battalion 14, 51, 88, 162, 166, 180, 194, 211, 229

15th (North Belfast) Battalion 47, 51, 189, 197, 205, 211, 219, 248

16th Battalion 47, 67, 70, 104, 241

Royal Army Medical Corps (RAMC) 74, 78, 144, 181, 219, 248; 110th Field Ambulance 155, 156

Royal Army Service Corps 74

Royal Engineers 42, 67, 69, 74, 97, 101, 103, 105, 112, 116, 127, 156, 159, 171, 197, 238

Royal Flying Corps 123, 154, 186, 237, 246

Bundoran 50, 51, 52, 55, 56, 57, 59

Burns, George 163, 167

Bussus 96

Caestre 184

Calvert, William (Billy) Henry 28, 102, 201

Cambrai 183, 186, 190, 191, 222

Candas 103, 147

Canizy 195

Cansdale, H 97, 102, 169

Carnduff, Thomas 5, 11, 30, 33, 38, 40, 41, 42, 43

Carson, Sir Edward 9, 11, 32, 33, 36, 38, 40, 43, 44, 45, 47, 48, 67, 78, 147, 191

Cheape, George Ronald 162, 163, 167, 171, 172, 173, 175, 182, 194, 246

Chichester, Robert Peel Dawson Spencer 24, 25, 28, 29, 30, 37, 38, 39, 41, 43, 48, 49, 50, 51, 62, 63, 68, 78, 79, 82, 98, 100, 101, 102, 120, 200, 202, 217, 219, 220, 236, 237, 242

Chichester, Dehra 98, 200, 201, 202, 203, 236

Church Lads 11, 15, 16, 18, 22

Churchill, Lord Randolph 10

Clyde Valley 41

Cobain, James 61, 62

Connaught 72

Connolly, Charles 86, 88, 89, 90, 91, 92

Constitution, YCV 16, 20, 21, 25, 39, 206, 207

Conteville 147

Corry, John Wallace 205

Couin 88, 92

Courtney, Edward 151

Courtrai 117, 119

Crawford, Major Fred 26, 40, 41

Crothers, Tommy 150, 154, 172, 176

Crozier, Rev Dr John Baptist 78, 102

Davis, HO 28, 29

Demicourt 185, 186

Derry Camp 158, 164

Domleber 147

Dorrity, George 114, 122

Douglas, Bob 76, 116, 141

Doullens 87, 191

Douvieux 194

Downey, Sydney HL 172, 247

Dranoutre 153, 154, 158, 235

Drought, Robert Victor 149, 154, 156, 157, 158, 245

Dublin 10, 22, 32, 34, 35, 47, 72, 125, 151, 153, 171, 176, 236, 237, 243, 244, 245, 246, 247, 248

Eastbourne 73, 74, 76

Elgin Avenue (trench) 122, 127, 132, 136, 137, 138, 139, 140, 142, 143

Elphick, Sergeant Major 55, 68, 70, 151, 239, 244

Emerson, James Samuel 189

Empress Queen 83, 240

Ergnies 97, 98, 101

Etricourt 188, 191

Falls, Cyril 81, 134, 180, 184, 246

Fienvillers 103, 147

Finner Camp 49–57, 58, 59, 66, 77, 131, 202, 238, 243, 244

Fitzsimons, James (Jim) 11, 12, 51, 90, 114, 115, 129, 136, 139, 143, 236, 244, 249

Flanders 74, 122, 177, 191, 234, 245

Follies, The Divisional 103, 123, 155, 156, 159, 167, 175

Fonquevillers 88, 92, 101

Football 28, 70, 75, 100, 103, 121, 123, 150, 159, 162, 163, 176, 193, 224

Forceville 105, 108, 121, 129, 130

Forth, Francis Charles 21, 55, 219, 236

Foy, Sergeant 147, 197

French, Sir John 87, 200, 201

Gas attack 14, 81, 90, 123, 127, 128, 135, 136, 143, 149, 152, 153, 155, 156, 205, 244

Gavin, Noel John Hay 146, 162, 167, 174, 181, 185, 245, 248

Geddes, Fred T 17, 19, 25, 26, 28, 39, 200, 210

Gladstone, William Ewart 10, 236

Gommecourt 90, 128

Gordon Castle dump 115, 127, 138

Gracey, Robert 57, 112, 131, 140, 144, 244

Grand Seraucourt 192, 193, 194

Greer, William A 98, 144, 245

Grouches-Luchoel 191

GS (General Stores) Wagon 149, 164

Gunning, Major JE 29, 39, 42, 44, 50, 97, 151, 241, 244

Hackney, George 6, 12, 59, 63, 64, 70, 73, 74, 75, 77, 79, 80, 81, 84, 87, 89, 96, 97, 99, 105, 118, 124, 126, 132, 137, 161

Haig, Sir Douglas 124, 159, 188, 238, 240

Hamel 108, 109, 111, 112, 113, 114, 134

Hamill, Rev Dr 78

Hanna, Captain 49, 102, 160, 169, 170, 238

Harper, J 29, 55, 79, 87, 99

Harrison, Samuel 12, 48, 52, 53, 54, 55, 56, 57, 59, 61, 64, 65, 69, 72, 77, 81, 86, 87, 89, 91, 95, 97, 98, 101, 103, 103, 104, 106, 108, 110, 113, 116, 118, 125, 130, 160, 171, 185, 239, 241, 249

Haute Pannee 175, 176, 177

Havrincourt 186, 189

Hayincourt 188

Heasley, W 149, 197

Hédauville 129, 146

Hermies 184, 185, 188

Herrissart 147

Herron, Company Sergeant Major 54, 62, 73

Hickman, TE 62, 63, 64, 70, 95, 119, 123, 124

Hill 60 179

Hill 63 161

Hogg, WF 139, 144, 166, 244

Hondeghem 175

Hooton, HH 99, 244

Hope, John Kennedy 14, 49, 50, 51, 52, 54, 55, 60, 69, 73, 76, 82, 83, 87, 88, 89, 90, 92, 100, 106, 107, 108, 111, 112, 119, 127, 131, 132, 136, 137, 140, 142, 143, 144, 152, 153, 155, 159, 164, 165, 168, 169, 147, 185, 187, 188, 189, 190, 191, 196, 197, 230, 238, 240, 242, 244, 245, 247, 248, 249

Hyndman, James Valentine (Val) 55, 87, 93, 102, 111, 114, 123, 132, 136, 137, 141, 244

Incinerator, The 66, 72, 98, 99, 102, 107, 119, 122, 124, 125, 126, 148, 212, 213, 222, 238, 241, 242, 244

Irish Parliamentary Party (IPP) 10

Irish Republican Army (IRA) 200

Jacquest, Regimental Sergeant Major 180, 248

Joffre, Joseph 87, 88

Jump Point 169, 170

Kemmel Hill 163, 167, 173

Kenning, J 99, 147, 163

King George V 45, 81, 82, 83, 87, 88, 216

King, Canon 78, 138, 240, 243, 244, 245

Kingsway (trench) 158, 164

Kinnaird, Sergeant 65–66, 239

Kitchener, Lord Herbert 46, 47, 78, 81, 83

Kortepyp Camp 159

La Grande Munque Farm 149

La Havre 83

La Plus Douve Farm Cemetery 161

Lack, Reginald Lambert 68, 99, 138, 139, 140, 149, 243

Lancashire dump 127, 129

Le Buisson 175

Lealvillers 122, 123, 125

Ledlie, Lieutenant 158, 180, 181

Lewis, Percy 160, 161, 246

Lindenhoek Crossroads 165, 166

Llewellyn, Major 120, 242

Lloyd, Lieutenant Colonel 160, 161

Locre 166, 167, 170, 173, 174

LOL 871 98, 147, 163

Mackay, JJ 112

Maricourt 128

Marteville 194

Martinsart 108, 115, 122, 125, 129, 130, 131, 144, 146

Maultsaid, Jim 12, 48, 110, 114, 115, 124, 132, 135, 136, 143, 149

Mayes, Thomas H 29, 55, 57, 95, 147, 163

McCammond, WEC 26, 32, 220, 237

McCullagh, Sir Crawford 43, 101

McFadzean, William (Billy) 19, 133, 195, 201, 216–219

McKee, James 29, 55, 70, 87, 99, 102, 133, 149, 152, 162, 168, 172, 203, 217, 247

McMordie, Julia 23, 200, 236

McMordie, Lord Mayor Robert 15, 16, 17, 18, 21, 24, 27, 29, 37, 236, 234

McRoberts, James 5, 60, 79, 80, 83, 84, 86, 95, 112, 114, 119, 138, 146, 153, 154, 155, 156, 157, 239, 240, 245, 249

Meehan, John Berryhill 131, 242, 243

Menary, CC 151

Mesnil 108, 111, 112, 115, 233–235

Messines 47, 149, 152, 163, 164, 166–172, 173, 178, 182, 197, 200, 203, 204, 227, 228, 245, 246, 247, 248

Méteren 162, 163

Metz-en-Couture 189, 190

Meyer, Robert 26, 27

Mezieres 192

Minenwerfer (Minnie) 94, 112, 119, 120, 149, 153, 155, 158, 165

Moeuvres 186, 187, 188

Monard, Stanley Hopkirk 12, 99, 100, 119, 120, 121, 135, 140, 144, 212, 219, 244, 243, 244

Mondicourt 191, 192

Montgomery, Allan 166, 246

Montgomery, Rev Henry 110, 163, 241

Moore, William 5, 12, 13, 100, 150, 151, 152, 159, 203

Moore, John Reid 5, 12, 13, 14, 96, 102, 145

Moreuil 192

Morrow, Lieutenant 168, 169, 189, 190

Mortimer, R 99

Mount Keep dump 109

Mountjoy II (see Clyde Valley)

Mulholland, Adjutant Alan 12, 57, 108, 111, 128, 132, 134, 137, 138, 140, 142, 143, 147, 148, 150, 155, 156, 160, 165, 167, 168, 171, 179, 181, 194, 203, 233, 234, 235, 242, 243, 244, 249

Mulholland, DO 154

Mullin, George 12, 46, 48, 49, 50, 51, 52, 53, 54, 55, 57, 59, 60, 62, 63, 65, 68, 73, 76, 80, 83, 84, 85, 87, 88, 95, 96, 97, 98, 101, 102, 103, 104, 106, 107, 108, 110, 112, 115, 116, 123, 124, 125, 127, 129, 130, 132, 136, 137, 141, 144, 149, 153, 154, 155, 156, 157, 158, 159, 160, 163, 164, 165, 166, 168, 171, 172, 173, 174, 175, 176, 177, 179, 197, 239, 243, 246, 247, 249

Murray, Sir AJ 78

Neuve Eglise 149

Nevin, J 163, 246

Newmarket Camp 166, 167, 172, 173

Notre Dame de Brebieres 116

Nugent, Oliver 81, 83, 85, 128, 130, 146, 149, 150, 163, 165, 166, 171, 176, 177, 190, 194

O'Brien, JD 156, 157, 158

Offoy 195

Oliver, Billy 85, 158

Onraet Wood 173, 174

Paisley Avenue (trench) 127, 128

Passchendaele 173–183, 248

Patton, Arthur 65, 174

Paysden, George 156, 245

Penman, Charles (Carl) 110, 111, 241

Pernois 95, 96

Ploegsteert 149, 152, 158, 161

Pond Farm 180, 245

Pont-Remy 96, 97

Poperinghe 177

Poulainville 85, 86

Powell, Herbert 64, 70, 81, 83, 239

Puchevillers 103

Radcliffe, George 139, 140, 243

Ramecourt 195

Randalstown Camp 58–66, 69–71, 72, 85, 202, 238, 239, 246

RE (see Royal Engineers)

Red Lodge 148, 149, 152, 153, 158, 161, 162

Regent Street (trench) 164, 169

Renwick, R 98, 112, 122, 164, 241, 242

Rethonvillers 192

Ricardo, Ambrose 33, 169, 171, 173, 175, 176, 177, 182

Richardson, Sir George 33, 34, 81, 128, 200, 219, 236

Robb, Victor H 29, 55, 97, 131, 144, 220, 244

Rocquigny 185, 191

Romarin 148

Route march 11, 26, 30, 43, 52, 53, 61, 63, 64, 66, 70, 79, 80, 85, 86, 94, 95, 103, 105, 115, 239, 245

Royal Navy 36, 75, 238, 240, 243

Rubempré 147

Sassoon, Siegfried 177

Scott Farm 169, 171

Scott, James 161, 163

Seaford 72–79, 99, 161, 202, 239, 240

Serques 147

Serre 128

Shane's Castle 58, 59, 63, 70, 239

Sheridan, Charles 12, 66, 68, 73, 79, 80, 87, 92, 95, 97, 132, 175, 180, 182, 197, 240, 249

Shuter, General 124, 149, 156

Slacke, Charles Owen 54, 55, 57, 131, 134, 144, 243

Smylie, Cecil Victor 205

Somme 11, 12, 22, 33, 35, 47, 117, 128–145, 147, 149, 158, 167, 172, 175, 182, 197, 201, 212, 222, 225, 227, 229, 235, 238, 239, 241, 242, 243–248

Sonen Farm 174

Sorel-le-Grand 188, 191

Souastre 88

Spanbroek 164, 169

Spree Farm 179

St George's Market 20, 21, 27, 28, 38, 48, 68, 200

St Omer 147, 175, 176, 236

St Pierre-Division 141

Stephenson, William (Billy) 55, 113, 115, 241

Stevenson, HG 15, 19, 29, 210, 236

Sunken Road 114, 135, 136, 143, 146

Thiepval Wood 12, 108, 117, 118, 123, 125, 127, 128, 129, 134, 136, 137, 139, 140, 142, 143, 144, 146, 182, 202, 216, 218, 219, 235, 243, 244

Treanor, Sydney 169, 170, 186

Ulster Hall 18, 27, 33, 68

Ulster Ladies' Work Society 201

Ulster Volunteer Force (UVF) 9, 10, 11, 12, 24, 31–39, 40–45, 46, 47, 48, 51, 67, 81, 107, 114, 128, 199, 200, 216, 218, 219, 236, 237, 238, 239, 240, 241, 243, 244, 245, 247, 248, 249

Ulsterwomen's Gift Fund 98

Unionist Clubs 10, 32, 33, 34

Uprichard, George 163, 203

Vacquerie 188

Varennes 103, 104, 105, 108

Verdun 128, 234–235

Verlaines 195

Victoria Barracks 32, 36, 150, 151, 245, 247

Victoria Cross 19, 133, 139, 189, 201, 216–219, 236, 239

Villers-Bretonneux 195

Villeselve 197

Vivian, Major OR 173, 175, 181, 246

Vlamertinge 179

Walker, Jerome (Jim) Lennie 115, 117, 119–120

Warneton Road 149

Watou 177

Watts, HE 177

Wee Joey 201, 202

Willis, Samuel 104, 113, 136, 140, 243, 244

Willson, WAP 102, 241

Winnezeele 177, 181

Wizernes 163

Wood, Lieutenant 166, 171, 172, 174, 176, 179, 180, 246

Woollcounte, CL 185

Workman, Frank 9, 17, 20, 25, 29, 39, 237

Wright, Matthew 112, 140, 148, 243

Wright, Rev John Jackson 129, 147, 244

Wulverghem 149

Wytschaete 166, 173, 174, 182, 235, 246

YCV Old Comrades Association 202

YCV Reunion Committee (see YCV Old Comrades
    Association)

Ypres 13, 117, 177, 178, 182, 183, 235, 246, 247

16734934R00090